MATTHEW

MATTHEW

O. WESLEY ALLEN JR.

Fortress Press
Minneapolis

MATTHEW

Fortress Biblical Preaching Commentaries

Scripture quotations are from the New Revised Standard Version Bible, copyright © 1989 by the Division of Christian Education of the National Council of the Churches of Christ in the USA. Used by permission. All rights reserved.

Library of Congress Cataloging-in-Publication Data is available

Print ISBN: 978-0-8006-9871-3

eBook ISBN: 978-1-4514-2645-8

The paper used in this publication meets the minimum requirements of American National Standard for Information Sciences—Permanence of Paper for Printed Library Materials, ANSI Z329.48-1984.

Manufactured in the U.S.A.

This book was produced using PressBooks.com, and PDF rendering was done by PrinceXML.

For
Howard Collins,
Stewart Jackson,
Rex Kaney,
Bill Kincaid
and Ron Luckey.

Some of the best of those
who have preached to me over the years.

All of whom make me want
to be a better preacher in the years to come.

CONTENTS

Series Foreword

A preacher who seeks to be creative, exegetically up to date, hermeneutically alert, theologically responsible, and in-touch with the moment is always on the hunt for fresh resources. Traditional books on preaching a book of the Bible often look at broad themes of the text with little explicit advice about preaching individual passages. Lectionary resources often offer exegetical and homiletical insights about a pericope with little attention given to broader themes and structures of the book from which the lection is taken. *Fortress Biblical Preaching Commentaries* provide the preacher with resources that draw together the strengths of these two approaches into a single text aid, useful for the moment of preparation halfway between full scale exegesis and a finished sermon.

The authors of this series are biblical scholars who offer expositions of the text rooted in detailed study and expressed in straightforward, readable ways. The commentators take a practical approach by identifying (1) what the text invited people in the ancient world to believe about God and the world and (2) what the text encouraged people to do in response. Along the way, the interpreters make use of such things as historical and cultural reconstruction, literary and rhetorical analysis, word studies, and other methods that help us recover how a text was intended to function in antiquity. At the same time, the commentaries offer help in moving from then to now, from what a text meant (in the past) to what a text means (in the present), by helping a minister identify issues, raise questions, and pose possibilities for preaching while stopping short of placing a complete sermon in the preacher's hands. The preacher, then, should be in a position to set in motion a conversation with the text (and other voices from the past and present) to help the congregation figure out what we today can believe and do.

The commentators in this series seek to help preachers and students make connections between the various lections from a given book throughout the lectionary cycle and liturgical year in their sermons and studies. Readers, preachers, and their parishioners will have a deeper appreciation of the book's unique interpretation of the Christ event and how that influences their approach to living the Christian faith in today's world. The most life-giving preaching is nearly always local in character with a minister rooted in a particular congregation, culture, and context encouraging listeners to think specifically about how the text might relate to the life of the congregation and to the surrounding community and world. *Fortress Biblical Preaching Commentaries* are set forth in the hope that each volume will be a provocative voice in such conversations.

PREFACE

Preaching Matthew is a hybrid of sorts, combining material usually found in different types of biblical, homiletical, and liturgical resources. From traditional books focused on helping pastors preach consistently through a biblical work, it keeps its eye on the overarching structures, themes, and theological claims that give Matthew its unique character. From commentaries that work passage by passage through a biblical work, it works through Matthew's material in the order Matthew presents it. But from homiletical helps for lectionary preachers, it gives most attention to readings from Matthew (lections) that appear in the Revised Common Lectionary (RCL). In this combination of approaches, preachers long familiar with Matthew may see elements of the First Gospel in a new light and may lead a congregation to experience the liturgical year based on Matthew (Year A in the RCL) in a new way.

This hybrid approach grows out of my understanding of the nature of biblical preaching. To preach biblically does not mean to go to the Bible, discover what it says, and simply repeat or translate it for a contemporary audience. Instead, the focus of biblical preaching (well, of any Christian preaching) is the good news of Jesus Christ—the grace, judgment, and call of God-with-us, here and now, as God has always been with the world. In the sermon, a biblical passage serves as the particular lens for the day for seeing a particular way God is with us and what it means for life in the world corporately as the body of Christ and individually as a disciple of Christ. In sermon preparation (and in the sermon itself), therefore, preachers should focus their gaze less *on* the text and more *through* it to look at life there and find the God made known in the Christ event in new and enlivening ways.

This type of focus changes the way preachers read a biblical text on behalf of a congregation. Critical exegesis is as important as ever, but it is a means to an end. Exegesis during sermon preparation is the process of turning the lens to sharpen the preacher's focus on the theological, ethical, pastoral, and existential needs of the congregation. Thus this book is exegetical in nature, but it is unapologetically exegesis in service to the pulpit. It does not attempt to be exhaustive in dealing with textual, historical, or literary issues involved in studying Matthew. It does not position the interpretation of different elements of Matthew in either the history of interpretation or among contemporary scholarship. While the nature of this approach means I have avoided the use of footnotes or references to scholarship, I hope the conversation I have had with Matthean scholarship and my dependence on the research of others is evident in the work. For a list of helpful research and important commentaries on the book of Matthew, an appendix indicating sources for further reading has been included.

So I have been selective in what I have included in this book, assuming that preachers who turn to it will (1) already be familiar with general issues related to Matthean scholarship from seminary or other biblical studies and (2) have done significant exegesis on a passage of interest using critical commentaries based in historical and literary criticism, Bible dictionaries, and other resources before turning to my discussion of that text. In other words, this homiletical, lectionary-oriented commentary on Matthew is meant to help preachers as they begin to turn from detailed, critical commentaries toward the pulpit. Preachers have not moved so close to the sermon that they are looking for sermon imagery and the like but close enough that synthesis of exegetical findings and theological possibilities is needed. In other words, while this book is not intended as a resource that fits the needs of preachers closely examining a biblical text for the first time in their sermon preparation, neither is it a resource for the final stages of sermon preparation where they are filling out their reading of a text with the "stuff" of the congregation. It stands in the middle of the week of the preparation, just at that point where the preacher is beginning to let go of reading the text for its own sake and moving toward interpreting it for the sake of a specific congregation set in a specific historical time and place.

But to open this book only on Tuesday or Wednesday each week to see what it adds to what one has already read about the Gospel lection for the week will be to miss some of what I hope it can offer the preacher working through Matthew throughout Year A of the lectionary cycle. The book is shaped by *a cumulative approach* to preaching week in and week out in the same congregation, an approach for which I have advocated in different ways in *The Homiletic of All Believers: A Conversational Approach* (2005) and *Reading and Preaching the Lectionary: A Three-Dimensional Approach to the Liturgical Year* (2007). Homileticians and biblical scholars are perpetual guest speakers and often write in such a way that assumes pastors experience the pulpit in the same way we do. But every parish pastor knows that the transformative power of the pulpit lies primarily in speaking and hearing the gospel and in reinforcing that message Sunday after Sunday to people who sit in the same seat each week. It is through repeated exposure that hearers assimilate the vocabulary of the faith and have their lives shaped by it. Pastor-preachers must be intentional in shaping their sermons so that the messages, concepts, imagery, and applications of their sermons across time overlap and reinforce one another. The lectionary's focus on a primary synoptic gospel for a whole year is helpful in doing this.

The lectionary has led preaching to be more biblical in recent decades than it was in the mid-twentieth century (when topical preaching reigned). Oddly, however, congregations seem more biblically illiterate than ever. While the lectionary cannot be blamed for this problem, the way it is shaped and certainly the way we use it in worship (especially in the Protestant pulpit) has contributed to this problem. Basically, each Sunday we look at an individual pericope and rarely get a sense of the whole scope and nature of the biblical work from which it comes. This disjointed relationship the congregation has with the Bible is exacerbated by the fact that preachers jump from Gospel to Old Testament to epistle to Gospel to psalm week after week. Taking into consideration the movement of the liturgical year and the constantly changing needs of a congregation, this jumping around makes good sense. But sustained homiletical focus on a single biblical book (say, on Matthew in Year A of the RCL cycle) can promote a cumulative approach to the work (and thus to a particular approach to the Gospel) and help increase biblical knowledge more broadly.

But even with sustained attention by the preacher and congregation, we need to recognize three ways the RCL uses the Gospels that get in the way of increased knowledge of that year's synoptic gospel. First, from Advent through Pentecost, the themes and movements of the liturgical year, not the themes and shape of the Gospel narratives, determine the choices of Gospel readings. In ordinary time, the lectionary does provide semi-continuous readings through the Gospel for the year. The problem is that the selections obviously omit those texts used in the first half of the year, which contain some of the key passages for understanding the gospel as a whole (for example texts from the opening and closing of the narratives) Second, the three-year cycle of the lectionary means that John does not get a year dedicated to it. The Fourth Gospel is broken into pieces across the three years, interspersed with the other three Gospels, interrupting the focus on the primary Gospel for the year and confusing the congregation about their differences. Third, even three years of Sundays is not enough to cover all of the material in all three of the Synoptic Gospels. Thus, the lectionary takes a harmonizing approach to how it uses much of the gospel material. If a pericope from one Gospel is used as a lection, its parallel is often omitted from the other Synoptics. Thus, for instance, Matthew's particular redactional take on a scene is lost if Mark's version is used. Since Mark is the shortest of the three Synoptics, a greater percentage of it is read during Year B than is read of Matthew in Year A or Luke in Year C. And because Mark is primarily narrative in content, much of the overlapping narrative material of Matthew and Luke is not read in Years A and C with a heavier focus instead on the sayings material of those Gospels.

To compensate for these problems, this book takes a cumulative approach to preaching Matthew, not just preaching in general. We begin with an introduction to Matthew, meant to serve as an overview to be read especially before beginning to preach on the gospel throughout Year A. The topics of the introduction are those found in most commentaries, but they are written in a way that assumes the reader has some of knowledge of the issues already and thus are here oriented toward the pulpit. How do the sociohistorical situation, theological worldview, and literary characteristics of Matthew influence how we preach the Gospel across a year's time in Year A of the lectionary cycle? Throughout the book, examination of individual lections will include references to these homiletically ripe, overarching exegetical observations.

In addition to this broad introduction to the First Gospel as a whole, each section of the narrative includes an overview. Preachers wanting to move deeper into a review of Matthew than the Introduction offers could read through these section overviews also at the beginning of Year A. Primarily, however, these section overviews are meant to be helpful to preachers in contextualizing lections that fall within that section. To preach cumulatively, pastors will need to keep aware of structures and themes within Matthew to which individual lections relate. Scanning the section overview before preaching on a single lection or perusing it carefully when dealing with a series of semi-continuous readings from a section will assist in this endeavor.

Finally, then, the most detailed examination comes in the comments on the individual lections. The comments will analyze the structure, themes and theological focus of the passage. Also, suggestions will be offered for connecting in sermons the Matthean lection of the day with the section of the gospel of which it is a part as well as with other places in the Gospel sharing concepts, vocabulary and theological perspective. Thus the overviews and the detailed commentary are meant to be in conversation in such a way as to strengthen the use of the text in the proclamation of the good news of Jesus Christ.

While it is not the focus of this book, it is strongly suggested that pastors who plan to preach a great deal on Matthew (be it in Year A of the lectionary cycle or taking a *lectio continua* approach to Matthew) sponsor Bible studies on Matthew outside of worship. Such studies can draw on these cumulative themes and reinforce the congregation's identification with them when they are raised in sermons.

Acknowledgments

While this commentary on Matthew has my name on the front cover, the work has been made much better by the aid of a number of friends throughout the journey of writing this book. I and the readers owe them thanks for making this a better work than it would have been had I written it in isolation.

David Lott started the journey by first suggesting to me that I write a preaching resource on Matthew for Fortress. I did my doctoral work so many years ago in Luke-Acts. Since reading Kermode, I have been fascinated with the literary skill of Mark. But Matthew? All those teachings just thrown together with key word connections and such overshadowing the narrative? I reluctantly agreed more because I was interested in creating a hybrid sort of lectionary commentary that could support a cumulative approach to preaching. But in the process of reading Matthew slowly and carefully in the company of many good scholars who have written before me, I fell in love with Matthew. What I had attributed to sloppiness on Matthew's part was inattentiveness on my part. Even though I had studied Matthew in the past, taught Matthew to my students, and preached on Matthew often through the many Year As of the lectionary cycle, I had not given the First Gospel its due as a unified narrative proclamation of the good news of Jesus Christ.

David, Ron Luckey, Ron Allen, and Jerry Sumney read materials I wrote in the early stages of the work. The support and questions I received from them definitively set some of the directions I would move in writing the bulk of the commentary.

Jerry and Emily Askew, colleagues at Lexington Theological Seminary, have had to endure many a times I wandered into their office with a random exegetical or theological question related to Matthew. Even though they would have been justified in doing so since I was adding to their significant workload, not once did they send me away without a helpful conversation. Jerry's fingerprints especially can be found throughout the commentary.

As the journey has drawn to an end, Lexington Theological Seminary hired a new dean of the faculty. Rich Weis has been nothing but supportive of my vocation of a scholar and protected time for me to complete this project. As I let go of the work, I place it in the very capable hands of Will Bergkamp, Susan Johnson, and Lisa Gruenisen at Fortress Press. They have been encouraging, held my feet to the fire, and have worked hard to make my ideas more presentable in book form.

Finally and always, thanks is due to my wife and daughter, Bonnie and Maggie, for their support across the whole of the journey. Over the last two years, they have rarely seen me without a Greek New Testament in my hand, a commentary by my side, and my computer on my lap.

Readings from Matthew in the Revised Common Lectionary in Order of the Liturgical Calendar, Year A

Liturgical dates are left blank when a Gospel other than Matthew is used.

Liturgical Date	Matthew	Pericope Title	Page Number
Season of Advent			
Advent 1	24:36–44	The Parables of the Flood and of the Thief in the Night	241
Advent 2	3:1–12	The Ministry of John the Baptist	34
Advent 3	11:2–11	Jesus and John the Baptist	124
Advent 4	1:18–25	The Birth of Jesus	28
Season of Christmas			
Christmas Eve/ Day 12/24/25			
Christmas 1	2:13–23	Conflict between Two Kings	31
New Year	25:31–46	Parable of the Judgment of the Gentiles	247
Season of Epiphany (Ordinary Time)			
Epiphany	2:1–12	The Magi	29
Baptism of the Lord	3:13–17	The Baptism of Jesus	36
Epiphany 2			
Epiphany 3	4:12–23, [24–25]	The Beginning of Jesus' Public Ministry	47
Epiphany 4	5:1–12	The Beatitudes	60
Epiphany 5	5:13–20	Salt, Light and Fulfilling the Law 1: Introduction	64

Epiphany 6	5:21–37	Fulfilling the Law 2: Antitheses 1	68
Epiphany 7	5:38–48	Fulfilling the Law 3: Antitheses 2	70
Epiphany 8	6:24–34	Trusting in God's Providence	76
Epiphany 9/ Proper 4	7:21–29	Trusting in Jesus as Messiah	78
Transfiguration of the Lord	17:1–9	The Transfiguration of Jesus	172
Season of Lent			
Ash Wednesday (ABC)	6:1–6, 16–21	Practicing Righteousness	73
Lent 1	4:1–11	The Temptation of Jesus	39
Lent 2	17:1–9 (Alt.)	The Transfiguration of Jesus	172
Lent 3			
Lent 4			
Lent 5			
Palm/Passion Liturgy of the Palms Liturgy of the Passion	21:1–11; and 26:14–27:66 or 27:11–54	Triumphal Entry The Passion	213 250 272
Holy Week			
Holy Monday			
Holy Tuesday			
Holy Wednesday			
Holy Thursday			
Good Friday			
Holy Saturday			
Season of Easter			
Easter Vigil	28:1–10	The Empty Tomb	273
Easter Sunday	28:1–10 (Alt.)	The Empty Tomb	273
Easter Evening			
Easter 2			
Easter 3			
Easter 4			

Easter 5			
Easter 6			
Ascension			
Easter 7			
Pentecost			

Season after Pentecost (Ordinary Time)

Trinity Sunday	28:16-20	The Great Commission	278
Proper 4: 5/29-6/4	7:21-29	Trusting in Jesus as Messiah	78
Proper 5: 6/5-11	9:9-13, 18-26	Tax Collectors and Sinners; a Dead Girl and a Sick Woman	98
Proper 6: 6/12-18	9:35-10:8, (9-23)	Sending of the Twelve	106
Proper 7: 6/19-25	10:24-39	Encouragement in the Face of Persecution	109
Proper 8: 6/26-7/2	10:40-42	Conclusion to the Mission Discourse	110
Proper 9: 7/3-9	11:16-19, 25-30	Jesus as the Revelation of the Father	126
Proper 10: 7/10-16	13:1-9, 18-23	Parable of the Sower	135
Proper 11: 7/17-23	13:24-30, 36-43	Parable of the Weeds in the Field	137
Proper 12: 7/24-30	13:31-33, 44-52	Parables of Growth and Discovery	140
Proper 13: 7/31-8/6	14:13-21	Feeding over Five Thousand	155
Proper 14: 8/7-13	14:22-33	Walking on Water	157
Proper 15: 8/14-20	15:(10-20), 21-28	Healing the Canaanite Woman's Daughter	160
Proper 16: 8/21-27	16:13-20	Peter's Confession	164
Proper 17: 8/28-9/3	16:21-28	The First Passion Prediction	168
Proper 18: 9/4-10	18:15-20	Overcoming Sin in the Church	183
Proper 19: 9/11-17	18:21-35	How Much Forgiveness in the Church?	185

Readings from Matthew in the Revised Common Lectionary in Order of Matthew's Narrative

(Liturgical dates are in Year A unless otherwise indicated.)

Matthew	Pericope Title	Liturgical Date	Page Number
Beginnings: From Bethlehem to Nazareth			
Birth			
1:18–25	The Birth of Jesus	Advent 4	28
2:1–12	The Magi	Epiphany	29
2:13–23	Conflict between Two Kings	Christmas 1	31
Preparation for Ministry			
3:1–12	The Ministry of John the Baptist	Advent 2	34
3:13–17	The Baptism of Jesus	Baptism of the Lord	36
Capernaum–based Ministry			
Beginning of Jesus' Ministry			
4:1–11	The Temptation of Jesus	Lent 1	39
4:12–23, [24–25]	The Beginning of Jesus' Public Ministry	Epiphany 3	47
Ethical Discourse			
5:1–12	The Beatitudes	Epiphany 4; All Saints 11/1 (or 1st Sun. in Nov.)	60

All Passages in Matthew, Including Those Not Used in the Revised Common Lectionary

9:32–34	97
9:35—10:23	106
10:24–39	109
10:40–42	110
11:2–11	124
11:12–17	119
11:16–19	126
11:20–24	119
11:25–30	126
12:1–14	120
12:15–21	121
12:22–37	122
12:38–45	123
12:46–50	123
13:1–9	135
13:10–17	135
13:24–30	137
13:31–33	140
13:34–35	135
13:36–43	137

Introduction

Most questions about the origins of the First Gospel can only be answered tentatively. *Who* wrote the narrative? We do not know. All of the Gospels were authored anonymously. The attribution to Matthew came later, based on the fact that the Gospel changes the name of the tax collector called to be a disciple by Jesus from Levi to Matthew (contrast Mt 9:9 with Mk 2:14; Lk 5:27). Answers to questions that follow, however, prove this answer to be untenable. Still, for convenience's sake, scholars continue to refer to the author as "Matthew," and we shall follow this convention as well.

Where was the First Gospel written? Again, we don't know. Biblical scholars have made many suggestions over the years. The most popular is Syria, specifically Antioch. The initial reason for considering Syria is interesting but not very reliable: Matthew 4:23-24 is a summary of Jesus' healing ministry in Galilee and the spread of his fame that follows the initial call of the fishermen as disciples. Mark, who narrates the same call story of the fishermen (Mk 1:16-20), does not have this summary afterward. So Matthew's paragraph would potentially hold unique clues to the author's interests. The structure of the comment that catches scholars' attention is this: Jesus did many healings in Galilee and thus his fame spread throughout Syria. Syria could be used in two different ways in the ancient world. Romans called the entire area of the eastern Mediterranean, "Syria," as a governmental region. Locally, and more traditionally, "Syria," referred to the part of this governed region on the northeastern coast of the Mediterranean Sea (north of Galilee). If in 4:24, Matthew is using "Syria" the first way, the passage makes sense. If he is using it the second way, it is odd that Jesus performs miracles in one region and his fame spreads throughout another. This would signal that Matthew might be referring to his home region—the location of the community from, to and for which he writes. This scholarly discussion does not add a lot of helpful information for preachers seeking to use a passage from Matthew as a lens through which to view God-in-Christ with us in the world today, but what it does add is important. First, it would put the author close enough to have some familiarity with the regions of Galilee and Judea without necessarily having intimate knowledge. This would explain some of the ways geographical and cultural details are named at times. Second, and more importantly, one of the reasons

Antioch in Syria makes sense is that it was a large city that in the later first century had both a large Christian population and a larger Jewish population. The tension between the synagogue and the church that is prominent in the First Gospel (see below) makes sense in such a setting. Knowing and sharing this can be important for the preacher because it helps avoid anti-Semitic, supersessionist *eisegesis* of Matthew in contemporary interpretation.

When was the First Gospel written? The label "First Gospel" refers only to canonical order, not chronological order. Almost all scholars agree that Mark was written first, around the year 70 C.E. in relation (at least in part) to the impending or just occurred destruction of the temple and the crisis of faith (i.e., theodicy) that it would have caused for Christians. Matthew uses Mark as his main source for writing his narrative. Approximately 90% of Mark appears in Matthew and about 50% of that shared material is word for word or nearly word for word. In addition to using Mark's content, Matthew seems to follow Mark's basic ordering of this material and thus the structure of his plot. Moreover, about two hundred of Matthew's over nine hundred verses are paralleled by Luke but not Mark. Most of this material is sayings/teachings of Jesus, and so most scholars agree that Matthew and Luke share a sayings source (commonly called Q) that they use independently to supplement Mark. (While I find comparison between Matthew and Luke's shared sayings material extremely helpful for preaching in conversation with Matthew's unique theology, I find claims about whether Matthew or Luke's version of a saying represents the original Q and discussion of the shape of "the Q community" based on insufficient evidence, forced and ultimately unhelpful for interpreting the text.) In sum, Matthew's composition looks something like this:

- 66% comes from Mark
- 22% is shared with Luke
- 12% is unique to Matthew

So Matthew likely wrote ten years or so after Mark (giving Mark time to have spread and become known by Matthew's community), editing Mark's material and adding material to Mark as he felt needed to meet the new situation of his community of faith in a new day.

The struggle to explain the relationships between Matthew, Mark, and Luke is called the synoptic problem. Every seminarian since the beginning of the twentieth century has learned about it. Yet hardly any of our laity have ever heard of it. When I first learned of it in college I was angry that none of the pastors I had grown up with had ever mentioned it. So I called them and asked why they had not explained in it the pulpit. Overall, the answers came down to a fear that such knowledge would weaken people's faith in scripture instead of build their faith. What happened for me in that first Introduction to New Testament course, however, was that my understanding of scripture was broadened and my faith in God was deepened. There is so much more of Matthew's theology from which to preach if the congregation learns that Matthew edited Mark and differs from Luke in the way in its attempt to faithfully present the gospel for a church facing particular circumstances in particular sociohistorical context. This knowledge sharpens the preacher's ability to draw analogies between Matthew's situation and ours, and the congregation's ability to follow the preacher in making that analogy and seeing God-with-us. Whether it be using a synopsis in a Bible study or a projection screen in worship, pastors can show laity the following kinds of things:

Matthew's concern for the fulfillment of scripture: point out that in contrast to Mark's version of the entry into Jerusalem (Mk 11:1-11), Matthew edits it so Jesus rides two animals at the same time (Mt 21:1-11);

Matthew's redemption of the portrayal of the disciples: for example, where Matthew adds in Jesus' praise for Peter after the good confession before he rebukes him and calls him Satan (Mt 16:13-23; cf. Mk 8:27-33);

Matthew's approach to Jesus' theology in the Sermon on the Mount (Mt 5-7) as compared to Luke's presentation in the Sermon on the Plain (Lk 6:17-49) especially as illustrated, say, in the beatitudes (Mt 5:2-12; Lk 6:20-26); and

Matthew's approach (My 28) to dealing with Mark's open-ending and lack of a resurrection appearance (Mk 16:1-8) in contrast with Luke's approach to the same problem (Lk 24).

By offering these sorts of examples over the course of preaching on Matthew throughout a year, laity likely will not feel threatened by them, will become convinced by the power of the cumulative evidence, and will learn to read Matthew (and the other Gospels) as theological narratives instead of trying to anachronistically press them into the service of modern journalistic, historical concerns.

Sociohistorical Tensions in Matthew

Much of biblical scholarship since the Enlightenment has focused on historical criticism—trying to answer questions about the historicity of references to events and characters in the biblical texts and the historical situations out of which those biblical works arose. (We have addressed some of those typical to Gospel studies in the previous section.) It has not always been clear to either scholars or preachers how or to what degree this historical research is useful to the proclamation of the gospel based on reading the Gospels as scripture. The answer preachers give to this question lies to a great degree in their theological orientation and that school of thought's view of the role of God in history and history as revelation.

For instance, in Gospel studies one of the long-debated historical issues relates to the historical Jesus—which stories and sayings come from the historical Jesus, which from the early church, and which from the hand of the author himself. To use classical theological terms, what is at stake is the relation of the Jesus of history to the Christ of faith. Does a miracle story, for instance, have authority in the pulpit today because it reflects what Jesus really did or because it makes a symbolic/metaphorical theological claim about Christ? Or does a particular parable have authority for the church because Jesus actually said it or because it reflects the church's understanding of the implications of living faithfully in the name of Christ? It is beyond the scope of this work to deal with this issue thoroughly, but it is important to name my approach. Without denying that there are historical elements to be discovered in the Gospels, I assume the best way to approach the text in service of contemporary proclamation of the gospel is to read the Gospel of Matthew as ancient proclamation rather than history. In other words, we will be focusing on the final form of the text's presentation of Jesus Christ instead of the historical issues behind the text.

This does not mean, however, that historical issues will never come into play in our reading of Matthew. Matthew did not offer his proclamation in a vacuum any more than today's preachers do. Understanding how Matthew shaped his presentation of his understanding of Jesus as the Christ to address his specific context will help us shape our sermons based on the First Gospel to better address our contexts. What drove Matthew as an author can (and should) influence our driving forces as preachers. Historical criticism in the latter part of the twentieth century shifted from dealing primarily with finding historical facts in and behind the biblical texts to consider the sociological, political, and cultural contexts out of which those texts arose and which is addressed by them. There are three such contexts—specifically, situations of tension—that are especially important for understanding Matthew's driving forces and that will come into play in lection after lection during Year A.

Rival Interpretations of Christ within the church: As we noted above, Matthew uses Mark as his main narrative source, but *edits* the Markan material significantly. Often scholars and preachers present Matthew and Luke's redaction of Mark in terms of the natural expansion of traditions. But let's be clear: Matthew did not expand Mark in some neutral manner by simply adding teaching materials to his narrative material. Matthew found Mark's narrative wanting when it came to meeting the ongoing needs of his church. Matthew's heavy dependence on Mark shows a great appreciation for Mark's presentation of the Christ event. But his willingness to omit some of Mark's material, change most of Mark's material he used, and add loads of material to what Mark compiled also shows Matthew's critique of Mark's final product. Even if the RCL takes a harmonizing approach to the synoptic material it selects over three years, preachers should not approach the lections using a harmonizing hermeneutic. Highlighting the different context in which Matthew wrote (as contrasted with the other Evangelists) and thus the different elements of content of the First Gospel (as compared with the other Gospel narratives) offers the congregation more gospel, not a divided gospel. By offering a congregation Matthew's unique theological approach to the Christ event, the hearers' understanding of God-in-the-world (that is, of God-in-their-lives) is expanded, whereas to only emphasize the theological elements the Gospels have in common distorts each Gospel's message and takes a reductionistic approach to the good news of Jesus Christ as proffered in the New Testament canon.

Throughout the commentary, however, on individual passages, we will examine specific redactional elements in Matthew's version of scenes and sayings that have parallels in Mark and/or Luke, but it will be good to examine a few of the more significant redactional elements in advance. First, Matthew changes the way the gospel story begins. Mark begins with John the Baptist and Jesus' baptism, so that Jesus *becomes* the messiah when God pronounces him to be God's Son at the baptism (Mk 1:1-11). Matthew extends the narrative backward to Jesus' ancestry and birth (Matthew 1–2). This addition does not simply represent biographical interest. Matthew changes Mark's christology, presenting Jesus as God's Son from his miraculous conception on. This identity (and the events confirming this identity) is a fulfillment of scripture. The narrative addition of the first two chapters changes the significance of Jesus' baptism and the interpretation of the stories that follow.

Similarly, and secondly, Matthew extends Mark's ending. In Mark the resurrection had been foretold and foreshadowed, but instead of narrating that resurrection Mark concludes with an open ending that presents only an empty tomb but no resurrection appearance (Mk 16:1-8). This is a major element of Mark's corrective christology in which the evangelist is reemphasizing the cross for a community that has been over-emphasizing the resurrection, perhaps in relation to Christian hopes and expectations related Jewish Revolt of 66–70 C.E. Their theology would have been seriously challenged when the Romans destroyed the temple, the strongest symbol of God's providential concern for the Jewish people (including Christians who saw themselves as related to Judaism—see below). Mark's surprise ending in which the women tell no one about the promise to meet the risen Christ back in Galilee works parabolically because all of the original hearers/readers presumably already knew and believed a story of the resurrection. Matthew, however, is not writing such a corrective narrative in relation to a crisis of theodicy. The author fills out the promised appearance of the risen Christ—the women tell the disciples of the open tomb, and they meet Jesus on a mountain in Galilee where Jesus gives them the "Great Commission" (Mt 28). Moreover, Matthew tells the story of guards placed at the tomb to counter charges presumably made by Jewish religious leaders, that there was no resurrection, only a stolen body (27:62-66; 28:4, 11-15).

Third, Mark often refers to Jesus' teaching in a way that gives it great narrative and christological importance. Oddly enough, however, Mark provides little content of that teaching. Matthew's redactional element that has received the most scholarly attention is the addition of a great deal of sayings of Jesus. Matthew collects most of these teachings into five discourses (perhaps modeled on the parables and eschatological discourses in Mark 4 and 13, and to a lesser degree on the mission instructions in Mark 6:6b-13). Each of the first four discourses end with a transition statement like, "When Jesus had finished saying these things . . ." (8:1; see also 11:1; 13:53; 19:1), and the last one ends with, "When Jesus had finished saying *all* these things . . ." (26:1) The five discourses, therefore, are as follows:

1. Ethical Discourse (Sermon on the Mount): Matthew 5–7
2. Mission Discourse: Matthew 10
3. Parables Discourse: Matthew 13
4. Community Discourse: Matthew 18
5. Eschatological Discourse: Matthew 24–25

At times in the past, scholars have tried to equate these five discourses with the five books of the Pentateuch, assuming Matthew is presenting Jesus as the new Moses. While there are significant elements of a Moses typology in Matthew's christological presentation of Jesus (especially in the first two chapters and the mountain setting that recurs in Ethical Discourse (chapters 5–7), the transfiguration (17:1-8), and the resurrection appearance (28:16-20; see also 14:23; 15:29) scholars generally agree that Matthew does not have a christology primarily shaped by a Moses typology and does not extend the elements of the Moses typology that are present to the structure of the discourses themselves. They are thematically connected discourses.

Rivalry between church and synagogue: As we mentioned earlier, Matthew was likely written ten or so years after the destruction of Jerusalem and its temple. The destruction of the temple itself was not the immediate sort of crisis for Matthew at this later period as it had been for Mark. But as went the temple, so did the sacrificial system in Judaism. The *torah* and its principles and practices had to be interpreted in new ways for the new context. The priestly class of Sadducees essentially disappeared, and so did the Essenes (who argued they were the rightful priests to serve the temple over against the Sadducees). That left two groups to vie for the role of heir and interpreter of the Jewish traditions—the Pharisees and the Christians.

Matthew has been rightly described as the most Jewish of the four Gospels. It has also been rightfully described as the most anti-Jewish (although this title could also be given to John). On the one hand, Matthew presents Jesus in the lineage of Abraham and David (1:1-17), narrates events in Jesus' life as the fulfillment of ancient scriptural prophecies using multiple, formulaic citations from the prophets (for example, the first such citation is found in 1:22), and has Jesus himself claim not to abolish the law and the prophets but fulfill it (5:17-20). On the other hand, in material unique to Matthew, Jesus attacks the Jewish leaders with great force (see especially 23:1-36) and presents the Jewish crowd in Jerusalem, spurred on by the religious leaders as calling for Jesus' execution while saying, "His blood be on us and on our children" (27:25).

This paradox grows out of the tension between Matthew's church and the synagogue over who has the best interpretation and application of the Jewish tradition in the post-temple, post-resurrection period. The break between the church (Matthew is the only Gospel that places the anachronistic term *ekklesia* on Jesus' lips; see 16:18; 18:17—chapter 18 is a church discipline of sorts) and the synagogue is especially evident in the fact that Matthew's narrator consistently describes Jesus as going to teach in *their* synagogues (4:23; 9:35; 12:9; 13:54; see also 11:1 where Matthew uses "their cities") as if Jesus as a Jew had no connection with the primary institution of Judaism in Matthew's day. More sharply, Matthew has Jesus accuse synagogues of being institutions that persecuted prophets and persecute the church (23:34; 10:17).

As we shall see in the commentary, Matthew does not present Jesus as a victim of unprovoked attacks by the Jewish religious authorities. Jesus makes the initial attacks on them. Both Matthew's vigilance in relation to the *torah* and his vehement attack of Jewish leaders should be understood as his attempt to legitimize the church and its faith in the midst of this struggle with the synagogue. Preachers will do well to highlight often this rivalry so as to help their congregation avoid using Matthew to support anti-Semitism. Indeed, it is Matthew's commitment to the idea that the Christianity of his day, including the inclusion of the gentiles in the church, is in continuity with the traditions and texts of Israel (over against the synagogue's claims that Christianity has broken with those traditions) that makes the rivalry so intense.

When this anti-synagogue/anti-religious leader theme shows up in lections, preachers will do well to help congregations recognize the role such rhetoric played in Matthew's struggle to defend and define the legitimacy of his church's life and faith. This can be done in such a way to affirm Christianity's continuity with Judaism today. Remember, both the church and Pharisaic Judaism were very young when Matthew was written in the late first century. Sibling rivalry can only occur if you are siblings. But usually as children mature, the siblings outgrow the rivalry while growing into new ways of valuing their relationship as siblings. In Western history, however, the church has sinfully and violently held on to the rivalry as the more powerful of the siblings in society. The costs to the church, to the Jewish people and to society have been enormous. Christians should not preach these texts in a post-holocaust age without humility and penitence in their hearts and on their lips. Moreover, with the dominant role the church occupies in Western society today, the preachers will often want to ask the congregation to identify and be convicted with the religious authorities/synagogue in the text instead of standing over against them.

Resisting the rival empire: One of the most common terms in the First Gospel is "the kingdom of heaven," (literally "of the heavens"). Matthew inherits the phrase and its significance from Mark—although Mark uses "kingdom of God"—but increases the emphasis on it in that he uses "kingdom" some sixty times compared to around twenty by Mark. Scholars have traditionally argued that the significance of Matthew's shift in phrasing is to make the term more appealing for a Jewish audience by using "the heavens" as a circumlocution which avoids uttering God's name. Since Matthew does use kingdom of God occasionally (6:33; 12:28; 19:24; 21:31, 43), this argument is not persuasive. Matthew's shift may reflect tradition or practice in his own community or a stylistic choice of his own, but the import of the term does not seem to have shifted significantly with the change of modifier.

Before we discuss the import of the phrase for Matthew, we need to recognize that the traditional translation of the Greek word *basileia* as "kingdom" is problematic for two reasons. First, the word "kingdom" is a spatial or territorial term. *Basileia* can refer to a place that is ruled by someone, but it can also refer to the act/power of ruling itself. Second, the word kingdom is not inclusive by today's standard of theological language. A kingdom is a place ruled by a male king, thus "kingdom of heaven" limits God by portraying God as male. Various terms—such as, reign, realm, rule, dominion—are in use as alternatives to kingdom, but none are without problems. In this commentary I will use "reign of heaven." Although we rarely speak of rulers as "reigning" these days and "reign" loses some of the force of the spatial qualities of *basileia*, this translation conveys the power, authority and regality of *basileia*.

The translation "reign of heaven" also helps congregations overcome the way this term if often misunderstood in the church. Intuitively, we understand the significance of much of our vocabulary in terms of contrasts. Words make sense over against their opposites. "Up" makes sense over against "down." "Yes" makes sense over against "no." But many words that represent more complicated concepts can be contrasted to more than one thing, and only context makes clear which contrast is at play. When I use the word "woman," I might be making a gender contrast over against "man" or an age contrast with "girl." In today's world when most people read or hear "kingdom of heaven," their mind is led to contemporary understandings of the afterlife and "heaven" as opposed to "hell." Or they hear it as a metaphor for the church over against the world—locating God in here with us but not out there.

In the ancient world, however, the heavens were the realm of God's transcendent power and holy will over against the corrupt powers and self-serving desires in the "world." This means that Matthew's "reign of heaven" as a metaphor for God's eschatological reign of justice and mercy should be understood as contrasted with the present reign of the world, especially although not solely, with the oppressive reign of Caesar. The reign of God represents God's just and merciful desire for and calling of the world over against the church's experience of life in the Roman Empire in which the vast majority had no political, social, or economic power. Matthew envisions a world transformed by the gospel of Jesus Christ. This transformation, for Matthew, is eschatological. It has begun in the birth, life, ministry, death and resurrection of Christ, but more is promised. The church is associated with the reign of God but is not a synonym for it, since the church has fully arrived but the reign of God has not. (See the discussion of eschatology below.)

This contrast between the reign of heaven and the reign of the world means that Matthew's Gospel is thoroughly political. Ironically, the phrase "the reign of *heaven*" shows God's concern for the *world*. Recall the Lord's Prayer:

> Your kingdom [reign] come.
> Your will be done on earth as it is in heaven. (6:10)

The evangelist is concerned that the church recognize that as they are not satisfied with the status quo, neither is God. Persecution of the church, economic disparity, exclusion of the unclean, oppression of those without power, lack of care for those who are ill and without means, peace forced on people by the sword, and so on and so forth cannot stand unchallenged by the gospel of Jesus Christ. The proclamation and work of the church should reflect God's desire that the world be healed—that the oppressed be saved and oppressors be judged. Preachers who deal with Matthew's messages only on individualistic terms and ignore its social and economic concerns are cheating key aspects of the First Gospel's presentation of the Christ event. While Luke's political agenda may be more obvious, Matthew's is no less significant for understanding the full import of the gospel for today's church. The very summary of the message of John the Baptist, Jesus and the church in Matthew is "Repent, for the reign of heaven has come near" (3:2; 4:17; 10:7). Presumably for Matthew, this means the reign has come near *in Jesus*. For Matthew, then, salvation known and experienced through the Christ event is not limited to, but certainly includes, a sociopolitical dimension.

Given these three tensions that play a role in the development and expression of Matthew's narratives—rival interpretations of the Christ event within the church, rivalry between the church and synagogue, and the church resisting the empire—preachers will do well to ask of every Matthean passage from which they will preach: With whom is Matthew in dialogue here? Implicitly or explicitly, is Matthew speaking against something in his world as he affirms something in the narrative scene or saying of Jesus? Which rivalry in Matthew is at play in this passage? Or, vice versa, when Matthew speaks against something, is there a group affirming it that Matthew stands over against? Locating Matthew properly can better help the preacher locate the congregation effectively in relation to the sermonic claim that will be offered.

NARRATIVE STRUCTURE OF MATTHEW

An important aspect of reading and preaching lections from Matthew in Year A of the RCL in a cumulative fashion is a sound understanding of the Gospel's narrative structure and plot development. Not only the content, concepts, vocabulary and images in the Gospel, but the very flow of the story of Jesus' birth, ministry, teachings, passion and resurrection is theological. While the First Gospel's structure has been greatly debated, we should remember that outlining an ancient narrative is as much a heuristic device helping us get a handle on a literary work as a whole as it is discovering what the author actually planned. Thus in the long run, for a preacher, it is more important to recognize key narrative connections and transitions in the gospel that help put any individual pericope in an insightful narrative and theological context in the aid of proclamation than it is to determine precise and detailed narrative divisions which are argued for in different scholarly commentaries.

Variations on two basic proposals for understanding Matthew's structure dominate the scholarly debate. One is that Matthew has three primary sections (1:1—4:6; 4:17—16:20; 16:21—28:20), divided by the phrase "from that time Jesus began to" in 4:17 and 16:21. The three sections are complex, involving a range of types of narrative scenes and teaching materials as well as a variety of theological themes. Still some generalization is helpful for getting the big picture. The first section involves the establishment of Jesus' identity through his birth, baptism and temptation. The second is initiated by public proclamation of the reign of heaven. The third is initiated by private instruction about and that leads to the passion and resurrection. Ultimately, however, this outline is not convincing. The phrase argued to be transitional is simply not that prominent to be the kind of marker proposed. (Moreover, part of the phrase, "from that time," appears also in 26:16 in reference to Judas.)

The second and older proposal focuses on the five discourses mentioned earlier (Ethical, 5–7; Mission, 10; Parables, 13; Community, 18; Eschatological, 24–25). As noted in that discussion, in the classical development of this proposal (which is no longer accepted) scholars argued that the discourses represented a new *torah*, as Jesus represented the new Moses. Rejecting this interpretation of the discourses, however, does not mean dismissing them as key structural elements in the Matthew's narrative. The concluding phrases to the discourses (a form of "when Jesus had finished saying these things" in 8:1; 11:1; 13:53; 19:1; 26:1) are more prominent than those observed in the previous proposal. The problems with this proposal are that (1) the gospel is presented as a pendulum between discourse and action that does not fully represent the flow of Matthew's story from beginning to end, resulting in the fact that (2) the discourses are interpreted as disconnected from the narrative context in which they are found. Moreover, (3) emphasis on the sayings material often translates into a diminishing of the importance placed on the narrative sections as if they add little to what Mark has already provided, so much so that Matthew has in some older readings been incorrectly considered to be of the genre of ancient manuals for Christian living instead of a narrative at all. (This ignoring of the narrative aspects of Matthew is seen, as well, in the RCL's favoring of the sayings material over the narrative material in Year A.)

I want to suggest a third option for looking at the structure of the First Gospel: attending to the *geographical movement* of the gospel as a way of (1) valuing the flow of the narrative plot and the thematic development of the five discourses in these two proposals and (2) heuristically seeing Matthew as a theological and narrative whole while preaching through passages chosen by the RCL. In the outline below, the main headings name the primary geographical progression of the story (with the discourses listed in italics):

- Beginnings: From Bethlehem to Nazareth (1:1—4:11)
    - Birth (1:2—2:23)
    - Preparation for Ministry (3:1—4:11)
- Capernaum-Based Ministry (4:12—18:35)
    - Beginning of Jesus' Ministry (4:12-25)
    - *Ethical Discourse* (5:1—7:29)
    - Healings and Following Jesus (8:1—9:34)
    - *Mission Discourse* (9:35—10:42)
    - Conflicts Building (11:1—12:50)
    - *Parables Discourse* (13:1-53)
    - Jesus as the Son of God Who Feeds the World (13:53—17:27)
    - *Community Discourse* (18:1-35)
- Traveling to Jerusalem (19:1—20:34)
- Passion, Death, and Resurrection in and around Jerusalem (21:1—28:15)
    - Entrance (21:1-17)
    - Jesus against the Religious Leaders in the Temple (21:18—23:39)
    - *Eschatological Discourse* (24:1—25:46)
    - Preparation for Dying (26:1-46)
    - Suffering and Death (26:47—27:61)
    - Resurrection (27:62—28:15)
- Beginning Again in Galilee (28:16-20)

One of the most striking things to notice from this arrangement of Matthew's material is that four out of the five discourses fall within the narration of Jesus' Capernaum-based ministry. For all of the space Matthew gives to the discourses, they do not drive the narrative as a whole. Matthew's plot is influenced by the discourses but not determined by them. The overarching story is moved along by *growing conflict* between Jesus and the disciples on the one side and the demonic powers and religiopolitical authorities on the other.

In the Beginnings sections, Herod (along with religious authorities summoned and supported by him) seeks to kill Jesus, but through divine providence Jesus is rescued. This conflict which leads Jesus from Judea to Egypt then to Galilee serves as a pattern for the traveling conflict that defines the rest of the story.

In the Capernaum-based ministry (on Jesus setting up headquarters in Capernaum, see the commentary on 4:12-25), Jesus begins critiquing religious authorities in the Ethical Discourse (as had John the Baptist; 3:7) by calling his followers to a higher righteousness than the religious leaders practice. After the discourse, Jesus begins healing and casting out demons, and the religious authorities begin challenging his works, practices and teaching even to the point of accusing him of using the power of Satan in performing exorcisms (9:34; 12:24) and ultimately scheming to destroy him (12:14). Twice in this section, Jesus predicts the final conflict in terms of his arrest, suffering and death at the hands of the authorities (16:21; 17:12; see also 17:22).

This prediction is repeated and expanded in the section in which Jesus travels to Jerusalem (20:17-19; see also 20:22, 28), as is increased testing by the religious authorities along the way (for example, the section begins with Jesus being tested, 19:3-9). Jesus' public and symbolically loaded entry into Jerusalem and his attack on the temple intensifies the conflict in the opening of the final major section of the narrative. The religious authorities respond by challenging Jesus on numerous issues while he teaches in the temple. But Jesus gets the last word with the strident condemnation of the religious authorities as powerful and oppressive hypocrites (chapter 23). (By setting this attack in the temple just before Jesus departs the temple for the last time and predicts its destruction in chapter 24, Matthew associates the post-temple synagogue leaders in his day with the now defunct temple, thus lifting up the legitimacy of the church in the strongest terms yet.) But the religious authorities (in cooperation with the political powers) have the last act—they arrest, try, brutalize, and kill Jesus. Yet the death is not the end of the conflict. The religio-political powers carry the conflict to the tomb by placing guards there. God, however, trumps all in the end by raising Jesus from the dead reducing their power to naught.

And in the final and shortest section of the narrative, in which Jesus and the disciples meet once again in Galilee, Jesus claims to have been given all authority in heaven and on earth (contrast Satan's claim to possess all the kingdoms of the world in 4:8-9) in a word that declares the conflict ended and won (28:18). It is not the discourses that drive the story, it is this conflict. And understanding where any individual passage is located in relation to this evolving conflict n Matthew will help the preacher name appropriately what is at stake in the scene. For instance, controversy scenes between Jesus and religious authorities are found in the Capernaum-based section, Travel Narrative, and Jerusalem section. But the tension is not equal in them, even if the clues within the passages themselves do not signal differences. The context should alert us that more is at stake for the plot in the conflicts in the temple than those at the beginning of Jesus' public ministry.

Given the weight preachers should place on context in interpreting passages as exemplified in the rising conflict of the First Gospel, we must be careful not to read its discourses as if context does not matter. The discourses play the most obvious role in the presentation of Jesus' itinerant ministry in and around Capernaum. Throughout this section Jesus moves in and out of the public arena in different ways and the discourses add to this dimension. The Ethical Discourse, the first example of explicit teaching of Jesus in Matthew, begins with Jesus withdrawing from the crowd to speak with his disciples (5:1) but ends with the crowds astonished at his teaching (7:28-29). The Mission Discourse is directed to the Twelve (10:5) but its focus is on sending them out in public ministry to the people of Israel. Jesus addresses the Parables Discourse to the crowds (13:2-3) but interprets the parables in private for the disciples (13:10-23, 36-43). The Community Discourse is fully addressed to insiders in private—Matthew uses Jesus' last word in Galilee to speak directly to his late first century church before Jesus departs from there heading to Jerusalem (19:1).

The fifth and final discourse is also addressed only to the disciples and is part of the last major section. Its placement at the height of the story's conflict signals that it has a different narrative function than the others. Following Jesus' teaching in the midst of conflict in the temple, this discourse interprets the fall of the temple (which was in Jesus' future and Matthew's past) in eschatological terms. On the other hand, as a prelude to the death and resurrection—that is, the eschatological moment of all moments—Jesus delivers the last discourse on last things, and its purview is much more cosmic in nature than the teaching in the earlier discourses (although they all have eschatological elements as well).

This signals that the conflict that drives Matthew's story of the Christ event and especially the divine resolution of that conflict (along with the presumed parallel tensions in Matthew's situation which the evangelist is addressing) are eschatological in nature. (See the discussion of eschatology below.)

MATTHEW'S THEOLOGICAL THEMES

In the commentary that follows I will often signal the theological character of a lection as a way to signal what the theological character of the sermon should be. A great deal of preaching today de-emphasizes theology and emphasizes instead exhortation with theological language added for seasoning. If biblical preaching, however, uses a scripture passage as a lens for viewing God-with-us and the implications of that claim for our way of life, we must use the lens properly. At the core of biblical preaching is analogy between the world behind and in the scriptural text and our contemporary world. While much has changed in human society since the composition of the biblical texts, and while in a postmodern worldview we may resist making universal claims, biblical preaching assumes that the character and will of God and the core human condition (and thus state of the world) are basically the same today as they were then. Otherwise ancient scripture would have little to say to us today. Thus when we preach on a biblical text, we do well to make sure our sermon is in the same theological category as the text we are using as a lens for our interpretation of the gospel in today's world.

As we have said, at its core, the First Gospel is proclamation. It is theological proclamation that was developed in a specific time and place for a specific people. It is proclamation offered in the light of certain sociological, religious, and political tensions that were part of that time and place, so that the narrative world and the author's world bleed into one another. It is proclamation in the form of a complex story instead of direct theological discourse. But it is proclamation. And we preachers claim that this proclamation is relevant for *our* specific time, place, and people. Matthew proclaims God's decisive engagement in the world in Jesus Christ, and thus offers us in his narrative a lens through which we can view God's continued engagement with us. Thus it is important to attend to recurrent theological themes in the First Gospel before we move to exegetical commentary on individual passages. By foreshadowing some of the more important theological aspects of Matthew's thought in this introduction, we will have data to use in preaching cumulatively from any individual reading from the RCL where these themes occur. Throughout the commentary, I will often note the theological arena of the passage to point preachers in a helpful direction.

Christology. First and foremost, Matthew is a christological work. In narrating the works of Jesus—the teaching, healings, death, and resurrection—Matthew proclaims something of the person of Jesus Christ.

Some of the most obvious clues to Matthew's christology are the titles he uses for Jesus. More than conveying distinct aspects of Matthew's theological understanding of Jesus' identity, these titles cluster and overlap to offer a broad picture of Jesus' theological significance. Matthew is filled with various christological titles, references and metaphors. We can only consider a few of the most important clusters here.

First is the name "Jesus" itself. As opposed to simply presenting "Jesus" as a proper name, Matthew etymologically connects the name with Jesus' purpose: saving his people from their sins (1:21; cf. 26:28). Thus to say that Matthew is a christological work is to say it is a soteriological one. Matthew also uses "Messiah/Christ" (Greek: *Christos*) as a proper name at times (in the phrase "Jesus Christ"), but more often as the title indicating Jesus as God's "anointed." This is a religiopolitical term implying a kingly figure in the line of David (and thus connected with the title "Son of David"). Jesus is no insurrectionist but the "king of the Jews" who suffers to save his people (2:1-6; 21:1-9; 27:11, 37, 42).

Second is "Son of God." This title is paired with Messiah in 16:16 and 26:63 so should not be seen as implying something radically different from that just discussed. It is, however, a more expansive term. Whereas in Mark, Jesus is claimed as God's Son at his baptism (Mk 1:11), in Matthew the voice at baptism (Mt 3:17) simply confirms what has been established earlier in the narrative through the story of the divine conception and virgin birth (1:19-24). Jesus claims this identity for himself in the story of the temptation, and (differently than in Mark where this identity is not affirmed by any human until it is revealed at the point of his death, 15:39) others use the title for him as well (14:13; 16:16; 27:54). Jesus as Son of God is "Emmanuel" (1:23), God's presence with God's people (see also 28:20). Thus Jesus authoritatively reveals God's will for the world as well as God's love for and judgment of the world.

Connected with "the Son of God" (Greek: *ho huios tou theou*) in terms of parallel linguistic construction is the Greek title *ho huios tou anthropou*, traditionally translated as "the son of man." This translation uses antiquated, male-exclusive language and simply does not convey the full sense of *anthropos*. Scholars have suggested terms like, "the Human One," or "the son/child of humanity." There is much to value in these, but they lose the linguistic parallel with "the Son of God." Therefore, although it is a wooden translation, awkward in English, and not necessarily recommended for the oral–aural arena of the pulpit, we are going to use the literal, "the son of the human" in this commentary.

"The Son of God" and "the son of the human" complement each other instead of naming different understandings of Jesus—we must be careful not to read later doctrinal formulations into "the Son of God" (fully divine) and "the son of the human" (fully human). Whereas "the Son of God" is established in the Beginnings section of the narrative, "the son of the human" does not appear until 8:20 during the Capernaum-based stage of Jesus' public ministry, because in the narrative it is only used by Jesus to refer to himself, and he does so thirty times from this point on (approximately twice the number of times reference to Jesus as God's Son are made). Hebrew and Aramaic predecessors to *ho huios tou anthropou* are simply poetic ways of referring to a generic person or likeness of a person. This is the case in the vision in Daniel 7, from which the Gospels' use of the term clearly comes (see Mt 24:30). In the first part of the vision recounted by Daniel (7:1-8), there are four beasts representing four kingdoms. But then two heavenly figures in human likeness appear, the Ancient of Days (7:9) and "one *like a human being* coming with the clouds of heaven" (7:13, NRSV, italics added to designate the phrase more literally translated "son of a human"; cf. Mt 24:30) to whom the former gave authority and kingship to bring judgment upon the beasts/kingdoms (Dan 7:14). In other words, the phrase "son of human" designates a celestial being appearing in the vision in the likeness of a human. By the time the Gospel writers use the term, however, the figure in Dan 7:13 was understood in Second Temple Judaism as a specific apocalyptic redeemer/judge, and thus they used the phrase as a title. While Jesus almost nonchalantly refers to himself as "the son of the human" in the way celebrities refer to themselves in the third person, by using the title in this way Matthew presents Jesus as an eschatological figure who brings judgment into the world (for example, 10:23; 13:41-43; 16:27-28; 19:28; multiple uses in ch. 24; 25:31; 26:64). But the apocalyptic judge is also the servant one who suffers and dies to give his life as a ransom for many (24:27; see also 9:6; 16:13,21; 17:12, 22; 20:18; 26:24, 64).

Whereas the Gospels present Jesus using "the son of the human" to refer to himself, the final title we should examine is used in Matthew only by Jesus' followers and those seeking aid from Jesus: "Lord" (8:2, 6, 8, 21, 25; 9:28; 14:28, 30; 15:22, 25, 27; 16:22; 17:15; 18:21; 20:30, 31, 33; 26:22; on calling Jesus "Lord" without submitting to him, see 7:21-22). The term is striking because it is commonly used for God as well as for Jesus. The Greek *kyrios* can simply be a title of common courtesy/respect, like "sir" in English, but it can also imply a more significant level of dependence and even subservience on the part of the one using it to address another. When applied to Jesus in Matthew, it certainly implies nothing of a divine nature and in fact adds little to the christological content we have already named. What it shows, however, is something of the posture Matthew assumes members of the Christian community should have toward Jesus given the authority of his teaching and works. We approach the Messiah, the Son of God, the son of the human, our teacher, healer, redeemer judge, with humility and subservience.

We preachers often sprinkle our sermons with such christological titles without explaining their significance to our congregations. Most likely, we assume the congregation is familiar with them. This may or may not be the case, but it is highly unlikely that our congregation recognizes that Matthew uses these terms in distinctive ways. One way to preach on a lection that is christological in nature is to use the christological title(s) in the passage as an entry way into everything else going on in the scene.

Characterization of God. As named above, in the Beginnings section Matthew goes a long way toward establishing the core content of his christology, especially in identifying Jesus as "the Son of God" in the stories of the conception by the Holy Spirit and the virgin birth. One of the reasons "the Son of God" is such an important christological title in Matthew is that it is the flip side of the characterization of God as "Father." Whereas Mark uses the title four times and Luke seventeen, Matthew presents Jesus as calling God "Father" over forty times. Jesus refers to God in a personal way using the language of *"my* Father" (7:21; 10:32-33; 11:27; 12:50; 16:17; 18:10, 19; 20:23; 25:34; 26:39, 42, 53), but he also includes his followers as children of God by speaking of God as *our* and *your* Father in the discourses (5:16, 45; 6:1, 4, 6, 8, 9, 15, 18; 7:11; 10:20, 29; 18:14; compare descriptions of the disciples as "sons of God/reign" in 5:9, 45; 13:38).

In contemporary preaching, this paternal metaphor for God is often sentimentalized or romanticized in a way that does not fit with Matthew's use. While "Father" does convey parental love, we must remember that the first century was a time of extreme patriarchy. (This patriarchy has been continued in the church through the use of "Father" as the dominant metaphor for God—a matter that needs great liturgical, homiletical and theological consideration but is beyond the scope of this commentary.) Fathers had significant power over their children and households. Matthew's use of "Father" for God, therefore, includes on the one hand, providential and salvific care for God's children, and on the other, it conveys God's authority and judgment over the world. It is very nearly equivalent to a kindly king. Therefore, we must be careful not to read too high a level of intimacy into this characterization of God. After all, while Matthew uses "Father" much more than does Mark, Matthew omits Mark's use "Abba" in Jesus' prayer in Gethsemane (Mk 14:36, Mt 26:39).

Perhaps most revealing, Matthew usually has Jesus speak of God as the Father *in heaven* or as the *heavenly* Father (5:16, 45, 48; 6:1, 9, 14, 26, 32; 7:11, 21; 10:32-33; 12:50; 15:13; 16:17; 18:10, 14, 19, 35; 23:9). Marking Father as a formal title for God instead of a form of intimate address, these spatial modifiers signal the transcendence of God. God is in heaven—distant, holy, Other. And this transcendence is part of what explains the eschatological nature of Christian experience. God is with us through Christ as Emmanuel (1:23; 28:20), but as we must await temporally for consummation of the reign of heaven, we wait (spatially) the coming of God's will on earth as it is in heaven (6:10).

While in a commentary on Matthew, one cannot avoid reference to the "Father" in the text, preachers should be careful in using this metaphor homiletically and liturgically. Matthew's use has clearly shaped the way the masculine term for God has become the dominant metaphor for the deity in Christianity (and thus limiting God) and the many subsequent ways women have been marginalized and oppressed in the church and in society. Given the theological and ethical problems with the term, preachers must ask whether they can any longer faithfully proclaim the reign of God made known in Jesus Christ using this metaphor.

Eschatology. It is difficult to exaggerate the apocalyptic dimension of Matthew (or of the New Testament as a whole, for that matter). Nearly every action and teaching of Jesus in the gospel has eschatological import (albeit to varying degrees). This eschatology is best understood in the context of Matthew's broad picture of salvation history. Although Matthew's plot extends from the conception to the resurrection of Jesus, his story world extends from Abraham (1:1) to the end of time (28:20). Put differently, at all times in his narrative, Matthew has in view both Israel's past and the church's future, and the story of Jesus serves as the hinge between the two. Israel's past has leaned in toward Jesus as seen in the fact that as the Messiah he is the fulfillment of scripture. And Jesus leans toward the future of the church (and indeed of the cosmos) in that even the death and resurrection narrated within the storyline is not the end of his work—the *parousia* is.

Matthew most explicitly refers to the *parousia* in the Eschatological Discourse in chapters 24–25. He inherits this discourse from Mark 13, but edits some of the language here and there, intensifies the expectation of the coming of the son of the human, and adds a significant amount of material (both "Q" material shared with Luke and material unique to Matthew) urging the disciples to be ready for the end. These elements are seen right from the beginning of the discourse. Mark's discourse begins when Jesus leaves the temple, predicts its destruction and then is asked when this will happen and "what will be the sign that *all these things* are about to be accomplished" (Mk 13:4). In Matthew, however, after Jesus predicts the fall of the temple, the question is different: "Tell us, when will this be, and what will be the sign *of your coming and of the end of the age*?" (Mt 24:3) Right from the outset, Matthew makes clear that the coming of Jesus and the end of times is absolutely connected.

When and how this *parousia* at the end of times will occur, however, are anything but clear. Matthew's intensification of Mark's eschatology might indicate that his hearers are less concerned about the *parousia* than he thinks appropriate. So Matthew names in strong terms the judgment that is part of the *parousia* with parables warning what happens to those not prepared (24:37—25:46).

Nevertheless, in attempting to raise his readers' eschatological awareness, Matthew does not overstate his knowledge of the end (24:36). He makes clear that the coming of the son of the human is not to be associated with natural disasters or human violence, especially the destruction of the temple or persecution of the church (24:4-28). It will be accompanied, instead, by cosmic signs described in scripture—that is, the destruction of the lights in the sky (24:29). This cosmic description of eschatological expectations shows that while Matthew is clearly persuaded a literal salvific judgment is in the future and wants to persuade his readers of such, he is more concerned with his readers living eschatologically in the present. As long as the sky is the same way it was yesterday, you need to keep living toward God's future.

This is the "already/not-yet" of eschatological existence. God's salvation and judgment have already arrived in Christ (as seen in the existence of the church), but they are not fully consummated (and seen in continuing evil in the world). For Matthew, it is incorrect to view the first coming of Jesus as historical and the second as eschatological. To speak the name Jesus is, in Matthew's view, to make an eschatological statement.

Notice that John's disciples ask Jesus—who stands before them in the present—"Are you the one to come?" in the future tense (11:3). And notice that the Gadarene demoniacs in 8:29 confront Jesus, recognizing him as the Son of God and asking a different question than is found in Mark 5:7: "Have you come here to torment us *before the time*?" (Greek for "time" here is *kairos*; while not all uses of *kairos* in Matthew have this weighty, eschatological sense, often it does: 11:25; 13:30; 16:3; 21:34, 41; 24:45; 26:18.) The demons seemed to think they had full reign until "the end of the age," but this is not the case. Matthew's story of Jesus is the story of the beginning of the eschatological age. The birth, teachings, healings/exorcisms, death and resurrection of Jesus as a whole mark the incursion of the end of the ages, in which we currently live and which we wait to see fulfilled. In Matthew's view, you cannot be a Christian and not experience existence eschatologically.

The same in-betweenness is found in language of *the reign of heaven.* As we have said, the reign of heaven is to be understood over against the reign of this world (especially the reign of Caesar), and thus is a thoroughly political concept. But it is more expansive of a concept for Matthew than a political reference alone can make clear. Jesus never defines the reign of heaven, but only describes it in parables that evoke questions about one's relation to the reign of heaven more than answer questions about the nature of God's reign itself. But clearly for Matthew, the coming of the reign of heaven cannot be separated from the coming of the son of the human/son of God. While Matthew speaks of the reign of God existing before Jesus' time, it has been suppressed by violence (11:12). The consistent proclamation of the approach (the Greek *eggizō* in the perfect tense can also mean "drawn near" or "has arrived") of the reign of heaven by John, Jesus and the disciples (3:2; 4:17; 10:7) and the parables comparing the reign of heaven to growth (13:24-33) indicate God is doing something new in Jesus. A new order has begun. But (as with Matthew's language of the *parousia*) this new order is not complete. Even though the reign of heaven has approached, the church is to pray for its coming (6:10).

Yet the First Gospel presents Jesus as predicting that the *parousia* will occur during the lifetime of some of those in the story (that is, in his generation—see 10:23; 16:28; 24:34). Matthew and Matthew's church, of course, know this did not occur, so why did the evangelist not edit or omit these sayings? While historical answers to this question are hard to find, the presence of this theme does show that Matthew at least suggests a metaphorical interpretation of his eschatological themes alongside any literal interpretation one might propose. After all, one does not edit Mark's Gospel to include teaching to inform the hermeneutics and practices of the church for the long run with the expectation that the son of the human is literally surfing in on the clouds any minute.

Thus in today's theological climate and given the passing of two thousand years without the *parousia*, preachers will do best to interpret these themes in experiential terms instead of chronological ones. Eschatological existence can be compared to driving a car on a lonely country road (with no street lamps) at night. With no oncoming traffic, you put your high beam lights on and ease toward the center of the road a little. But then as you begin to rise up a slope, you see headlight beams coming from the other side of the hill. You move back to the right some and turn off the high beams. This is a simplified version of already/not-yet. You have not yet met the vehicle coming your way, but you have already adjusted your driving in relation to its approach. To be a Christian shaped by the Christ event but living in a world shaped also by evil forces is to live everyday with the headlights but not the full reality of the vehicle.

Ecclesiology. The church for Matthew is the eschatological community formed by Jesus and living in the already/not-yet of the last days in light of his teaching, healing, death and resurrection. The church is not alone in this time. Even while awaiting the *parousia*, they have the promise that Jesus is with them (1:23; 18:20; 28:20). That Matthew is especially concerned for the church is seen in the fact that the fourth discourse focuses, to a great degree, on life in the church (the Community Discourse; chapter 18). In fact, as we have noted earlier, in this discourse Matthew anachronistically puts the word church (Greek *ekklēsia*) in Jesus' mouth (18:17; see also 16:18).

Jesus formed the church for Matthew in that he called the disciples, taught them, empowered/authorized them and sent them out as his emissaries. The disciples represent the church in Matthew's narrative, or conversely, the readers are led to identify with the disciples in the narrative. Understanding how Matthew does this will help preachers invite their congregation to identify with the disciples appropriately in different lections from Matthew.

This identification between the church and the disciples is found in Mark as well, but in Mark the disciples start off in a positive manner—obediently responding to Jesus' call (1:16-20)—only to misunderstand who Jesus is (for example, 4:41), and to eventually abandon him at his arrest (14:26-31, 50, 66-72). A key Markan passage in showing the disciples as flawed is Peter's confession in 8:27-33. When asked who the disciples think Jesus is, Peter uses the correct words: "You are the Messiah." But something is signaled as wrong when Jesus immediately (and sternly) orders the disciples to keep this silent; then foretells his suffering, death and resurrection using not Peter's title of Messiah but "the son of the human;" and then rebukes Peter to the point of identifying him with Satan when Peter tries to rebuke Jesus. This flawed understanding of the Markan disciples is likely a literary technique to help the Markan readers see their own flawed christology.

Matthew, however, redeems the disciples to a great extent. They certainly misunderstand Jesus at times, and they certainly abandon Jesus at his arrest

(26:31–35, 56, 69–75). But they are much more aware of who Jesus is than in Mark's version. As a group, they profess him as the Son of God (14:33). And Peter does so in the confession at Caesarea Philippi, expanding Mark's "Messiah" to "You are the Messiah, the Son of the living God." Instead of immediately silencing Peter, Jesus blesses him, explicitly founding the church. Matthew then continues with the Markan material in which Jesus orders the disciples to tell no one, predicts his death and rebukes Peter by calling him Satan (16:13–23). But the dye has already been cast a different color and the scene has a much more positive tone. Matthew's disciples are a positive model for the church to emulate.

Indeed, the authority given to Peter when Jesus praises him for his confession is the same authority Jesus gives to the church just a couple of chapters later in the Community Discourse. Jesus says to Peter, "And I tell you, you are Peter [Rock], and on this rock I will build my church… And I will give you the keys of the kingdom of heaven, and whatever you bind on earth will be bound in heaven, and whatever you loose on earth will be loosed in heaven" (16:18–19). Likewise, when Jesus describes the role of the church in conflict between Christians, he says, "Truly I tell you, whatever you bind on earth will be bound in heaven, and whatever you loose on earth will be loosed in heaven" (18:18).

Matthew's use of the disciples as representatives of the church in his gospel means that not only is the discourse of chapter 18 directed especially to the church, so are the other discourses. Only the Parables Discourse (chapter 13) is addressed to the crowds instead of the disciples, but even it contains private interpretation offered only to the disciples. Matthew's expansion of Mark with teaching materials grouped into these discourses for the disciples/church shows that the evangelist is concerned with creating a document that will undergird the ongoing life of the community of faith in a way he assumes Mark's narrative does not. He provides the church with instructions for their ethical life, their missionary outreach, their understanding of the reign of God, and their eschatological existence. With the RCL's emphasis on these discourses during Ordinary Time of Year A, preachers will do well to imagine with their congregations ways these teachings name who the church is and who it is to become in accordance with God's will and Jesus' ministry as opposed to reading them in ways that laity hear the lections as addressing individuals alone.

Part of Matthew's goal in narrating and providing teaching for the church in these ways is to locate the church within the scope of his vision of salvation history. As we described earlier, Matthew views Jesus as the hinge between Israel's past and the church's future. A theological problem in connecting those two for the New Testament writer is the fact that the church contains gentiles. How can a gentile-filled church be part of Jesus as fulfilling instead of abandoning the *torah*? In addition to having Jesus exhort the disciples/church to hold on to a higher righteousness than the scribes and Pharisees in observing the law in the Ethical Discourse (5:20), Matthew answers this question with a two-stage mission. When Jesus sends the disciples out to exorcise demons, heal sickness and proclaim the approach of the reign of heaven in the Mission Discourse, he begins with the explicit instruction, "Go nowhere among the gentiles, and enter no town of the Samaritans, but go rather to the lost sheep of the house of Israel" (10:5-6). This is striking given Matthew's distancing of Jesus from the synagogue discussed above. In other words, the mission of the disciples (historical representatives of the church) is narrated as initially being directed only to the Jews. Mark does not contain this element in his form of the sending of the twelve (Mk 6:7-13), so Matthew has made an intentional theological move in adding it. Mark concludes the mission with the disciples reporting what they had done and taught (Mk 6:30), but Matthew never reports the apostles' return. Omitting this detail is likely also intentional, signaling to the reader that the mission to the Jews has not ended. Thus when expounds upon the parable of the vineyard, claiming, "the kingdom of God will be taken away from you and given to a people that produces the fruits of the kingdom" (21:43), the "you" refers to religious leaders and not Israel as a whole. After the resurrection, however, Jesus returns to Galilee of the gentiles (4:15) and instructs the disciples now to go and make disciples *of all nations* (28:19). The gentile mission does not replace the mission to Israel but supplements it. In spite of his church's conflict with the synagogue, Matthew views Jesus's concern as being universal—not either/or but both/and. And he assumes the church's concern should be the same. The church today that reads Matthew, therefore, should have an evangelistic fervor to proclaim the good news of the reign of God known in and through Jesus Christ but without anti-Semitic or supersessionist tones to the proclamation.

1

Beginnings: From Bethlehem to Nazareth (1:1—4:11)

The First Gospel begins at the beginning. The opening words in Greek are *biblos geneseōs Iēsou Christou*, literally, "the book of genesis [beginning, creation, birth] of Jesus Christ" (1:1). *Biblos geneseōs* may serve as the title for the whole Gospel, name the opening chapters narrating everything leading up to the beginning of Jesus' ministry (1:1—4:11), introduce the material telling of Jesus' origins and infancy (1:1—2:23), or only start the genealogy that immediately follows the verse (1:2-17). Regardless, the reference to the beginning of God's story with God's people is unmistakable. From the first stroke of his stylus, Matthew connects the story of Jesus Christ with the whole of God's story told in Hebrew scripture. Preachers should always keep this wide angle view of salvation history in mind when focusing on individual passages in this Gospel.

In 1:1—4:11, Matthew prepares the reader to encounter Jesus through the works of his ministry and teaching, death, and resurrection, by introducing his very character as God's messiah through stories leading up to and through his birth and childhood (1:1—2:23) and preparation for ministry (3:1—4:11). The connections with Israel's ancestry, the numerous messianic titles, and the density of prophecy fulfillment citations in these chapters set the christological tone for the whole of Matthew's story. Put differently, these chapters are no mere prelude to what follows in the Gospel (as has been asserted by scholars in the past). Instead, all of the stories that follow these opening chapters unpack the theological conception of Jesus as the Christ offered here. Nowhere is this more evident than in the fact that before Jesus is born, Matthew announces that he is Emmanuel, God with us (1:23, from Isaiah 7:14), and at the end of the Gospel the risen Christ promises to be with his disciples "always, to the end of the age" (28:20). In all stories in-between, therefore, (without reading in trinitarian theology that developed centuries later in the church) whatever we see Jesus doing, we see God doing. In Jesus's actions and teachings, in his very person, we see God's salvific presence. To help a congregation get a sense of central christological emphases of the First Gospel, a preachers should not only spend time focusing on the language and images offered in the opening chapters and found in lections that are used early in the liturgical year but can also reference them often while preaching on other passages in Matthew with similar emphases throughout Year A.

BEGINNINGS: JESUS' BIRTH AND CHILDHOOD (1:1—2:23)

INTRODUCTION

This section is commonly labeled a "birth narrative" (see 1:18), similar to Luke 1:1—2:40. But in truth this is a misnomer. There is a lot of detail about Jesus' lineage, the betrothal of Joseph and Mary in relation to her pregnancy, and the response to Jesus' birth by the Magi and Herod, but technically speaking there is no birth scene. The birth is certainly reported; it is just not narrated (which is why the gospel reading for Christmas Eve/Day is drawn from Luke 2 every year and not Matthew even in Year A). Matthew's interest here is not in establishing biographical facts, other than presenting Jesus as born in Bethlehem and growing up in Nazareth—biographical details we also find in Luke. What is at stake instead is theological: connecting Jesus as messiah with a lineage extending through David to Abraham, showing Jesus' coming as the fulfillment of God's prophecies in the Hebrew Bible, and naming the significance of his coming through the use of various titles and a geographically-oriented midrash of the Moses/exodus story. In other words, this section is thoroughly christological in intent, not historical, and thus stories related to Jesus' birth are told even if the birth itself is mentioned only in passing.

This section can be outlined as follows:

> 1:1-17 Genealogy
> 1:18—2:23 – Infancy
>> 18a – Heading
>> 18b-25 – Parents' Response to the Birth Beforehand
>> 2:1-23 – Magi and King's Response to Birth Afterward

PASSAGE OMITTED FROM THE LECTIONARY

The RCL gives much attention to the infancy stories, but omits the genealogy altogether. Lists of "begats" do not usually make exciting texts to read in liturgy and on which to preach. But this genealogy is key to understanding Matthew's christology and especially the scandal of Jesus' being born of a woman who got pregnant out of wedlock. The genealogy is structured in three series of fourteen generations, from Abraham to David, to the exile, to Jesus. As Christ, Jesus is not only the son of David, with whom God made a covenant concerning the rule of Israel, but also the son of Abraham, with whom God made the covenant establishing the people of Israel in the first place. The numerological construct conveys that God has chosen and prepared for the time of this birth. Jesus is no mere coincidence of history—he is the eschatological culmination of history. And God has chosen his birth to occur through the virgin Mary, in the same way that God continued blessing Israel through a scandalous woman forced to take the role of a prostitute to seduce her father-in-law in order to have a child (Tamar, v. 3), a prostitute who betrayed her people of Jericho in order to assist the invading Hebrews (Rahab, v. 5), a Moabite widow of an Israelite, who seduced her husband's kin so he would marry her according to Levirate marriage customs (Ruth, v. 5), and a woman seduced by David himself while her husband was fighting David's war (the wife of Uriah, v. 6). Jesus Christ is the epitome of the cliché, "God works in mysterious ways," and Matthew's story is a narrative through which we can interpret and proclaim those ways (1:1-17).

LECTIONS

The three lections taken from this section of Matthew are really parts of one intricate narrative. Repeated vocabulary, themes, and structures link all of the scenes of chapters 1–2 together. The three passages are, however, read neither on three consecutive liturgical occasions (with Christmas Eve/Day lections coming from Luke 2) nor in sequence during the liturgical year (the order is Advent 4—1:18-25; Christmas 1—2:13-23; Epiphany—2:1-12). In sermons on these three passages, preachers will need to reference the connections explicitly to enhance the cumulative effect of preaching from Matthew during this early part of the church year.

LECTION: THE BIRTH OF JESUS
1:18–25; ADVENT 4

Preachers may experience two very different hurdles as they approach this text.[1] The first is that congregations have heard it so many times, they already know (or at least they think they already know) what it is about. The second is that the passage is so chock-full of theological goodness that it is difficult to pick a singular homiletical focus.

While Luke focuses on Mary as the active parent in dialogue with the angel of the Lord, Matthew chooses Joseph. As interesting as Luke's choice of using the female character is, so is Matthew's choice of emphasizing the faithfulness of the non-father in the role of Jesus' birth. Joseph is a righteous man whom Matthew presents as presuming Mary to be unfaithful when she is found to be pregnant. But an epiphany sets him straight and he obediently takes Mary as his wife and serves as Jesus' legal father, even to the point of accepting the responsibility for naming in accordance with God's will.

Preachers will do well to invite their congregation to identify with Joseph. He is, however, neither the focus of the scene nor its main character. Anybody who has ever been in a play knows that the primary characters get the most lines. Joseph does not speak. Instead, the angel of the Lord and Isaiah speak. The focus is what they speak about: the coming messiah. On the Fourth Sunday of Advent, the congregation should be located where Joseph is: learning who the child is that is about to be born. Preachers attend to lesser elements of the story if they attend primarily to Joseph's epiphanic experience and his response of obedience. A sermon on this text will not ordinarily be ethical in character (that is, concerned with the congregation's behavior being modeled on Joseph's), but christological, even while it continues the eschatological emphasis that dominates Advent.

Notice all that is told of this child in this space of a few short verses.

He is of divine origin (conceived by the Holy Spirit) (vv. 18, 21). Again, while we should not read later Trinitarian claims into this language, we should recognize that this language is one of the sources used to make that claim.

---

1. All liturgical dates refer to Year A of the RCL in which Matthew is the primary Gospel read unless otherwise specified.

At the same time that Jesus is from God, he will be the son of David (a messianic title as well as a genealogical descriptor) by virtue of being claimed as Joseph's son (v. 20). This language connects the scene with the genealogy in 1:1-17.

His name is symbolic of his role: Jesus (a common Jewish name (Greek for the Hebrew Joshua, derived from the verb to "save") will save his people from their sins (v. 22). Matthew does not at this point specify who "his people" are or what "their sins" are. By virtue of following the genealogy, the reader is set up to assume "his people" is Israel. This is certainly true, but as the narrative of the Gospel unfolds with its attention on the sick, the poor, the tax collectors, the oppressed and finally the gentiles, we will find this assumption to be too limited. Differently, contemporary readers are likely to assume that Matthew's understanding of sin is individual based on individualistic themes in contemporary society and individualistic readings of Paul's theology of justification. Clearly here, though, sin is corporate. Thus the salvation Jesus is to bring is social and political (even cosmic) in nature.

Jesus is the fulfillment of scripture. Vv. 22-23 comprise the first of many prophecy fulfillment citations in Matthew.

The prophetic text which Jesus fulfills is Isaiah 7:14. As commentators on both Matthew and Isaiah will point out, in the original Hebrew text the emphasis is not on a virgin birth, but simply on a symbolic birth. The LXX translation of the Hebrew changed "young woman" to "virgin." This translation was used to shape the story of Mary as Jesus' mother. But Matthew's emphasis is not on Mary; it is on Jesus as Emmanuel. Not only does Jesus come *from* God, Jesus will manifest God's presence *with* the people he is coming to save from their sins.

The preacher would do well on the Fourth Sunday of Advent to begin the sermon with claims that we all already know this story, quickly narrate it again in almost ho-hum tones (locating the congregation to see with Joseph's perspective), and then pan out to show the congregation just how much christological theology is packed into this little scene. This will allow preachers to raise the question of Christ's eschatological, saving presence in today's world.

LECTION: THE MAGI:
2:1-12; EPIPHANY, YEARS ABC

The lectionary preacher has several significant problems when wanting to effect a hearing of Matthew's story of the Magi. The first is that, as we have named, this passage is not an isolated pericope that stands alone. It is the first half of chapter 2, which is a lengthy (in Synoptic Gospel terms), complex story. As with chapter 1, chapter 2 as a whole is focused on christology but the christological lenses have switched from lineage and messianic titles to politics and geography. A second problem that is related to the first is that in the lectionary cycle, we read the two parts of Matthew 2 in reverse order. On the First Sunday of Christmas we read the second half of the story (Herod's slaughter of the innocent), and then on Epiphany (or Epiphany Sunday—the Sunday before January 6) we read this story. A third problem is that because the story of the magi is associated with the feast of Epiphany, tradition pushes us to preach the passage in terms of the first revelation of the Christ to the gentiles. While this is an element of the story, it is not the primary focus for Matthew.

Matthew 2 unpacks the political significance of having demonstrated that Jesus is the "son of David" in chapter 1. We often think of Luke as the Gospel most interested in a social, political agenda, but Matthew here from the beginning also shows that the birth of Jesus as the Christ, Son of God and Son of David, has significant political ramifications. Herod is the bad guy in the story, but he is also absolutely correct in his assessment of the situation: Jesus is a threat to his power, Jesus' birth (and the reign of God he will proclaim as arriving) is a challenge to Caesar's empire. Herod knows that when the mage call Jesus a king, they are right. It is cliché for preachers to say that Jesus was not the kind of Messiah expected in Second Temple Judaism. He does not assemble an army to overthrow Rome; he does not try to take the throne; and he does not try to reestablish Israel as an empire. This is all true. But none of this means that his preaching, his healings, his associations, his critique of religious leaders (who benefitted from the empire's benevolence toward them while oppressing others), his death and his resurrection were not a condemnation of and attempt to transform the status quo. Indeed, in this story, Jesus is a passive infant—his very being, not just his later actions, is a challenge to the powers-that-be.

But the fact that a star announces Jesus' birth shows that Matthew interprets the reach of Jesus' impact as going far beyond the political borders (and thus power) of Herod in Judea. The appearance of a star was a common element in legends concerning the birth of a new emperor. But Jesus' star even appears beyond the bounds of the empire. It appears "in the east," an intentionally ambiguous term pointing to an oriental location outside the "western," Roman purview. Jesus' will save his people from their sins, that is, he will liberate his people from oppression with a global, or better, cosmic impact.

The magi, then, are not the main characters of the story. They serve to bring the conflict of the story forward. As eastern (gentile) magicians, they are odd choices to bring news (in the form of a question) to Herod that a new king of the Jews has been born. They are not kings as the Christmas carol says. In fact, the Bible consistently looks down on *magoi* (for example, consider Simon and Bar-Jesus in Acts 8 and 13). Yet, similar to the night-shift shepherds in Luke's birth narrative (Lk 2:8-20), God has revealed the birth to and through these undesirables. Jesus is of scandalous lineage, born of a virgin, and now given testimony by palm readers and horoscope writers—God works through mysterious ways. Moreover, the obedient response of the magi to the angel (coupled with Joseph and Mary's obedience) serves as a model for readers while Herod's machinations reveal the lengths to which those in power will go to destroy good news from reaching those under their power.

Preachers may naturally ask their congregation to identify with the magi, inviting them to respond to the good news of who Jesus is in similar fashion. The theological focus of an Epiphany sermon, however, should not usually be on those who receive the revelation. It should be on the one revealed, on the character and impact of the revelation. In other words, a sermon on this text will be christological, but it should also be political. The sociopolitical claims of the text should expand a congregation's view of the salvation God brings through Christ *and* should call for a response to those claims that require something different of us than it did of the magi. As the church on the post-resurrection side of hearing this story, we cannot be content with going home by a different way to protect the newborn king. As Christ's church (see 16:18), we must confront the oppressive and destructive powers of the world empowered by the saving presence of God-with-us.

LECTION: CONFLICT BETWEEN TWO KINGS
2:13-23; CHRISTMAS 1

Preaching on the story of the slaughter of the innocents on the First Sunday of Christmas is difficult because the narration of the scene in Matthew presumes the story already told in 2:1-12, which the congregation will not hear in worship until the celebration of Epiphany. The preacher will have to remind the congregation of this story without going into an in-depth interpretation that upstages visiting the Gospel lesson on Epiphany.

As with the story of the magi's visit to Herod and then to Jesus, this story for Matthew is primarily christological. It raises the stakes of the political nature of the Christ event in a number of ways. Most striking is the use of midrash in telling the story as an echo of the story of Moses and the exodus. Midrash draws on elements of a known story and refigures them to tell a new story. In midrash, the elements shared between the stories need not be exactly parallel (say, in the way in an allegory each element lines up symbolically with a reference). The point of reframing the elements in a new way is not to say this is the same story with the same meaning as the older, referenced story. Indeed, midrash works more like metaphor than allegory: the new story is *and* is not like the reference story. The intent of midrash is that by drawing older, familiar elements into a new story, the older story influences the interpretation of the new one. Hearers/readers are struck by both the similarities and the differences so that new (parabolic) insight is gained. So Herod killing all boys under the age of two in Bethlehem (similar to Pharaoh killing all newborn males in Exodus 1:15-22), Jesus escaping the slaughter (as Moses was saved in Exodus 2:1-10), and Jesus being called out of Egypt (as God used Moses to lead the Israelites out of slavery in Egypt in Ex 12ff), all point to Jesus as a political liberator like Moses. But following on the heels of chapter 1, it is clear that Jesus is more than Moses. Jesus is the Moses-like messiah, who is also the Son of David and Son of God.

Remember that while God was working through Moses in Egypt (before the first Passover and the crossing of the Red Sea), the oppression and suffering of the Israelites was increased by Pharaoh. This is the reality of evil's response to God's presence. So we should not be surprised to find that the good news of the birth of the messiah is met with horrific violence by those who have benefitted from the hierarchical political and economic structures of society. The advent of Christ does not mean the removal of evil from the world. Indeed, in this scene the birth of the Son of God is the impetus for violence.

To be sure, Matthew presents God as being in control through the angel's interventions and instructions. But we should be clear. God is in control, not of all events in the scene, but specifically of Jesus' destiny. Notice that the scripture fulfillment formula is different in this scene than in the others in chapters 1–2. Elsewhere, Matthew says that such and such happens *so that* (Greek *hina*) the word of the Lord through the prophet was fulfilled. In v. 18, Matthew quotes Jeremiah, a text that when heard in isolation this way is filled with angst and grief. In v. 17 Matthew does not say that those two year old and younger boys were killed "so that" this scripture would be fulfilled. The narrator simply says, "Then [Greek *tote*] was fulfilled what was spoken through Jeremiah the prophet." In other words, for Matthew the slaughter of the innocents is a fulfillment of scripture but not of God's will, in that scripture often names that which resists God's desire for the world. The good news is that God's providence is overarching and the likes of Herod cannot stop what is planned for Jesus. (Ironically, God protects Jesus from being killed at this point so that he can be killed at the right time, as a ransom for many, 20:28). The reality, though, is that Herod can still do a lot of damage along the way. Jesus has come to save God's people, but if this passage is to be taken seriously, that salvation will occur *in the midst of* the struggle between good and evil in the world, not in the creation of a utopia that does not match our experience of reality.

This is not an easy text to preach during the twelve days of Christmas, but it is important not to ignore or avoid it. Despite the carols playing on the radio, the greens hanging in the sanctuary, the parties, and the gift-giving, the holiday season celebrating the nativity is not without pain and turmoil. Every pastor knows that addiction, mental illness, and family dysfunctions cause increased problems in the lives of their parishioners during this "joyous" season. In spite of the fact that individuals and churches feel good (and should feel good) about all the food and clothes charities with which they participate during the holiday season, huge numbers of people sleep in the cold on the streets during Christmastide, just like the rest of the year and about 80% of the population worldwide live on less than ten dollars a day. Even though we sing peace on earth and goodwill to all, wars, ethnic cleansing, gang violence, and infanticide do not take a break from December 25 through January 6.

The good news to be proclaimed is that God's providence and salvation through Christ is not erased by such tragic circumstances, by horrific violence. The good news is that Christ was born into just such a world to save us from these sins. The good news is that this good news is not proclaimed as pie-in-the-sky theology that does not take the real world seriously. But in preaching this good news, preachers should not pass too quickly over the pathos of the scene. Many congregants will find the honesty of naming suffering and despair in the face of "Joy to the World" instead of the denial asked of them by most of the world liberating in and of itself.

Beginnings: Preparation for Ministry (3:1-4:11)

Introduction

A significant shift in setting sets off this section from the previous one. A shift in time is signaled with the words, "In those days" that opens this new section (3:1). While the words mark a new phase in the narrative they are (intentionally?) ambiguous. How much time has passed since Joseph brought Jesus and Mary back from Egypt and settled in Nazareth? The place is also ambiguous: "the wilderness of Judea." Wilderness is a symbolic space of isolation. In isolation is danger but also the potential of revelation from God.

This section opens with John preaching and baptizing in the wilderness and closes with Jesus being tested in the wilderness.

Here Matthew continues to develop the christological approach of the infancy stories by giving us new insight into the character and purpose of Jesus, especially in the words of John the Baptist in 3:11-12 and with the heavenly voice speaking at his baptism (3:17). But with Jesus now in adulthood, the stories also set the stage for Jesus to begin his eschatological ministry. Jesus prepares by being baptized by John and being led by the Spirit to be tested by Satan.

LECTIONS

The RCL uses all parts of this section in Year A, dividing it appropriately into three passages. The three passages appear in order early in Advent, early in the Season after Epiphany, and early in Lent.

LECTION: THE MINISTRY OF JOHN THE BAPTIST
3:1-12; ADVENT 2

It is intriguing that the New Testament church's proclamation of Jesus as the messiah begins consistently with one who is not the messiah—John the Baptist. The early church struggled with the relationship of Jesus and John because Jesus being baptized by John makes it appear as if Jesus was John's disciple, that John was the greater of the two. So the Gospel writers needed to show continuity between the ministries of the two without presenting Jesus as John's subordinate or presenting them as equals and needed to interpret Jesus' baptism as something other than placing Jesus under the authority of John. (Compare Matthew's approach with Luke's. Luke 1–2 presents Jesus birth story as paralleling John's, but consistently shows that Jesus is the greater of the two. Then Luke 3:18-22 presents Jesus' baptism *after* having already told of John's imprisonment.)

Matthew adapts Mark's presentation of John and the baptism of Jesus in different ways to achieve these two goals. Like Mark 1:2-3, Matthew quotes scripture to identify John as the forerunner of Jesus—as the one who prepares the way of the Lord—while cleaning up Mark's conflation of words from Exodus, Malachi and Isaiah and assigning them all to Isaiah (v. 3). And like Mark 1:4-6, Matthew describes John in ways that make him appear to be the return of Elijah (clothing, food, location), which was popularly believed to occur before the coming of the messiah (vv. 1, 4). Matthew, like Luke, adds to Mark's account in John's own mouth testimony to Jesus ("one coming after me") as greater than he is (vv. 7-12). (For ways that Matthew adapts Mark's version of the baptism story to accomplish these goals, see the commentary on the next passage.)

But Matthew also adds something unique that is found in neither Mark nor Luke. He summarizes John's preaching with the exact words he later uses to summarize the preaching of Jesus and the disciples: "Repent, for the kingdom of heaven has come near" (v. 2; cf. 4:17; 10:7). (See the Introduction and the comments on 4:12-25 below for a fuller exploration of the concept of the "reign of heaven.") For Matthew, then, the difference between John and Jesus is not their message but the role they play in relation to that message. In his address to the Pharisees and Sadducees, John *announces* the coming judgment. Jesus, on the other hand, *is* the eschatological judgment. John baptizes with water (like cleansing in the form of washing the surface of something), but Jesus baptizes with fire (like purification in the form of refining or smelting metal to remove unwanted elements).

This new christological portrayal of Jesus as judge may seem at odds with the angel's claim that Jesus is to save his people from their sins (1:21), but in truth salvation and judgment are two poles of the same magnet. Many of us pastors like to preach about justice but avoid any talk of divine judgment. If God decides between what is just and unjust, then God is judge. If God decides that we need to be saved from our sin and liberated from oppression, then God has judged our sinfulness and our situation as not according with God's will. God's mercy and love are meaningless, if God cannot choose to see us and our situations in different ways. For Matthew, to meet and know Christ is to be judged and saved at the same time. The proper response is repentance. This theological claim and existential response will need to be central to an Advent sermon on this lection.

It is important to notice who comes out to be baptized by John. Matthew says the people of Jerusalem, all of Judea, and all of the region around the Jordan (vv. 5-6). Recall that "all of Jerusalem" was troubled with Herod at the news of the birth of a new king (2:3). Both in the earlier scene and here, Matthew uses hyperbole to show the level of impact the birth pangs of the Gospel are having at the center of Israel's religious and political life. This also shows that Matthew is not anti-Jewish. John seems to accept the repentance of and baptize all these people. It is only the religious leaders with whom he takes issue. And although preachers often speak of such leaders as adversaries of Jesus who challenge and attack him in the Gospels, in Matthew they are not the ones to strike the first blow. John challenges them, not the other way around. This sets the stage for Jesus to do the same (for example, see Jesus' similar use of "brood of vipers" and "good fruit" when addressing the Pharisees in 12:33-34.)

This is not an easy text to preach in Advent or any other season. The difficulty is not in identifying what is emphasized in the text but because what is emphasized is so clear. The problem is that what is emphasized is so hard to hear and to respond to appropriately. Three points of identification invite three different sermons in relation to eschatological advent of judgment/salvation and the invitation to repent. The easiest approach may be to ask our congregation to identify with the faceless crowds who come out to be baptized by John. By doing so, we call our hearers as individuals to prepare for the coming of Christ with repentance and confession of sins. In other words we call them to change their lives and to be open to Christ changing their lives.

Second, if we ask the congregation to identify with the religious leaders, we must be willing to name honestly that we religious folks may be the ones most challenged by Jesus' coming. We have domesticated the gospel into polite news for the middle class instead of being saved by confrontation with our judge. In a sense, this identification leads to the same kind of sermon as the first but with a stronger call to reflect on the need for the *church* to repent, not just the individuals gathered into it.

Third, we can also ask the congregation to identify with John himself, placing ourselves in the role of those who are to prepare the way for the coming of the Lord, the arrival of the saving judge who baptizes with fire and the Holy Spirit. In this case, we call the church (and individuals within it) to take up a critical role toward the world, our particular society, and indeed our church. We call the church to speak words of judgment and work radically for justice *so that* all might know God's forgiving and providential care.

LECTION: THE BAPTISM OF JESUS
3:13-17; BAPTISM OF THE LORD

As noted in the discussion of the previous passage, the early church struggled with the relationship of Jesus and John because Jesus' baptism makes it seem as if Jesus was John's disciple. So the Gospel writers needed to show continuity between the ministries of the two without presenting Jesus as John's subordinate or presenting them as equals and needed to interpret Jesus' baptism as something other than placing Jesus under the authority of John. John's own proclamation about the one coming after him dealt with the first issue (3:7-10). The second is dealt with in this pericope.

In Mark's version of the baptism, the voice that calls Jesus God's Son makes it clear that Jesus is more than a disciple of John's (Mark 1:11), but there is still a question of why Jesus responded to John's message of repentance and a baptism for the forgiveness of sins at all. Did Jesus need to be cleansed of sin? Matthew inserts into Mark's version of the scene a dialogue between John and Jesus in which John resists baptizing Jesus because Jesus is the greater of the two. Jesus responds by saying that he needs to be baptized to "fulfill all righteousness" (3:14-15). These are the first words of Jesus in the Gospel of Matthew, and they are loaded, yet ambiguous, words.

"Righteousness" (Greek: *dikaiosunē*) and its cognate "righteous" (Greek: *dikaios*) are key terms for Matthew. "Righteousness" is never used in Mark and only once in Luke (Luke 1:75) while in Matthew it shows up in the mouth of Jesus seven times (Matt. 3:15; 5:6, 10, 20; 6:1 {the NRSV poorly translates *dikaiosunē* here as "piety"}, 33; 21:32). Similarly, "righteous" appears in Matthew twelve times without parallels in Mark or Luke. Scholars are not in agreement about Matthew's nuanced understanding of the concept of righteousness. We can say that to be righteous or to possess righteousness in Matthew is related to observing the Torah but not limited to it. To be righteous is to be an ethical, good person, but it is more than that. The righteous are juxtaposed to sinners. The righteous are paired with but not equated to prophets. Jesus came for the sinners instead of the righteous but nonetheless called his followers to be righteous. So when Jesus is fulfilling all righteousness by being baptized, Matthew is not making a claim about his need for repentance or forgiveness. Instead, he presents Jesus as setting an example for the church, not simply a ritual example but one that leads *us* to recognizing our sins and reorienting our lives toward the good.

While the dialogue between John and Jesus is key for understanding what is at stake for Matthew in this passage, it will probably be in the background instead of the center of a sermon on Jesus' baptism. Clearly, the emphasis in the story is on the epiphany that occurs when God's Spirit descends on him and the heavenly voice announces that he is the God's beloved Son. In Mark 1:11, the voice speaks only to Jesus: "*You* are my Son, the Beloved; with *you* I am well pleased." But in Matthew the voice speaks of Jesus in the third person: "*This* is my Son, the Beloved, with *whom* I am well pleased" (v. 17). Matthew presents the epiphany as public. Presumably John and "the people of Jerusalem and all Judea…and all the region along the Jordan" (3:5) heard God's testimony to the true identity of Jesus. This statement is the narrative climax of the christological focus of the entirety of 1:1—4:11. What the angel declared to Joseph, what the magi understood the star to mean, what the prophetic texts confirm, and what John himself proclaimed is now summed up once for all in God's own voice.

Moreover, this declaration in which God claims Jesus as God's Son stands in direct contrast to the common use of the same language in which the state claimed that the emperor was God's chosen son. So following John's challenge made to the religious leaders whose privilege rests on Roman authority in the previous passage, this scene continues Matthew's undercurrent that the person and ministry of Jesus as God's Son is a challenge to socio-political status quo.

Given what we have said, there are two significantly different sermonic approaches invited by this text that fit well with a celebration of Baptism of the Lord. The first involves a christological focus that accords both with Matthew's christological emphasis throughout the early part of his narrative and with the epiphany theme of the manifestation of God's Christ. In such a sermon, the preacher could proclaim (perhaps in a way that draws together the christological threads woven through Advent, Christmastide, and Epiphany sermons on Matthew) the manner in which Christ's submission to baptism and the divine voice's declaration work together to reveal the relationship of Jesus to God. It is important not to read Trinitarian theology back into Matthew, but a preacher can unpack ways this text helps the contemporary church better understand Trinitarian theology. Or, more closely connected with Matthew's own purposes, the preacher can highlight how even the "common" language used to refer to Jesus (that is, the Son of God) is a countercultural, political statement.

The second possibility is a sermon that uses Christ's baptism as a lens for interpreting the church's baptism. This is especially appropriate given the growing practice of using Baptism of the Lord as a Sunday for rituals of the renewal of baptism. This sermon requires a hermeneutical move in which what happens to Jesus in his baptism is not viewed as *sui generis* but as a model for our sacrament. This does not mean that the church baptizes because Jesus was baptized (see 28:21-20). It does assume, however, that the Gospel writers in general, and Matthew specifically, constructed the story of Jesus' baptism to accord with their community's practice and theology of Christian baptism. Assuming baptism is a conversation of sort between God on the one hand and the baptizand and the church on the other, this type of sermon draws an analogy not only between Jesus' desire to fulfill all righteousness and reasons why we should seek (and remember) baptism, but would assume as well that the divine speech concerning Jesus is analogous to the way in which God claims every person as God's own through (or witnessed to by) baptism.

LECTION: THE TEMPTATION OF JESUS
4:1-11; LENT 1

While most of the lections from Matthew 1:1—4:11 fall in the cycle that extends from Advent to Epiphany, this last passage from the section that presents Jesus as preparing for his ministry as the messiah is read on the First Sunday in Lent. The temptation story has long been associated with Lent due to Jesus' fasting in the wilderness for forty days as a biblical model for the forty days of Lenten discipline. While this liturgical connection offers much for preaching this text on Lent 1, the distance of numerous weeks or even a couple of months between reading 3:13-17 on Baptism of the Lord and reading 4:1-11 on the Sunday after Ash Wednesday causes a literary disconnect the preacher must work to mend for hearers. This disconnect is exacerbated by what is read on the Sundays of Ordinary Time following Epiphany—passages taken from the beginning of Jesus' ministry, especially his first discourse, the Sermon on the Mount. For Matthew, the temptation story is the final story of Jesus' preparation for ministry and flows directly out of the baptism story. (Contrast the placement of the story in Luke 4:1-13 where the genealogy [3:23-38] separates the baptism [3:21-22] and temptation story so that the temptation story serves as Jesus' *first* act of ministry).

For preachers, the temptation story seems to be a ready-made three-point sermon. With one point per temptation, all you have to do is add two jokes and a poem, and you have your sermon. While focusing on the different tests the devil poses to Jesus is a perfectly legitimate exegetical and homiletical approach, I propose that attending to the context in which Matthew places this story and the similarities between the temptations offers a more focused approach to the text.

Matthew places the temptation story on the heels of the baptism story (3:13-17). In that story, Jesus goes out to be baptized by John in the wilderness, and the Spirit descends upon Jesus just before the voice announces that he is the Son of God. In this passage the Spirit leads Jesus into the wilderness (presumably *deeper* into the wilderness since he is already in the wilderness with John) where in the first two temptations the devil begins testing Jesus with the words, "If you are the Son of God." The wilderness, the Spirit, and the title Son of God intimately connects the temptation with the baptism. As we noted at the first mention of wilderness in 3:1, the wilderness is a symbolic space of isolation. In isolation is danger but also the potential of revelation from God. Danger and revelation may well be holding hands in the wilderness where Jesus is tested.

Here the Spirit leads Jesus into this danger. Even though the scene is thick with apocalyptic mythology, we should assume that the danger is very real.

The telling of the story may be fanciful but what is at stake is not, otherwise Matthew would not give the Spirit such a prominent place in initiating the story and fill the scene with so much scripture. What is at stake is whether Jesus will appropriately, fully, and faithfully claim his identity as God's Son. Jesus' identity, significance and purpose was revealed to Joseph and the magi before his birth. It was revealed to John and the crowd (and Jesus) at Jesus' baptism. Now Satan gives Jesus every opportunity to deny who he is, or better, whose he is. He poses the temptation as if he were giving Jesus the opportunity to fulfill his destiny, or at least to use or prove his identity: *If* you are the Son of God, then . . . But he is in reality inviting Jesus to be less than what God intends, indeed, to be Satan's instead of God's. After all, the last temptation (which does not begin with "If you are the Son of God") is the climax of the scene because the tempter invites Jesus to worship him directly (contrast Luke's order of the tests in which the temptation in Jerusalem is the final and climatic temptation [4:9-12] related to the fact that Jerusalem is at the center of the narrative and theology of Luke-Acts). The conditional clause is not necessary because the act of worshiping that which is evil, violent, decadent and oppressive would negate the messianic identity altogether.

As with the other lections from the beginning chapters of Matthew, the temptation scene is christological in terms of its theological focus. Jesus *does* claim the title of Son of God and thus dedicates himself to the healing, liberating, challenging, nonviolent, and merciful mission that is God's will for God's people. Only now is he finally ready to take up the proclamation of the advent of God's reign and the call to repentance. One will do well to preach this text with this focus as a way of preparing a congregation to hear Jesus' claims about his identity according to John in the Gospel lections that follow in the rest of Lent, even while contrasting John's christology with that of Matthew in those sermons (Lent 2: John 3:1-17; Lent 3: John 4:5-42; Lent 4 John 9:1-41; and Lent 5: John 11:1-45).

The placement of this reading at the beginning of the season in which the church is taking on Lenten disciplines and preparing catechumenates for baptism, however, also encourages the preacher to interpret Jesus' temptation as a model for the Christian struggle with temptation. In this case the passage is read ethically—that is, in terms of Christian behavior. Temptation is, for all of us all of the time, a question of who and whose we are. Thoughts of cheating, revenge, stealing, lying, and so on and so forth are really questions about whether we are God's or are possessed by something else, something less. So in one sense, Lenten disciplines are temptation practice. We are led by the Spirit to give up or take on something to test whose we are. After all, since the

Spirit led Jesus to be tested *before* his ministry began and Jesus did not give in to Satan's invitation, we can be sure that when he is in Gethsemane praying, "My Father, if it is possible, let this cup pass from me," he will go on to say, "yet not what I want but what you want." (26:39). We desire such strength for ourselves as well.

2

Capernaum–Based Ministry
(4:12—18:35)

As noted in the introduction, there are a range of ways one might outline the Gospel of Matthew and break it into manageable sections for reading and study. The major divisions we use in this book represent broad geographical, temporal movements in the narrative. In the first movement, the narrator presented Jesus' identity, character and purpose through stories leading up to his birth, dealing with his childhood, and jumping to his adult preparation for ministry.

In the narrative movement to which we turn our attention now, Matthew offers the readers episodes from Jesus' ministry based out of his home in Capernaum (4:13). The section is usually referred to as narrating the period of Jesus' Galilean ministry. While Jesus travels outside of Galilee proper a number of times in this section—across the sea to the "land of the Gadarenes" (8:18, 23-34); across the sea to a deserted place (14:13-33); to the district of Tyre and Sidon (15:21-28); and to Caesarea Philippi (16:13ff, the point at which Matthew envisions Jesus returning is unclear, either after 16:28 or after 17:20)—the bulk of his actions and teachings is focused on the Jewish people of Galilee. And clearly the use of the formula quotation in 4:14-16 emphasizes that Jesus fulfills scripture (and thus God's will) by locating in Galilee (compare the geographical significance of scriptural citations in 1:5-6; 2:15, 23). But it is specifically the city of Capernaum within Galilee as Jesus' home base that gets special attention in Matthew. Matthew follows Mark in locating Jesus in Capernaum but raises the stakes. For instance, at the beginning of this section (4:13) Matthew changes Mark's notice that Jesus "went" (*eisoporeuontai*) to Capernaum (Mark 1:21) to the stronger claim that Jesus "dwelt" or "made his home" (*katoikeō*) there. Similarly, Matthew changes Mark's notice that Jesus returned to Capernaum (Mark 2:1) to say that Jesus came to his "own city" (*idian polin*, 9:1). Moreover, Matthew mentions Capernaum three times not found in Mark at all (8:5; 11:23; 17:24). If this were not enough, Matthew uses "house" (*oikos/oikia*) a number of times seemingly to indicate Jesus's home in Capernaum (9:10, 28; 13:1, 36; 17:25). This is important data for the preacher because it reminds us that Matthew paints Jesus' itinerant ministry differently than we usually do in the pulpit. Matthew's original readers would have recognized that Jesus having a house as a base of operations located him in a social class that was similar to artisans and tradespeople (like those in the fishing industry) instead of peasants of lesser economic means. It is important to remember that in the ancient Mediterranean world, the home was also the place of business for such people. One's house was a public space of work as well as having private dwelling space. (Thus we find Jesus withdrawing to the wilderness for private prayer, presumably because his "home" allowed for little such privacy.)

Note how the above passages make it clear that others recognized Capernaum as Jesus' home and sought him there. Thus, as opposed to wandering aimlessly (that is, homelessly) around Galilee calling disciples, proclaiming the reign of God, healing the sick and possessed, and debating the religiopolitical leaders, Jesus' ministry is headquartered in a central location in Galilee from which he goes out to do ministry and to which he returns. Jesus does not just happen upon this town or that situation, upon this person or that conflict. He strategically moves out from his headquarters to visit and minister in an area and then returns to his home base. And, therefore, when he sets out for Jerusalem (19:1) it is also a strategic move that fits with the agenda of his ministry and life, not simply a coincidental visit during Passover of which the powers-that-be take advantage.

This narrative of Jesus' Capernaum-based ministry is the largest section of Matthew. Because the section is so large, and because Matthew has gathered so much of this material from other sources, we will not find as concentrated a theme or theology in it as we did with the christological focus of the opening section. Matthew here is expanding upon Mark's material in diverse ways (but especially with additional saying materials gathered into discourses) to equip and undergird the theology, faith and lives of his readers in ways that he assumes Mark's Gospel does not. One would expect such an agenda to require more diverse topics and issues to be addressed than we find in Matthew's first section or in parallel materials from the Gospel of Mark.

This does not mean, however, that the material in this section is so episodic that it does not hold together, although a congregation can certainly get this idea from our practice of reading and preaching one an episode at a time in worship. Throughout the section, Matthew brings his christology into clearer and clearer view. Moreover, the plot thickens throughout the section as conflicts between Jesus and religious/political stakeholders arise and increase.

As we saw with John the Baptist in 3:7ff, it is not simply that the religious leaders attack Jesus in this section. Jesus is the one to strike the first rhetorical, ideological blow. As we will see, he takes the (nonviolent) fight to them, if you will. This rising conflict will carry the narrative forward in the later sections as Jesus heads to Jerusalem, the center of religious and political power in the region, and to the cross.

Lectionary preachers will have to work to make their congregations aware of these broad strokes, because the shape of the liturgical year does not allow for reading the bulk of this section before Holy Week. During the Sundays after Epiphany in Year A (depending on how many Sundays there are given that Easter is a movable feast), the RCL has the church reading only from the first part of this section (primarily from the Ethical Discourse/Sermon on the Mount). After Ash Wednesday (on which the gospel reading is also taken from the Sermon on the Mount in all three years: 6:1-6, 16-21) and the First Sunday in Lent (on which the reading is Matthew's version of the temptation story found in the Beginnings section as part of Jesus' preparation for ministry, 4:1-11), the gospel readings for Lent switch to the Fourth Gospel to give John a chance to appear in the three year lectionary cycle (although Matthew 17:1-9 is an alternate gospel reading for Lent 2). Then on Palm/Passion Sunday, we return to Matthew to hear his version of the events in Jerusalem without having experienced much of the groundwork Matthew laid in chapters 8–18 for understanding the reason those events occurred. Indeed, our congregations will not have even heard Jesus' passion and resurrection predictions (16:21; 17:12, 22-23; 20:18-19; see also 26:2) before he enters Jerusalem. Preachers who want to preach cumulatively in such a way that their congregations experience the fullness of the gospel as portrayed in Matthew's narrative will need to draw back on this dynamic when they preach on chapters 8–18 during Ordinary Time after Pentecost.

To see the lectionary's separation of this material better we can outline the section in terms of the way it alternates between narrative and discourse in relation to the liturgical year:

UP TO SEVEN LECTIONS FROM THIS SECTION ARE USED BETWEEN
EPIPHANY 3 AND 8 (DEPENDING ON THE LENGTH OF THE SEASON):
> Beginning of Jesus' Ministry (4:12-25)
>> *Ethical Discourse* (Sermon on the Mount, 5:1—7:29)

UP TO FIFTEEN LECTIONS FROM THIS SECTION ARE USED AFTER
PENTECOST (DEPENDING ON THE DATING OF TRINITY SUNDAY),
PROPERS 5-19:
> Healings and Following Jesus (8:1—9:38)

Missionary Discourse (10:1-42)
Conflicts Building (11:1—12:50)
Parables Discourse (13:1-53)
Jesus the Son of God who feeds the world (13:53—17:27)
Community Discourse (18:1-35)

When a preacher and congregation return to this section after Lent and Eastertide have passed, they will need to remind themselves of the first two parts of it read after Epiphany as well as highlighting the growing conflicts mentioned above as leading to the cross and resurrection, already celebrated in Holy Week. In this extended period, preachers should also be able to point out the pendulum between narrative and discourse as a clue to Matthew's organization of his material without trying to tie Matthew down to too specific of a narrative or theological theory about why he alternates material this way or how the alternation works. There are no strict parallels between the narrative material and the discourse that follows. The thematic character of the discourses is at times looser than a reader might wish. Matthew does not reserve all of Jesus' teaching for the discourses—the narrative sections are filled with logia and pronouncement stories that proclaim and elaborate on the reign of God. And while Matthew draws on Mosaic typology in his christology, the five discourses throughout the whole of the gospel are not presented as a new Torah. Nevertheless, the pendulum does give Matthew a way of grouping materials he has gathered and developed in such a way that invites readers to look for meaningful connections within the groupings and for the advancement of the plot toward its climax in the crucifixion, empty tomb, and resurrection appearances.

CAPERNAUM-BASED MINISTRY: THE BEGINNING OF JESUS' PUBLIC MINISTRY (4:12-25)

INTRODUCTION

The opening subsection of the narrative of Jesus' Capernaum-based ministry is a short piece that sets the tone for and in a sense summarizes all that follows. It has three elements that work together in a sandwich fashion.

4:12-17 – Summary of the Beginning of Jesus' Ministry
4:18-22 – The Call of the First Disciples
4:23-25 – Summary of Jesus' Ministry and the Spread of Fame

Because of the summary nature of the two pieces of bread in the sandwich, preachers are likely to be most attracted to the more vivid narrative filling in the middle. However, the first piece especially holds significant potential for the pulpit and both outer parts help sharpen an understanding of the role the call of the first disciples plays in Matthew's narrative.

VERSES OMITTED FROM THE LECTIONARY

The RCL assigns most of this section to be read as a single lection for the Third Sunday after Epiphany (following two Sundays on which Matthew and John's versions of the baptism story are read). Only verses 24-25 are omitted, presumably because the reading is already long in terms of liturgical needs. But the two final verses do add to the impact of hearing the summary of Jesus' accomplishments in ministry, and it would be worth adding the verses back in. So in the section that follows, we will consider the section as a whole, rather than examining the omitted verses and the lection separately.

LECTION: THE BEGINNING OF JESUS' PUBLIC MINISTRY
4:12-23[24-25]; EPIPHANY 3

The opening verses of the section (4:12-17), or the first piece of bread of the sandwich, summarize the beginning of Jesus' ministry in terms of John's arrest, Jesus' chosen headquarters (see above), and the core content of Jesus' proclamation. Matthew follows Mark in opening with this summary but edits it significantly for his own narrative and theological purposes. First, he adds a scriptural quotation (from elements of Isaiah 8:23—9:1) to show that Jesus' choice of location fulfills God's will for the Messiah (for a fuller discussion of the significance Matthew gives to Jesus' location, see above in the introduction to 4:12—18:35). And, second, he alters the summary of Jesus' preaching. Whereas Mark summarizes Jesus' preaching as "The time is fulfilled, and the reign of God has come near; repent, and believe in the good news" (Mk 1:15), Matthew reads, "Repent, for the reign of heaven has come near" (Mt 4:17). This language parallels exactly John's proclamation in 3:2 (see also the same proclamation, with the exception of the call to repent, assigned to the Twelve in 10:7), whereas in Mark the messages of John and Jesus are not the same.

While preachers will do well to note the summary concerning Jesus' location to frame later sermons on Jesus' ministry in and around Galilee, a sermon that attends to this material will likely focus on the content of Jesus' proclamation. Matthew has moved the word "repent" to the opening of the proclamation, giving it heightened emphasis. This theme might have been explored on the Second Sunday of Advent when preaching on 3:1-12.

Revisiting it now several weeks later would allow the preacher not only to highlight a key parallel in Matthew but also to build on a homiletical theme that could be a small thread running from Advent through the Season of Epiphany toward Lent. (For more on repentance, see the discussion of 3:1-12 above.)

Perhaps of more homiletical importance would be to spend time unpacking Jesus' claim concerning the advent of the reign of heaven (and why that would lead us to repent). There is terrible misunderstanding in the pews of what "the reign of heaven" refers to and a loss of an eschatological worldview that is found on every page of the New Testament, especially when the reign of God is mentioned. This problem is exasperated by the fact that in all of the Gospels Jesus is portrayed as describing the reign of God (primarily in parables) but never as defining it. Matthew's choice to use "reign of heaven" more than "reign of God" often leads contemporary readers to think Jesus is talking about heaven in the popular sense of that a word—God's dwelling place to which souls ascend after death. Nothing could be further from Matthew's mind. His concern is not otherworldly, but God's will, justice and mercy replacing the status quo of this world. The reign of heaven (*hē basileia tōn ouranōn*) is a political term. It is intentionally juxtaposed to reign/reign of Caesar (as seen in violence and oppression) and to the reign of Satan (as exhibited in the narrative through demonic possession and attacks). Notice how later in Matthew, Jesus teaches his followers to pray, "Our Father *in heaven* . . . Your *reign* come. Your will be done on earth as *in heaven*" (6:9-10).

So in his proclamation, Jesus announces that with his ministry, God's will draws near to earth—near to us, here and now— judging and challenging the ways of oppression, violence, and suffering (that is, the ways of death). The connection between Jesus and the reign of heaven is explicitly stated in 12:28 where Jesus defends himself against the accusation that he is casting our demons by Beelzebul. As part of his argument, Jesus says, "But if it is by the Spirit of God that I cast out demons [which it is], then the reign of God has come to you [which it has]." In Jesus, the reign of heaven has come near. And since we Christians believe the world has been transformed by this drawing near, we repent—not to avoid judgment but because we have experienced judgment *and* grace in Christ already. But we Christians are not ignorant of pain and inequality that still exists in the world. The already/not yet quality of Matthew's eschatology is highlighted by the fact that he omits Mark's reference to the time being fulfilled. Without diminishing the already element of Matthew's understanding of God's salvific act in Jesus Christ, Matthew holds in tension with it the not-yet aspect of God's reign. Thus the church continues to pray for the full consummation of the divine reign on earth, and we penitentially respond to Christ's call to cooperate with God's reign. This leads us to the next section.

If the opening verses of the lection serve as the first piece of bread in Matthew's sandwich, the middle of the sandwich (vv. 18-22) is the call of the first disciples to leave their livelihoods and follow Jesus, sharing in his mission. It is important when preaching on this scene that we correct some contemporary pictures of the disciples that do not accord with the Gospels' presentation of them. We caricature the fishermen as poor. Perhaps they are best thought of using the analogy of small family-business owners. Any first century reader of the First Gospel would have known that to fish professionally, one had to have means to catch the fish, pay taxes on fish caught, be able to process (and perhaps transport) the fish, a place from which to sell the fish, and personnel (often family) to work in both the boat and the store. Thus, when the four men leave behind their nets, boats and family, they are not simply leaving behind a job; they are leaving behind their business.

But every reader wonders why they are willing do this. The way Matthew (following Mark 1:16-20) tells the story, we have no sense that the four men have met or even heard of Jesus before. Jesus does not persuade them to follow. He does not invite them to follow. He commands that they come with him and learn a new trade: fishing for people. Historically, this may not make sense, but it does narratively. Jesus has just moved to town and begun his ministry. As 4:17 is a summary of Jesus' proclamation, so is v. 19 a summary of his call to the disciples. Their obedient response is the first success of Jesus' proclamation (even if the narrator does not indicate that they heard the proclamation). If repentance is not simply a feeling but a reorientation of one's life, the disciples have exemplified faithful penitence in light of the arrival of the reign of heaven in Jesus Christ by leaving their livelihoods and following Jesus . . . wherever and whatever that may come to mean. Matthew clearly intends for the disciples (in this scene and throughout the narrative) to serve as models for his readers, that is, for Matthew's church. The readers should respond faithfully to God's call as did Peter, Andrew, James and John. This fact is emphasized by Matthew's reference to Simon as "who is called Peter/Rock." Matthew offers this detail (even though an explanation of the import of the name is not given until 16:18) in a way that it is clear that the original readers already know Peter. Presumably, they have already claimed him as a founder of their community and thus as a model to emulate (see 10:2; 16:18-19; 19:27). Today's preacher will likewise do well to offer the four disciples as models of faithful repentance in light of Jesus as the sign of the advent of God's reign for contemporary Christians as well.

The specific success of calling the first disciples in the middle of the sandwich leads to the second piece of bread, which is a summary of Jesus' continued (initial) success. There is not much theological content here to serve as the basis for a sermon. The text, however, deserves mention in relation to preaching on the earlier portion of the lection because it serves as an exclamation point at the end of the opening movement of this major section of Matthew's narrative and points forward to what is coming. In other words, it names the success at proclaiming the gospel of the reign of heaven, teaching, and relieving suffering due to disease and demonic possession. This initial success and the fame that accompanies is the context in which all of which follows in the gospel is set. The reader knows in very broad strokes now, the fullness of Jesus' ministry. What follows in the rest of the narrative section dealing with Jesus' Capernaum-based ministry (and beyond) are specific examples of his teaching, healing and confrontation of destructive powers.

There are two narrative details here that might not make their way into the center of a sermon, but which should be of interest for preaching through Matthew in a cumulative fashion. First, in v. 23, Matthew uses the phrase "in *their* synagogues" for the first time. While this summary passage does not bring the conflict between the early church and the synagogue into full view, it foreshadows texts where that will occur. It also highlights Matthew's emphasis on the house in Capernaum as the headquarters for his ministry over against the established religious structure of the day in Galilee—the synagogue. Second, while Jesus is described as going about Galilee in v. 23, Matthew says his fame spreads throughout Syria in v. 24. Syria here may be used in the imperial sense of referring to the whole of eastern region of the Mediterranean with its capital in Antioch but which would include Galilee and Judea. Or, as many scholars argue, Matthew may mention Syria here in the sense of the northern region on the eastern side of the Mediterranean Sea because that is where he writes and where his community of faith is. In other words, he mentions Syria to legitimate his church having received word of Jesus (and thus word of the gospel of the reign) at a very early point.

Capernaum-based Ministry: Ethical Discourse (5:1—7:29)

Introduction

In the first four chapters of the Gospel, Matthew establishes his christological view of Jesus and puts him in the appropriate place to begin his ministry. The beginning snapshot of his ministry has included a summary of his preaching, his calling disciples, and his healing work. Now we get down to specifics. And the first specific Matthew offers is a lengthy discourse commonly called the Sermon on the Mount. It is important to recognize that given the summary of Jesus' words and works that has preceded, Matthew chooses to begin his specifics with speech. Proclamation and teaching precede action when it comes to understanding the significance of the Christ event.

The RCL gives a significant amount of attention to the Sermon on the Mount, reading through it in a semi-continuous fashion during the period of Ordinary Time that follows Epiphany and extending into the beginning of the season after Pentecost if Easter is especially early. In truth, the amount of attention this discourse can be given by the lectionary preacher is dependent on the date of Easter during any given Year A of the lectionary cycle.

While the church has named this discourse the Sermon on the Mount in relation to its setting, we would do well to also refer to it in relation to its content as we consider preaching through Matthew in a cumulative fashion. In terms of contrasting this first speech to the other four that follow in the Gospel, its focus is ethical. The others are the Missionary (10:1-42), Parables (13:1-53), Community (18:1-35) and Eschatological Discourses (24:1—25:46). By "ethical," we mean less that the discourse deals with ethical dilemmas and decision-making and more with the praxis of the Christian life as oriented toward the kingdom of heaven and the will of God.

The Ethical Discourse is perhaps the most interpreted New Testament passage in the history of the church, making preaching on passages drawn from it somewhat intimidating. The amount of attention it has received by the likes of Augustine, Aquinas, Luther, the Anabaptists, Calvin, Bonhoeffer, and myriad biblical scholars using different critical methods in the twentieth century demonstrates both the importance accorded it as central to the church's understanding of the Christian life and the complexity of the text in determining just what kind of Christian life it pictures.

A key question that has arisen over the course of this history of interpretation is whether the ethical praxis presented in the discourse is a straightforward, practical ethic to be followed by Christians and others; an idealistic, unattainable ethic that drives readers to God's grace; or an eschatological ethic that only fits within the first century's apocalyptic worldview. What in the discourse is to be understood as literal instruction and what is metaphorical or provocative in forming the reader?

These questions are complicated by the fact that a similar discourse is found in Luke 6, commonly called the Sermon on the Plain. All of the blocks of materials in Luke's version of the discourse are found in Matthew's in the same order with the exception of the "golden rule":

5:3-12 Beatitudes	6:20-26 Beatitudes and Woes
5:38-42 Turn the other cheek; 5:43-47 Love your enemies	6:27-35 Love your enemies & turn the other cheek
5:48 Be perfect as your Father...	6:36 Be merciful as your Father...
7:1-5 Hypocrisy	6:37-42 Hypocrisy
7:12 Golden Rule	(6:31 Golden Rule)
7:15-20 False Prophets/Good Fruit	6:43-45 Good Fruit
7:21-27 Not everyone who says Lord, Lord...Build house on rock	6:46-49 Not everyone who says Lord, Lord...Build house on rock

While much of the language within these parallel blocks is identical or nearly so, both Matthew and Luke clearly edited the material to fit their theological and ethical outlook. Moreover, Matthew has much more material in his version, most of which is found in some form or another in other places in Luke. So whether Matthew and Luke shared a common source that contained the core skeleton of the sermon (which Matthew significantly expanded or Luke significantly shortened), or the two had different sources with some common heritage, or one read the other is up for debate. Although these source-critical questions need not detain us here, the relationship of the two versions of the discourse raises the question: how does knowledge of the parallel in Luke affect the way we interpret and preach on the discourse in Matthew?

Preachers may not need to know the whole history of interpretation of the Sermon on the Mount or take a stance on every critical issue that has been part of the debate concerning the material in the discourse. But to preach in a cumulative fashion through the semi-continuous lections, they will need to determine a basic stance that (1) helps relate all of the individual passages to a sense of the purpose of the whole discourse and (2) applies a common hermeneutic to all the different passages. The stance I offer for your consideration before we turn our attention to individual passages within the discourse is as follows:

The Ethical Discourse is a mixture of different types of sayings materials. Some offer general principles for the Christian life and some are more narrow examples of Christian living. Some expressions are literal directives for the church and others provoke ethical reflection similar to the ways parables function. Some sayings Matthew inherited, some he redacted significantly, and some he created to fit with those he inherited. Knowledge of Luke's use of some of the same material can help us get a handle on some of these issues, but as we shall see, Matthew has his own aim and the final form of the discourse embedded in Matthew's narrative is what primarily drives our reading.

The ethic Matthew presents is practical, idealistic, and eschatological all at the same time. That the material here is thoroughly eschatological is undeniable. The "reign of heaven" is mentioned eight times in the discourse (5:3, 10, 19 [twice], 20; 6:10, 33; 7:21), the confrontation with evil is a prevalent theme of the discourse (for example, 5:11; 6:13), and preparing readers for God's judgment is a clear intent of the speech (emphasized especially at the end: 7:13-27). Likewise, there are idealistic expectations in the discourse that seem beyond the reach of any normal, finite, sinful human or human community—summed up in the expression, "Be perfect, therefore, as your heavenly Father is perfect" (5:48).

But these eschatological, idealistic elements give the discourse its practical force instead of competing with it. They join together to evoke a vision in which God's will is done on earth as in heaven. They evoke a vision of the reign of heaven as being located on earth (indeed, the word earth [Greek: $g\bar{e}$] is used six times in the discourse; 5:5, 13, 18, 35; 6:10, 19). They invite individual Christians and the church as a community to embrace a vision of righteous and just living as disciples of Jesus Christ to which to aspire in all aspects of their daily lives (various words related to the Greek root for right/righteous/just [dikaios] can be found in 5:6, 10, 20, 25, 45; 6:1, 31).

The Sermon on the Mount is not some otherworldly oriented ethic. Just consider, for instance, how much of the figurative language of the discourse is related to the human body:

- Body: 5:22-23, 25
- Clothing: 6:25, 28-30, 31; 7:15
- Eating, taste, food, drink: 5:6, 13; 6:11, 16ff (fasting), 25, 31; 7:9, 10
- Eye, sight: 5:8, 16, 28, 29, 38; 6:1, 22-23, 26; 7:3-5
- Hand: 5:30; 6:3
- Head/face/cheek/tooth: 5:36, 38, 39; 6:16, 17
- Heart: 5:28; 6:21.

It is hard to imagine a discourse filled with so much bodily imagery not being concerned with the everyday aspects of physical, communal life.

The fact that Matthew mixes idealistic, eschatological, and practical considerations in a compilation of materials employing literal and figurative language does not mean the discourse is simply a hodgepodge of unrelated ethical teachings. While commentators disagree about the structure of the

Sermon on the Mount, most agree that the author intended it to be understood as a unity, and, therefore, they propose outlines with which to get a picture of the whole. I will do no less.

The discourse is framed by narrative pieces describing its setting and audience. We have already seen in 4:24-25 that Jesus has attracted a large crowd to Capernaum. In this scene Jesus pulls away from the crowd, up a mountain, to teach his newly called disciples (5:1-2). Interestingly, however, when the discourse is finished, the narrator describes the reaction of "the crowd," not the disciples—they are astonished at the authority with which he teaches (7:28-29). One might surmise that the ethical discourse is directly spoken to the church but is an ethic to which all are invited (cf. the discussion below on 16:19).

The opening section of the discourse proper is 5:3-16. The Beatitudes (vv. 3-12) serve as the opening address of the audience—sort of a "Friends, Romans, countrymen," if you will. But these are not throw-away lines that have no connection with what follows. Significant vocabulary in the Beatitudes is found dispersed through the rest of the discourse.

Verses 13-16 contain the sayings in which Jesus tells his audience, "You are the salt/light of the earth." These verses often receive much less attention by commentators than either the Beatitudes before or the material that follows. It is my contention, however, that they represent the core theme of the discourse. So important is this theme that Matthew has Jesus assert the theme twice—once using the metaphor of salt and once using light. Salt and light are metaphors for "good works" (see v. 16). The ethic offered in the discourse as a whole and lived into by followers of Christ, therefore, is a testimony that will lead witnesses to give glory to God in heaven. All that follows in the discourse, in different ways unpacks this theme. (It is a shame that the RCL assigns these verses to a lection that includes the following passage since both are so important to the Sermon on Mount narrowly and the narrative as a whole more generally).

The first section following the introduction to the speech, then, is the hermeneutic for interpreting the law (5:17-48) as the basis for a call to higher righteousness (5:20). The primary hermeneutical approach is described in vv. 17-20, a central passage not only for the Sermon on the Mount but for the whole of the Gospel. This is both an interpretative and christological statement. We are to interpret and live out the law in certain ways because Jesus is the fulfillment of the law and prophets. This hermeneutical principle of fulfillment is then exemplified in six case studies (usually called antitheses) concerning murder/anger (vv. 21-26), adultery/lust (vv. 27-30), divorce procedure/forbidding divorce (vv. 31-32), swearing falsely/forbidding swearing (vv.

33-37), just retaliation/turn the other cheek (vv. 38-42), and love of neighbor/ enemy (vv. 43-47).

Each section of the Ethical Discourse is concluded with a statement that sums up and puts an exclamation point at the end. This first section is punctuated with the striking, "Be perfect, therefore, as your heavenly Father is perfect" (5:48).

The next section of the discourse deals with being righteous (literally "doing righteousness"–the NRSV has the misleading translation of "practicing your piety") while trusting in God's providence (6:1-34). The opening verse sets the theme of the section clearly before the reader: we are to do righteousness in a way that is rewarded by God, not by those who see us. This serves to limit the witness of good works called for in 5:13-16. While the Christian's and the church's good works are to be a testimony to God's glory, having them seen for *our* sake is not an end unto itself. Verses 2-18 unpack this principle in relation to three case studies—charity, prayer and fasting. Contrasted through these is the reward we get by being seen by others and the reward we get from God. In the material that follows (vv. 19-33) Jesus explores further what we can expect from God when we trust in God instead of our own means. The reward is named with the metaphorical contrast between treasure on earth (recognition received from others?) and treasure in heaven (given by God who sees in secret?) (vv. 19-21). That we should not take heaven as a reference to the afterlife is seen by the fact that God's reward of the righteous (that is, providence) is compared to God's care for the birds and lilies of the earth.

This section is concluded, summed up and punctuated with the statement: "So do not worry about tomorrow, for tomorrow will bring worries of its own. Today's trouble is enough for today" (6:34).

The third movement of the discourse (7:1-12) is shorter than the first two. It deals with judging others and is often misinterpreted. Vv. 1-5 are often quoted as if they mean Christians are called not to judge others at all. This is simply an unfair reading of this passage specifically and Matthew in general. The principle being laid forth here is to judge *as* you will be judged (similar to the line in the Lord's Prayer asking that we be forgiven *as* we forgive, 6:12, 14-15). It is a warning, not against judging in general, but against hypocrisy (compare the use of "hypocrites" as a contrast to proper ways for "doing righteousness" in 6: 2, 5, 16; see also 15:7; 22:18; 23:13, 15, 23, 25, 27, 2; 24:51). That judgment of others is not only allowed but required is clear in the very next line (v. 6), where Jesus calls hearers to avoid giving that which is holy to the dogs and casting pearls before swine. Notice the shared language concerning swine trampling pearls under their feet here and the reference to tasteless salt being trampled underfoot in 5:13. In the context of the Sermon on the Mount as a whole, the holy and pearls which Jesus calls followers to withhold from the unaccepting/unworthy is the testimony of good works symbolized by salt and light in the opening of the discourse.

In vv. 7-11, Matthew offers the saying concerning, asking, seeking, knocking and it will be given, found, and opened. In other contexts, this language seems to be about faith during prayer (compare Luke 11:9-13 as part of 11:1-13; and Matthew 21:22). If Matthew had wanted to use the *logia* in this way, you would have thought he would have placed it in the previous section focused on God's providence. Placed in this section of the Ethical Discourse dealing with judgment, however, it would seem that which is promised in this line is that God will give proper discernment in judging others.

The section is then punctuated with the "Golden Rule" in v. 12. The connection between treating others as you would have them treat you and judging others as you wish to be judged should be obvious, although we often separate this saying from its context.

The fourth and final movement of the discourse grows out of the third but also serves as a conclusion to the whole speech. It calls for the reader to judge appropriately between two ways of life offered by different sources. In other words, 7:13-27 serves as the closing exhortation to heed Jesus' words and follow his ethic in the Sermon on the Mount. It may be harder than other options, but it is secure. Each part of this section is built on a contrast:

- Vv. 13-14 Narrow gate/hard way leading to life vs. wide gate easy way leading to destruction.
- Vv. 15-20 Good trees bearing good fruit vs. bad (literally "evil") tree/ false prophets bearing bad fruit that are thrown into the fire (cf. good fruit here to "good works" in the opening statement of the theme of the discourse in 5:16; see also 3:8-10).
- Vv. 21-23 Those who do the will of God and enter the reign of heaven vs. those who say to Jesus "Lord, Lord" and are sent away from him as evildoers.

As with the previous sections, this last one also ends with a saying that serves as an exclamation point summing up the section. But this one refers explicitly to the whole discourse: "Everyone then who hears these words of mine and acts on them . . ." (7:24). The concluding contrast is the exclamation point for the whole discourse: Vv. 24-27 Those who hear and do Jesus' words/build a house on rock that lasts vs. those who hears these words and do not do them/build a house on sand that is destroyed.

5:1-2   Narrative Frame-Setting: disciples as audience   5:1-12   EPIPHANY 4
                                                                         AND ALL SAINTS
5:3-16   **Introduction**
    3-12 Beatitudes
    13-16 Theme of the discourse: Salt and light of the world   5:13-20 EPIPHANY 5

5:17-48 **Hermeneutic of the fulfillment of the law**
    17-20 Hermeneutical principle—Jesus Christ fulfills
            the law and prophets
    21-48 Examples applying the hermeneutic (antitheses)   5:21-37 EPIPHANY 6
        21-26 Murder/anger   (PROPER 1)
        27-30 Adultery/lust
        31-32 How to divorce/do not divorce
        33-37 Do not swear falsely/do not swear
        38-42 Just retaliation/no retaliation   5:38-48 EPIPHANY 7
        43-47 Love of neighbor/love of enemy   (PROPER 2)
     48 Concluding Statement: be perfect

6:1-34   **Doing Righteousness while trusting
            in God's providence**
    1-18 Do righteousness to receive a reward from   6:1-6,16-21 ASH WED.
            God instead of from people   (ABC)
     1   Statement of general principle
     2-18 Examples apply general principle
        2-4 Charity
        5-15 Prayer (including the Lord's Prayer)
        16-18 Fasting
    19-33 God's providence in light of doing righteousness
        19-21 Treasures on earth/treasure
                in heaven
        22-23 Eye is lamp of the body
        24-34 Choosing between trusting God or wealth   6:24-34 EPIPHANY 8
         24   No one can serve two masters   (PROPER 3)
         25-33 Compare the birds and the lilies   6:25-33 T'GIVING (B)
     34 Concluding Statement: Do not worry
            about tomorrow

7:1-12   **Judging Others**
    1-5 Against hypocrisy in judging
    6   Do not give holy to dogs or pearls to swine
    7-11 Ask, seek, knock
    12 Concluding Statement: Do to others
            as you wish them to do to you

7:13-27 **Closing Exhortation: Choose between two ways**
    13-14 Narrow gate/hard way or wide gate/easy way
    15-20 False prophets/bad trees producing bad fruit
            or good tree produce good fruit
    21-23 Will those who say "Lord, Lord" but do not   7:21-29 EPIPHANY 9
            do God's will or those who do God's will enter   (PROPER 4)
            the reign of heaven?

    24-27 House built on rock or house built on sand

7:28-29 **Narrative Frame: crowds astounded at Jesus'
            authoritative teaching**

Attending to this understanding of the discourse's structure (or one proposed by another scholar) will help the preacher locate each lection within the purpose and movement of the whole. However, the preacher will also struggle with the fact that the lectionary often makes choices concerning the boundaries of readings for liturgical instead of exegetical reasons, thus combining materials from more than one pericope or cutting off material the exegete would rather include in a pericope. This can be seen in the table above.

PASSAGES OMITTED FROM THE LECTIONARY

The table above also helps us see clearly what materials in the Ethical Discourse the RCL ignores. All of chapter 5 is included in the readings for the Sundays after Epiphany. A major portion of chapter 6 (vv. 1-6, 16-21) is used for all three years of the lectionary cycle on Ash Wednesday, but the Lord's Prayer is omitted from the reading. Otherwise, only vv. 22-23 of this chapter are missing from the lectionary. The majority of chapter 7 (the first twenty of the twenty-nine verses) is excluded from the lectionary. Perhaps some justification for these omissions is that much of Luke's parallel version of these materials is read in Year C:

6:7-15   // Luke 11:1-13 (Proper 12)
6:22-23 // Luke 11:34-36 (Not in RCL)
7:1-20   // Luke 6:27-38 (Epiphany 7); Luke 6:39-49 (Epiphany 8);
               Luke 11:1-13 (Proper 12; see above as parallel to Mt 6:7-15).

We now glance at these omitted passages from the Sermon on the Mount briefly before turning to the passages that do appear in the RCL.

LORD'S PRAYER (6:7-15): OMITTED FROM LECTIONARY

The Lord's Prayer in Matthew is embedded in the tripartite pericope dealing with almsgiving, prayer and fasting (6:1-18). These three parts have an obvious shared rhetorical pattern which the Lord's Prayer breaks and expands in the second piece on prayer. The Ash Wednesday lection (6:1-6, 16-21) omits the Lord's Prayer to help the congregation hear the parallel structures and make connections between "doing our righteousness" in relation to the three topics and the invitation to Lenten discipline.

But praying some form of Matthew's version of the Lord's Prayer is a central practice to much of Christian worship. Moreover, a number of scholars who propose a different outline for the Sermon on the Mount than the one offered above see the Lord's Prayer as the center of the discourse. Clearly, the prayer deserves attention in the pulpit. A preacher can make much with our familiarity with the prayer over against our lack of understanding of its content. The prayer is through and through an expression of eschatological faith. So many contemporary congregations have lost a sense of eschatological hope as they attempt to resist literal understandings of apocalyptic imagery in the Bible that highlighting the eschatological language we use in worship each week may be a way to invite them into an informed, contemporary theological appreciation of Christian eschatology that is found throughout the Sermon on the Mount, and indeed the whole of Matthew.

EYE AS THE LAMP OF THE BODY (6:22-23): OMITTED FROM LECTIONARY

Preachers may be thankful that these verses are omitted from the lectionary simply because they are so confusing. If we assume (as I think we should) that the references to the eye and body are not to be taken literally, the metaphorical or parabolic sense of the saying is still not clear. Indeed, Luke uses the saying in a very different context (11:34-36 in conjunction with other figurative language related to seeing and light [see 11:29-36]) and thus suggests very a different interpretation than does Matthew.

For Matthew, the saying supports Jesus' teaching concerning trusting in God's providence as part of doing righteousness. The contrast between light and darkness reinforces the contrasts that are part of related teachings—treasure in heaven or on earth (6:19-21); choosing to serve God or wealth (6:24); trusting in God or trusting in oneself (6:25-33).

EXHORTATION ON JUDGING AND FOLLOWING CHRIST (7:1-20): OMITTED FROM LECTIONARY

While the omission of the Lord's Prayer is problematic because of its importance for Christian practice and spirituality, the RCL's omission of 7:1-20 is significant because it represents such a large piece of the closing portions of the Ethical Discourse. As noted above, lectionary preachers will have the opportunity to attend to Luke's parallels of much of the material in Year C, but the way in which these materials draw to a close Jesus's opening discourse in Matthew will be lost. The omission is even more striking when we realize that 7:21-29 (Epiphany 9 for traditions that do not celebrate Transfiguration on the last Sunday after Epiphany; or Proper 4 if needed following Trinity Sunday) is rarely needed given the range of dates within which Easter usually falls in the calendar. The last third of the Ethical Discourse is then, for all practical purposes, missing from lectionary-based worship. In truth, this omission reflects the fact that the first two-thirds (and especially chapter 5) have been much more influential on the church throughout the history of interpretation than has chapter 7.

Still, the call to and hermeneutic for appropriate discernment of God's ways, including the Golden Rule (7:1-12) and the contrast of two ways (7:13-27), support and add to the earlier material in the Sermon in significant ways. Especially important for understanding the role and impact Matthew intended for this teaching material to have on the church's praxis are the concluding verses (7:24-27).

LECTIONS

While important parts of the Sermon on the Mount are missing from the RCL, there is much to preach on in the Sundays after Epiphany (as well as on Ash Wednesday and All Saints). If preachers bring depth to their interpretation of the Beatitudes (5:1-12, Epiphany 4) and the hermeneutic and case studies for reading and living out the law (5:17-48, Epiphany 5-7) in Ordinary Time after Epiphany and then transitions into Lent with the call to do righteousness (6:1-18, Ash Wednesday), they have used the stretch of three to six worship services well.

LECTION: THE BEATITUDES
5:1-12; EPIPHANY 4; ALL SAINTS

This lection has two parts, the narrative introduction to the Ethical Discourse as a whole (vv. 1-2) and Jesus' opening address to the hearers/readers—the Beatitudes (vv. 3-12). Clearly, the Beatitudes make up the meat of the reading, and preachers should focus on them. But they will not want to ignore altogether the description of the setting, especially if they are preaching on the text as the beginning of a series during the season after Epiphany. Congregations will be well served if pastors spend a few minutes in the sermon (perhaps in the introduction) to use the opening verses as an opportunity to

1. locate the Sermon on the Mount in Matthew's narrative as the first specific action/words of Jesus' ministry, introduce the discourse as a whole, and name this as the first of five discourses

2. connect the mountaintop setting with the elements of Matthew's christology that draw on the Moses tradition as well as to highlight the importance of mountains in Matthew (for example, in the temptation story, 4:8; the transfiguration story, 17:1; the eschatological discourse, 24:3; Jesus' prayer before his death, 26:30; and the scene of Jesus' resurrection appearance to the disciples, 28:16)
3. mention the tension between the disciples as the direct audience and the crowd/world as an indirect one (see 7:28-29).

In fact, preachers may wish to introduce language as part of this brief focus on the opening verses of the lection to which they will return in later sermons on the Ethical Discourse in order to build continuity across the series.

Preachers will find a plethora of different interpretations when they turn to commentaries for help in understanding the Beatitudes. Some of the primary questions that are debated are as follows:

- Is the language of the Beatitudes drawn from the Hebrew Bible/LXX or from the early church?
- Has Matthew redacted the Beatitudes or has Luke (6:19-28)?
- Do the Beatitudes stand on their own or are they part and parcel of the Sermon on the Mount?
- Do the Beatitudes address the followers of Jesus or all of those for whom the language is applicable?
- Does each beatitude name a different group or does the collection as a whole name a single group in different ways?
- Do the Beatitudes bless those in a certain situation or do they exhort hearers to take up a certain behavior or attitude?

I am not trying to be coy when I say that, in a very real sense, the answer to all these questions is Yes. While Matthean scholars must choose a place to stand on each question, preachers can comfortably stand in the ambiguity of both/and as a way of embracing the (almost overwhelming) richness of this passage. There are good reasons to consider the language of the Beatitudes as coming from Isaiah 61:1-11; Psalm 37:11; 24:3-4; 107:9; and the like; as well as seeing that same language as related to early Christian rhetoric and paraenesis (for example, compare the vocabulary in 1 Peter 1:8, 22; 2:10; 3:4, 11, 14; 4:13, 14). Those named in the opening clause of each beatitude are clearly insiders to Matthew's Christian community, but the language at the same time evokes the situations and characteristics of people outside the community. There are obvious differences between the various blessings (the "poor in spirit" and "peacemakers" are not synonyms) but at the same time they overlap ("poor in spirit" can be seen as an overarching, yet loose, label for all of the descriptors that follow).

Answering yes to the question of whether Matthew's beatitudes function as true blessings on those in difficult circumstances or as paraenesis calling readers to embrace certain attitudes and behaviors requires some deeper discussion for the sake of the pulpit. It is a very different thing to preach a word of blessing on hearers' lives than it is to preach a challenge calling hearers to live in a way they are not. The first is a blessing that functions prophetically—offering eschatological hope to the subjugated and downtrodden. The second is a blessing that functions like a proverb—offering instruction in the form, "You will be blessed *if* you _____." The first sounds like, "Blessed are those in pain, because God will make it right." The second sounds like, "Blessed are those who do good, because they will be rewarded." In preaching on the Beatitudes, do you, then, call people to *become* poor in spirit (assuming this language means something like humility) or offer comfort to those who are poor in spirit (assuming the phrase points to a state of being distressed)? Is hungering and thirsting for righteousness a quality of seeking inner goodness and obedience to God's will (a quality a preacher would want to inspire) or desiring what is right from the world when they (and others) are not receiving it (a situation to which the preacher would want to bring hope)? While some descriptors of those addressed could be read in either terms of situation or calling (for example, poor in spirit, meek, hunger and thirsting for righteousness), others seem clearly to be negative terms you would not want to aspire to (for example, mourning, being persecuted) or moral/ethical labels which do not call for a blessing as a cure (for example, the merciful, the peacemakers). The choice between blessing and exhortation can certainly be both/and when preaching the Beatitudes, but given the difficulties named, the preacher must choose exegetically and theologically how the two relate in conversation with this text.

Exegetically, one approach is to relate blessing and calling structurally—in other words, allowing the form of the Beatitudes to determine which of the verses should be read as prophetic blessings and which as wisdom blessings. As with the Ethical Discourse as a whole, there is no scholarly consensus concerning an outline for the Beatitudes. Some of the details to be accounted for in any outline include the identical repetition of the apodosis, "for theirs is the kingdom of heaven," in the first and eighth beatitude (vv. 3, 10); the repetition of *dikaiosunē* (righteousness or justice) as the last word of protasis in the fourth and eighth (vv. 6, 10); and the shared theme of the eighth and ninth beatitudes along with their shift in person from third person to second person (vv. 10-12). With all of these different connections, clearly the eighth beatitude is of thematic and structural importance. Readers can assume that Matthew's version of the Beatitudes is shaped primarily to address those who are oppressed and persecuted for their Christian faith. The eighth beatitude forms an inclusio with the first beatitude around the six beatitudes in-between urging us to interpret both poor in spirit and persecuted as overarching categories for the whole list. The less obvious connection between the eighth and fourth beatitude suggests a break in the middle of those in-between beatitudes, so that vv. 4-6 and vv. 5-7 form two groups. The first group can be read as focusing on conditions of the persecuted hearers in need of God's help—grief, meekness (not as an attitude of humility but as a name for being forced to be meek), and the desire for what is right (when the world is not right). The second group calls those persecuted to "keep the faith," if you will: be merciful, pure in heart, and work for peace. Finally, the similarities between the eighth and last beatitude suggest that the two together form the exclamation point at the end of the list. The shift from "they" to "you" along with the only two actual imperatives in the whole list—rejoice and be glad—suggest that the Beatitudes serve as encouragement to the church to hold to a Christian ethic that trusts in God's providentially care and eschatological promise even (or especially) in light of the evil and suffering they face in the world. This, one might argue, is the theme of the entire Sermon on the Mount. See page 64 for a diagram of the structure of the Beatitudes.

Theologically speaking, it is significant that the two groups of blessings within the inclusion (that is, vv. 4-6 and 7-9) start with promise and then move to exhortation. Grace precedes (and informs) ethics. The irony here, of course, is that the grace proclaimed is eschatological in nature. In vv. 4-5, the protases name current conditions but the apodoses name future salvation. We are blessed *now* for what we *will* receive in God's time. So future grace precedes the call to an ethic of discipleship in the present! Preachers who unpack this theological claim in relation to the specific blessings in the Beatitudes will prepare their congregation well to relate eschatology and ethics throughout the Sermon on the Mount.

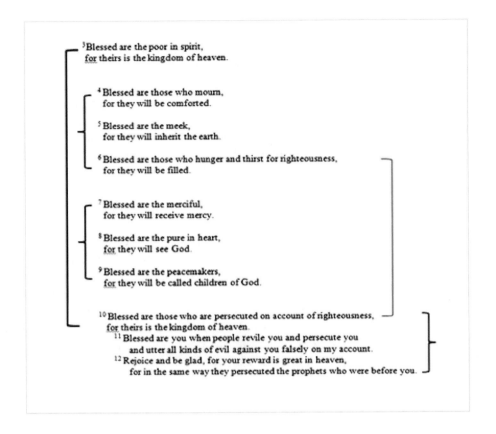

³Blessed are the poor in spirit,
for theirs is the kingdom of heaven.

⁴Blessed are those who mourn,
for they will be comforted.

⁵Blessed are the meek,
for they will inherit the earth.

⁶Blessed are those who hunger and thirst for righteousness,
for they will be filled.

⁷Blessed are the merciful,
for they will receive mercy.

⁸Blessed are the pure in heart,
for they will see God.

⁹Blessed are the peacemakers,
for they will be called children of God.

¹⁰Blessed are those who are persecuted on account of righteousness,
for theirs is the kingdom of heaven.
¹¹Blessed are you when people revile you and persecute you
and utter all kinds of evil against you falsely on my account.
¹²Rejoice and be glad, for your reward is great in heaven,
for in the same way they persecuted the prophets who were before you.

Lection: Salt, Light, and Fulfilling the Law 1:
Introduction 5:13–20; Epiphany 5

This lection contains not one but two very important passages for understanding the purpose and central claim of the Ethical Discourse. The problem is that the preacher cannot preach both and do them justice, but to preach one and ignore the other also does injustice to the importance of either passage for interpreting the sermon as a whole. One homiletical approach that may help overcome this problem is to begin a sermon with a quick look at the whole lection naming the two distinct parts but then focusing for the rest of the sermon on vv. 13–16. Then next week use the first antitheses about murder and anger as a launching pad to actually back up and preach on vv. 17–20. With that suggestion in mind, I will focus, in the following discussion of this lection, on the two pericopes separately.

We start, then, with the sayings in which Matthew has Jesus compare his hearers (disciples) to the salt and the light of the world (vv. 13-16). The two metaphors of salt and light do not compete but highlight the same thing: the call to do good works that can be witnessed by humanity for the glory of God. Part of what joins these two figures together is that neither salt nor light serve themselves; they are means to an end. Salt flavors (or preserves) food. Light illumines its subject (here the house or a city built on a hill). Similarly good works serve the glory of God, instead of the good works (or better the good workers) serving themselves (compare the discussion of practicing righteousness so that it can only be seen by God in 6:1-18). The good works with which Matthew is concerned are the types of behaviors and attitudes spelled out in the rest of the Sermon on the Mount. But it is important to remember that the specifics of the Ethical Discourse are exemplary, not exhaustive. Salt and light are metaphors for the whole orientation of the ethical life to be exhibited by the Christian community and its members, not simply for the individual ethical acts.

This is emphasized in a striking way by a clue in the Greek of v. 13 that is lost in the English translation. Instead of asking what can be done if the salt has "lost its taste," the Greek literally asks what is to be done if it "has become foolish (*mōranthē*)." The English translation is not wrong—it is simply unable to show that a figurative idiom is at play. The reason this word play is important is that the Ethical Discourse ends with a contrast between good fruit (good works) and bad/evil fruit (7:16-20) and between the wise and the foolish (*mōros*, 7:24-27). To be foolish is to fail to heed Jesus' instructions and follow them, thus failing in the church's witness to life of discipleship offered by Jesus Christ. In other words, the hortatory nature of the discourse introduced with the call to be salty and not foolish, light and not be hidden, hints at a two ways choice that becomes explicit in the final verses of the discourse (7:13-27). Preachers will do well to offer their congregations this choice between two ways over and over while preaching on the Sermon on the Mount. To do so is not to preach salvation by works, but to offer the congregation ways of faithfully and ethically responding to the gospel of Jesus Christ.

We turn now from this thematic opening charge of the discourse to the specific hermeneutic of Jesus fulfilling the law offered in 5:17-20. As mentioned earlier, this passage opens the section of the discourse that contains the six examples (antitheses) of applying the hermeneutic in vv. 21-48. Because these examples comprise the gospel lections for the next two weeks, and because this passage is absolutely key for understanding them, the Sermon on the Mount as a whole, and indeed the entirety of Matthew, the preacher should deal with these verses carefully.

Remember we have said that Matthew can be characterized as both the most Jewish and the most anti-Jewish of the Gospels because his church is in an intense sibling rivalry with Pharisaic Judaism after the destruction of Jerusalem and the fall of the temple in 70 C.E. Both are arguing that they are proper heirs of Israel's faith and tradition, but they offer radically different interpretations and applications of that faith and tradition in their day. Here Matthew makes a case for how the church understands itself in relation to Israel's scripture as understood in light of the person and works of Jesus Christ and in its own social life.

Too often this and other passages in Matthew have been preached by taking language reflecting the early church's struggle with the synagogue out of its context and distorting the gospel into anti-Semitic claims. The preacher can name the battle for legitimacy between the late first century church and synagogue as a backdrop for a contemporary interpretation of the hermeneutic without demonizing the Jews or exaggerating the church's persecution in the process. For example, often in modern pulpits, we characterize the Jewish religious leaders, especially the Pharisees, as attacking Jesus. But in Matthew, it is not the Pharisees who strike first. Remember, John the Baptist first called out the Pharisees and Sadducees when they came seeking his baptism (3:7–12). And now in 5:20 Jesus also pokes at the Pharisees and scribes by claiming that the righteousness of his disciples (that is, the church) must exceed that of the scribes and the Pharisees (that is, the synagogue) even though they have not spoken against him yet at this point in the narrative. As Matthew presents it, it is not the religious leaders who create the tension between Jesus and other religious leaders—it is John and Jesus. But notice the nuance of Jesus' claim here. He says only those whose righteousness exceeds the righteousness of the scribes and Pharisees will enter the reign of heaven. He does *not* claim that these Jewish leaders are not righteous. On the contrary, the statement only has rhetorical force if the reader assumes they are a righteous group. Jesus throws down the gauntlet, if you will, but names the church's competition as a worthy of significant praise. In other words, what is at stake for Matthew is claiming the church's rightful inheritance from Israel more than discounting the synagogue's inheritance. (Indeed, in the antitheses that follow, Matthew does not try to show that synagogue's interpretation of the *torah* is illegitimate, only that Jesus' radicalizing interpretation and application of the law is.)

In vv. 17–20, the way Matthew names this legitimacy of the church is to argue (probably against accusations directed at the church) that Jesus did not abandon (and thus the church has not abandoned) the law and the prophets. Indeed, Jesus *fulfills* the scripture. We have already seen this in the formula citations of infancy narrative in which Matthew says Jesus or some event surrounding Jesus fulfilled a prophecy. But even though the prophets are mentioned here, the emphasis is really on the fulfillment of the law. The question is what is meant by "fulfillment." *In what way* did Jesus fulfill the law? Matthew could simply mean that Jesus kept the law, that is, followed the mandates of the *torah*. The antitheses show, however, that fulfilling the law is not simply the opposite of abolishing it—it is more than just keeping it. To keep the law is to have the righteousness of the Pharisees and scribes. Matthew presents Jesus as going a step further. In the person and works of Jesus Christ, the church discovers the fullest (that is, fulfilled, filled-up) meaning and application of the *torah*. This leads to neither a literal nor a libertine interpretation of scripture. It is a "next step" sort of hermeneutic. Study the law. Determine its foundational intent. And ask, what is the next step of ethical behavior and attitude to which this leads us, especially as we consider it as illumined by the life, ministry, death and resurrection of Jesus Christ? The case studies that follow avoid any simple equation of "*the* way" the next step is taken. Instead, they illustrate a variety of ways that the church is called to fulfill the law as heirs of Israel's faith that encourage the church to continue the reflective, interpretive process taught by Jesus.

Another connection the preacher can make to help the congregation experience the weight of what it means for us that Jesus fulfilled the *torah* is the use of "fulfill" in Matthew's version of the baptism story. In all of the references to events in the gospel story fulfilling a scriptural/prophetic passage, the Greek word for "fulfill" is used in the passive voice—such and such took place to *fulfill* what the Lord had spoken through. . . . In those cases, one assumes God is the actor, making these "historical" events occur in accordance with divine will. But in the baptism story and our passage, "fulfill" is used in the active voice—that is, Jesus speaks of himself as intentionally fulfilling all righteousness/the law and the prophets. There is active intent on Jesus' part to fulfill God's will that serves as a model for the church. Thus, Matthew seems to imply that whereas fulfillment in the "historical" arena is God's doing, in the ethical arena fulfillment is left up to us, following Christ.

LECTION: FULFILLING THE LAW 2: ANTITHESIS 1
5:21-37; EPIPHANY 6

These seventeen verses comprise a lection obese with content. It includes four of the six antitheses that exemplify the hermeneutic that Matthew has Jesus offer in 5:17-20. The next lection (for Epiphany 7) contains the last two. This weight is likely due to the fact that the final two are broader in scope and have had a stronger influence on the tradition of Christian ethics than the first four. (Matthew, however, seems to divide the antithesis into groups of three, indicated by the repetition of the full formula, "You have heard from ancient times...but I tell you" in vv. 21 and 33, and by the use of "again" in v. 33.) The antithesis as a form is unique to Matthew, but some of the sayings Matthew uses to compose his six antitheses are found in Luke. In the discussions of this and the next lection, we will focus on Matthew's use of this material within his own narrative context but preachers will do well to compare and contrast Matthew's use of these sayings with Luke's (especially those found in the Sermon on the Plain) to get a handle on the full force of Matthew's distinct aim:

Matthew		Luke
5:25-26	//	12:57-59
5:32	//	16:18
5:39-42	//	6:29-30
5:44	//	6:27-28
5:45-47	//	6:32-35
5:48	//	6:36

The first case study (vv. 21-26) shows how the ethic of Jesus' disciples must move beyond the prohibition against murder which is liable to judgment in the courts (found in Exod 20:13; 21:12; Lev 24:17; Num 35:16-21; Deut 5:17). Not only this sort of violence, but anger is prohibited. So much is expected of disciples that if they call anyone a fool in anger (Greek: *raka* or *mōre*) they are to be judged by both humanity and God. These terms for "fool" are not especially egregious terms, and that is just the point. Even small insults that harm a fellow human being are outside the boundaries of Christian ethics. The antithesis closes with two examples of extending the principle at play here to making amends when one has offended another in the manner prohibited—seek reconciliation before you appear in front of a human or divine judge. Although the formula varies slightly from one to the next antitheses, they share a common structure and logic: they open with a reference to a commandment or ethical practice found in the Pentateuch, and then move to an intensification (that is, fulfillment) of the interpretation and application of the original piece of the *torah* for the church. While space does not allow us to explore the complexities in each antithesis, we can name how each antithesis functions in this intensification.Preachers cannot do justice to all four of the pericopae in this lection in a single sermon. There are two basic homiletical options available. One is to focus on one of the four pericopes. Preachers would probably choose such a focus based on a connection between some pressing issue in the congregation or the world that is related to one of the passages. The sermon might begin with a wide-angle view of the whole lection (reminding hearers of the hermeneutic read in last week's lection) and then zoom in on the chosen pericope. A second option, which was discussed in the commentary on the previous lection, is to use these four passages exactly as Matthew intended—as examples of the hermeneutic in 5:17-20. In other words, the lection would serve as a lens (or properly as four lenses) for examining Matthew's hermeneutical approach to the law as fulfilled (brought to its fullest meaning) in the person and works of Jesus Christ instead of focusing on the lection itself. The sermon could work inductively, moving from the specific examples of the antitheses (as sermonic illustrations) back to the hermeneutical principle of a fuller righteousness as a still-valid guide for the church's approach to biblical ethics today.

The second case study (5:27-30) involves the prohibition against adultery found in Exodus 20:14 and Deuteronomy 5:18. Jesus "fulfills" this by prohibiting lust as well. This mode of radicalization is the same as the first one. In it anger, the passion that can lead all the way from calling someone a fool to murder, is prohibited. Here, lust, as the passion leading to adultery, is forbidden. Again, as Jesus uses hyperbole in the first antithesis (prohibiting even calling someone a fool), here Jesus uses hyperbole to illustrate the importance of avoiding lust (that is, plucking out your eye or cutting off your hand; see 18:8-9 for a different application of the saying in vv. 29-30).

While the fourth case study follows the structure and logic of the first two, the third (5:31-32) is a little different. It is likely placed here because of the connection with the second in dealing with adultery (Matthew often connects logia due to shared key words and themes). This subordinate nature is evidenced by how much shorter this antithesis is than the other three in the lection. This third example of the hermeneutic of fulfillment starts with divorce. Unlike the ancient traditions cited in the first two antitheses, this one is not a prohibition. Deuteronomy 24:1-4 details the procedure a man must go through to be allowed to divorce a woman. But Jesus radicalizes this procedure by saying that divorce (unless done because of adultery) is the same thing as adultery. In Matthew 19:3-9, Jesus is presented as more fully detailing why Moses allowed divorce but Jesus prohibits it—because of hard-heartedness. This later parallel in Matthew supplements our understanding of what we find in the antitheses—Matthew presents Jesus' hermeneutic as being related to an understanding of the *intent* behind different commandments in the *torah* instead of only the words in the commandment.

As mentioned, the fourth case study in the lection (5:33-37) follows the structure of the first two antitheses (reference to ancient commandment, Jesus' fulfillment of the commandment, and further exposition of implications of the fulfillment). It also follows their basic logic of intensification with the move from prohibiting swearing falsely (related to Exod 20: 7, 16; Lev 19:12; Num 30:1-15; Deut 5:20) to a prohibition against swearing *at all*. As anger potentially leads to murder and lust to adultery (and, in a different way, divorce to adultery), swearing can lead to swearing falsely.

Clearly, any of the four antitheses in this lection contains details not discussed here that hold potential for the pulpit. What I have tried to do is show similar threads in all four for the second preaching option suggested above—presenting Matthew's hermeneutic of Jesus as the fulfillment of scriptural ethics as a standard for Christian behavior today. If preachers take this homiletical path, they can push their congregation toward a reflective ethic in which one moves beyond a morality of A is wrong and B is right to a consideration of consequences—how action C is to be avoided because it can lead to greater harm in action D.

Lection: Fulfilling the Law 3: Antitheses 2
5:38-48; Epiphany 7

On the Seventh Sunday after Epiphany (in years when the season stretches this long), preachers will not need to use this lection to illustrate the hermeneutic of fulfillment found in 5:17-20 since they have had opportunity to explore it for the last two weeks. The logic can be reversed in this sermon: the hermeneutic can be the starting point to show what is at stake in these last two, and weightiest, antitheses.

The first case study in the lection (the fifth in the series of antitheses as a whole) comprises vv. 38-42. Dealing with a radicalization of the commandments for appropriate distribution of retributive justice, it follows the same structure we have seen before: 1) reference to ancient *torah*; 2) statement of intensification; 3) examples. Similar to the case study involving divorce, at first glance it seems as if Matthew presents Jesus as overturning the ancient practice of eye for an eye (found in Exod 21:24; Lev 24:20; Deut 19:21). But, as you recall from the discussion of that earlier antitheses, Matthew's hermeneutic shows Jesus as intensifying (that is, fulfilling) the ethic under examination in relation to the *intent* behind the commandment. The intent of the ancient practice was to make the punishment fit the crime so that retaliation was not excessive. In other words, this sense of justice lowers the response from a life for an eye to an eye for an eye. Jesus pulls the Christian's response back even further so that no retaliation is allowed. What is presented is an ethic of nonviolence and nonresistance. With this lection coming just before Lent, it is instructive to consider how some of the examples in the antithesis find echoes in the passion story:

If anyone strikes you on the right cheek, turn the other also (v. 39)	Jesus rejects use of sword at his arrest (26:51-52) and is struck but does not stroke back (26:67-68; 27:26-31)
If anyone wants to sue you and take your coat, give your cloak as well (v. 40)	Jesus' clothes are taken and divvied up by those crucifying him (27:35)
If anyone forces you to go one mile (that is, military conscription for transportation), go also the second (v. 41)	Simon of Cyrene forced to carry Jesus' cross (27:32)

Clearly for Matthew this case study is at the heart of the Christian ethic. The preacher must, however, recognize and speak with sensitivity about this sort of ethic because it can and has been used throughout the centuries to keep the oppressed in their place. The proclamation of the gospel should never be heard by those suffering at the hands of others as: "Thus saith the Lord, 'Grin and bear it.'" There is a radical difference between the way an abusive husband might hold this passage over his wife's head and the way a leader of a nonviolent protest might cite it. It is important to remember that the intent of the original commandment which is intensified here is justice, not maintenance of the status quo. One way to preach a sermon on this passage is to start with rejecting various misuses of the ethic and then move to a proper interpretation of and exhortation to follow it.

The last antithesis in the lection and in the series as a whole (5:43-47) intensifies the commandment to love one's neighbor. Again we start with the ancient commandment—love neighbor and hate enemy. The command to love neighbor is found in Leviticus 19:18, but in truth nowhere in the Hebrew Bible is there the command to hate enemies. Hatred of enemies is simply the natural opposite of love for neighbors and thus hatred is the common sense attitude toward an "enemy." The way Jesus radicalizes the commandment to love our neighbor is to expand who our neighbor is, even to the point of including our enemy! "Enemy" should not be lightened to mean just anyone we do not like. Matthew qualifies enemy with the phrase "those who persecute you." In Matthew's day, the church (like the Jews) was economically, socially and militaristically persecuted by the Roman empire. Matthew's church further struggled with the synagogue over being a legitimate heir to post-temple Judaism, and experienced this struggle as persecution. To achieve the higher righteousness Jesus requires of his followers, the church must love these sorts of enemies—those who threaten their well-being and very existence.

But what is meant by "love." We must not reduce the biblical command to love to a modern sense of love as a "feeling." In the ancient sense of something commanded, love is a conscious and chosen attitude that leads to action that benefits the other. Take the first example in the text: pray for those who persecute you. To pray for someone is to lift up their well-being to God's providential care. One who is willing and chooses to pray in this manner will also act on behalf of that person's well-being. To act for the well-being of an enemy of the church is indeed a radical ecclesial ethic.

One can choose to preach on one of the two antitheses in this lection or preach on them together drawing on the common theme of an ethical stance toward those who stand over against us. Such a radical approach to human behavior belies any attempt to reduce the Christian way of life to offering someone a smile or a good word along the way. This is more, much more. To offer well-being to those who would take away yours is no small thing. But again it does not mean supporting the status quo if you are under the thumb of your enemy. When you pray for those who persecute you, you assume their well-being will be increased if they cease being a persecutor.

On a tangential note, the statement in this last antithesis (v. 45) that God makes the sun rise and sends rain on both the evil and the good, the righteous and the unrighteous is worthy of a sermon all on its own. Matthew uses this statement as a theological rationale for a human ethic that extends to one's enemies. But on its own, the statement names the character of God's providential care that gets at the heart of questions of theodicy. How often are we preachers asked, "Why did God do so and so?" or "Why did God allow such and such to happen?" Preachers could develop a sermon that works backward from the general ethic to focus on theological rationale.

Finally, while 5:48 draws the final antithesis to a close by extending the call to be children of God (in v. 45), it is a concluding statement to the whole section of the ethical discourse that began in v. 17. It puts an exclamation point on the hermeneutic of fulfillment, the call to a higher righteousness. Luke's version of this saying (Lk 6:36) is a call to be merciful as God is merciful, but Matthew calls us to imitate God's perfection. This line alone has allowed readers to dismiss the Sermon on the Mount as an idealist ethic that is impossible to achieve. But recognizing Matthew's use of figurative, hyperbolic language in other places in this section (for example, 5:29-30) helps us see that this line functions as a true call for readers (ancient and modern) to strive for the holiest of lives, for an ethic with transformative potential, for a righteousness that improves the well-being of all.

LECTION: PRACTICING RIGHTEOUSNESS
6:1-6, 16-21; ASH WEDNESDAY ABC

With this lection, we move into a new section (6:1-34) of the Ethical Discourse. The opening verse that sets the theme of the section, however, is closely connected with what has preceded in that Jesus here gives instruction on "doing righteousness." The NRSV's translation of *dikaiosunē* as "piety" fails to signal to the English reader that the term here is the same as that used in 5:6, 10 and especially 5:20 where Jesus calls his disciples to a higher righteousness than that held by the scribes and Pharisees. That Matthew is still concerned here with a *higher* righteousness is evidenced by the contrast in each of the three parts of the lection concerning almsgiving, prayer and fasting, similar to the contrast in the antitheses between what "you have heard" and what "I say to you," 5:21-47. The threefold division of the lection technically involves only 6:1-18. Verses 19-21 really start a new section and are considered part of the discussion of the next lection. There is the way hypocrites do these things and the way Jesus calls his hearers to do them.

Remember our observation that in Matthew Jesus first attacks the Jewish religious leaders instead of first being attacked. In 5:20, with the call to higher righteousness, Jesus acknowledges the righteous behavior of Jewish leaders but intensifies the requirements for his followers. The scribes and Pharisees are righteous but not righteous enough. In 6:1-18 the hypocrites are engaging in acts of righteousness but for the wrong motivation—gaining glory from people instead of serving God. Jesus calls for a higher righteousness—engaging in these acts in ways that do not draw attention to oneself but draws one closer to God. That the hypocrites here are likely to be understood as the religious leaders is supported by the fact that outside the Sermon on the Mount ("hypocrite" also appears in 7:5), "hypocrites" always refers to them (15:7; 22:18; 23:13, 15, 23, 25, 27, 29; 24:51). Again, it is important to contextualize this strong language in light of the conflict between Matthew's church and the Pharisaic synagogue over who is the proper heir and interpreter of Judaism after the fall of the temple, because in truth what Jesus teaches here about not drawing attention to oneself accords with Jewish teaching of the day. In other words, Matthew does not present Jesus as critiquing Jewish acts of righteousness so much as arguing that the religious leaders do not follow their own teaching (see 23:3). Matthew is not anti-Jewish; he is simply in a struggle to defend the integrity of his movement over against leaders of another movement that grew out of the same ashes of mid-first century Judaism.

The lection opens with the general principle or warning concerning appropriate motivation for doing acts of righteousness (v. 1) and then gives three case studies involving almsgiving (the Greek term *eleēmosunē*, can mean acts of mercy in general or specifically charitable giving, vv. 2-4), prayer (vv. 5-15), and fasting (vv. 16-18). With the exception of the Lord's Prayer inserted into the section on prayer (see above on passages omitted by the RCL), the case studies follow the same rhetorical pattern:

	Almsgiving (vv. 2-4)	Prayer (vv. 5-6)	Fasting (vv. 16-18)
Introduction of Topic	So whenever you give alms,	And whenever you pray,	And whenever you fast,
Negative Example of hypocrites	do not sound a trumpet before you, as the hypocrites do in the synagogues and in the streets,	do not be like the hypocrites; for they love to stand and pray in the synagogues and at the street corners,	do not look dismal, like the hypocrites, for they disfigure their faces
Negative Motivation	so that they may be praised by others.	so that they may be seen by others.	so as to show others that they are fasting.
Present Reward	Truly I tell you, they have received their reward.	Truly I tell you, they have received their reward.	Truly I tell you, they have received their reward.

Positive Instruction	But when you give alms, do not let your left hand know what your right hand is doing,	But whenever you pray, go into your room and shut the door	But when you fast, put oil on your head and wash your face,
Positive Motivation	so that your alms may be done in secret;	and pray to your Father who is in secret;	so that your fasting may be seen not by others but by your Father who is in secret;
Future Reward	and your Father who sees in secret will reward you.	and your Father who sees in secret will reward you.	and your Father who sees in secret will reward you.

This pattern shows that the individual topics of almsgiving, prayer, and fasting are not the primary foci for Matthew. As appropriate to the genre of narrative, most pericopes in the Gospels function with the climactic claim coming at or near the end. In this passage, however, the logic flows deductively, with the general principle coming first and specific examples and applications following. In other words, this lection sets the stage for a three-point sermon! Like the topics of the antitheses, acts of mercy, prayer and fasting are simply lenses through which we can examine the principle of v. 1: when we do acts of righteousness appropriately, in ways that are not self-serving and do not seek admiration from other people, we will be rewarded by God. Notice that the reward we get from other people is in the form of immediate gratification, but God's reward is future, eschatological. (Matthew also uses the Greek word for reward, *misthos*, in 5:12, 46 in the discourse and later in 10:41,42; 20:1, 8, always with an eschatological emphasis). But also notice that the principle does not assert we are to be righteous *in order to* get a reward from God. The contrast in the examples is not between seeking praise from people and seeking a reward from God. The contrast is between doing righteous acts "so that they may be praised by others" (v. 2; cf. vv. 5, 16) and "so that your alms may be done in secret" (v. 4; cf. vv. 6, 18). To change strategies simply to get a better reward is still self-serving. Matthew wants the reader to get the point: doing acts of righteousness is "not about us." We do acts of righteousness because they are "right." As Matthew presented a hermeneutic in the antitheses that was concerned with the intent of ancient *torah*, so here Matthew presents the flip side of the coin: concern for the intent behind contemporaneous acts of righteousness.

The RCL follows a longstanding ecclesial practice in assigning this passage as the gospel lection for Ash Wednesday for all three years of the lectionary cycle. The traditional connection between the passage and Ash Wednesday is that the description of these acts of righteousness in Matthew serves to illuminate the purpose of and appropriate approach to Lenten disciplines. In Year A, preachers can connect their invitation to Lenten disciplines to the wider emphasis on the life of discipleship as one of a higher righteousness proffered in the earlier readings from the Ethical Discourse during the Sundays after Epiphany. In Years B and C, the homiletical connections made to the broader context of the Sermon on the Mount will probably not be as strong, but they can be made. Still the passage invites the contemporary church to rethink spiritual disciplines. Spirituality these days has become awfully self-serving. It may not be as crass as clearing our throat as we drop our check in the offering plate so everyone notices, but we do often do acts of charity, prayer, abstinence, study and worship with a consumerist mentality. What do I get out of it? How will it give me a higher level of satisfaction? Matthew's Jesus says, "It's not all about you." Do it because it is right, and you never know what God will do with it in the future.

Lection: Trusting in God's Providence
6:24–34; Epiphany 8; 6:25–33; Thanksgiving B

The boundaries of this lection are unfortunate. You may recall from the previous discussion of the lection for Ash Wednesday (6:1-6, 16-21) that it improperly included vv. 19-21 instead of stopping at v. 18. The verses designated for the Eighth Sunday after Epiphany and for Thanksgiving in the United States and Canada (Year B), on the other hand, only make sense in light of vv. 19ff. While preachers may decide that adding in these extra five or six verses would make the lection too long to read, at least vv. 19-21 need to be considered during sermon preparation and be referenced in the sermon itself.

In the opening verses we can see the pattern from the previous lection of contrasting immediate gratification of praise from humans (you have your reward-present tense) and reward from God in secret (future tense) extended. If we fail to attend to this pattern, we may think Matthew is presenting Jesus as starting off on a completely new topic. But the contrasts here between treasure [treasure = reward?] on earth and in heaven (vv. 19-20; compare the request that God's will be done on earth as in heaven in the Lord's Prayer in relation to the coming of the reign, 6:10); between light and darkness (vv. 22-23);

and between serving God or wealth/mammon (v. 24) continue to illustrate the difference between the higher righteousness required of Jesus' disciples for entry into the reign of heaven (5:20; 6:33) and the righteousness of the religious leaders Matthew is debating.

As Matthew is concerned with intent behind the *torah* (as we saw in our discussion of the antitheses; 5:21-47) and with the motivations behind doing acts of righteousness (6:1-18), Matthew is also concerned here with the inner life of Christians. The language of interiority is explicit in the claim that wherever your treasure is so will your heart be (v. 21; cf. 5:8, 28) and in the discussion of the body as full of darkness or light (vv. 22-23).

In some ways the passage seems to move from a metaphorical expansion of 6:1-18 in vv. 19-23 to a more literal focus on money in vv. 24ff. However, as the issues of murder/anger, adultery, divorce, swearing, retributive justice and love of enemy in the antitheses (5:21-47) and the acts of righteousness of almsgiving, prayer, and fasting were case studies, so are material concerns of food, drink and clothing in this passage. The discussion of livelihood and the accumulation of wealth, in other words, focuses the readers on the call to trust in God more than on a condemnation of wealth. (In this way the lection can serve as a reflection on the petition of the Lord's Prayer asking God for daily bread, 6:11. Compare especially the connection between *daily* bread and v. 34's emphasis on focusing on today instead of tomorrow.)

Perhaps the focus is best understood through the Greek word *merimnaō* that appears six times in this passage (vv. 25, 27, 28, 31, twice in 34) and only twice elsewhere in Matthew (10:19; the noun form appears in 13:22). The NRSV translates the word as "worry" (the noun form in 13:22 is translated as cares [of the world]). While *merimnaō* can have a different force in different contexts, here the kind of worry that seems implied is anxiety, even obsession about the likes of material needs and desire such as food, drink and clothing, because it is the kind of worry that implies trusting in one's own endeavors over God's providential care. The birds and flowers do not worry or work, and God takes care of them. So we, who are more valuable to God, should not worry for nutrition, clothing, or wealth.

This is a difficult text to digest (pardon the pun) much less to preach. If read literally, it presents a picture of God's providence that simply does not accord with historical, human experience. Plenty of people who have trusted in God's benevolence have suffered and/or died because of hunger, thirst, and exposure—in other words, of the results of poverty. This might lead one to the view that Matthew presents an idealist instead of realist approach to the Christian life in the Sermon on the Mount. But remember, Matthew is quite realistic about the troubles of the hungry, thirsty and naked (see 25:31-46). He presents Jesus here as using hyperbolic, figurative language in an almost parabolic fashion to lead readers to put their heart, their treasure, in God's hands instead of their own. One can work for a living, eat, drink and dress decently and give God thanks (in secret?) for that which has been gained. Or one can work for a living, eat, drink and dress decently and still be obsessed about having more, relying only one's own ability and good fortune.

To preach this text in closest connection with Matthew's original use of the material is to focus on the contrast of trusting God and trusting self in dealing with the world and especially possessions. This is a necessary (but hard to hear) word for today's materialistic, commercialistic world, and fits with the fact that all passages from the Ethical Discourse invite hortatory preaching. It is especially needed to counter the prosperity gospel that is so sinfully prevalent in the church and on the airwaves these days.

On the other hand, one should be careful to pass by such a passage as this and not address the issue of theodicy. Why doesn't God feed the hungry, and give drink to the thirsty and clothe the naked if God loves us all more than birds and flowers? To help a congregation re-imagine what God's providence looks like in a modern, theological world-view will greatly enhance any ethical dialogue and action in which the church engages.

Lection: Trusting in Jesus as Messiah
7:21-29; Epiphany 9/Proper 4

In most Protestant congregations, this lection will not be used in the season after Epiphany because it is part of a set of readings offered as an alternative to lections chosen for the Last Sunday after Epiphany as the celebration of Transfiguration Sunday. Only traditions that read the transfiguration story on the Second Sunday in Lent and/or celebrate the feast of the Transfiguration on August 6 will turn to this lection on the Last Sunday after Epiphany, and only then if Easter is very late in the year. Conversely, the set of lections of which this gospel lesson is one are possible for the Sunday following Trinity Sunday but only if Trinity has been celebrated by May 22—that is, only if Easter is very early in the calendar year.

This likely means that a congregation that uses the RCL will not hear a reading from the last third of the Sermon on the Mount. While this material is probably not as weighty and certainly has not been as influential in the history of the church as the Beatitudes (5:3-12), the antitheses (5:17-48) or warnings about practicing righteousness in secret (6:1-18; and especially the Lord's Prayer in vv. 9-13), it is the climax or at least hortatory conclusion of the ethical discourse.

As such, the closing reiterates in a new way the central exhortation that we have seen in all of the lections discussed above. The Sermon on the Mount stands as part of the rhetorical tradition that places before readers/hearers two ways. Matthew offers this choice over and over in different ways in the material we have reviewed above:

salt vs. foolish/tasteless salt (5:13)
light vs. hidden light (5:14-15)
abolish the law vs. fulfill the law (5:17-19)
higher righteousness vs. righteousness of scribes and Pharisees (5:20)
> do not murder vs. do not get angry (5:21-26)
> do not commit adultery vs.do not lust (5:27-30)
> divorce in this way vs. do not divorce (5:31-32)
> do not swear falsely vs. do not swear (5:33-37)
> eye for an eye vs. turn the other cheek (5:38-42)
> love your neighbor vs. love your enemy (5:43-47)
doing righteousness to be seen by humans vs. seen by God in secret (6:1)
> giving alms in public vs. giving alms in secret (6:2-4)
> praying in public vs. praying in secret (6:5-6)
> fasting in public vs. fasting in secret (6:16-18)
storing treasures on earth vs. storing treasure in heaven (6:19-21)
> body full of light vs. body full of darkness (6:22-23)
> serving God vs. serving mammon (6:24)
>> anxious about food and drink vs. birds of the air (6:25-27)
>> anxious about clothing vs. flowers of the field (6:28-32)

Here at the end of the discourse, this choice is offered again in no uncertain terms. In fact, the eschatological consequences of choosing incorrectly are laid out strongly. Prior to our lection, the concluding choice is named in 7:13-14 using the metaphorical contrast between the wide gate leading to destruction and the narrow gate leading to life. Few choose the latter. Next comes the warning about false prophets (vv. 15-20) that includes the contrast between good trees bearing good fruit (related to the call for good works at the beginning of the discourse in 5:16) and bad trees bearing bad fruit (the Greek translated "bad" throughout this passage is actually *ponēros*, evil; compare 5:11, 37, 39, 45; 6:13, 23; 7:11) and thus being thrown into the fire (fire as a symbol for eschatological judgment is common in Matthew (3:10-12; 5:22; 13:36-43, 50; 18:8-9; 25:41).

Our lection contains the final, and perhaps strongest, two contrasts of the discourse. The first contrasts those who profess Jesus as "Lord" but do not do the will of the Father in heaven and those who do God's will (see 12:46-50). One cannot help but recall the line asking that God's will be done on earth as in heaven in the Lord's Prayer (6:10). Like the two sayings discussed in the previous paragraph, the contrast between the two choices serves to highlight the consequences of the choice—being sent away or entering the reign of heaven (recalling 5:20). What is new in this passage as compared with most of what we have reviewed in the ethical discourse is that here the choice is described as explicitly related to how one responds to Jesus. The call to righteousness in the Sermon on the Mount is not a call to a general way of life but to a righteous path of following Christ as his disciple.

The second contrast (vv. 24-27) narrows the focus of response to Jesus even more narrowly to responding to Jesus' words *in this discourse*. Those who heeds the teaching offered in the sermon ("these words of mine," vv. 24, 26) will stand solid like a house built on rock and those who do not will be destroyed like a house built on sand. The strong eschatological tone at the end of the discourse emphasizes the importance of the ethical way of life presented throughout the whole.

Preachers should be careful not to interpret this emphasis literally in terms of reward and punishment in the end times. The future tense highlights the present potential that a higher righteousness in Christ offers. It offers stability, life, the reign of God. The call to higher righteousness may appropriately be presented homiletically as exhortation, but it is gift not burden. A higher righteousness does not lead us to Jesus. Jesus graces us with a life of higher righteousness. To preach this message at the end of the lectionary sequence drawing from the Ethical Discourse will draw together many hanging threads and prepare the congregation for a different approach to the invitation to Lenten disciplines and to a different appreciation of what follows in Matthew.

Capernaum-based Ministry: Healings and Following Jesus (8:1—9:34)

INTRODUCTION

Following the Ethical Discourse, Matthew's pace speeds up to the pace of a poodle who just drank a pot of cappuccino with its mixture of healing, discipleship and conflict stories in chapters 8–9 that give readers their first real exposure to Jesus' itinerant ministry before slowing down again with the Missionary Discourse in chapter 10. Indeed, because of the lack of clearer chronological comments, readers could almost draw the conclusion that the events of the two chapters happen within the scope of a few days. In preaching on a passage here or there on Sunday mornings, we can miss the way Matthew portrays Jesus' movements and actions as piled one on top of the other in short order to offer a cumulative picture of his ministry.

Remember that just before the Sermon on the Mount, Matthew summarized Jesus' ministry in terms of his going throughout Galilee teaching in "their" synagogues, proclaiming the good news of the reign of heaven and performing healings (4:23-25) although the reader had yet to see any specific examples of these actions (other than the call of the disciples) or have any sense of Jesus' actual movement (other than his locating in Capernaum [4:13] and walking beside the Sea of Galilee [4:18]). Having offered the readers the first major exposure to Jesus' teaching in chapters 5–7, now the narrator gives them a glimpse of what Jesus' Capernaum-based ministry looked like. An outline emphasizing Jesus' movements shows how this section flows out of the Ethical Discourse and leads into and beyond the Mission Discourse:

8:1: Jesus *comes down the mountain* followed
by great crowds and heals a leper.
8:5: Jesus *enters Capernaum* and heals a centurion's child
(Greek: *pais* can mean either of servant/slave or child; contrast
the use of *doulos* in Luke's version of the story (7:2) which
clearly means slave) from a distance.
8:14: Jesus *enters Peter's house*, heals his mother-in-law
and later many who were brought to him there.
8:18: Because of the crowds, Jesus *decides to go to the other side*
(of the sea) but discusses following him with a scribe and
a disciple before departing;
8:23: While *crossing the sea*, Jesus calms a storm.
8:28: On the other side (in the gentile *country of the Gadarenes*),
Jesus exorcises demons from two demoniacs and is
immediately *asked to leave*.
9:1: Jesus *crosses back over the sea* and returns to "*his own town*"
(Capernuam) and immediately has brought to
him a paralytic, whom he heals.
9:9: *Walking along* (by or from the sea) Jesus calls Matthew
the tax collector to follow him.

9:10: Immediately following this, Jesus eats dinner with tax collectors and sinners in *"the house"* (that is, Jesus' house or headquarters) and answers a question about fasting.

9:18: Jesus (and his disciples) *leave the house* to follow a leader/ruler to his house (presumably still in Capernaum) to raise his dead daughter and encounters a woman with a hemorrhage on the way.

9:27: As Jesus *went on from there*, two blind men follow him to *"the house"* (again, returning to Jesus' house) where he heals them and immediately afterward exorcises a demon that causes a man to be mute.

9:35: Jesus goes about *"all the cities and villages"* (that is, around Capernaum in Galilee) teaching in "their" synagogues, proclaiming the good news, and healing the sick (echoing 4:23-25 before the Ethical Discourse).

10:1: While traveling, Jesus names, commissions, and *send out* (further) the twelve.

11:1: "Now when Jesus had finished instructing the twelve disciples,he *went on from there* to teach and proclaim his message *in their cities.*"

When preaching on an individual passage within this section, preachers should not lose sight of the way Matthew uses this section as a whole to exemplify Jesus' Capernaum-based ministry. Likewise, it is important to recognize that this section advances a number of key thematic elements of Matthew's story and theology—christology (specifically the authority of Jesus), the continuity between Israel's tradition and the newness of the Jesus movement (extending the theme of fulfillment/intensification in the Ethical Discourse), following Jesus (as a prelude to the discourse in the following chapter), and the introduction of religious leaders opposing Jesus (to begin shaping the conflict that will lead to Jesus' death). We shall look at each topic in turn.

Christology. Christologically speaking, in this section Matthew is primarily interested in establishing Jesus' authority as the Messiah. Matthew had first named that the crowds recognized Jesus' authority in relation to his teaching in the conclusion to the Ethical Discourse: "The crowds were astounded at his teaching, for he taught them as one having authority, and not as their scribes," (7:28-29). This recognition of Jesus' authority is echoed again in this section in relation to Jesus' authority to forgive and heal: "When the crowds saw it, they were filled with awe, and they glorified God, who had given such authority to human beings" (9:8).

As we saw earlier, the opening chapters of Matthew focus on establishing Jesus' identity in terms of christological titles and a geography that fulfills scriptural typology. Matthew uses similar approaches here. The use of titles supports Jesus' authority in terms of how other characters address Jesus in this section and Jesus' response to them:

Kyrios (The Greek can mean either "Lord" or "sir")

8:2: The person with the skin disease addresses Jesus as *kyrios*, recognizing Jesus' authority to choose whether to cleanse him or not.

8:5,8: The centurion who explains that Jesus does not need to come to his house to heal his child because of his level of authority calls Jesus *kyrios*.

8:21: The disciple who wishes to depart to bury his father before following Jesus calls him *kyrios* only to have Jesus place commitment to him over the man's commitment to his father.

8:25: When the storm rises on the sea, the disciples ask Jesus to save them, calling him *kyrios*. When Jesus calms the storm, they recognize his authority even over the wind and sea.

9:27: The two blind men who follow Jesus asking for his mercy, call him Son of David. When Jesus asks if they have faith he can heal them (that is, has authority to do this) they answer in the affirmative and call him *kyrios*.

Teacher/The Son of the Human

8:19: The lone scribe who expresses a desire to follow Jesus wherever he goes addresses him as teacher (this is the first time this form of address is used in Matthew, and afterward it is always placed on the mouths of those outside Jesus' circle); but when Jesus explains there is no end destination, he refers to himself as the Son of the human (as if correcting the scribe in thinking he is only a teacher; and this is the first time this title appears in Matthew).

9:6: When some of the scribes question whether Jesus blasphemes when he forgives the sins of the paralytic, Jesus explicitly names that the son of the human has authority to forgive sins and demonstrates that authority by healing the paralytic.

9:11: The Pharisees ask Jesus' disciples why their teacher eats with sinner and tax collectors

Son of God

8:29: The demons who are scared of what Jesus can do to them (and thus recognizing his authority over them) call him Son of God.

Son of David

9:27: The two blind men who follow Jesus asking for his mercy, call him Son of David. When Jesus asks if they have faith he can heal them (that is, has authority to do this) they answer in the affirmative and call him *kyrios*.

These titles, coupled with Jesus' miracles and teaching in and around Capernaum, show that his authority is not limited by geographical boundaries (including Jewish or gentile territories) and extends over his community of followers, illnesses, demons, and even nature. Indeed, at this point in the narrative, readers would be hard pressed to name what Matthew sees Jesus as not having authority over. Thus while preachers working on any passage in this section will likely invite their congregation to identify with those encountering Jesus, they should be careful to make sure their sermons have strong christological emphases. For Matthew, the stories in this section are less about the situations and needs of those encountering Jesus—they are, after all, fairly flat characters—and how those situations and needs are addressed, and more about how those encountering Jesus serve to highlight his saving power and authority. Of course, we should be careful not to go so far in this christological direction that we ignore the soteriological dimension of the both healing and the call stories. Jesus' authority as the Christ is that through which we are healed, forgiven, and called into discipleship.

Continuity between the Old and the New. In the Ethical Discourse, Matthew presents Jesus as claiming not to wish to abolish the law and the prophets but to fulfill them and expecting his followers (that is, Matthew's church) to keep the law (5:17-20). But as the antitheses that follow this claim show, the way in which the law is to be kept may seem new given the hermeneutic of intensification (fulfillment) that Jesus models (5:21-48).

In this section Matthew extends the dynamics introduced in the Sermon on the Mount by presenting Jesus as holding in tension the old and the new. For example, in the opening healing story Jesus does something new that shows a break with traditional interpretation of the law: he touches someone considered unclean because of a skin disease. But this break with old is coupled with Jesus maintaining the tradition of the priests declaring the person to be clean (8:2-4).

Similarly, in 8:5-13, when the centurion seeks healing for his child, Jesus seems to consider going to the gentile house, an act clearly forbidden in first century interpretation of the law. But Jesus respects the man's wishes to heal from afar and does not go. Then he adapts the traditional eschatological image of many from the east and west (that is, gentiles) being gathered on the temple mount (see Isa 2:2-4; 25:6; Micah 4:1-4; Zech 8:20-23) to many being gathered to feast with .faith (and implicitly of the inclusion of gentiles in the church).

The paradoxical relation of the old and the new found in Jesus' eschatological ministry is most directly named when John's disciples question Jesus concerning fasting (9:14-17), a story Matthew gets from Mark 2:18-22. Jesus answers that they should not fast while he is with them as wedding guests should not fast while the bridegroom is still at the party, emphasizing the new thing Jesus represents and is doing and which should be celebrated (and thus why it would be inappropriate for the disciples to fast). Jesus builds on this answer with the somewhat confusing metaphors of a new (unshrunk) patch of cloth ripping an old piece of clothing or new wine causing old wine skins to burst. The point seems to be that the new and the old are not compatible. But Matthew adds something peculiar to the end of Mark's version of the scene. He has Jesus say (with italics marking the redactional addition), "Neither is new wine put into old wineskins; otherwise, the skins burst, and the wine is spilled, and the skins are destroyed; but new wine is put into fresh wineskins, *and so both are preserved*." Within the metaphor, "both" refers to the new wine and the old wine skins. So while Matthew rejects the idea that the new that Jesus represents should simply be added to the old, he also lifts up the continuing value of the old for his community of faith.

Discipleship. In 4:18-22, Jesus called his first disciples, and due to their obedient response (and presumably the community of faith's prior knowledge of the disciples), they serve as role models for the readers. In the Ethical Discourse (chs. 5–7), Jesus withdraws from the crowd and teaches his disciples on the mountaintop (although the crowd overhears the discourse, 7:28-29).

Thus by the time the readers get to chapters 8–9, the disciples are in clear view as well as something of what is expected of them (and thus the readers whom they represent) is known. That picture is complicated in this section.

Throughout the section, the disciples are presumably with Jesus, watching and listening as he heals the sick and converses with various people. Thus all of the stories in chapters 8–9 can be seen as shaping the disciples. But there are two groupings of material that explicitly deal with issues related to following Jesus.

The first grouping is 8:18-27, Jesus' dialogue with potential disciples and the crossing of the sea. Jesus has healed the crowds at Peter's house (that Jesus visited Peter's house and heals his mother-in-law indicates a significant level of intimacy between Jesus and his disciples, 8:14-17) and now gives orders (that is, to his disciples) to go across the sea. At this moment, two different men express interest in following Jesus (to the other side). The first is a scribe (see the discussion of conflict below), who expressly says he will follow wherever Jesus goes, without reservation. Too often Jesus' response is seen as a critique of the scribe, but the text does not indicate so. Jesus simply elaborates on what the scribe's commitment would mean—those who go with the Son of the human, have no place to lay their head. Then a disciple (someone already following Jesus!) asks to go bury his father before he follows Jesus to the other side of the sea. Jesus' response to his follower is a critique of that desire: "Follow me, and let the dead bury their own dead." Both of Jesus' responses have a depth of meaning beyond what we can discuss in this context, but we can say that they both indicate the high levels of commitment required of disciples. They must be prepared to leave commitments to home and family behind them. Note that the narrator does not tell the readers whether the scribe or disciple followed Jesus to the other side or not. This open-ended quality to the dialogue serves as an invitation to the readers to follow.

Coupled with this dialogue is the story of Jesus and his disciples crossing to the other side. In the midst of the storm, the disciples become fearful, Jesus calls them "you of little faith," and when he calms the storm they say, "What sort of man is this, that even the winds and the sea obey him?" In addition to establishing Jesus' authority over nature, this scene presents the disciples as human. The flat characters are rounded somewhat through the narrator showing that they can be afraid (that is, of little faith) even when with Jesus and are unsure who it is that they are following. In Mark, this story follows the Parables Discourse (4:1-34), in which the disciples are presented as ones who should understand the parables but do not, thus leading the readers to wonder whether the disciples (and we who have identified with them) are insiders or outsiders. Their fear in this story, therefore, evokes from Jesus a more stern response in Matthew (Mark has Jesus question why the disciples have "*no* faith?" instead of being of "*little* faith"). This is part of Mark's use of the disciples to challenge the christology of his community. What we see in Matthew, then, is a softening of the critique of the disciples he found in Mark but still a complicating of their characterization.

The second grouping of materials dealing with discipleship is 9:9-17 and includes the call of Matthew, the dialogue about Jesus eating with tax collectors and sinners, and the dialogue about why Jesus' disciples do not fast. This material complicates the picture of the disciples (and of discipleship) further. In calling a tax collector to follow him and then defending his practice of eating with tax collectors and sinners, Jesus makes clear that his band of followers representing the church and being called to a higher righteousness than the scribes and Pharisees (5:20) is not your typical religious group. Indeed, Jesus has come to make them (and not those who are already righteous) disciples (8:12-13).

The picture is complicated further in the second grouping in the dialogue in which John's disciples ask why Jesus' disciples do not fast the way they and the Pharisees do. The new thing Jesus Christ represents/is doing translates into a joyful discipleship in which it is inappropriate to fast. However, Jesus has already prescribed how his followers are to fast in the Ethical Discourse (6:16-18), so readers are surprised to find Jesus' followers not fasting and Jesus defending the practice of not fasting by using the analogy of wedding guests in the presence of the bridegroom. But Jesus goes on to say, "The days will come when the bridegroom is taken away from them and then they will fast," (9:15). While Matthew has clearly established the disciples as points of contact with the story for his readers, he also distinguishes between the period of discipleship with Jesus and discipleship following Jesus' death and resurrection.

Introduction of Conflict. Matthew uses the conflict between Jesus and the religious leaders in the narrative as a literary mirror for viewing and addressing the conflict between his church and the synagogue in the late first century after the fall of the temple. Since both are presenting themselves as proper heirs to Israel's tradition, Matthew presents Jesus and John as initiating the conflict so it does not look like the church is simply at the synagogue's mercy.

We have noted in a number of places earlier that contrary to common presentation of Matthew in the pulpit and other settings, the religious leaders do not initiate the conflict with Jesus. John the Baptist and Jesus begin by critiquing them. In fact, until now (nearly a third of the way through the narrative) the religious leaders have not challenged Jesus at all. With great literary skill, Matthew introduces their resistance to Jesus as part of the same section where he emphasizes Jesus' growing authority and where he highlights the tensive connection between the old and the new in Jesus' eschatological movement. It is instructive to note how the resistance develops in the section.

In 8:19 a scribe expresses a desire to follow Jesus wherever he goes. In the Greek, the character is explicitly described as *one* scribe (*heis grammateus*; contrast this with Luke's version where it is simply "someone"—Greek *tis*—who says this to Jesus, Lk 9:57). Perhaps the modifier "one" is a hint that this scribe is not stereotypical of scribes as future characters in Matthew's story. The scribe calls Jesus "teacher," which as we have seen earlier, is not a valued christological title for Matthew. Nevertheless, there is nothing in the way Matthew narrates the scribe's approach to Jesus that should lead the reader to assume he is insincere. Jesus does not call the scribe to follow him (as he later does Matthew—perhaps, part of his calling not the righteous but sinners, 9:9, 12-13) but neither does he reject the scribe's request. Jesus (v. 20) simply raises the stakes in terms of what is required to follow, as he does also when one of his own disciples wants to put a condition on following Jesus in the next two verses. Remember as we said above that we are not told how the scribe (or the disciple that dialogues with Jesus next) responds to Jesus. Matthew is highlighting the demands of discipleship, but for all we know the scribe accepted those demands.

In 9:2, Jesus forgives the sins of a paralytic. "*Some* of the scribes" (Greek, *tines tōn grammateōn*) say to themselves that Jesus is blaspheming (v. 3). There are three things to note about this description of the religious leaders. First, in contrast to the one scribe of 8:19, we now have "some" of the scribes. The numbers are increasing, and clearly more are against Jesus than are interested in following him. Second, their concern that a teacher/healer is placing himself equal to God in having authority to forgive sins is well placed. Were this story about someone other than the one we recognize already as God's Son we would also consider it blasphemy. And, third, they do not attack or challenge Jesus with their concern. They simply "say to themselves" that Jesus is blaspheming. It is Jesus who calls them out publicly for what they are privately thinking (referring to the thoughts as "evil"), not they who challenge him. So we see movement from one scribe wanting to follow Jesus to some scribes having internal questions about him and being confronted by him.

The scribes do not appear again in this section (see 12:38 for their next appearance paired with the Pharisees). Instead, the Pharisees step onto stage with Jesus next. In 9:11 they have questions about Jesus' practice of eating with tax collectors and sinners. Like the scribes they do not confront Jesus directly, but they have moved beyond questioning inwardly to questioning

Jesus' disciples. Jesus overhears them and answers that he has come for sinners, not the righteous (9:12-13). Again, Jesus offers the first direct confrontation.

In the very next scene, John's disciples ask Jesus why his disciples do not fast (9:14-17). The question does not need to be read as an accusation. It can well be seen as a sincere inquiry. It does, nevertheless, distinguish Jesus' movement from John's. Jesus also distinguishes his movement from that of the Pharisees (who are presumably still in the house following the dialogue described in the previous paragraph), since John's disciples named both themselves and the Pharisees as fasting often. Jesus' movement is something new that should not just be grafted onto the old represented by the Pharisees.

The Pharisees do not show up again until just before the transitional summary of healings at the end of the section (9:35-38) setting up the Mission Discourse. In the meantime Jesus has healed five people—the woman with the hemorrhage, the dead girl, two blind men and lastly the man with a demon causing him to be mute. The Pharisees comment on this final healing in a way that surely is a challenge to his authority exhibited in all healings (9:34; some ancient manuscripts do not include this verse, but the stronger textual and literary evidence supports its inclusion). The verse reads, "But the Pharisees said, 'By the ruler of the demons he casts out the demons.'" Note two things. First, they do not claim Jesus is hoax and not really healing people but only challenge *how* (that is, by whose power and authority) he exorcises demons. Matthew revisits this accusation and has Jesus respond to it in 12:22-32. Here he simply allows it to stand unanswered as the beginning of the religious leaders attacking Jesus, which will eventually lead to his arrest and execution. Second, Matthew does not specify the audience to whom the Pharisees speak. It could be inward or public, but it seems clear they have not yet addressed Jesus directly with their concerns. This will begin with the Sabbath controversies in chapter 12, leading up to the confrontation concerning Jesus' authority to cast out demons just mentioned. Regardless of the audience to whom they address their accusation, the accusation itself characterizes religious leaders for the rest of Matthew's narrative: they are against Jesus and misrepresent him and his ministry.

Passages Omitted from the Lectionary

Only one reading from Matthew 8:1—9:34 is found in the RCL. It is 9:9-13, 18-26 and is assigned to Proper 5, which is scheduled for June 5-11 but is only used in years when Trinity Sunday falls on a date earlier than June 5.

This means that in most cycles of the RCL, this section is completely missing from Year A focusing on Matthew. One should not assume that this gap in the lectionary's use of Matthew means the texts are unimportant for Matthew's theology and/or plot. Remember, the RCL works with a harmonizing approach: to have as many of the stories of Jesus as possible read in worship across the three year cycle, they rarely choose parallel versions of stories from different Gospels. This is illustrated well by this section of Matthew:

Passage	Matthew	Mark	Luke
Cleansing Man with Skin Disease	8:1–4 (not in RCL)	1:40–45 (Epiphany 6B)	5:12–16 (not in RCL)
Healing Centurion's Son	8:5–14 (not in RCL)	No Markan parallel	7:1–10 (Proper 4C)
Healings at Peter's House	8:14–17 (not in RCL)	1:29–39 (Epiphany 5B)	4:38–41 (not in RCL)
Desiring to Follow Jesus	8:18–22 (not in RCL)	No Markan parallel	9:51–62 (Proper 8C)
Stilling the Storm	8:23–27 (not in RCL)	4:35–41 (Proper 7B)	8:22–25 (not in RCL)
Exorcizing the Gadarene Demoniacs	8:28–34 (not in RCL)	5:1–20 (not in RCL)	8:26–39 (Proper 7C)
Forgiving/ Healing a Paralytic	9:1–8 (not in RCL)	2:1–12 (Epiphany 7B)	5:17–26 (not in RCL)
Calling Tax Collectors and Sinners	9:9–13 (first part of Proper 5A)	2:13–22 (Epiphany 8B)	5:27–32 (not in RCL)
Jesus' Followers not Fasting	9:14–17 (not in RCL)		5:33–39 (not in RCL)
Healing Woman with Hemorrhage and Raising Dead Girl	9:18–26 (second part of Proper 5A)	5:21–43 (Proper 8B	8:40–56
Healing Two Blind Men	9:27–31 (not in RCL)	No exact parallel– closest 8:22–26 (not in RCL)	No parallel
Exorcizing Demon Causing Muteness	9:32–34 (not in RCL)	No parallel	No parallel

Most of the passages from Matthew 8:1—9:34 not used in the lectionary have a parallel in Mark or Luke that is used at another time in the three year cycle. This means congregations may hear the basic stories found here in the course of three years, but they will not hear Matthew's particular take on that story. Moreover, without great care on the preacher's part, the themes emphasized in this section (named earlier) can go unnoticed by a congregation working through Matthew in Year A. Preachers concerned about the cumulative picture of Matthew they are offering the congregation throughout the year will need to find ways to name these themes while preaching on other passages. Especially important will be properly framing the beginnings of conflict to understand its development later in the narrative.

(Note: It is intriguing that the two final Matthean passages in the list above do *not* have parallels in Mark or Luke but still do not appear in the RCL. Yet both parts of the one Matthean lection from this section do have parallels in Mark, which are also chosen by the lectionary in Year B.)

CLEANSING A MAN WITH SKIN DISEASE (8:1-4):
OMITTED FROM LECTIONARY

Although the narrator has introduced miraculous healing earlier as a constitutive part of Jesus' ministry (along with proclamation of the reign of God and the gathering of followers; 4:12-25), it is not until after the lengthy Ethical Discourse, that we read of a specific healing. The first is this story of Jesus cleansing a man with a skin disease. Given the tension between Jesus doing a new thing while also claiming to fulfill the law in the Sermon on the Mount, it is an interesting first choice for the way it combines ignoring issues of *torah* observance (touching a man who is unclean) with *torah* observance (sending the healed man to be declared clean by the priests).

In Mark's version (1:40-45), this story introduces the motif of the messianic secret—Jesus orders the man to tell no one of the healing except to show himself to the priests, but instead he goes and spreads the word widely. Matthew's story ends with Jesus' command to the man to tell no one but show himself to the priests. We are told nothing of the man's response so the natural conclusion is that Matthew wants us to assume he obeyed Jesus. This means the narrator keeps the focus clearly on 1) Jesus ability to heal and 2) his relation to the *torah*. Preachers should likewise focus on Jesus' characterization in the story.

HEALING THE CENTURION'S SON (8:5-13):
OMITTED FROM LECTIONARY

This story follows well on the heels of the previous one in terms of relating Jesus' healing ministry to issues of *torah* observance. Here a gentile asks Jesus to heal his son (the Greek word *pais* can also mean "servant," but "son" is likely the more accurate translation in this case). Whereas the man in the previous story was unclean by virtue of his ailment, this man is unclean by virtue of his personhood—that is, not being Jewish. Key to interpreting the story is v. 7. The NRSV translates Jesus as saying, "I will come and cure him." This presents Jesus as willing to enter a gentile home, which could have been seen as breaking the boundaries of purity codes (see Acts 10:28). But Jesus' line can also be translated as a question: "Shall I come and cure him?" The implications of the question is more ambiguous. Jesus may be offering to come, but he may be questioning the appropriateness of his coming. This would better explain the centurion's speech about Jesus' authority and ability to heal from afar.

Indeed, Jesus being able to heal from a distance does emphasize his power and authority. But preachers will notice that in this story the healing seems to be lens instead of the focus of the story. The mention of the son being healed at the end serves as an explanation point to the discourse that has taken place between the centurion and Jesus, with Jesus getting the last word. But that word points back to the faith of the centurion. Sermons on this passage should allow the narrator to focus the congregation's attention on the centurion's faith in Jesus' authority as a model offered to us even today.

HEALINGS AT PETER'S HOUSE (8:14-17):
OMITTED FROM LECTIONARY

Overall, this scene serves simply to strengthen the picture of Jesus as healer established in the previous two stories. The summary of healings in v. 16 echoes back to the summary at the beginning of Jesus' ministry (4:23-24). The healing of Peter's mother-in-law is only two verses long (vv. 14-15). Preachers may wonder whether there is enough to preach on here.

Matthew's source for this scene is Mark, and the bulk of the story is the same as Mark's version. But at the end of the scene the narrator offers something not found in Mark—a scripture fulfillment citation. The reader has not seen one of these since 4:15-16 at the beginning of Jesus' ministry. That citation of Isaiah 9:1-2 was used as support of Jesus' ministry in Galilee. In the Sermon on the Mount, Jesus demonstrates how his teaching is a fulfillment of scripture (5: 17-48). And now the citation in this scene comes from Isaiah 53:4 (the first use of a suffering servant passage in Matthew) and is used as scriptural support for Jesus' healing ministry. Matthew wants the reader to know that everything about Jesus, his very person and his ministry, are fulfillment of God's will found in scripture.

DESIRING TO FOLLOW JESUS (8:18-22):
OMITTED FROM LECTIONARY

It is a shame that the RCL omitted this passage from its readings from Matthew. There are a number of things in the text that invite homiletical reflection. First, as mentioned earlier, the "one" scribe to speak here of his willingness to follow Jesus complicates the picture of religious leaders, helping us not demonize them in our reading of Matthew. (Luke simply has "someone" say this line to Jesus instead of a religious leader, Luke 9:57.) Second, Jesus' answer to the scribe about the son of the human not having a place to lay his head invites a struggle of interpretation given that Matthew presents Jesus as being headquartered in Capernaum. Third, the disciple's request to bury his father before following Jesus (across the sea) names a very real existential dilemma of the conflict of commitments that authentic religious devotion can entail. Fourth, Jesus' response to the scribe and disciple are often preached as if Jesus is chastising them, but this is anything but clear. Jesus seems better characterized as laying out the demand (a radical demand to be sure!) for them and allowing them to choose.

Given this invitation to choose, it is striking—and this is a fifth reason this passage makes for a good homiletical springboard—that the narrator gives the readers no clue as to how the scribe and disciple respond to Jesus' words. Too often preachers characterize them as shrinking away with their heads hung low, but this is not the case. As mentioned in relation to the story of the man with the skin disease above, if the narrator does not describe disobedience, the reader should assume the flat characters respond as instructed. At the very least, the open (ambiguous) ending allows the preacher to invite hearers to "finish" the story by responding to Jesus' call appropriately.

STILLING THE STORM (8:23-27):
OMITTED FROM LECTIONARY

The story of Jesus calming the storm plays such a key role in Mark's Gospel (4:35-41) in establishing the disciples' misunderstanding of who Jesus is following on the heels of the Parables Discourse that it can seem insignificant by comparison in how Matthew uses it. Matthew's use is more nuanced, but is nevertheless important for the development of his plot and characterization of both Jesus and the disciples.

Jesus gave orders to cross the sea back in v. 18 but was delayed by dialogue with "one" scribe and a disciple about the requirements of following Jesus. That discussion with individuals about the commitment required in discipleship sets up reading this story as characterizing the disciples as a group (and thus representing the church) who go with Jesus (across to the gentile side of the sea) as appropriately committed, similar to the fishermen jumping up and following Jesus in 4:18-22. Their fear (vv. 25-26), Jesus' reference to them as having "little faith" (v. 26; not as strong as Mark having Jesus say the disciples have "no faith," Mk 4:40), and their closing question about what kind of person Jesus is (v. 27), however, show that commitment and understanding are not always equal partners. Preachers have much to work with if they ask a congregation to identify with the disciples in this scene.

But while the characterization of the disciples is sharpened here, the clear focus is on Jesus, given that the last line raises the question of his identity. The narrator assumes the readers should know what the characters in the story do not, that is, just what kind of person Jesus is. And in this story Jesus' authority established in the healing stories earlier in the chapter extends over nature itself. Thus even if preachers use this story to focus on commitment and understanding in discipleship, they should do so specifically in relation to christology.

Exorcizing the Gadarene Demoniacs (8:28-34): Omitted from Lectionary

Matthew has pared down Mark's twenty-verse long version of this story (Mark 5:1-20) to seven verses. Much of the drama is lost in the process. In Mark's version, the focus is on the demoniac and his transformation. Strikingly, at the end of the story, the healed gentile asks to follow Jesus. Jesus denies the request but instead sends him forth to tell what the Lord had done for him. This is the only person Jesus sends forth after a healing to spread the word instead of ordering them to tell no one. Add to this the not so subtle jab at Rome's militaristic reign by calling the demon Jesus defeats, "Legion" (which Matthew omits), and you have a story full of nuances that make preachers tremble with excitement on Monday morning when they have just begun the process of sermon preparation.

Preachers will likely feel much less excitement if they focus on Matthew's version of this exorcism, but there is still good homiletical meat here to share. For Matthew, the edited version of the Gadarene demoniacs (now two men instead of Mark's one—cf. 9:27-31, where Matthew has two blind men healed), focuses more squarely on Jesus, establishing further his authority. After all, while Matthew has mentioned that Jesus has been casting out demons before now (4:24; 8:16), this is the first explicit exorcism narrated in the Gospel. Jesus is evidently able to approach the demoniacs when others could not. The demons recognize him immediately, but think Jesus has come early—"before the time"—thus establishing Jesus' ministry as an eschatological event. Jesus needs no dramatic actions, but says only, "Go," to cast out the unclean spirits. And Jesus (humorously) allows the demons to pick their own demise in going into a herd of (unclean) swine only to have them drown immediately after.

But the ironic punch line to the story is that the townspeople (or in Matthew's hyperbolic style, "the *whole* town") come out and ask Jesus to leave. Contrast this with the previous scene of the stilling of the storm, (8:23-27). Jesus' followers are scared of the storm not recognizing the power and authority of the one they are following. The Gadarenes recognize the power and authority of Jesus and reject him for it.

Forgiving/Healing the Paralytic (9:1-8):
Omitted from Lectionary

With this story Matthew reaches the high point of establishing Jesus' authority in chapters 8–9. Readers have seen Jesus exert his power and authority over impurity, illness, nature and even the demonic. Now Jesus shows that the son of the human also has authority to forgive sins. The healing in this scene is simply a literary technique used to highlight Jesus' ability to offer forgiveness.

A key to preaching this text is to characterize appropriately "some of the scribes" as basically being correct in thinking that only God has the authority and ability to forgive sins. Jesus' words and actions should not be read as countering the scribes' claim but as indicting them for failing to recognize that he is God's Son. As God's unique (messianic) representative, Jesus has been given God's authority to forgive sins, as sure as he has the ability to order a paralytic to walk. Establishing this christological claim in this scene sets up what follows in vv. 9-13 (part of the lection for Proper 5 discussed below), justifying that Jesus eats with and calls as followers tax collectors and sinners. He can forgive them and lead them into righteousness.

Why Jesus' Followers Do Not Fast (9:14-17):
Omitted from Lectionary

The structure of this passage, which Matthew takes from Mark 2:18-22, is simple: Jesus is asked a question about why his disciples do not fast (v. 14), and he answers it (vv. 15-17). The simplicity, however, ends there. Jesus' answer is filled with metaphors (and perhaps allegory) that are not clear in their application. Jesus speaks about fasting but shifts the subject in a way that readers cannot be sure he is concerned with fasting at all (the Lukan narrator makes a clear distinction between the sayings about the patch and the wineskins and the preceding dialogue about fasting; Luke 5:36).

As mentioned above in the introductory comments for chapters 8–9, this passage deals with the tension in the relationship of Jesus' movement to traditions of Judaism it inherits. There is newness here, but without a complete abandonment of the old. One does significant damage to Matthew's theology to preach a text like this with a supersessionist tone.

On the other hand, Matthew also uses this story to highlight the increasing conflict starting to evolve around Jesus and his followers. In 9:3, some of the scribes questioned Jesus forgiving sins. In 9:11 the Pharisees question Jesus eating with tax collectors and sinners. And here John's disciples question why Jesus' followers do not fast. One way of more clearly defining who Jesus and his followers are is by showing who they are not.

Healing Two Blind Men (9:27-31):
Omitted from Lectionary

The source(s) behind this story are difficult to determine. Most commentators note the similarities with the healing of the blind beggar at Jericho just before Jesus enters Jerusalem (Mark 10:46-52//Matthew 20:29-34) and assume Matthew has created a doublet from that story. On the other hand, Matthew's placement of this story early in the narrative seems related to the healing of the blind man at Bethsaida in Mark 8:22-26 for which Matthew has no other parallel. These problems indicate that the preacher will do better to interpret this scene within the context of Matthew's narrative than to draw conclusions by comparison with the evangelist's primary source, Mark.

The section (Matthew 8–9) draws to a close with five healings (or better three healing stories). More than adding new elements to Matthew's christological emphasis of the section, they intensify what has already been demonstrated. In this scene, Jesus returns to "the house" (that is, his headquarters) and heals two blind men who have faith in his healing ability.

Faith is a recurring theme in this section with homiletical potential (cf. 8:3, 10, 26; 9:22, 28).

Exorcizing Demon Causing Muteness (9:32-34): Omitted from Lectionary

The healings in chapters 8 and 9 close with an exorcism that is not even a story. A demoniac is brought to Jesus in his house right after the healed blind men leave. The narrator does not describe what Jesus says or does, but just names that the demon left and the man who had been mute spoke.

The reason Matthew tells the story this way is the healing simply serves as the set up for the real focus of the scene, the rising conflict of the narrative. The crowds express amazement that "Never has anything like this been seen in Israel" (v. 33). The attentive reader will realize that the crowd is placed to comment on the entirety of chapters 8–9, not just this particular healing—compare the similar statement at the close of the Ethical Discourse (7:28-29). But whereas the positive assessment following the Sermon on the Mount is the final word, here the Pharisees get the final word and offer a different appraisal of Jesus' work: he casts out demons by the power and authority of Beelzebul (v. 34; instead of by the power and authority of God).

What is striking about this accusation is that it is left to hang in the air without a response or resolution. Matthew will return to the accusation and have Jesus display the irrationality of the claim in 12:22-32. But for now, there it is. The readers obviously know it is incorrect. Matthew leaves it there to establish a turning point in the conflict. While the questions by religious leaders in the preceding scenes might have been viewed simply as questions, we now have a full-force assault underway. Preachers working through Matthean lections (or through Matthew as a whole) in some cumulative fashion, will want to highlight this moment.

Lections

It is a shame that so much happens in Matthew 8–9 to establish Jesus' authority, and the RCL selects only one reading from the section. The lection has significant homiletic potential, but it does not highlight some of the stronger themes of the section.

It should be noted, moreover, that the lection is really two separate passages (9:9-13: Jesus associating with tax collectors and sinners; and 9:18-26: Jesus healing the dead girl and the woman with the hemorrhage) with an omission (the dialogue about fasting, 9:14-17) between them. The fact that the passages are thematically unrelated coupled with the second passage combining two intercalated stories makes this an extremely difficult lection for preachers to get their hands around. They will have to choose to focus on either the first or the second passage.

LECTION: TAX COLLECTORS AND SINNERS; A DEAD GIRL AND SICK WOMAN 9:9-13, 18-26; PROPER 5

Because this lection is really composed of two separate pericope, the commentary that follows will deal with each passage separately.

9:9-13: Tax Collectors and Sinners. Although short, this is a complex scene. Matthew's source for this scene is Mark 2:13-17. As usual, Matthew makes editorial changes to the scene he inherits, but they are not theologically significant changes. Two changes are important to note, however. The first is that the Gospel writer changes the tax collector's name from Levi to Matthew (v. 9 / Mk 2:14). Some scholars have suggested they are two different names for the same person (for example, a name and a surname) and others have suggested the Gospel writer is actually talking about a different person than Levi. This is a historical conundrum that cannot be resolved. But the reason the change is important for preachers is that this change is likely the reason the First Gospel was attributed to Matthew. Indeed, laity may be familiar with this but have heard it as historical proof that Matthew wrote the Gospel as an eyewitness. Preaching on this text gives pastors a chance to offer a counter understanding of the authorship of the Gospel in passing.

The second editorial change Matthew makes concerns the setting of the story. In Mark 2:13-14, Jesus comes out of his home in Capernaum where he has just healed a paralytic (Mk 2:1-12) to teach by the sea and sees Levi. After calling Levi as a disciple, Jesus attends a dinner at Levi's house that includes tax collectors and sinners (Mk 2:15). In Matthew, however, Jesus has returned from the other side of the sea (where he exorcised the Gadarene demoniacs, 8:28—9:1) when he is met (by the sea) by a paralytic (9:2). After forgiving and healing him, Jesus walks along (that is, finally heading away from the sea) and sees Matthew in his tax booth there (where he would collect taxes on fish caught for commerce, 9:9). After calling Matthew as a disciple, Jesus is then found in "the house" at a meal with tax collectors and sinners. The fact that Matthew changes Mark's reference to Levi's house shows that he means the reader to assume this is Jesus' home/headquarters in Capernaum. So Jesus does not simply eat with tax collectors and sinners when in their house, he invites them into his own home.

There are three movements to the story. The first is the calling of Matthew (v. 9). The call resembles that of the fishermen (4:18-22) in that the narrator gives no explanation for why the tax collector responds positively to Jesus' call. There is no hint that he has heard Jesus preach or witnessed any miracles. Instead, Jesus simply calls, and he simply obeys. But, of course, there is nothing simple about such following as the readers know from having just recently heard Jesus' response to two would-be followers in 8:18-22, where Jesus makes clear how hard it is to be one of his followers—no place to lay your head and no chance to bury your dead.

The obedient response of the tax collector leads into the next movement of the story (vv. 12-13), in which we see Jesus (and presumably Matthew) sitting down for a meal with other "tax collectors and sinners." Without explaining why they are there as well, the narrator portrays the Pharisees as questioning Jesus' disciples about why he eats with such people. Before we attack the Pharisees from the pulpit, we need to recognize that it is a fair question. Jesus has taught a higher righteousness (5:19-20) but now appears in intimate fellowship (eating with someone in ancient Mediterranean culture had a strong symbolic significance) with those who in no way live a life of such righteousness. By sinners, Matthew really means sinners, not simply good people who made a bad choice here or there. Tax collectors were Jews who over-collected from their own people to pay the oppressive Romans. In other words, they profited significantly by the oppression of their own people. The Pharisees' question, then, need not be read as mean-spirited or attacking Jesus (although this tone will increase as the narrative progresses). It is justified in light of the characterization of Jesus thus far in the narrative.

The third movement, then, is Jesus' rationale for why the one who calls his followers to be perfect as God is perfect (5:48) eats with those who are more than just a little imperfect. Since the first two movements serve to set up Jesus' pronouncement as the climax of the scene, this final part should be the focus of the sermon. Notice, first, that Jesus in no way defends those with whom he is eating as if they have been falsely accused. His language clearly acknowledges that the Pharisees' description of his dinner companions is correct: they are sinners. What Jesus does instead is to say that is for them that he has come. In other words, Jesus shifts the focus from their character to his.

First, Jesus answers in soteriological terms using the analogy of a physician. The logic is common sense: it is the sick instead of the healthy who need a doctor. (The analogy reminds readers of the connection made in the previous story where Jesus first forgives a paralytic of his sins and then to prove that he has authority to forgive also heals the man of his physical ailment, 9:2-8). Second, Jesus answers in ethical terms by quoting Hosea 6:6 which contrasts mercy and sacrifice. This is often interpreted as an attack on the legalism of the Pharisees and it is indeed a challenge to the religious leaders (that, as we have seen, grows out of the conflict between Matthew's church and the synagogue of the late first century). But it is important to remember that the focus here is on Jesus' character. More than attacking the Pharisees, Jesus explains how his actions that seemingly contradict what he himself has taught before are actually a fulfillment of scriptural mandate. Then, third, Jesus shifts from analogy and scripture references to an explicit declaration of his purpose: he has come to call not the righteous but sinners (as manifested in both the call of Matthew and the dinner).

The word call here, however, is extremely important. To accept the call means a significant level of commitment and radical change of life. In other words, Jesus calls sinners so that they might become righteous. God's grace made known in Christ is a transforming grace. It would be superfluous to call the righteous so that they might become righteous. Sinners, however, need change. This is as much a defense of the composition of Matthew's church (Jew, gentile, sinner, saint) as it is of Jesus' ministry. Jesus and the church call those who are outside the reign of heaven *so that* they might be able to enter it.

In sharing this christological and ecclesiological vision of salvation, preachers will have to decide with whom in the story the congregation should identify. Some congregations might be most like the religious leaders, drawing boundaries around the church between saints and sinners that offer transformation to no one. Other congregations might be most like the sinners, welcomed to the table and invited to share in much more. And still other congregations might best experience this story from the perspective of the disciples, those struggling to follow Jesus in offering mercy to the world and being reminded of those to whom the mercy is to be extended.

CAPERNAUM-BASED MINISTRY: MISSION DISCOURSE (9:35—10:42)

INTRODUCTION

Following the Ethical Discourse (chapters 5–7), Matthew presented Jesus as moving around Galilee in a mixture of healing, discipleship and conflict stories in chapters 8–9. The narrative pace slows down again here with the second of Matthew's five discourses—the Mission Discourse. As 11:1 shows, however, Jesus keeps traveling around in "their" cities after this discourse. Thus the discourse is part and parcel of (or better an expansion of) Jesus' itinerant ministry, not a diversion from it. Moreover, the themes of the Mission Discourse are closely related to those found in the narration of Jesus' ministry. As Jesus has traveled around preaching and healing, so he sends the disciples out to do the same.

One of the interpretive questions that surrounds this discourse is the identification of those Matthew intends to instruct. Most scholars agree that Matthew has anachronistically taken issues involved in the church's outreach in his day and shaped Jesus' instruction to address them in a fairly transparent manner. In other words, in the narrative world Jesus instructs the Twelve, but the apostles are clearly representatives of people in Matthew's community. The question is who these people in Matthew's community are. Is Matthew concerned with literal guidelines for the behavior of itinerant charismatic prophets commissioned and sent out by the church or is he writing to the church as a whole with instructions for outreach that are perhaps to be understood in a bit more figurative fashion? In truth, the answer may be more of a both/and than an either/or situation. Likely, the instructions (or better, pieces of the instructions) reflect a specific historical situation in the early church (different elements and forms of the instruction are found in Mark, Q, Matthew and Luke), but as time went on they were applied to broader circumstances. Our homiletical interest, of course, is less in the historical investigation of First Century missionaries and more in how Matthew's particular configuration of the instructions inform the mission of the church today as well as advance his narrative.

The Mission Discourse is, of course, thoroughly ecclesiological in nature. It can be seen as containing Matthew's core ecclesiological teachings concerning the church's engagement of the world in tandem with Matthew's core ecclesiological teachings concerning the church's inner workings found in the Community Discourse in chapter 18. As an ecclesiological/mission ethic, the instructions and teachings of the discourse are exemplary as opposed to being intended as exhaustive. Much as the antitheses serve as case studies of Matthew's core hermeneutic in the Ethical Discourse (5:17-48) instead of hard and fast rules, these teachings serve to set the framework for the church's outreach. Preachers must look beyond the details to the big picture to grasp what is at stake in the ethic and theological underpinning of this discourse.

As mentioned, mission instructions are found in all of the Synoptics and presumably in Q since some mission material is shared by Matthew and Luke that is not found in Mark. If we take a close look at Matthew's discourse with an eye toward its relationship to the materials found in the other two

Gospels, we find a complicated situation. Clearly, Matthew's primary source for the discourse is Mark, but the Markan materials he uses to compose the discourse are varied in type and found scattered throughout Mark's narrative: the primary source material comes from the naming of the Twelve (3:13-19); the sending out the Twelve (6:6b-13); and elements concerning suffering in the eschatological discourse (13:9-13). Not only has Matthew moved these materials together into a new context, he has taken a very free hand in editing them to fit his socio-theological purposes. Moreover he has added to Mark's material instructions he found elsewhere (compare "Q" materials used in the discourse found in Luke 6:40; 10:3, 16; 12:2-9, 51-53; 14:25-27; and note that Luke has two formal commissioning scenes—the sending of the Twelve in 9:1-6 and the sending of the seventy in 10:1-17). While little of the material in the discourse is unique to Matthew, the configuration of the discourse and the shaping of the language of passages within it are.

In spite of the variety of source material Matthew uses in composing his Mission Discourse, there is significant unity and order to it. Recognizing the structure can help the preacher better interpret the function of individual passages as Matthew uses them (in contrast to ways we might be familiar with the same material in Mark or Luke). The configuration can be identified as follows:

9:35–38 **Setting and description of need for the**
Apostles to be sent out
10:1-4 **Introduction to the Discourse**
40 Authorizing the Twelve
2-4 Naming the Twelve
10:5-15 **Instructions for itinerancy**
5-6 Scope of the mission
7-8 Tasks of the mission
9-15 Behavior during the mission
10:16-23 **Hardships to Expect**
16-18 Warning of persecutions
19-23 Behavior during persecution
10:24-42 **Encouragement**
24-25 Rationale for persecution
26-31 Exhortation to courage
32-33 Jesus' affirmation of those who acknowledge him
34-39 The need for enduring commitment
40-42 Conclusion (with vv. 11-15).

Matthew delineates the major sections of Jesus' actual speech by concluding each section with a saying including the words, "Truly [Amen] I say to you" (vv. 15, 23, 42). The end of the discourse as a whole is then marked with Matthew's standard formula for concluding the five discourses: "*Now when Jesus had finished* instructing the twelve disciples (11:1).

Notice how the movement exhibited in this outline moves in the opposite direction of most contemporary preaching. Preachers today are prone to move from proclamation to exhortation/application, but here the basic movement of Jesus' actual speech (10:5-42) moves from instruction to promise. The ethical/ecclesiological weight is at the beginning of the passage, but the theological weight is at the end.

Another structural issue important for the preacher to keep in mind when working through this discourse is how the mission fits into Matthew's narratively constructed structure of salvation history. As named in the Introduction, Matthew views Jesus as the hinge between Israel's past and the church's future. A theological problem in connecting those two for the New Testament writer is the fact that the church contains gentiles. How can a gentile-filled church be part of Jesus' fulfilling instead of abandoning the *torah* (5:17-19)? In addition to having Jesus exhort the disciples/church to hold on to a higher righteousness than the scribes and Pharisees in observing the law in the Ethical Discourse (5:20ff), Matthew answers this question with a two-stage mission.

In this discourse, Jesus sends the disciples out to exorcise demons, heal sickness, purify the unclean, and proclaim the approach of the reign of heaven with the explicit limits, "Go nowhere among the gentiles, and enter no town of the Samaritans, but go rather to the lost sheep of the house of Israel" (10:5-6). This exclusion of the gentiles is striking given Matthew's sibling rivalry with the synagogue. In other words, the mission of the Twelve (as transparent representatives of the church) is narrated as initially being directed only to the Jews. Mark does not contain this element in his form of the sending of the Twelve (Mark 6:7-13), so Matthew has made an intentional theological move in adding it. Another change Matthew makes to Mark illustrates why Matthew defines the mission of the Twelve this way. Mark concludes the mission with the disciples reporting what they had done and taught (6:30), but Matthew never reports the apostles' return. (The closest such reference may be in 17:22 where the Jesus and the disciples are said to have been gathering [*sustrephomenōn*] in Galilee—an odd reference since they have been operating in and around Galilee throughout Jesus' Capernaum-based ministry and since the disciples are explicitly mentioned as being with Jesus often in the interceding chapters. Even more odd, Matthew never explicitly says that disciples went out after being commissioned. In 11:1, it is Jesus who goes out.) Omitting the conclusion of the mission signals to Matthew's church that the mission to the Jews has not ended. After the resurrection, Jesus returns to Galilee of the gentiles (4:15) and instructs the disciples now to go and make disciples *of all nations* (that is, gentiles; 28:19). For Matthew, the resurrection makes the gentile mission possible and thus the gentile mission does not replace the mission to Israel but supplements it. In spite of his church's conflict with the synagogue, Matthew views Jesus' (and the church's) concern as being universal—not either/or but both/and. Thus, the instructions given in chapter 10 are limited to the mission to Israel only in the context of the narrative world. Matthew intends them to be instructive for the ongoing mission of the church in its outreach to all.

Another major narrative/theological aspect of the mission instructions which the preacher should emphasize if preaching on the lections taken from the discourse is signaled in vv. 24-25: "A disciple is not above the teacher." The work of the apostles (and thus of those sent out by the church) as well as the response to their ministry is modeled on the work of and in response to Jesus. In the introduction (10:1), the narrator makes clear that Jesus gives the twelve disciples authority to do the work the reader has seen him doing in the previous chapters—casting out demons and healing the sick. This is reiterated and expanded in Jesus' voice in v. 7: "As you go, proclaim the good news, 'The reign of heaven has come near.' Cure the sick, raise the dead, cleanse the lepers, cast out demons." Matthew has offered summaries of Jesus doing this sort of work (4:23-24; 8:16; 9:35), but notice how he has also presented explicit examples of each of these:

Proclaim the good news, 'The reign of heaven has come near.'	4:17 – Jesus preaches the same eschatological message of the advent God's reign with the addition of the call to repent (cf. John's proclamation of the same message in 3:2).
Cure the sick	The centurion's child (8:5-13); Peter's mother-in-law (8:14-15); The paralytic (9:2-8); The bleeding woman (9:20-22); Two blind men (9:27-31)
Raise the dead	The ruler's daughter (9:18-19, 23-26)
Cleanse the lepers	The man with the skin disease (8:1-4)
Cast out demons	The Gadarene demoniacs (8:28-34); The mute demoniac (9:32-34).

What these parallels show is that in the section offering instructions for itinerant ministry, those being sent are being called to imitate Jesus in ministry as just illustrated in the previous section of the narrative.

The flip side of this imitation is seen in the next section of the discourse in which Jesus describes hardships those sent out will face (10:16-25). Here they are being told to imitate Jesus in expecting to be persecuted and facing that persecution. But, of course, Matthew's church had already been facing such persecution, so this section of Jesus' speech (expressed in future tense) interprets the present experience of Matthew's original readers. Their persecution follows Jesus' persecution. Consider, in terms of the narrative world, how the persecutions named here foreshadow aspects of Jesus' passion to appear later in the story:

They will hand you over to councils (10:17)	Jewish authorities conspiring to arrest Jesus (26:1-5); Jesus before the council (26:57-68)
You will be dragged before governors and kings (10:17)	Jesus before Pilate (27:1-2, 11-26)
Brother will betray brother to death (10:21)	Judas betraying Jesus (10:4; 26:20-25, 47-50; 27:3-4).

This two-sided imitation of Jesus (in ministry and in persecution) forms the crux of the Mission Discourse (vv. 5-15 and 16-25, respectively). But it is the next section of the discourse, intended to encourage those whose ministry leads them into situations of persecution in that same way it did Jesus (10:26-39), that serves as the climax of the speech. In sum, Jesus exhorts those in his ministry to have no fear of persecution. The call to courage is not rooted in a denial of the power of evil or the very real suffering that will result from persecution. Instead it is based on the idea that God's sovereign providence is stronger than anything evil can do. So while expressed in a rhetoric of imperative, the force of the section is really declarative.

LECTIONS

The RCL offers three lections drawn from the Mission Discourse during Ordinary Time. These are 9:35—10:8 (9-23); 10:24-39; 10:40-42. If a congregation reads the longer option for the first lection (the optional verses are included in parentheses), the entire Mission Discourse is covered. The problem is that including those verses makes for a very long liturgical reading and a lesson far too long to deal with in the pulpit. Thus even if the whole lection is read, the preacher will be forced to choose some focus on the text that excludes some elements of it. On the other hand, to read the shorter option for the first lection is to omit the center of the discourse (speaking both figuratively and literally). And a smaller problem is added to this significant problem: the break between the first and second lection is not in the most logical place. If one wishes to follow the basic semi-continuous plan of the RCL in Year A, but has the freedom to redraw the boundaries of the lections, a better division would be: 9:35—10:15; 10:16-23; and 10:24-42. In what follows, however, we will discuss the lections as the RCL defines them.

Lection: Sending of the Twelve
9:35—10:8 [9-23]; Proper 6

As can be seen from the outline of the Mission Discourse above, the shorter option for this lection includes the setting, introduction and part of the instructions for itinerant ministry while the longer option adds the rest of the instructions and most of the description of hardship to be expected by those sent out. Because either option includes too much material for a congregation to digest in a single sermon, preachers should focus on one part of the lesson. They can start with an overview and then zoom in, but to say everything risks saying nothing. I will comment on the material section by section to aid preachers who choose different foci.

9:35-38 is a transitional passage that can be seen as both a conclusion to the previous section and its concern for healing those in need and as setting the stage for the next section with the sending out of the Twelve. Jesus is presented as assessing the situation to which he has been attending (in the past) and naming that the need is greater than one person can meet (in the future).

The way in which Matthew names the need is interesting. Jesus has compassion on the crowds because they are, according to the NRSV, "harassed and helpless" (v. 36). The Greek is more literally translated as "troubled, bothered, or annoyed" (Gk. *skullō*) and "thrown down" (Gk. *riptō*). The question for the interpreter is to what the terms refer in their figurative use here. One option is to read the terms as referring to the kinds of situation seen in the previous section of Matthew: illness, uncleanness, demon possessed. The terms could also refer to situations of being oppressed. The ambiguity may be intentional. In other words, for Matthew illness, demon possession, being ritually unclean, and economic/political oppression are all related.

The modification of the next line is helpful to contextualize these terms. Matthew describes the crowd using language taken from the Hebrew Bible: they are "like sheep without a shepherd." This indicates that Matthew's concern is for Israel and foreshadows 10:5-6. If the crowd is a shepherd-less Israel, then this opening is meant, at least in part, as an indictment of Jewish leadership for its failure to alleviate the people's suffering. Jesus' proclamation of God's reign, his healings and exorcisms—about to be extended to the work of the apostles/church—are assumed to be the help the people really need. Thus this discourse is set up as part of the sibling rivalry between the synagogue and Matthew's church. Whereas before we have seen Matthew portray Jesus as establishing the church as the proper heir to and interpreter of Israel's faith and traditions, now we see the Gospel writer naming the church more explicitly in this role in terms of its evangelism.

Nevertheless, Matthew is a realist in the sense that he knows in the current state of his church's work, many are still "harassed and helpless." Similar to the sheep image, the language of the harvest is taken from the Hebrew Bible, but this metaphor is used eschatologically in the tradition. Thus Matthew offers instructions for the mission of the church in eschatological terms. The mission, and the reign of heaven that it announces, foreshadows the ultimate alleviation of trouble and oppression. We often do not talk about the church in eschatological terms these days. This has significant homiletical promise.

10:1-4 introduces the discourse in that it names the authority Jesus gives to the Twelve and names who the Twelve are. There is little of significant theological or homiletical help in this section (especially given that the endowment of authority is repeated and expanded in the next section. Scholarly interest in this material has been of the historical sort. Was there really a group of twelve apostles or is this a symbolic group related to the twelve tribes of Israel? If there really was a group of Twelve, who were they given that the lists of names in the different Gospels have so many variants (as seen in Mk 6:16-19; Lk 9:14-16; and Acts 1:13)?

10:5-15 provides the primary instructions for the Twelve/church. Everything before has set the stage for these instructions and everything that follows unpacks the implications of the life represented in these verses.

In vv. 5-6, Jesus limits the scope of the mission to the lost sheep of the house of Israel. This lection shows up at the beginning of Ordinary Time. If one is going to begin working through Matthew in a semi-continuous fashion, focusing on this section has potential for a cumulative approach to

Matthew's paradoxical relationship with Judaism. Such a sermon could relate the historical conflict between Matthew's church and the synagogue after the fall of the temple to Matthew's two-staged mission presented here and in the Great Commission (28:16-20) and raise questions about contemporary Christianity's relationship with Judaism.

In vv. 7-8, Jesus gives the Twelve/church instructions about the tasks they are to perform in ministry. This section concludes the shorter option for the lection and can serve well to ground an ecclesiological sermon. Indeed, drawing on the parallels listed above concerning the way the work of the Twelve imitates the work of Jesus, preachers can offer the congregation a vision of the contemporary church's mission as imitating the works and character of Christ. Instead of asking, "What would Jesus do?" we ask "What *did* Jesus do?" This theme of imitation can be double-sided in relating to the last verses of the lection as well (vv. 16-25). As Jesus suffered in ministry so will/should we, if we are really following his example in ministry.

In vv. 9-15, Jesus deals with the behavior of those sent out in relation to the response they receive. The opening verse is often read as instructing the disciples to carry nothing with them as they go out in ministry. But the verb translated as "take" by the NRSV does not mean "carry" but means "acquire." In other words, the concern is not what the apostles start out with but how they are compensated while out and about in ministry. In a sense, Matthew is saying that those sent out should only receive food and lodging, no pay, clothes or other gifts. Compare where Luke 10:7 has Jesus say to the seventy he sends out, "The laborer deserves to be paid," with Matthew's "Laborer's deserve their food" (v. 10).

Matthew's intent behind this limitation of hospitality received is unclear. Comparing these instructions for the apostles to Paul's intent in similar discussions (1 Cor 9; 2 Cor 11:7-11; 1 Thes 2:9; 2 Thes 3:7-9) can be instructive, but we cannot be sure Matthew's concerns are analogous to Paul's. Speaking homiletically, however, at the very least, the contemporary church has something to learn about what we should expect from those to whom we minister. One way or another, this passage puts all the weight on meeting their needs as opposed to their in any way meeting our needs.

On the other hand, the section closes (vv. 11-15) with high expectation for acceptance of Jesus' proclamation. Those who accept the ministry of Jesus' emissaries are to be offered peace. Those who do not are judged in a way that exhibits rejection being returned for rejection. But notice that the disciples are to do nothing more than leave those rejecting the gospel totally behind—leaving even their dust behind. Judgment is left to the eschaton and to

God's will. Such is not the church's concern. The church moves on to others in need.

10:16-23 provides the primary warnings for the apostles/church in parallel to the previous section containing the primary instructions of the chapter. As noted above the forms of persecution named are meant to foreshadow those faced by Jesus in his passion. Thus the church is to imitate Jesus in suffering as well as in ministry (because the latter will naturally result in the former). And this was, to some degree, the historical experience of the early church. In other words, the language of the section likely reflects not only Matthew's narrative purposes, but also the realities of conflicts and hardships endured by first century missionaries (as is similarly portrayed throughout Acts).

What is significant for preaching this text is less the historical identification of such suffering and more the recognition that to follow Jesus in proclaiming the good news of the reign of heaven and to offer healing to the troubled and oppressed masses is a risky endeavor that will get the attention of the powers-that-be. This raises a question concerning the flipside of this assertion: if the church is not being pursued by those who benefit by the status quo (that is, the reign of Caesar and "throwing down" of those at the bottom of the social ladder), are we actually participating in Jesus' ministry as Matthew calls us to do? "That'll preach," as they say, but we must careful not to sentimentalize the suffering envisioned here—mock trials leading to the threat and loss of life. While the instructions of the chapter need not be taken literally, the weight of what Matthew offers should not be lightened for contemporary Christians. Being the church in the world is serious business, so be wise as serpents and innocent as doves.

LECTION: ENCOURAGEMENT IN THE FACE OF PERSECUTION
10:24-39; PROPER 7

The opening two verses of the lesson (vv. 24-25) really serve as a transition between the previous section and this one. They offer the basic rationale of the entire discourse: as with Jesus, so with the church. In ministry the church imitates Jesus. And thus the church faces the same consequences as Jesus—persecution. Matthew makes the point with two metaphors: disciple/teacher and slave/master. But the point is driven with force by a direct reference to an accusation against Jesus made by the religious leaders, that is, that he casts out by Beelzebul (9:34). This controversy will arise again in 12:22-32, where Jesus will deconstruct the logic of the accusation. The reference here (v. 25) stands in between the initiation of the controversy and its escalation. So will the persecution of the church that follows Jesus in ministry be escalated.

The core theme of the section, however, is to assert that persecution in the end falls short in its ability to overcome the grace and providence of God. The comparison of the church's worth to the worth of sparrows recalls the reference to birds of the air in the Sermon on the Mount (6:26), where the theme also had to do with trusting in God's providential care. The apostles/church are exhorted to have courage not because God will erase all hardships. (After all, Matthew has Jesus in this section name that his very mission creates conflict instead of establishing peace; vv. 34-36.) They can be fearless because in Jesus life itself has been redefined in such a way that the powers-that-be cannot threaten it (v. 39), a fact seen in the crucifixion and resurrection of Jesus himself (notice the cross language in v. 38).

While the instructions in vv. 5-15 clearly serve as the didactic focus of the Mission Discourse, this section serves as the theological foundation for it. It is written in the form of imperatives ("Have no fear" is stated three times; vv. 26, 28, 31), but it is not meant as instruction. The proclamation is that we can trust our very being, the meaning of our existence, to God because God is on our side, *pro nobis*, and bigger than anything that can be thrown in our direction. This God who saves and provides for us ultimately is worthy of our ultimate devotion.

When we preach on this lection, it is important to remember that Matthew's concern here is not about theodicy in general or even individual suffering at the hands of persecutors (even though the language used often refers to individuals). The context of the discussion of providence here is the ministry of the apostles as a group, of the church as a whole. The evangelist's concern is with persecution brought on the church as a community of Jesus' emissaries in bringing good news and healing to a world broken by evil. Keeping this focus helps the sermon stay in the theological category of ecclesiology where it belongs instead of slipping into other areas.

LECTION: CONCLUSION TO THE MISSION DISCOURSE
10:40-42; PROPER 8

The RCL has made a strange choice in concluding its reading of the Mission Discourse with a lection that includes only three verses after opening the discourse with a lesson that spanned 24 verses. Nevertheless, these few verses are complex. They concern the reward to be received by those who welcome those sent out by Jesus/the church.

They do not represent a section of the discourse on their own but a subsection of the larger final movement focused on encouraging the readers and giving them courage/confidence (10:24-42). But as the passage concludes this movement, it also serves as the conclusion to the whole discourse. Notice that while the passage does not simply repeat the sentiments found in vv. 11-15, it does overlap so much that one asks why Matthew places the saying here instead of in that section.

The answer lies, at least in part, in the shift of focus exhibited in the passage. Throughout the discourse the focus has been on those sent out—who they are, what their tasks are, how they are to behave, what hardships they are to expect, and why they need not fear those hardships. In this passage, however, the focus is on the reward to be given to those who receive the ministry of those sent out. Or does it really shift?

It is important to remember that Matthew is an insider-document, a narrative written for the church. The discourse as a whole and this passage particularly is written for the church, not for outsiders. The audience of the discourse has not shifted suddenly at the end. Matthew still presents Jesus as speaking to the Twelve who represent the readers/church. So the preacher should ask, how does this passage function in the hearing of the church?

It is actually the climax of encouragement. After naming the hardships that will be part of the church's mission, which means that many will reject the proclamation and service of the church, naming the reward of those who welcome the ones sent out signals that in spite of the hardships, the mission will ultimately be successful. There is no need to talk about rewards if this is not the case.

But it is important to notice as well that for Matthew the language of rewards is eschatological (recall, for example, the Beatitudes in 5:3-12). What this ultimately means is that the success of the mission is not dependent on how well those sent out do their job. God is responsible for the success of the mission. The emissaries represent Christ who represents God. When the emissaries are welcomed God is welcomed. God offers the good news of God's own reign. God heals. God defeats the demonic. God cleanses. God rewards.

But even as the passage wraps up the symphony with God banging on the tympani and crashing the cymbals, another subtle, but intriguing note is sounded softly from somewhere in the woodwind section. Interpreters throughout the history of the church have struggled with who is being named in the list of "prophets," "the righteous," and "the little ones" (v. 41). Many have proposed three classes of missionaries. This seems doubtful, but at the very least Matthew makes a distinction between the first two in the list and the last. Notice how the grammatical structure of v. 42 speaking of the little ones breaks with the parallel structure speaking of prophets and righteous ones in v. 41 (the shift in English represents well the different structure in Greek). The rhetorical force of this break in the pattern is to put the emphasis on the little ones. But who are they? Matthew uses language in other places that makes clear these are ordinary, vulnerable Christians (see 18:6, 10, 14; cf. 25:40, 45). They are not leaders. They are not super-faithful. For some reason or another, they are those in the community of faith who are vulnerable. They are the ones likely to "stumble" (that is, sin) and are in need of assistance in keeping the faith (see the commentary on 18:6-10). And yet they are the last ones mentioned in the discourse. Jesus starts by naming the Twelve and ends with a passing mention of the "little ones." If there was any question whether the Mission Discourse was meant to be instructive for the church—that is, the whole church—there is no longer. All are to imitate Christ in ministry and bearing hardship. And all represent Christ (and thus God) in the successes of that ministry.

CAPERNAUM-BASED MINISTRY: CONFLICTS BUILDING (11:1—12:50)

INTRODUCTION

Preachers are in good company with some commentators if as they turn from the Mission Discourse to this narrative section, they see the materials here as only loosely connected—Jesus and John the Baptist, woes to the Galilean cities, invitation to take up Jesus' easy yoke, conflicts concerning healing on the Sabbath, Jesus the healer as fulfillment of Isaiah, the Beelzebul controversy, and Jesus' true family. Indeed, the sense that these pericopes are thrown together to provide some narrative material between the Mission Discourse (ch. 10) and the Parables Discourse (ch. 13) is supported by noting the sources Matthew uses to construct the section. Matthew takes material from Mark 2:23—3:35 and adds in "Q" material along with some small pieces unique to Matthew:

Matthew	Sources
11:1	Unique to Matthew
11:2-19	Lk 7:18-35
11:20-24	Lk 10:12-15 (piece missing between this and the next is the return of the 70)
11:25-27	Lk 10:21-22
11:28-30	Unique to Matthew
12:1-21	Mk 2:23—3:12 (piece missing between this and the next is appointment of the 12)
12:22-37	Mk 3:22-30 (cf. Lk 11:14-23 for connection with following 2 pericopes)
12:38-42	Mk 8:11 + Lk 11:29-32

12:43-45	Lk 11:24-26 (Mt's order of this and the preceding pericope are reversed from Lk's and is missing Lk 11:27-28)
12:46-50	Mk 3:31-35 (omitting Mk 3:19b-21)

To interpret the pericopes in chapters 11–12 as isolated from one another, however, is to cheat the section from the cumulative effect it has on Matthew's overarching plot development. While we will discuss the import of some of these phenomena later, notice the repetition of key vocabulary across pericopes (and across sources) that gives the chapters a sense of being interwoven:

- deeds (*erga*) — 11:2, 19
- reed — 11:7; 12:20
- repent — 11:20, 21; 12:41
- born (*gennētos*) — 11:11; offspring (*genēma*) — 12:34; generation (*genea*) — 11:16, 12:39, 41, 42, 45
- their cities — 11:1; their synagogue — 12:9
- *krisis* (sometimes translated "judgment," and sometimes less helpfully as "justice") — 11: 22, 24; 12: 18, 20, 36, 41, 42)
- Sabbath — 12:1, 2, 5 (twice), 8, 10, 11, 12
- *Exeimi* ("it is permitted") — 12:2, 4, 10, 12
- David — 12:3, 23
- Son — (son in relation to the Father) 11:27 (three times); (the son of the human) 11:19; 12:8, 32, 40; (the son of David) 12:23; (your sons) 12:27.

While not exactly the same thing, Matthew also repeatedly uses the grammatical form of the comparative throughout this section:

- 11:9: More than a prophet
- 11:11: No one born greater, yet least in reign of heaven is greater
- 11:20: More tolerable for Tyre and Sidon than for you
- 11:24: More tolerable for Sodom than for you
- 12:6: Something greater than the temple here
- 12:41: Something greater than Jonah is here
- 12:42: Something greater than Solomon is here
- 12:45: Seven spirits more evil; last state is worse than the first

Given these sorts of repetition uniting the material in chapters 12–13, when preaching on an individual pericope in this section, preachers will do well, then, to pay attention to the relation of that passage to the whole section in order to get a sense of the full import Matthew placed on the passage.

There are two interrelated developments to which Matthew seems to want his audience to attend in this section. This first is the increasing conflict between Jesus and others that starts turning the narrative from simply portraying Jesus' itinerant ministry in and around Capernaum as being for its own sake and portraying it as leading toward the final conflict that will occur in Jerusalem later in the narrative. In the Mission Discourse, Jesus made clear that he brings conflict for his followers—their persecution imitates his experience of persecution. In this section we see Jesus drawing lines in the sand based on rejection and the religious leaders now bringing the conflict to him. Preachers can see this dynamic by outlining the structure of the section in relation to the way Jesus' conversation partners change.

11:2-6: Jesus begins by identifying himself to *John's disciples* (or better to *John the Baptist* himself through John's disciples)

11:7-19: After John's disciples leave, Jesus continues discussing John with *the crowd*. Here he praises John but clearly distinguishes himself from John. Nevertheless, he accuses the crowd of rejecting both John and Jesus.

11:20-24: In an apostrophe (a literary technique of direct address to someone not present) Jesus chastises the Galilean cities of *Chorazin, Bethsaida,* and *Capernaum* for their failure to repent. This passage functions as an intensification and expansion of the accusation of *the crowd*, who continues to be Jesus' real audience.

11:25-30: In vv. 25-27, Jesus prays to the *Father*, but the prayer functions much like the apostrophe of the previous passage in that *the crowd* is really still the audience. This is seen in the shift to speaking of God in the third person in v. 27 and further with the shift to Jesus calling people to take up his yoke in vv. 28-30 without any identification of an audience.

12:1-8: With a change in setting, Jesus is next confronted by
the Pharisees over his disciples picking and eating grain
on the Sabbath. Earlier in the narrative we saw that Jesus first
took shots at the religious leaders, not the other way around.
But now they begin to attack him.

12:9-14. Next Jesus is challenged about healing on the Sabbath in
their synagogue. The people who ask Jesus about this are only
named as "they" (v. 10), but by the end of the scene, it is the
Pharisees who are conspiring against Jesus to destroy him.
Thus Matthew connects Jesus' conflict with religious leaders in
Jesus' day with his church's conflict with the synagogue in his
own day. Moreover, Matthew makes explicit that the conflict
Jesus is facing is building toward the ultimate conflict that will
result in his execution.

12:15-21. This is the only scene in the two chapters that does not
present Jesus as being in dialogue. It is an interlude offered by
the narrator but it again involves Jesus with *the crowds*. Jesus
withdraws from the Pharisees who are plotting against him and
heals "all" of those in the crowds following him. This serves as
the basis for the longest scripture fulfillment citation in the First
Gospel (from Isaiah 42:1-4, 9). While there are a number Of
things this citation does for Matthew, one to be noted in
relation to the building conflict is the twofold mention of the
gentiles in the passage. After having sent the Twelve nowhere
among the gentiles but only to the lost sheep of the house of
Israel and after having been in conflict with the religious
authorities to the point that they seek to destroy him, this
turn to the gentiles justifies the inclusion of gentiles in
Matthew's church.

12:22-37: Without a change in setting, Jesus heals a demoniac,
which leads *the Pharisees* to reappear and accuse Jesus of
casting out by Beelzebul. Even though, Matthew takes over this
material from Mark, the high importance of this accusation
for Matthew can be seen in the other references to it
(9:34; 10:25), which are not found in Mark. Jesus gives
a lengthy response to the accusation which both shows
its logical flaws and condemns the religious leaders for
the attack.

12:38-45: In a connected scene, the opponents of Jesus are expanded to include *the scribes and Pharisees*. They seek a sign from Jesus, but he offers only his death and resurrection as the sign of Jonah as a condemnation against them.

12:46-50. The narrator's opening line of this passage—"While he was still speaking . . ." —lead readers to connect this scene with what has gone before. Jesus' family appears outside wishing to speak to him, but Jesus does not engage them as conversation partners. Instead he speaks with his *disciples* for the first time since chapter 10, and says they are his family when they do the will of his Father.

The rising conflict throughout this section (and especially the notice in 12:14), shows that it marks a turning point for Matthew's narrative. Jesus is not yet headed to Jerusalem, but everything is beginning to point in that direction. Moreover, the accusations and rejection presented clearly mirror those being experienced by Matthew's community at the time he wrote his story. So preachers must be careful to locate the conflict in both the narrative and socio-historical contexts to properly interpret it. But there is also another context to consider: the eschatological one. Matthew uses all of these groups (John and his disciples, the crowd, and the religious leaders) to represent the broader category of "this generation" (11:16; 12:39, 41, 42, 45). This is a chronological term that might lead one to identify the groups historically. But recall that we have argued above that Matthew uses temporal language and imagery in eschatological contexts to speak figuratively of Christian experience. "This generation" represents all those of all time who bring judgment (*krisis*, 11:22, 24; 12:18, 20, 36, 41, 42) upon themselves by rejecting Jesus and the church.

But judgment is not the only word offered here. Indeed, in the Bible, judgment is rarely pronounced for its own sake—it almost always implies a call to repentance. Such is the case in this section. Even while Matthew lists all those who stand over against Jesus as part of "this generation," he intersperses more positive notes in the section which signal that there is the possibility of people accepting Jesus' (and the church's) ministry. After accusing the crowds of rejecting both John and Jesus and condemning the cities for being unrepentant,

Jesus gives thanks for what has been reveals to "infants" (through him) and invites all who are weary to come to him (11:25-30). After Sabbath conflicts with the Pharisees and their synagogue, Jesus heals all those in the crowd who are ill and is described as fulfilling scripture (12:15-21). And after rebuffing the religious leaders' accusation that he casts out demons as a demon and rejects their test that he give them a sign, Jesus calls his disciples his true kin because they do his Father's will (12:46-50). We have already seen this pattern of naming the reality of conflict in ministry followed by the promise of success in ministry in the very structure of the Mission Discourse, in which the blessing at the end reminds the church that some will welcome them and their ministry (10:40-42).

The second development in this section is christological and is closely related to the first. As Matthew presents Jesus' conflicts as increasing in number and severity, he also gives us more insight into who Jesus is. In other words, lines are drawn in the sand between Jesus and the groups named above specifically because of who Jesus is. We saw earlier how the opening chapters of Matthew (1:1—4:11) presented christology in terms of messianic titles and a typological geography. Titles are not absent from this section (see the list above concerning the repetitive use of "son" in chapters 11–12), but here the primary christological emphasis is on Jesus' deeds. In 11:2-3, the narrator says that John has heard "what the Messiah was doing" (literally "the deeds of the Christ" [Greek *to erga tou christou*] a unique phrase in Matthew), and sends his disciples to ask if he is "the one to come" (literally "the coming one" [Greek *ho erchomenos*]). Jesus answers (vv. 4-5) in terms of the results of what he has been doing in his ministry—the blind see, the lame walk, those with skin disease are cleansed, the deaf hear, the dead are resurrected, and the poor have good news proclaimed to them. This list resembles the actions readers witnessed in chapters 8–9 as well as the instruction given to the Twelve about what they are to do in ministry (in imitation of Jesus' ministry; 10:1, 7-8). The monologue concerning the role of John the Baptist relative to Jesus is concluded when Jesus says, "Yet wisdom is vindicated by her deeds" (v. 19), thus connecting Jesus' work with that of wisdom itself.

The fact that John sends his disciples to Jesus even after what he professed and witnessed at the baptism (3:13-17) shows that while he is a significant figure in salvation history, he is in no way Jesus' equal. Indeed, Jesus characterizes John as an eschatological prophet, but all to prepare for his coming. John is Elijah (11:14), but Jesus is the son of the human (v. 19). Moreover, Jesus is the Son of God the Father who alone reveals God (v. 27) and who is related to others who do God's will (12:50).

As the son of the human, Jesus' deeds include being lord of the Sabbath (12:8); fulfilling scripture in having God's spirit upon him and extending God's *krisis* to the gentiles (vv. 17-21); casting out demons by the Holy Spirit (v. 28); and (foreshadowing the climax of the narrative) being raised from the dead (v. 40).

PASSAGES OMITTED FROM THE LECTIONARY

The RCL offers two readings from this section that cover a significant amount of chapter 11 but none of chapter 12. As we can see in the table below, this is due in part to the fact that the lectionary uses most of the parallel material found in Mark in Year B. However, none of the parallel material in Luke ("Q" material) is used in Year C focusing on Luke.

Matthew	Parallels	Lectionary
11:1	Unique to Matthew	
11:2-19	Lk 7:18-35	Mt 11:2-11, Advent 3 Year A; Mt 11:16-19, 25-30, Proper 9, Year A
11:20-24	Lk 10:12-15	
11:25-27	Lk 10:21-22	(See above for Proper 9, Year A)
11:28-30	Unique to Matthew	(See above for Proper 9, Year A)
12:1-21	Mk 2:23—3:12	Mk 2:23—3:6, Proper 4, Year B
12:22-37	Mk 3:22-30	Mk 3:20-35, Proper 5, Year B
12:38-42	Mk 8:11 + Lk 11:29-32	
12:43-45	Lk 11:24-26	
12:46-50	Mk 3:31-35	(See above for Proper 5, Year B)

I will comment briefly on those passages from chapters 11–12 not included in Year A before focusing more in depth on the two lections that are taken from this section.

JOHN AND JESUS (11:12-15): OMITTED FROM LECTIONARY

The RCL includes most of the passage dealing with John the Baptist but it is split into two pieces (11:2-11, 16-19). This division omits vv. 12-15 in the middle of the unit. Preachers may be relieved that this piece is omitted given the difficulty with interpreting v. 12. Translators and scholars debate what Matthew means with the references to violence here. The difficulty of the line is likely a main reason the RCL omitted the verses.

These verses focus more on John the Baptist than on an explicit comparison of John and Jesus, but the comparison is implicit. John is clearly presented as Elijah to underscore his role as precursor to the Messiah, instead of being the Messiah himself. This was an important issue in the first century because there were likely still disciples of John around during Matthew's day.

For the contemporary preacher, what is important about this text for understanding Matthew is the schema of salvation history that is presented. John marks a turning point in history completed and fulfilled in the person of Jesus as the Christ. Whatever the elusive line about the reign of heaven suffering violence until John means, it is clear is that for Matthew the reign of heaven was not initiated by Jesus. With Jesus the eschatological advent of God's reign occurs in a *new* way.

WOES TO THE UNREPENTANT GALILEAN CITIES (11:20-24): OMITTED FROM LECTIONARY

The second lection drawing on the contrast between Jesus and John is an indictment of the crowd for rejecting both John and Jesus. That indictment is expanded to all of Galilee with this passage. Jesus pronounces judgment on three Galilean cities (including his headquarters of Capernaum) for failing to repent when witnessing the deeds he has performed there. While Jesus continues to minister (at least somewhat successfully) in Galilee (see 12:15), this pericope opens the door for the conflict heating up in 12:14 and the mention of gentiles in 12:18, 21. The conflict does not mean Matthew and his church turn their backs on Israel (see the comments above on the Mission Discourse being to Israel alone) but it does name the tense relationship the church and the synagogue.

Preachers dealing with this text need to be careful not to name the judgment on the cities in a way that moves in the direction of anti-Semitism. The way to avoid this is to have the congregation identify with the crowds/

Galilean cities. In what ways have the "deeds" of God's healing grace in our lives/world gone unheeded so that we have failed to turn from self-serving ways? What would real repentance on our part look like in our materialistic, class-driven, violence-promoting world? It is important to remember that the Bible rarely speaks of God's judgment in a way that it is an end unto itself. Judgment is expressed for the very purpose of inviting repentance so that God may judge the reader differently.

SABBATH CONTROVERSIES (12:1-14): OMITTED FROM LECTIONARY

This section actually includes two pericopes, both of which deal with conflicts with the religious authorities concerning the sabbath. In vv. 1-8, the precipitating issue is the disciples' action of plucking grain as they walk through a field and in vv. 9-14 the issue is Jesus' act of healing a man with a withered hand.

Preachers should be careful not to see the issue with which Matthew is concerned as to whether his community should observe the sabbath. Matthew assumes the sabbath is to be observed. What is at stake is a hermeneutical issue—*how* are the commandments concerning Sabbath observation to be fulfilled. These scenes, then, serve as narrative case studies similar to the antitheses in 5:21-48 illustrating the hermeneutic laid out in 5:17-20. Jesus fulfills the law by working toward an underlying intent in the commandments.

It should be noted that Jesus' interpretation of what is allowed on the sabbath as exhibited in these stories is not unique. In and around the first century, various Jewish groups and individual rabbis asserted very similar understandings of sabbath practice. In other words, the controversy stories here do not represent Jesus over against the Judaism of his day, but conflict between different Jewish groups.

Of course, for Matthew the debate is not purely academic. The stories end with the explicit statement of the religious leaders' intent to "destroy" Jesus (v. 14). This is a key statement both for understanding the stakes at play in Matthew's day in terms of his church's argument with the synagogue over whether the church is a proper heir and interpreter of Israel's tradition and for advancing the plot line of the narrative.

JESUS AS GOD'S CHOSEN ONE (12:15-21):
OMITTED FROM LECTIONARY

It is a shame that the RCL omits this passage. It is a key christological notice in the Gospel.

Immediately after the religious leaders begin plotting to "destroy" Jesus (v. 14), Jesus "withdraws." The Greek word for withdraw in v. 15 is *anachōreō* and is used by Matthew numerous times to indicate not simply leaving a place or seeking to be alone but escaping from danger (see 2:12, 13, 14, 22; 4:12; 14:12; 15:21). Matthew uses this withdrawal from threats as a chance to reflect on how the reader should understand Jesus' actions at this point in the narrative. The narrator's voice breaks in to comment on the story in a way similar to the opening chapters (1:1—4:11). Indeed, Matthew returns to the technique of quoting scripture used in those chapters. Here we find the ninth and longest formula citation in the Gospel, taken primarily from Isaiah 42:1-4.

Preachers may well wonder what to do with this quotation. Matthew does not seem to anchor it well in his narrative. It does not deal with healing, which seems to be the focus of the context. Instead, Matthew likely locates it here to connect the silence of the servant in the text with Jesus' command to the crowd not to make him known (v. 16). While this connection highlights Matthew's attempt to shape Mark's messianic secret motif to his own purposes, it can obscure the larger theological significance of the Isaiah text. It serves a christological purpose in that affirms Jesus as God's chosen, beloved *pais* (which can mean both "servant" and "child") with whom God is well-pleased. This text stands behind (and nearly halfway between) God's similar declaration concerning Jesus in the scenes of Jesus' baptism (3:17) and transfiguration (17:5). Standing in the middle of this section of chapters 11–12, in which conflict is building, Matthew uses this scriptural citation to assert that the distance being established between Jesus, the disciples and Matthew's church on the one side and John/John's disciples, the crowds, the Galilean cities, the religious leaders, the synagogue and even his own family on the other is directly related to Jesus' unique identity as God's Son.

In addition to the christological function of the quotation is an eschatological/ecclesiological one. With the mention of God's chosen one as bringing judgment and hope to the gentiles/nations (Greek *ethnoi*), the text foreshadows the developing role of gentiles in Matthew's narrative and church. The judgment of the gentiles/nations reappears in the most dramatic form in 25:31-46, and then becomes hope in the Great Commission (28:19).

THE BEELZEBUL CONTROVERSY (12:22-37):
OMITTED FROM LECTIONARY

This scene is omitted by the RCL because Mark's version (Mk 3:22-20) is used in Year B. While Matthew is clearly dependent on Mark's version (although there are agreements between Matthew and Luke against Mark in some of the language in this pericopes), Matthew shapes the material to his own purposes. Matthew shapes this controversy to be a critical christological/ecclesiological lens. The accusation that Jesus casts out by the power and authority of Beelzebul was first made in 9:34 and was referenced again by Jesus to explain the persecution against the apostles/church in 10:25. This repetition of the accusation along with the length of Jesus' response to it debating the illogical nature of the accusation (twelve verses!—12:25-37) shows how important the issue was for Matthew's community of faith.

Preachers today may have a difficult time relating to the issue, however. After all, people are not accusing the church today of performing exorcisms by the power of Satan. But under the specific accusation is the issue of defaming Jesus as not of God. It stands over against the Isaiah quote in the previous scene, which specifically names Jesus as God's Son/servant. Matthew wants to affirm in the strongest possible fashion that Jesus uniquely acts by the power of the Holy Spirit (v. 28; see earlier v. 18) and embodies the reign of heaven. The text, in other words, serves as a critique of any outside (or inside) interpretation of Jesus that makes him less than this. To declare Jesus simply a good man/prophet is reductionist in the same manner as the religious leaders' accusation.

If this passage were read in worship, however, it is likely that people will be more interested in the "unforgivable sin" than the accusation concerning Jesus' exorcisms. But we should resist the temptation that has plagued the history of interpreting this passage to try to identify the specific content of "blasphemy against the Holy Spirit." The language of an unforgivable sin here should be read as a rhetorical hyperbole used for effect in dealing with the first century conflict between the church and synagogue instead of an eternal doctrine.

REQUEST FOR A SIGN (12:38-45):
OMITTED FROM LECTIONARY

Because the Pharisees have begun to conspire to "destroy" Jesus (12:14) and have accused him of casting out demons by Beelzebul (12:24), the reader is primed to recognize their their (and the scribes') request of Jesus for a sign as anything but a sincere search for truth as part of a journey of faith. Their request serves as a taunt, challenge or even a dare, as if they were saying, "So you say you cast out by the power of the Holy Spirit . . . then prove it." Jesus rejects their test with the same type of intense judgment language used against the Galilean cities earlier in the section (11:21-24).

Moreover, Matthew uses the request to make yet another christological claim with soteriological implications. "This generation" (that is, every generation that rejects Jesus/the church, as we noted above) is given a sign: the death and resurrection of Jesus. It is a sign that calls for repentance, a reorientation of one's life and commitments.

The description of the condemnation (*krisis*) of "this generation" here is striking. Matthew does not use his stock language of being thrown into the outer darkness into weeping and gnashing of teeth (as found, for example, in 8:12; 13:42, 50; 22:13; 24:51; 25:30). Instead he draws on exorcism language related to the previous Beelzebul controversy (12:22-37). The image of an unclean spirit departing from a person but then returning with seven more evil spirits is essentially a way of saying that the judgment of those who reject Jesus receive is to be left to suffer the consequences of that rejection. In other words, the punishment for rejecting the evil-defying salvation found in Jesus is simply to not receive that salvation.

JESUS' DISCIPLES AS HIS TRUE FAMILY (12:46-50):
OMITTED FROM LECTIONARY

As if Jesus' separation from and conflict with John and his disciples, the crowds, the Galilean cities, and the religious leaders were not enough, Matthew concludes the chapter with a division between Jesus and his family. Unlike Mark 3:21, 31-34, however, Matthew does not tell us that the family came to see Jesus because they thought he was "beside himself." Matthew provides no motivation for the family visit whatsoever. This is a clue to preachers that the family simply serves as a foil for the narrator here. They are the set up for the pronouncement that follows. The real focus is on the disciples, whom Jesus claims make up his family *when* they do the will of his Father.

Preachers may recognize in the placement of this story a pattern similar to that found in the Mission Discourse (see the discussion of 10:40-42 above). In that discourse, after naming all of the rejection and persecution that the apostles/church would experience, Matthew signaled that nevertheless the mission would be a success (that is, some would welcome those sent out). Similarly, Matthew concludes this section that has presented Jesus as being in so much conflict that it will lead to his death (12:14, 39-40) with a scene that presents a faithful community in intimate relation with Jesus. Preachers can use this image, in contrast with the wider narrative context, to offer congregations a picture of their true selves. Given the way Matthew so transparently overlays his story of Jesus on the situation of his church, it is not surprising that a section so thoroughly focused on christology ends on a climactic ecclesiological note.

LECTIONS

There are two lections taken from this section of Matthew. Both are taken from the first half of the section, dealing with John the Baptist, so there is a connection between the two. However, they are not read in subsequent weeks. The first is used in Advent, and the second follows the semi-continuous readings from the Mission Discourse used in Ordinary Time, which we examined in the previous section.

LECTION: JESUS AND JOHN THE BAPTIST
11:2-11; ADVENT 3

The pattern for the gospel readings in Advent every year is the same. The text for the first Sunday comes from the synoptic eschatological discourse. We begin the liturgical year with the end of time. We do not turn our attention toward the birth narrative until the Fourth Sunday of Advent. On the second and third Sundays of the season (in between the end and the beginning), the gospel readings focus on John the Baptist. The Second Sunday of Advent deals with the description of John's ministry as a precursor to Jesus' baptism. On the third Sunday of the season, for which this lection is assigned, the gospel reading focuses on the encounter between John (through his disciples) and Jesus later in Jesus' ministry. These readings on John are used in Advent because they lead the church in its expectation of "the coming one" (v. 3). One would be hard pressed to preach on the whole of this passage. Preachers will do well to focus on either vv. 2-6 or 7-11.

This first scene opens immediately after the Mission Discourse (11:1) with a flashback to John being in prison, which Matthew had noted as the impetus for the beginning of Jesus' ministry in 4:12. Jesus' fame has spread even there.

John sends his disciples to ask Jesus if he is the "coming one." The peculiarity of this messianic title makes this a perfect text for Advent. The title is future oriented but used to describe Jesus who is present. In Advent we paradoxically *wait* for the one who has *already* come. This captures well the already/not yet aspect of eschatological experience that characterizes the Christian life.

John's question is puzzling given his recognition that he should not baptize Jesus (3:14) following his proclamation of the coming of the one "stronger" than he (3:11-12). Preachers should be careful not to assume doubt or a lack of faith underlies John's question. Matthew simply uses John's question as a set up for Jesus' pronouncement affirming that he is the one to come and to name the distinctive roles of John and himself in relation to one another. This was an important issue in Matthew's day for there were likely still disciples of John around (see Acts 18:25-26; 19:3-4) proclaiming his as the messiah. For the contemporary pulpit, John's question can simply be used to help the congestion identify with the fact that even the faithful can have questions about the fullness of Jesus' identity.

The focus in the first half of the lection (vv. 2-6) is on the way that Jesus' deeds (*erga*, v. 2) show him to be the Christ, whereas the readings associated with the birth narrative (which appear earlier in Matthew's narrative but some of which will be read later in Christmastide) focus on messianic titles and geographical symbolism to unpack the author's christology. Jesus' answer to John's question both reflects deeds we have already seen (summaries of healings have already been noted in 4:24; 8:16; 9:35) and echoes language from Isaiah 29:18-19; 35:5-6; 42:7, 18; 61:1 (cf. Mt 8:17 where Matthew quotes Is 53:4 to show that Jesus' healings fulfill scripture).

This three layered connection between Isaiah, the birth narrative, and this description of Jesus' ministry presents Jesus as the center of salvation history: the one to come (in the future) is performing deeds (in the present) that fulfill prophetic expectations (of the past). This paradoxical tension between the past, present and future is tailor made for an Advent sermon.

The second scene shifts from focus on the work of Jesus to the place of John in Matthew's salvation history that centers on Jesus. John's disciples leave and Jesus begins to talk *about* John to the crowds. In truth, John is not the focus of the passage. He is the lens through which Jesus invites the crowd (that is, through which Matthew invites the readers in his church) to see themselves. This may not be evident if preachers miss that the RCL inappropriately cuts off the lesson before Jesus' train of thought has reached completion. Verses. 12-15 follow from v. 11 and lead directly into vv. 16-19 (which the RCL assigns to the following lection used in Ordinary Time). Nevertheless, v. 11 makes the point. After discussing who John is with laudatory terms (not only a prophet, but more than a prophet . . . one who fulfills scripture), Jesus throws in an unexpected twist. While earlier John had said that the one coming after him would be "stronger" *ischuroteros* than he (3:11-12), Jesus goes further now in saying that even though no person born of a woman is greater than John, even the least (*microteros*) in the reign of heaven is greater (*meizōn*) than he. Given Matthew's use of the "the reign of heaven" as both present and future, the identification of the "least" here is ambiguous. It is likely the same kind of phrase as "babes" (11:27 later in this section), "little ones" (10:42; 18:6, 10, 14) or "least of these" (25:40, 45) as references to those in the church. Nevertheless, the point is unmistakable: Jesus invites his hearers into God's eschatological reign to live in the experience of the already/not yet of God's salvation. This invitation is punctuated with the judgment on "this generation" that follows (starting in v. 16—biblical pronouncements of judgment are almost always offered as invitations to change one's ways).

Preachers focusing on this second scene during Advent, then, should resist the temptation to offer a historical look at the role of John the Baptist and instead focus on the way Matthew calls the church to be more (greater) by embracing more (the coming one who is stronger) as we live in and simultaneously long for the reign of heaven.

Lection: Jesus as the Revelation of the Father
11:16-19, 25-30; Proper 9

This lection divides up and combines portions of Matthew 11 in a terrible manner. Verses 16-19 flow out of 11:2-15's discussion of the relation of John the Baptist and Jesus. The passage pronounces judgment on "this generation" for rejecting both John and Jesus. This judgment is extended to the Galilean cities in vv. 20-24. Verses 25-30, on the other hand, offer an indication that some (that is, "babes," v. 25) have accepted the revelation of God through the Son (v. 27) and an invitation for all to find rest in Jesus (vv. 28-30). We have observed earlier the pattern of Matthew highlighting rejection of Jesus and his apostles in the Mission Discourse and repeated in Matthew 11–12 (see the Introduction to this section above). Preachers, then, may wish to focus on the second half of lection (which is the climax of the broader passage) and only use the first half of the lection to provide the setting of rejection of this generation as a contrast for the grace offered by Jesus. We will focus the comments that follow on the second half.

The problem with preaching on the second half of the lection, however, is that vv. 28 and 30 are so well known that it may difficult for a congregation to hear the lines anew. Highlighting their context will help with this.

It is important to note that the paragraph opens with Jesus addressing God (v. 25). The NRSV introduces the prayer with the words, "At that time Jesus said." A more wooden translation of the Greek text is, "At that time, answering Jesus said." This is important to note simply to see that for Matthew, Jesus' prayer is a response to the rejection of the Galilean cities (vv. 20-24) and the condemnation of "this generation" more generally. In other words, Jesus answers those who reject him by praying to God. But notice that even though Jesus pronounces woes upon the cities, he does not pray that they be damned. He instead turns his attention to those who accept his words and deeds, indeed his very person as a revelation of the Father.

The "Q" language Matthew has Jesus use to define his relationship with the Father here (v. 27; cf. Lk 11:22) sounds like it belongs in the Gospel of John instead of Matthew (see Jn 1:18). We must be careful not to read later Trinitarian theology into this language (for example, compare Exod 33:12-14 for similar language related to God and Moses having reciprocal knowledge of each other followed by a promise of rest) but still recognize that it is a fairly high christology that helped fund the development of such language. It recalls the language of Jesus as God's son, Emmanuel in 1:20-23.

This language, however, is not an end unto itself. In other words, while it is strong christological content, its rhetorical function is to establish the character of the one who offers the soteriological invitation in vv. 28-30 (which is unique to Matthew). This is signaled by the fact that Jesus shifts from praying to God in vv. 25-27 to addressing the crowd without any notice from the narrator of the shift. The one who invites us to come to him speaks to God on our behalf and speaks for God in calling us. Put directly, Matthew wants his readers to know that to come to Jesus is to come to God.

One way preachers can help congregations hear this passage anew is to clarify to whom the invitation is extended. Those "who labor and are heavy laden" are not simply those who work hard at their middle class jobs and are tired. Matthew has in view those oppressed under the reign of Caesar—those dispossessed, the sick, the demonized, the impoverished, the starving, the imprisoned. The language of salvation here is not language of a vacation from a bad day, but liberation from the evil structures of society that kill and destroy. Given this, some congregations might be invited to identify with Jesus here in extending God's respite to the world as those sent out by Jesus. After all, this passage falls not long after we read that the one who receives us (as sent out by Jesus) receives the one who sent us and thus receives the one who sent Jesus (10:40 and 11:27 are companion sayings of sorts).

But, of course, the invitation to receive God's liberating care in Jesus is extended to all, and the preacher may want to have the congregation identify with those invited by Jesus. One way to provoke a new hearing of the invitation in this homiletical approach is to emphasize v. 29. The respite offered by the humble one involves teaching. This is odd, to say the least. One thing we do not need to be taught how to do is rest! The use of rest here foreshadows the sabbath (that is, day of rest) controversies in the next chapter (12:1-14). In those scenes we see the disciples gathering food to relieve their hunger and Jesus healing a man with a withered hand. This "work" on the sabbath shows that the eschatological rest indicated here is not idleness. One should think more of peace in the midst of the work we are called to do than respite from that work. Remember that we noted in the Introduction that the image of eschatological salvation is one in which the saved are left behind with more responsibility instead of being relieved of work in the world (for example, 25:21, 23).

This idea of peace within the work to which we are called is supported by the use of the mention of the "yoke," which in the first century was a common metaphor for obedience and service. Jewish leaders often spoke of the yoke of the *torah* or the yoke of the commandments. Since Matthew has Jesus present himself as the fulfillment of the law (5:17-20), he here speaks of "my yoke" not as a replacement of the *torah* but as an interpretation of it. Jesus' interpretation (and thus the church's interpretation) of the *torah* is the offering of rest/peace. This rest is both a gift we receive and something we must learn (and do).

CAPERNAUM-BASED MINISTRY: PARABLES DISCOURSE (13:1-53)

INTRODUCTION

Following the Ethical Discourse (Mt 5–7), Matthew presented Jesus as moving around Galilee in a mixture of healing, discipleship and conflict stories in chapters 8–9. The narrative pace then slowed down again with the Mission Discourse of chapter 10. After this, Matthew offered a series of scenes in which conflict between Jesus and others (especially the religious leadership) builds (chs. 11–12). Now we come to the third of Matthew's five discourses—the Parables Discourse. While the pace again slows down with the shift from narrative to speech, it would be as much a mistake to read the material in chapter 13 as if it was isolated from its literary context as would have been the case with the first two discourses. Matthew places the discourse where he does both to offer a window into the content and method of Jesus' proclamation and to advance the plot of his story. Indeed, it is noteworthy that this central discourse is the only one that opens with an indication that it is addressed to the crowds instead of the disciples. (In truth, however, the bulk of the discourse consists of private instruction to the disciples: vv. 10-23, 36-52.)

Before we focus on how the material of this chapter relates to broader theological issues and narrative developments in Matthew, it is important for preachers to have in hand a working definition of parables in general to be able to understand and explain the unique way this type of material functions in the Synoptic Gospels. Too often laity see parables as sermon illustrations or "earthly stories with a heavenly meaning." The implication is that they are stories meant to clarify abstract points.

Parables, though, are more evocative metaphor than narrative explanation. A metaphor compares two dissimilar things to help you view the first item in the comparison in a new way. "Politics are a circus," and "Politics are war," can both be true at the same time, but they do not function syllogistically in a way that it would also be true to say, "A circus is war." This is because metaphors do not function in the same way that propositional statements do. The metaphors in the above example do not help us understand a circus or war differently; each illuminates a different characteristic of politics. The comparisons do not define or explain politics, but they do invite hearers to make meaning of the concept politics in a way they might not have before.

We speak of metaphors *inviting* hearers to make meaning because they do not dictate meaning. They evoke reflection on meaning. Take the first metaphor, "Politics is a circus." Does that mean politics are entertaining the way a circus is? Does it mean politics are chaotic? Does it mean politics look chaotic but really all is choreographed by a ring master? While context may help clarify which nuance is correct, metaphors are open-ended and multivalent by their very nature. Indeed, metaphors are powerful *because* their meaning is not singularly clear, but this is also their danger. Preachers know well that we have much less control over how hearers interpret a metaphor we use than if we develop in a few explicit sentences our analysis of the current political atmosphere. The second is more precise, but metaphors are more engaging. They illuminate, but do so by raising questions about (1) how the hearer understood the subject in the first place and (2) how the metaphor is to be interpreted or applied.

We can draw on this understanding of the evocative power of metaphors to adapt a classic definition of parables offered by C. H. Dodd, *The Parables of the Kingdom* (New York: Scribner, 1936). A parable is "a narrative metaphor, drawn from nature or common life, which arrests the hearer by its vividness or strangeness and leaves the mind in sufficient doubt about its precise interpretation or application to tease it into active thought even to the point of altering one's worldview."

Let us look more closely at the elements of this definition. First, by *narrative metaphor drawn from nature or common life*, we mean that the whole of the narrative is the metaphor. Usually the primary referent for parables is the reign of God/heaven. But it is not that the reign of heaven is being compared to, for instance, good seed (13:24). The *entire* narrative situation and development (13:24-30) serves as the metaphor, not just one element of the story. (A note is necessary here. Some parables function in the Synoptics as allegories and many others have been interpreted allegorically. An allegory is a story in which each element of the story is symbolic of something outside the story world. As a general rule, unless Jesus offers an allegorical interpretation of a parable, preachers should first look for a broader metaphorical reading of a parable before turning to an allegorical interpretation.) But whether a narrative metaphor or an allegory, the terms of comparison in the parable (that is, the symbols or the content of narrative image) will be familiar to the hearers. This is why in Jesus' ancient preaching to an agrarian society, so many of the parables relate to farming.

Second, by *arrests the hearer by its vividness or strangeness*, we signal the fact that most parables include a twist, an unexpected element. Something uncommon appears in the image drawn from common life. The familiar subject matter becomes evocative by the introduction of something that does not fit with the hearers' experience of that subject matter. For example, any person living in the agrarian society of the ancient Mediterranean world would have known that there is no such thing as a mustard "tree" (13:32). There were large mustard shrubs, but not trees. So when Matthew presents Jesus as speaking of the mustard tree, he assumes his audience recognizes and is intrigued by the discrepancy.

Third, *leaves the mind in sufficient doubt about its precise interpretation or application* signals that parables do not normally function as example, moralistic or illustrative stories. Instead of creating an "Aha!" experience, parables often evoke an initial "Huh?" from the hearers/readers. In other words, parables are supposed to raise questions as much as they are meant to provide answers. The question is about the first item in the metaphoric comparison (I thought I understood the reign of heaven but what is its real nature?) not the second (I thought I understood mustard plants but what are their real nature?) The journey to new realization comes by way of the path of puzzlement. (After all, in the ancient world, the word "parable" could be used to refer to a riddle.)

And, finally, *to tease the mind into active thought even to the point of altering one's world-view* indicates that parables intend to create puzzlement not simply about the inner logic of the narrative. Because the reign of heaven is a broad and encompassing term, a narrative metaphor describing (but never defining) some characteristic of God's reign in an unexpected fashion leads the hearer/reader to reflect on and reconsider previously held interpretations of God, self, and world. These are earthly stories with a worldly (in the large sense of that word) meaning.

Given this understanding of parables in general, how does the *collection* of parables in the discourse in chapter 13 function in Matthew's narrative? Remember, as Matthew 24–25 is an expansion of the eschatological discourse in Mark 13, this discourse is an expansion of the collection of parables found in Mark 4. (These two discourses in Mark likely served as the model for Matthew's five discourses.) Consider the following table:

	Matthew	Mark	Luke
Parable of the Sower	13:1–9	4:1–9	8:4–8
Purpose of Parables	13:10–17	4:10–12	8:9–10
Interpretation of Parable of Sower	13:18–23	4:13–20	8:11–15
Not Hiding a Lamp	Cf. Mt 5:14–15;10:26; 7:2; 13:12	4:21–25	8:16–16
Parable of Seed Growing Secretly		4:26–29	
Parable of the Weeds	13:24–30		
Parable of the Mustard Seed	13:31–32	4:30–32	*13:18–19*
Parable of the Yeast	13:33		*13:20–21*
Use of Parables	13:34–35	4:33–34	
Interpretation ofParable of the Weeds	13:36–43		
Parable of the Hidden Treasure	13:44		
Parable of the Pearl	13:45–46		
Parable of the Net	13:47–50		
Scribes of the Reign of Heaven	13:51–52		

"When Jesus had finished these parables…"	13:53		

We see in this comparison that Matthew takes (and edits) from Mark two parables (the Sower and the Mustard Seed), an interpretation of the first of those parables, a discourse about the function of parables, and a description of the extent of Jesus' use of parables from Mark. Matthew uses material similar to Mark 4:21-25 in other places in the narrative, and omits one of Mark's parables (4:26-29). Only one short parable (Yeast) in Matthew's discourse is paralleled in Luke but not in Mark (signaling that the Mustard Seed and Yeast parables may have been combined in a source shared by Matthew and Luke apart from Mark's use only of the Parable of the Mustard Seed). The rest of the material (approximately half of the discourse, most of which is added to the end of the Markan material) is unique to Matthew. Moreover, the bulk that is added to the end of Mark's version is presented as being offered to the disciples in private (v. 36ff).

It is not only the material Matthew adds that gives the Parables Discourse a unique flavor, when compared to Mark's material. In his expansion and redaction of Mark 4:10-12, Matthew (13:10-17) explains the function of parables within Jesus' ministry and thus within the narrative of the First Gospel quite differently than Mark had viewed parables. Drawing on language from Isaiah 6:9-10, Mark presents Jesus as claiming that parables are offered to "those outside" (Greek, *ekeinois tois exo*) "in order that" (Greek, *hina*) they can see but not perceive, hear but not understand, so that they cannot turn and be forgiven (Mark 4:11-12). In other words, Mark presents Jesus as using parables to draw a dividing line between those inside and outside of the reign of God. Those inside already understand the mystery of God's reign and can understand the parables (v. 10), but the outsiders will not be able to enter God's reign by way of the parables. This seemingly odd use of parables sets up two literary-theological foci of Mark: (1) the disciples seem at first to be insiders but the fact that they need Jesus to interpret the parables for them makes them appear as outsiders; and (2) it is only through the cross that we can truly understand who Jesus is and enter the reign of God. In some ways, this turns the entire narrative of Mark into a parable focusing on the cross.

Matthew views parables somewhat differently. Let us see how Matthew changes Mark's language:

Matthew 13:11-13	*Mark 4:11-12*
[11] He answered, "To you it has been given to know the secrets of the kingdom of heaven, but to them it has not been given. [12] For to those who have, more will be given, and they will have an abundance; but from those who have nothing, even what they have will be taken away. [13] The reason I speak to them in parables is *because** 'seeing they do not perceive, and hearing they do not listen, nor do they understand.'	[11] And he said to them, "To you has been given the secret of the kingdom of God, but for *those outside,*
[14] With them indeed is fulfilled the prophecy of Isaiah that says: "You will indeed listen, but never understand, and you will indeed look, but never perceive. [15] For this people's heart has grown dull, and their ears are hard of hearing, and they have shut their eyes; so that they might not look with their eyes, and listen with their ears, and understand with their heart and turn—and I would heal them.'	everything comes in parables; [12] *in order that* 'they may indeed look, but not perceive, and may indeed listen, but not understand; *so that they may not turn again and be forgiven.'*
*The NRSV has been changed here to translate better the Greek *hoti* as "because" instead of "that."	

First, instead of only drawing on the language of Isaiah 6:9-10 to interpret the function of parables, Matthew presents Jesus' use of parables as a *fulfillment* of this prophetic text. Or more properly, it is the crowds' lack of understanding of Jesus' parabolic proclamation that fulfills scripture (see Matthew 13:14-15). Thus the parables themselves are not responsible for the misunderstanding. (Interpreters should recognize in the crowds' lack of understanding Matthew's concern with the conflict between the church and the synagogue.)

The fact that the parables are not the cause for the crowds' lack of understanding of the mysteries of the reign of heaven is seen all the more clearly in that Matthew changes Mark's language of "those outside" simply to "them" and "in order that" to "because" (Greek, *hoti*). Moreover (and most importantly), in the initial explanation of the purpose of parables that draws on Isaiah's language before Matthew quotes the passage in full, Matthew omits the reference to the crowds not turning and being forgiven altogether. Matthew may have lines drawn in the sand between insiders and outsiders similar to Mark, but they are not as deep and can be moved. Indeed, the parables can do the moving. For Matthew, the parables hold the possibility of offering understanding instead of only distinguishing those who do and do not understand Jesus' message concerning God's reign. So when Matthew's Jesus interprets some of the parables it is not meant to highlight the disciples' misunderstanding but to demonstrate their (and the readers') being brought further into God's reign through the offer of new understanding (compare Matthew 13:18 to Mark 4:13).

This positive view of the potential effectiveness of the parables is important to note because it helps us understand why the Parables Discourse is placed where it is. Jesus' parabolic invitation into the eschatological reign of heaven in chapter 13 serves as a stark contrast to the dividing lines drawn in the previous two chapters highlighting conflict between Jesus and the authorities. That section ended with praise of disciples who do God's will as Jesus' true kin, and this discourse invites others into discipleship. This discourse then begins with a parable in which understanding of Jesus' word of God's reign (13:19) is equated with bearing fruit (13:23).

Moreover, Jesus' ministry from its beginning has been characterized as focused on the proclamation of the reign of heaven (4:17; similarly with the ministry of John the Baptist in 3:2 and those sent out by Jesus in 10:7 in the last discourse). Following these and other references to the reign of heaven, chapter 13 gives content to the concept in a different way than the Ethical Discourse had in chapters 5–7. Thus to preach on lections drawn from this discourse is less to be about "explaining" parables and more to invite hearers into a mode of discipleship that embraces and experiences the radical view of God's reign with all of the evocative force one can muster in imitation of Jesus' own use of parables. Indeed, the phrase, "the reign of heaven" is used 78 times in Matthew, twelve of which occur in Parables discourse. This is more than in any other discourse, including the longer Eschatological Discourse in chapters 24–25. To enter the metaphorical world of a parable is to risk entering into God's eschatological reign.

PASSAGES OMITTED FROM THE LECTIONARY

All of the parables of chapter 13 are used by the Revised Common Lectionary. Interestingly, what is omitted is Matthew's explanation for the purpose of parables given in vv. 10-17 and 34-35. This is a shame, given that in this material Matthew provides his unique understanding of Jesus' parables. If this material is left unattended, the preacher loses some important clues about how to interpret the Parables Discourse as a whole as and the individual parables both in the discourse and in other parts of the narrative. This unique Matthean perspective on the parables is discussed above in the introduction to this discourse, so we will not look at these verses in detail here. It should be noted, however, that the first lection discussed below is intimately connected with this material, in that the Parable of the Sower is concerned with the reception of parables themselves.

LECTIONS

Although the RCL omits Matthew's explanation of why Jesus preaches in parables, it does a good job of including the bulk of this discourse in a three week span in the Season after Pentecost. The first week, the Parable of the Sower and its interpretation is read (13:1-9, 18-23), omitting material that deals with Matthew's explanation for the purpose of parables (vv. 10-17). The second week, the Parable of the Weeds and its interpretation is read (13:24-30, 36-43), which involves skipping over a couple of parables (vv. 31-33) and further insight into Matthew's unique view of parables (vv. 34-35). And on the third Sunday, the RCL returns to the two parables drawing on the metaphor of growth skipped over in the previous lection and combines them with three discovery-themed parables that conclude the discourse (13:31-33, 44-52).

Lection: Parable of the Sower
13:1–9, 18–23; Proper 10

In Proper 9, we read the scene concluding chapters 11–12 in which Matthew presents the conflict between Jesus and the religious authorities as ramping up significantly. That final scene, however, serves to contrast the success of Jesus' ministry with that conflict by focusing on the identification of disciples who do God's will as Jesus' true family. A similar dynamic is at play as we transition to our first lection from the Parables Discourse. The Parable of the Sower contrasts three failures with one success. Moreover, the success identifies understanding the word of God's reign with the bearing of good fruit (that is, doing the will of Jesus' Father).

Historical critics have struggled to determine an original meaning of the Parable of the Sower (vv. 1–9) apart from the allegorical interpretation assumed to be added later by the church (vv.18–23). Many twentieth-century commentaries rooted in form criticism urged preachers to ignore the allegorical interpretation and preach on an earlier construction of the parable. Without engaging these arguments in detail, let us say that while most parables should not be read allegorically, some seem to have been allegories from their beginning. The Parable of the Sower draws on traditional Greek and Jewish imagery (such as sowing seed as proclamation) in ways that invite an allegorical interpretation. Moreover, we are primarily interested in the final form of the canonical text when it comes to preaching, and all versions of the parable include the allegorical interpretation. Preachers, therefore, should focus on the interpretation of the parable Jesus offers to the disciples as the center of the sermon.

Indeed, the allegorical interpretation likely describes authentically the experience of a mixture of failure and success of Matthew's community in its attempts to propagate Jesus' proclamation. Moreover, the interpretation has strong connections with materials found in other places in Matthew. For example the religious leaders exemplify those who hear but do not understand Jesus' word of the reign of heaven. In both the Ethical Discourse (5:11–12) and the Mission Discourse (10:16–39), Matthew is concerned with those who will and will not faithfully endure persecution. Again, in both of the earlier discourses, Matthew has shown concern for those in the faith who will be consumed with worries and desire for wealth (6:19–34; 10:8–10; see also 8:18–22). But Matthew has also repeatedly signaled success in Jesus' (and the church's) ministry by presenting moments in which some truly listen to and understand Jesus' proclamation and produce good fruits (4:18–22; 7:24–27; 9:9; 10:40–42; 11:25–30; 12:46–50).

This last parallel requires us to pause. So often this parable (and other elements of Matthew) is preached in a way that congregations get the idea that Jesus experienced and thus the church should expect more failure than success. After all, in three types of soil the seeds fail and in only one does it take root and produce fruit. But any ancient hearer/reader would have recognized in this image drawn from common life that only a small amount of a farmer's seed falls on the various types of poor land (around the edges of good field). Most will fall on the good soil. Matthew presents conflict over and over again to move his plot along toward Jesus' passion, not to give the impression that Jesus' mission fails. These conflicts are outweighed by the crowds that flock to him for healing and indeed for hearing his proclamation (13:2). As Jesus has clearly indicated, the harvest is great (9:37-38; 13:8, 23). The fact that three-fourths of the parable focuses on failure is not meant to put the weight of interpretation on failure but to highlight the surprisingly great harvest at the climax of the parable all the more. (Compare the other three parables that highlight great harvest/growth, 13: 24-33).

Traditionally, this parable has been preached in hortatory sermons where listeners are urged to reflect on what kind of soil they have been and to become the good soil. There is nothing in our observations to argue against this homiletical approach. The parable and its interpretation invites the kind of critical self-analysis such a sermon calls for. On the other hand, it is noteworthy that Jesus, in his interpretation of the parable, does not himself turn to exhortation. As an introduction to the Parables Discourse, the Parable of the Sower simply *explains* why some hear and understand and some do not. In a day when we worry so much about shrinking denominations and dying congregations to proclaim this parable as a "This is simply (theologically) the way things are" type of message could be received as much needed good news. It will be good news, because the emphasis in the parable is on the success of the word of the reign of heaven. Preachers who can help congregations celebrate God's great harvest that is occurring in the face of most of the story-telling in the church these days being focused on lost seed will have well-earned their salary this week.

LECTION: PARABLE OF THE WEEDS IN THE FIELD
13:24-30, 36-43; PROPER 11

In our discussion above of the Parable of the Sower we noted the scholarly debate concerning whether the allegorical interpretation was a later addition. The same situation is found with the Parable of the Weeds, except that the answer is clear: the interpretation is later. Nevertheless, Matthew does want his readers to understand the parable through the lens of this particular interpretation and the RCL includes the interpretation offered to the disciples (separated by two other public parables and a narrator's interlude, vv. 31–35) as part of the lection for the preach to consider.

First a word about the context of the parable. It is connected to the Parable of the Sower in a significant amount of shared vocabulary, but the interpretation makes it clear that the terms function as symbols of different things here. Nevertheless, there is a common picture of reality shared by the two parables that help preachers relate their sermons on succeeding weeks. That is, both parables picture the world as divided into two groups: those who are in the reign of heaven and those who are not. In the first parable, the reason for this division is that some understand and accept (and do) Jesus' word of God's reign and some do not, putting the responsibility on the hearer. In the second parable, the responsibility is on the evil one who sows children of the evil one among children of God's reign (vv. 38–39), which picks up and expands upon a similar image from the interpretation of the Parable of the Sower, in which the birds who eat seed that falls on the path represent the evil one snatching away what is sown in the hearts of those who hear but do not understand (vv. 4, 19). The shift in responsibility is not contradictory. With these two parables Matthew makes clear that our inclusion or exclusion from the reign of heaven is both something we do and something that is done to us. Both grace and responsibility and victimization and responsibility are pairs that cannot be easily separated.

As the Parable of the Weeds is related to the parable that precedes it, so is it connected with the two short parables that follow (and which are part of the next lection, vv. 31–33). All three parables, unlike the Parable of the Sower, are presented as metaphors for the reign of heaven. Moreover, all three, like the Parable of the Sower, emphasize growth. The image of future growth indicates a strong eschatological theme. In the case of this parable, the seed is *already* planted and growing but has *not yet* been harvested. Thus the parable names the current situation of the mixture of wheat and weeds, of good and evil, as the eschatological reality of Christian experience. Naming this present reality in light of God's future is a key element of preaching the good news of Jesus Christ.

But Matthew's interpretation of this parable goes beyond simply naming the already/not yet of Christian eschatology in the same way, say, the parables of the mustard seed and yeast do. This can be seen by considering how well the parable exemplifies the definition of parables we offered earlier. The image of farming wheat and dealing with weeds is drawn from common life. But much seems out of the ordinary. If you want to ruin someone's field, is the best strategy to plant weeds? And surely every gardener knows that you pull weeds as soon as you see them to help your crop grow better. But the householder waits until the harvest is ready to gather, separate and burn the weeds.

Mediterranean agricultural practices are being twisted here to set up the climax and application of the parable. The "evil one," presumably the devil, does not for Matthew have power to ruin the crop sown by the Son of the human. The best Satan can do is wreak havoc in the in-between time. Evil/bad seed is sown amongst the good so that the weeds (their roots?) get so entangled with the wheat that destroying the weeds would result in destroying the wheat. Thus, as dealing with the weeds is delayed, so is the eschatological culmination of the Christ event and the resulting judgment on those outside the reign of heaven.

One way to preach this parable is to contrast this view with the traditional interpretation of the parable in which the field is seen as the church with the impossibility of knowing who in the church is saved and who is not. Jesus makes clear that the field is a symbol for the world, not the church. Matthew casts his gaze farther and wider than most preachers have when speaking of this text. The parable is not about who gets into heaven and who does not.

Notice that when Jesus interprets the parable as an allegory and lays out the symbolic meaning of different images, there is an important one missing. The sower is the Son of the human. The field is the world. The good seed are the children of God's reign. The enemy is the evil one and the bad seed is children of the evil one. And the reapers are the angels of God's judgment who will purify God's reign. But who are the slaves? Matthew's omission of the slaves in the allegorical tally may be intentional. Within the narrative itself, the omission invites the disciples seeking an explanation of the parable to identify with them. For Matthew's original readers, the church was clearly meant to identify with the disciples and thus the omission invites the church to see themselves represented in the parable by the slaves.

Preachers today, therefore, should draw on Matthew's literary technique to ask their congregations to identify with the slaves. The parable as interpreted allegorically presents Matthew's eschatological view of salvation history. In the present some already experience God's reign but only in the midst of sin and evildoing. The question of the parable ultimately is not when or how God will resolve this situation. The slaves asked if they should do something about the weeds and were told no. The parable, therefore, reminds us that we cannot and should not attempt to resolve the tension between the already and the not yet. That is God's to do.

This is not, however, license for apathy in the face of oppression or evil. While the interpretation names the Son of the human as the one who sows, the implication of the slaves questioning the householder about the state of the field implies they have some responsibility for the field. The original hearers of the parable would have presumed that a farmer who had slaves would have had those slaves sow his fields. Thus our responsibility is to continue sowing good seed in the world in our devotion to and imitation of Christ, but unlike Christ we cannot claim responsibility or power over the ultimate results of that sowing.

Lection: Parables of Growth and Discovery
13:31-33, 44-52; Proper 12

Any preacher coming upon this lection will immediately be struck by the impossibility of preaching on all of the parables included in this single reading. One could choose to preach on a single parable included in the lesson. But a way to include a little more material but still focus the sermon thematically would be to preach on related parables. Consider the following outline of the material included in the lection:

Parables of Growth (13:31-33)
 Parable of the Mustard Seed
 Parable of the Leaven
Parables of Discovery (13:44-50)
 Parable of the Hidden Treasure
 Parable of the Pearl of Great Value
 Parable of the Separation of the Fish Caught in the Net
Conclusion to the Discourse: Scribes of the Reign of Heaven (13:51-52)

The two parables of growth are basically synonymous. The same is true of the first two parables of discovery. The third parable in this section is related but in some ways is more similar to the Parable of the Weeds of the Field than to the first two in the section. The last section, the conclusion to the Parables Discourse, is important for Matthew but likely will not catch the preacher's eye as the most profitable part of the text on which to concentrate. Thus in the comments to follow we will focus first on the two parables of growth as a potential homiletical unit and then on the first two parables of discovery as a second option.

Parables of Growth. Whereas growth was an element in both the Parables of the Sower and the Parable of the Weeds in the Field previously considered, Matthew here makes it *the* focus of two shorter parables (13:31-33). Again, when we preach on the parables of the mustard seed and leaven, we need to remind ourselves that the entire narrative of the parable is a metaphor for the reign of heaven. In other words, it is neither the mustard seed at the beginning of the parable nor the tree at the end that is like God's reign. The reign of heaven is like the *whole* story that begins with the seed *and* results in the tree in which the birds of the heavens nest. (Often the focus on the mustard seed is due to the use of the same image in the saying recounted in 17:20. But the image there is a metaphor for faith and here is part of the metaphor for the reign of heaven.)

Both of these parables are drawn from the most mundane and common areas of knowledge of ancient hearers and to Jesus' public audience. All would have been familiar with mustard plants and with the process of leavening dough to make bread. At first glance, then, it might appear that Jesus presents the image of the growth of the reign of heaven as a natural process. But, as we recall, parables usually have a twist or anomaly in the story that makes the interpretation puzzling. This is the case in both of these parables, but the strange element can easily be missed by modern readers. In the first, the puzzle is that the small seed grows not only into a mustard shrub but into a tree. Every person in the Mediterranean, agrarian culture knew that large mustard plants might grow to five or six feet, but never would these have been considered trees. What does this hyperbolic image of the tree mean? In the second parable, the puzzle is related to the amounts specified in the parable. As the image opens with a woman using leaven, hearers would assume the daily task of making a loaf of bread for a family. But suddenly Jesus has her leavening "three measures" of flour (NRSV; Greek *sata tria*). While the NRSV is a literal translation of the Greek phrase, the NIV better highlights the excessive amount of flour with the translations, "about sixty pounds" of flour. This would create enough dough for over a hundred loaves of bread. What does this hyperbolic measurement mean?

Both parables are built on the image of contrast—tiny beginnings lead to endings grown beyond our imagination. In the past, preachers have often interpreted these parables to be about the successful expansion of the church or Christendom. Or they have been interpreted on a more individualized level that small beginnings of faith lead to big things. But the image of growth is as metaphorical as is the mustard seed and the leaven. The thing to highlight is how radically different (and more) is the end than the beginning. These parables are eschatological and describe Christian experience of the already/not yet entailed in the phrase "the reign of heaven," which is a metaphor itself. To be a follower of Christ is to know God's reign on earth already but not fully, to know the mustard seed but not yet the mustard tree. We live in the light of God's salvific and liberating providence but in the midst of the oppression of the reign of Caesar with all of the poverty, suffering, evil and death that comes with it. To preach these parables we should focus less on offering some pie-in-the-sky vision of what will be and more on the tension of the in-between, with both its joy and struggle.

A final note about homiletical use of these parables is worth making. In the parable of the leaven, the main character who acts is a woman. This is significant because women are so rarely used in such a positive fashion in the ancient, patriarchal texts of the New Testament. We must be careful not to allegorize the parable and make of the woman a symbol for God. But we should emphasize her role in a way that we might not highlight the man who sows the mustard seed in the first parable as a counter to the relative absence of women in scriptural and homiletical proclamation of the gospel.

Parables of Discovery. After Jesus' explanation of the Parable of the Weeds in the Field to the disciples, Matthew presents Jesus as narrating three more parables about the reign of heaven without any break (13:44-50). In other words, these parables are part of the private instruction to the disciples (see 13:36) following the public proclamation that ended with the parables of growth (13:31-33). While Matthew groups these three parables together, the first two (the Parables of the Hidden Treasure and the Pearl of Great Value, vv. 44-46) have a parallel structure and field of meaning that are different from that found in the third parable (the Parable of the Separation of Fish Caught in the Net, vv. 47-50). This is not to assert that there is no connection between the third and the first two parables. Indeed, a case can be made that vv. 44-52 as a whole (including the concluding exhortation to the disciples, vv. 51-52) comprise a section for Matthew given the use of "treasure" in vv. 44 and 52 as an *inclusio*. Nonetheless, the stronger connection between the opening two parables warrant homiletical focus on them alone in contrast to the possibility of overextending oneself in trying to preaching on all of this material.

Like the two previously examined parables of the reign of heaven, these also present the eschatological experience of the already/not yet of God's reign. But whereas the parables of the mustard seed and leaven imaged the already/not yet in terms of tiny beginnings contrasted with ultimate growth, these parables do so in terms of an object being present but hidden. God's reign is here, but not fully possessed.

The parables of the hidden treasure and the pearl of great value, however, do more than give metaphorical attention to the already/not yet experience of the reign of heaven. Unlike previous two parables examined, these two give the readers characters with whom to identify. There are differences in the actions of the characters. In the Parable of the Hidden Treasure, the unidentified person finds a treasure on someone else's property, buys the field without telling the person, and acquires the treasure to boot. Scholarship has debated the legal and moral implications of this characterization. The merchant in the Parable of the Pearl of Great Value, on the other hand, makes a fair deal aboveboard for a pearl he has found in the course of his trade. For preachers to attend to the differences other than to tell the stories well as part of the sermon, however, is to focus on the wrong elements. Matthew has paired the parables so that readers will notice the similarities:

- Both characters find their prize accidentally. (If we draw on the conclusions of the parables of the mustard seed and leaven—a mustard *tree* and three measures of dough leavened—we can presume that the characters could not have imagined finding such prizes, so why would they have been looking for them?)
- Both sell all they have to obtain their prize.

If the *experience* of God's reign is being described here, we can say that the reign of heaven cannot be found by our own efforts, but once it comes our way we should do everything within our means to obtain it. In other words, these parables proclaim the eschatological experience of the reign of God, but underneath the proclamation is implied exhortation about how to respond to that experience.

But as preachers invite congregations to identify with these two parallel characters, we should be careful not to turn their actions into radical sacrifice. We should especially not preach about the need for economic sacrifice in relation to these texts. While this theme certainly shows up in other places in the Gospels where disciples are called to leave their livelihood behind (for example Matthew 19:16-30), here the financial imagery is metaphorical. But the parable does not present the characters as giving up anything. Sacrifice implies loss. While it is true that the characters in the parables sell everything they have, this action is simply to get something more. Obtaining the reign of God then does not require us to give up something so much as it requires us to trade up, if you will. Both characters take extraordinary action in their trading up. This dynamic of the eschatological experience is that into which Matthew invites his readers and into which preachers should invite their congregations.

CAPERNAUM-BASED MINISTRY: THE LAST STAGE OF JESUS' ITINERANT MINISTRY (13:54—17:27)

INTRODUCTION

Following the Parables Discourse, Matthew gives us the longest narrative section since the opening four chapters of the Gospel. With only the exception of the final pericope, however, all of the materials in this section of Matthew are taken from Mark 6:1—9:32. Matthew omits a few passages from this portion of Mark and edits the material he uses, but overall he follows Mark closely including using the material in the order found in the Second Gospel. Thus preachers might well expect that the logic of this material is really Mark's logic and contributes little to the unique theology and plot development of Matthew. This is indeed partially true. While the individual stories are new to the reader who has been working through Matthew from the genealogy on, few of the theological elements or of the trajectory of the narrative carry any surprises.

This does not mean the material is extraneous to Matthew's purposes, however. Even though the material comes from Mark, Matthew uses it in a way that makes it his own. For instance, the section reinforces the picture of Jesus Matthew has already presented and solidifies the advancement of the story toward its already foreshadowed end in Jerusalem. This material in 13:54—17:27 echoes themes and events already narrated in earlier Matthean passages. The following chart is not exhaustive but illustrates some of main Matthean elements that resonate in this section:

Rejection of Jesus at Nazareth 13:53-58	Nazareth – 2:19-23; 4:13; Jesus' family – 1:1-17, 18-25; 12:46-50
Jesus and the Death of John the Baptist 14:1-12	The relation of Jesus and John – 3:1-17; 4:12; 11:2-19. Political opposition – 2:1-18, 19-22; 10:18
Feeding Over Five Thousand 14:13-21	Compassion for the crowds – 9:35-38; see also for 14:34-36 below. Eating – 4:3-4; 6:25-33; 9:10-17; 10:10
Walking on Water 14:22-33	Nature miracle – 8:23-27
Summary of Healings 14:34-36	Individual healings and exorcisms – 8:1-4, 5-13, 14-15, 28-34; 9:2-8, 18-26, 27-31, 32-34; 12:9-14, 22. Summaries of Healings – 4:23-25; 8:16-17; 9:35; 10:8;

Controversy over Defilement 15:1–20	Ritual/purity/legal conflict – 5:17–48; 6:1–18; 9:2–8, 9–13, 14–17; 12:1–8, 9–14
Healing the Canaanite Woman's daughter 15:21–28	Ministry to gentiles – 2:1–12; 4:15; 8:5–13; 8:28–34; 10:5–6. See also for 14:34–36 above.
Summary of Healings 15:29–31	See for 14:34–36 above.
Feeding of Four Thousand 15:32–31	See for 14:13–21 above.
Controversy over Seeking a Sign 16:1–4	Seeking a sign – 12:38–42. Conflict with religious authorities – 2:3–6; 7:28–29; 9:2–8, 10–13, 14–17, 34; 10:16–31; 11:25–27; 12:1–8, 9–14, 22–37, 38–45.
Beware the Leaven of the Religious Leaders 16:5–12	See above for 16:1–4.
Peter's Confession 16:13–20	Peter: 4:18–22; 8:14–15; 10:2–4; see also below for 17:1–9.
The First Passion Prediction 16:21–23	Religious Leaders conspire to destroy Jesus – 12:14–15; also see for 14:1–12 above
Instruction on Taking up One's Cross and Following Jesus 16:24–28	Following Jesus – 4:18–22; 8:18–22; 9:9
Transfiguration 17:1–9	Jesus as God's Son – 2:18–25; 3:13–17; 4:1–11
Instruction on the Role of Elijah 17:10–13	See above on 14:1–12.
Exorcism of Convulsing Boy 17:14–20	See for 14:34–36 above. Mustard seed – 13:31–32. Faith – 8:10; 9:2, 22, 29
Second Passion Prediction 17:22–23	See for 16:21–23 above.
Instruction on Paying the Temple Collection 17:24–27	

Even though the material of the section is overwhelmingly Markan, this list of echoes shows the section as a whole has become Matthean. Indeed, 16:13-28—in which Peter confesses Jesus as the Messiah, Jesus blesses Peter as the Rock upon which he will found his church, foretells his coming death and resurrection, and describes the nature of discipleship in terms of gaining life through losing one's life—does not simply repeat themes already raised in the narrative. It pulls together christology, soteriology, ecclesiology, discipleship, and eschatology in a way that has not yet been seen and becomes a central scene for the whole gospel.

Matthew has also made this section of Markan material his own through the manner in which he embeds it within his narrative. Recall that Matthew's Parables Discourse just before this section is itself modeled on and an expansion of the collection of parables in Mark 4. After the parables, Mark includes several stories of mighty deeds. Instead of using them here, Matthew has moved them to earlier points in his narrative:

> Stilling of the Storm, Mk 4:35-41//Mt 8:23-27
>
> Exorcising the Gerasene Demonic Mk 5:1-20//Mt 8:28-34
>
> Raising Jairus' Daughter and Healing the Hemorrhaging Woman, Mk 5:21-43//Mt 9:18-26.

The story of the Stilling of the Storm in Mark presents the disciples as not knowing who Jesus is, reinforcing the picture of their inability to understand the meaning of the parables. For Matthew, however, the disciples do understand the parables (Mt 13:51). Matthew's moving of this material results instead in the story of the Rejection of Nazareth (Mt 13:54-58) placed on the heels of the Parables Discourse. As opposed to Mark's focus on the disciples' misunderstanding, the rejection by the people in Jesus' hometown in Matthew reinforces the picture of *the crowd's* lack of understanding the parables. Moreover, the references to Jesus's family in this scene set in Nazareth echoes back to the discussion of Jesus' true family (12: 46-50) immediately prior to the Parables Discourse. This forms an *inclusio* showing that Matthew intends the reader to see the narrative as a single thread that includes the discourses as integral pieces to the advancement of the story. So we should not make the mistake of thinking of Jesus' teaching as asides. The five discourses work with other materials to move the story along. So preachers should make sure to read 13:54—17:27 as proceeding from the Parables Discourse in chapter 13 and leading toward the Community Discourse in chapter 18.

We can see further how Matthew edits the section to lead into the Community Discourse. Mark drives the wider unit of his narrative along through three passion predictions, each of which is followed by an inappropriate response on the part of the disciples:

8:31-33, First Passion prediction and Peter's Rebuke

9:30-37, Second passion prediction and argument over which disciple is the greatest

10:32-45, Third Passion Prediction and the request of John and James.

Matthew, however, includes only the first two of the passion predictions in the section we are currently examining (16:21-23; 17:22-23). The third follows the Community Discourse and does not appear until 20:17-19. Moreover, Matthew separates the argument over greatness from the second passion prediction (inserting in-between the discussion of the temple collection, 17:24-27), so that instead of being a response to foreshadowing of Jesus' death, it serves as the introduction to the fourth discourse (18:1-5). Thus while the passion predictions are clearly important for Matthew thematically, there are not used structurally as in Mark.

Instead, the placement of the discussion of the temple collection as the conclusion to this section is significant. As noted above, this is the only material in the section that is unique to Matthew. Notice that in the chart of echoes between 13:54—17:27 and earlier materials in Matthew, we indicated no such parallels for this passage. Certainly a case could be made that this scene relates to earlier stories of conflict with the religious authorities. But those characters who have been appearing in such roles are not named here—literally these new characters are simply called "those collecting the double drachma" (17:24). Thus the import of this unique scene is that it introduces the temple for the first time into Matthew's story. In other words, the scene concludes the section by pointing ahead to all that will happen in and around the temple in Jerusalem.

Moreover, Matthew breaks with the Second Gospel at Mark 10:1, which says, "He left that place and went to the region of Judea and beyond the Jordan." Matthew picks this thread up again after the Community Discourse, so that chapter 18 brings to an end the focus on Capernaum as the home base of Jesus' itinerant ministry in Galilee. He actually begins to head geographically toward the end of the story in chapters 19–20.

In sum, Matthew retains Mark's new emphasis on Jerusalem and the passion in this narrative section (and the next) but restructures how that emphasis plays itself out. This emphasis is seen as well in relation to the conflict that occurs in the section. Earlier we read of conflict building with the religious authorities (especially in chapters 11 and 12) even to the point that the Pharisees began to conspire to destroy Jesus (12:14). In this section, Matthew points toward the end of that conflict more strongly and explicitly. Consider the following progression:

- A political ruler, Herod the tetrarch, hears reports about Jesus (14:1).
- Jesus is again in conflict with Pharisees and scribes, but this time they are described as coming to Jesus in Galilee "from Jerusalem" (15:1).
- The Sadducees (who controlled the Jerusalem temple) appear for the first time in Jesus' ministry alongside the Pharisees as testing Jesus (16:1; the only earlier time Matthew has mentioned Sadducees were as part of the audience of John the Baptist preaching in the wilderness alongside the Jordan in 3:7). The presentation of the Pharisees and Sadducees as united against Jesus is striking given that they were rival sects within Judaism.
- Jesus leaves Galilee for Caesarea Philippi (that is, a city named for the emperor), is declared the Son of God by Peter (that is, a title often used to describe the emperor), and announces he must go to Jerusalem to suffer, die and be raised (16:13-23).
- Jesus then describes discipleship in terms of taking up one's "cross" (16:24-26).
- After the Transfiguration, at which the heavenly voice declares Jesus God's Son, Jesus tells the disciples to tell no one what they have seen until after he has been raised from the dead (17:9).
- Jesus again foretells his betrayal, death and resurrection (17:22-23).
- Finally, Jesus names that Christians, as God's children, should not have to pay the temple collection, but does so in order that the collectors (from Jerusalem?) are not scandalized (17:24-27).

The problem with preaching through Matthew 13:54—17:27 using the lectionary is that much of this thematic emphasis and narrative progression of the section is easily missed. As we have seen in the past, some of the RCL's choices involve a harmonizing approach in which lections are chosen so that parallel material from the different Synoptics is not used each year. But there is also significant overlap between the use of Matthean and Markan material in this section because the RCL has focused on key dramatic scenes such as Peter's confession and the transfiguration due to traditions of the church and liturgical needs. Consider the following table of Matthean and Markan parallel sections with the lectionary choices noted:

	Matthew	Mark
Rejection of Jesus at Nazareth	13:53-58	6:1-6, Proper 9B (6:1-13)

Jesus and the Death of John the Baptist	14:1–12	6:14–29, Proper10B
Feeding Over Five Thousand	14:13–21, Proper 13A	6:32–44, First Part of Proper 11B (6:30–34)
Walking on Water	14:22–33, Proper 14A	6:45–52
Summary of Healings	14:34–36	6:53–56, Second Part of Proper 11B
Controversy over Defilement	15:1–20 (vv. 10–20 are optional part of Proper 15A)	7:1–23, Proper 17B (vv. 1–8, 14–15, 21–23)
Healing the Canaanite Woman's daughter	15:21–28, Proper 15A	7:24–30, Proper 18B (7:24–37)
Summary of Healings	15:29–31	7:31–37, Proper 18B (7:24–37)
Feeding Over Four Thousand	15:32–39	8:1–10
Controversy over Seeking a Sign	16:1–4	8:11–13
Beware the Leaven of the Religious Leaders	16:5–12	8:14–21
Peter's Confession, the First Passion Prediction, and Instruction on Taking up One's Cross and Following Jesus	16:13–28, Proper 16A (vv. 13–20)	8:27–9:1, Proper 19 (vv. 27–38)
Transfiguration	17:1–9, Last Sunday after Epiphany; Transfiguration	9:2–10, Last Sunday after Epiphany; Transfiguration (vv. 2–9)
Instruction on the Role of Elijah	17:10–13	9:11–13
Exorcism of Convulsing Boy	17:14–20	9:14–29
Second Passion Prediction	17:22–23	9:30–32, Proper 20B (9:30–37)
Instruction on Paying the Temple Tax	17:24–27	
Disciples' Argument over Who is the Greatest	18:1–5	9:33–37, Proper 20 (9:30–37)

While some significant pericopes from Matthew 13:54—17:27 are used by the lectionary, the choices do not help congregations get a sense of the cohesiveness of the section and the way it moves the narrative along. Preachers will need to fill in the blanks of context to help congregations understand and experience the full import of the lections as part of Matthew's Gospel. Helping congregations hear these passages as playing a role in Jesus preparing the disciples to head toward Jerusalem will allow them to find things in the lections they would otherwise miss.

PASSAGES OMITTED FROM THE LECTIONARY

More of Matthew 13:53—17:27 is ignored by the lectionary than is used. Given what we have said above about the nature of this section reinforcing theological themes already offered by the Gospel, this is not a completely unwise choice. Nevertheless, there is a cumulative development in the omitted materials that preachers will want congregations to note—that is, the shifting weight toward foreshadowing what is coming in Jerusalem.

REJECTION OF JESUS AT NAZARETH (13:53-58):
OMITTED FROM LECTIONARY

Since some version of this story appears in all three Synoptics and since it has traditionally been a fairly popular text with preachers, it is likely that most congregations know the basic premise of Jesus being rejected by his hometown fairly well. What they likely do not know is the unique way the story is shaped and used in each Gospel.

For Matthew, the story follows on the heels of the Parables Discourse (13:1-52) in which the crowds are presented as misunderstanding Jesus and his message of the reign of heaven. This scene intensifies that presentation by presenting his hometown not just as misunderstanding Jesus but rejecting him (notice the shift from surprise to offense in vv. 54 and 57). As we mentioned above, this rejection is highlighted all the more by the contrast between familial language in this scene and that in 12:46-50.

It is also interesting to consider that Matthew places this homecoming scene at the beginning of the section that starts turning the reader's focus toward Jerusalem. In other words, Matthew places the scene here to begin cutting ties with Galilee—Jesus', the disciples' and the readers' ties. Even in

Nazareth, Matthew refers to the synagogue as "their synagogue" (v. 54). This scene clearly marks this section as transitional.

Jesus and the Death of John the Baptist (14:1-12): Omitted from Lectionary

This is one of the few gospel scenes in which not only is Jesus not the main character but he is not even an actor. He is off stage during this flashback to John the Baptist. Nevertheless, it is important for preachers to recognize that the reason the story is included is likely because there were still disciples of John the Baptist in Matthew's day claiming that John was the messiah. Matthew starts the story with a notice that Herod is confused about Jesus' identity (as have been the crowds hearing the parables and the people in Nazareth). He is so confused that he equates Jesus and John. The story of John's death is told in a narrative about Jesus in order to demonstrate the difference between John and Jesus. It also foreshadows the imperial threat to Jesus—if rulers are willing to kill John in such a revolting manner for speaking about the inappropriateness of his marriage (even though Mark and Matthew get the historical details of the marriage wrong), how much more will the powers-that-be go after one who declares the reign of God over against the reign of Caesar.

Still, John is a heroic figure here, and Jesus' strong connection with him is shown in the fact that John's disciples immediately respond to John's death after burying him by going to Jesus to tell him what has happened. (14:12-13).

Summaries of Healings (14:34-36; 15:29-31): Omitted from Lectionary

There are two summaries of Jesus' healing activity in this section. Matthew uses summaries such as these throughout his narrative to keep in the readers mind that his story of Jesus is selective. Much happens that is not narrated in detail. These two summaries do not make for the most exciting texts to preach on, but they can be used to remind a congregation of the portrayal of Jesus' widespread success that would keep him in the eye of the religious and political authorizes. Indeed, the crowds gathering around Jesus stand in stark contrast to the rejection he receives from religious leaders and in "their" synagogues.

CONTROVERSY OVER DEFILEMENT (15:1-9 [10-20]):
OMITTED FROM LECTIONARY

In an odd division of Matthew's text, the RCL breaks this scene (15:1-20) in two and connects the second half (vv. 10-20) with the following scene in which Jesus heals the daughter of the Canaanite woman (14:21-28). While the theme of uncleanness in the first passage may offer something for reading the story of the Canaanite woman, the stories are clearly separate pericope.

The controversy with religious authorities concerning whether eating with unclean hands makes you unclean has in it two historical backgrounds that are at play. The first is the issue of ritual purity in terms of the categories of unclean, clean and holy. Jesus' response here does not completely negate those categories, but he does redefine them significantly. This makes sense given that Jesus has already crossed over lines dividing the clean and unclean (for example, in his first healing where he touches the person with the skin disease, 8:3) and given that Matthew is concerned with keeping the faith in a post-temple world (and purity codes focused, to a great extent, on ritual participation). In other words, Jesus is presented as shifting the focus from ritual purity to moral purity.

The second issue is that of adherence to tradition. Jesus' response to the Pharisees and scribes echoes back to the hermeneutic for interpreting the law offered in 5:21-48 in which Jesus is concerned about the intent of the commandments and presents a view in which not all commandments are equal (for example, notice the difference in v. 4, "God said," and v. 5, "you say;" this is reminiscent of the antitheses in 5:21-48). Tradition, especially in the form of purity codes, is not to be held for the sake of tradition but only when and because it leads to a deeper ethical life (see 9:13). (It should be noted that the logic of this passage is dependent on ancient Jewish disputes concerning the interpretation of the oral *torah*, in which the early church comprised of Jewish-Christians would have participated. To preach on this passage, one will need to consult a commentary that examines these socio-historical issues in detail.)

In terms of advancing Matthew's plot, this scene significantly raises the stakes in the conflict with the religious authorities. Jesus condemns the authorities as blind leaders. Put in the context of Matthew's sibling rivalry with the synagogue, this is really an argument for the legitimacy of the church and its practices (probably including the inclusion of the "unclean" gentiles) over against the synagogue of the late first century.

Feeding Over Four Thousand (15:32-39):
Omitted from Lectionary

The RCL does not use this pericope because it is a doublet of the feeding of over five thousand in 14:13-21, which is to be read for Proper 13. The feeding stories emphasize Jesus' desire and power to care for the masses. By telling this story so soon after the earlier one, the narrator means to impress the readers all the more with this fact. Telling such a story once makes the point. Telling two such stories elicits amazement on the part of the reader, recognition that the first time was not a fluke and Jesus can do such things anytime he wishes.

Another element to be recognized in this passage is that even after the first feeding scene, the disciples are portrayed as still surprised at Jesus' actions. Lifting up this element when preaching on 14:13-21 will serve well if the preacher is inviting the congregation to identify with the disciples in that story.

Controversy over Seeking a Sign (16:1-12):
Omitted from Lectionary

As with the previous omitted pericope, the opening controversy story of this passage (vv. 1-4) is a doublet. In 12:38-42, the religious authorities seek a sign. Jesus condemns them for the test (of him and of God) and declares they will only be given the sign of Jonah, a reference from the Hebrew Bible that is used to foreshadow Jesus death and resurrection. The scene in 16:1-4 is slightly shorter, and has a much shorter reference to the sign of Jonah.

The new material in the doublet is what is intended to attract the attention of the readers. Earlier the religious authorities represented the "evil generation," but here the condemnation is pointed more directly at them *as* religious authorities. Indeed, the fact that Sadducees have now joined the Pharisees (rival groups in Second Temple Judaism) in their opposition of Jesus highlights the emphasis on religious leaders over against the people as a whole. As religious authorities, they especially should already be interpreting the signs of the times and recognize who Jesus is. Again, this conflict both pushes the narrative toward the show down in Jerusalem and reflects the late first century struggle between Matthew's church and the synagogue (even though the Sadducees ceased to be a Jewish force once the temple was destroyed in 70 ce).

Also new in the doublet, as compared with the first time religious authorities seek a sign from Jesus, is Jesus' commentary on the leaven of the Pharisees and Sadducees with the disciples (vv. 5-12). Preachers need to help the congregation avoid using texts such as this one (and the previous ones discussed that portray the Jewish religious leaders in a negative light) to support anti-Semitism. Even though Matthew's source for this passage is Mark 8:14-21, the First Gospel's use of the warning must be heard against the historical situation in which the late first century church was struggling to defend its legitimacy as an heir of Israel's faith over against the synagogue and its threat of persecution. Matthew consistently portrays Jesus as striking against the religious *leaders* not against the Jews as a people.

INSTRUCTION ON THE ROLE OF ELIJAH (17:10-13):
OMITTED FROM LECTIONARY

Following the story of the transfiguration in which Elijah and Moses appear with Jesus, Jesus discusses with the disciples the role of Elijah in contemporary thought. Because he was carried away to the heavens instead of dying (2 Kings 2:11), tradition had claimed Elijah would return to prepare the way for the day of the Lord (see Mal 4:5-6) and thus for the messiah. Jesus is not presented as countering that tradition but, instead, as explicitly applying it to John the Baptist.

This emphasis on John echoes back not only to earlier materials prior to this section but the scene of John's death in 14:12. As with that scene, by naming John as Elijah what Matthew is really doing is highlighting Jesus as the Christ.

EXORCISM OF CONVULSING BOY (17:14-20):
OMITTED FROM LECTIONARY

This exorcism that follows the transfiguration is omitted from the lectionary in both Year A and Year B (Mark 9:14-29) and appears only as optional verses to be added to the reading for Transfiguration in Year C with Luke 9:28-36 (37-43). This is a shame because it is a unique story whose emphasis is less on the healing itself and more on the issue of faith, specifically the faith of the disciples—Jesus has accused them of "little faith" already in 6:30; 8:26; 14:31; 16:8. It is at least in part Matthew's answer to why healing miracles do not continue after Jesus' time—the church does not have the faith of Jesus. While the scene does condemn the "faithless and perverse generation" (v. 17)—language used just verses earlier for the religious authorities, 16:4—the hyperbole in Jesus' speech can be seen as especially highlighting the unique character of Jesus as the one who can truly order a mountain to move (v. 20).

Beyond the way the scene functions internally, it also plays a role in pushing the narrative toward Jerusalem. In addition to building the conflict in which Jesus defeats Satan and Satan's demons, Jesus cries out, "How much longer must I be with you?" after having just told the disciples a third time about his coming passion. Matthew wants the reader to know without a doubt that the answer to Jesus' question is, "Not much longer at all."

THE SECOND PASSION PREDICTION (17:22-23): OMITTED FROM LECTIONARY

Jesus foretelling his suffering, death and resurrection twice in this section of the narrative is key to the advancement of Matthew's plot. It makes sense that the RCL chooses only the first of these to be read during Ordinary Time, since the second prediction adds little new information to the first. The doublet, however, serves to give a sense of the foreboding pathos Matthew creates in this section, exemplified in the disciples' sadness (v. 23). Indeed, this emphasis on the upcoming tragic death is so important that Matthew adds a mention of the passion at 17:12 not found in Mark.

LECTIONS

While the RCL does not select readings from Matthew 13:54—17:27 that help congregations get a full sense of the section's purpose as a whole within the Gospel's plot development, it has chosen passages with dramatic, theological and existential import. Some of the selections have been popular homiletical choices throughout the history of the church, and others have received relatively little attention until recent years.

LECTION: FEEDING OVER FIVE THOUSAND 14:13-21; PROPER 13

There are two feeding miracles in this section of Matthew, both of which come from Mark (Mark 6:30-44; 8:1-9). While focusing attention on the details of 14:13-21, preachers will do well to mention the doublet in 15:32-39 (see comments above) as evidence of the importance this miracle holds for the Synoptic tradition in emphasizing Jesus' desire and power to care for the masses.

Unlike Mark who sets the purpose of the withdrawal to an isolated place as a chance for the disciples to rest upon their return from their mission (Mark

6:6b-13, 30-31), Matthew's scene opens with the notice that Jesus withdraws upon hearing news of the death of John the Baptist. Matthew uses the Greek word found here (*anachōreō*) in other places to indicate an escape from danger (2:12, 13, 14, 22; 4:12; 12:15). This withdrawal by boat, then, coupled with the crowd's following by foot makes a clear contrast: Jesus is viewed as a threat by the political powers (14:1-2) but has great appeal to the masses who hunger and thirst for righteousness and are filled, 5:6; 14:20). And it is for these masses that Jesus has compassion (14:14; cf. 9:36; 15:32).

The story of compassion is structured in three movements: an introduction or setting of the scene (vv. 13-14), a dialogue between Jesus and the disciples about feeding the crowd (vv. 15-18), and the miracle proper (vv. 19-21). Formally speaking, this scene is a miracle story with the miracle coming at the end. But, in truth, the greatest weight is on the dialogue, with the miracle serving to confirm what is said there. This punctuating use of miracles is seen in other places (for example, in 9:2-8 healing the paralytic serves to support Jesus' ability to forgive sins). Therefore, in preaching this text, without ignoring the miracle, the sermonic focus belongs on the middle section.

This dialogue is all about characterization of both Jesus and the disciples in relation to the crowd. After Jesus has healed those sick in the crowd, the disciples suggest that Jesus dismiss them so that they can go to the village to buy something to eat (v. 15). In Mark's version of the story, this suggestion demonstrates the disciples' desire to be alone with Jesus, but not in Matthew. Here their suggestion is an act of concern for the crowd—with evening having arrived, the crowd needs to eat. The disciples are not trying to get rid of the people but to make sure their needs are met, which they naturally assume cannot be met in such a deserted place.

Jesus' compassion is now portrayed as extending from those in the crowd who are sick to the crowd as a whole. His response is not a rebuke of the disciples but a recognition of the appropriateness of their concern, even while redirecting their strategy for dealing with the needs of the crowd. He instructs the disciples to feed the crowd themselves. But they, of course, name correctly that they do not have the resources to do this. Unlike in the second feeding story where the disciples should expect Jesus to feed the crowd (15:33), here their response about having only five loaves and two fish is simply giving an account of their resources.

But then Jesus takes charge of the resources at hand. Notice that the reader is not shown the miracle itself. We never know exactly how or when the food multiplies. This has led many a modern interpreter to attempt to rationalize the miracle and turn it into a stewardship story: once the little amount of food began to be distributed, people in the crowd began sharing what they brought with them. That would be a nice story with a good moral, but it is not this story. The synoptic tradition clearly views the event as a supernatural miracle that demonstrates Jesus' power in the same way that healings do.

Even though readers are not told how the miracle occurs, we are brought into a rich world of intertextual echoes at this point. The miracle evokes from the Hebrew Bible images of manna being provided for Israel (Exodus 16) and of Elisha multiplying a first fruit offering to feed a hundred (2 Kings 4:42-44). The story evokes eschatological hope for the messianic banquet and parallels the gospel story and the early church's practice of the Lord's Supper (26:26) with Jesus *taking* the bread, *blessing* it (in the doublet Jesus *gives thanks*, 15:36), *breaking* it, and *giving* it (14:19). This story, then, calls forth memories of all the expressions of ways God providential feeds God's people.

But notice what Jesus does here. He does not feed the crowd. Having performed these actions (which also resemble a traditional Jewish blessing at the start of a meal), he gives the food to the disciples and *they* distribute it to the people. Then, as with the parables of the mustard seed and leaven (13:31-33), the small beginnings grow so that all (five thousand men plus women and children; in other words, five thousand households) are filled and an abundance of leftovers are collected.

Like all miracle stories, this one has a christological purpose—it highlights Jesus' compassion and power. Even though we should not rationalize the story by offering a naturalistic explanation, neither should we literalize it by focusing on the supernatural miracle. The way the story echoes other biblical feeding stories and the fact that the story is essentially told twice is an indication that Matthew wants the readers to move below the surface level to something more. The role of the disciples in the story points to this something more. Since the disciples serve in Matthew as representatives of the church, this is essentially an ecclesiological story. What Jesus provides, the church is to distribute to the masses. We are to extend the mercy of Christ to all who would take it and be filled.

We must be careful not to flip this message over and say the church is able to meet all the needs of the masses—this simply does not match the reality of poverty and suffering in the world alongside the existence of the church. Instead, as with the disciples in the story, we are not left to our own resources. Whatever we offer the world is more than we have to offer because God takes it and blesses it.

Lection: Walking on Water
14:22-33; Proper 14

Matthew gets the story of Jesus walking on the sea and calming the winds from Mark 5:45-52 (cf. John 6:1-21 for related versions of the feeding miracle followed by Jesus walking on water). Completely unique to Matthew and inserted into the Markan story (vv. 28-31), however, is the element of Peter joining Jesus out on the water. The placement and vividness of Peter's exchange with Jesus makes it the climax and focus of the story in contrast to Mark's story where the demonstration of Jesus' miraculous ability to walk on water is the clear emphasis of the scene. In addition, Matthew changes the end of Mark's story. In Mark, when Jesus gets in the boat and the winds cease, the disciples are filled will astonishment and confusion (Mark 6:52). But in Matthew's edited version, when Jesus and Peter get in the boat and the winds cease, the disciples worship him and proclaim him to be the son of God (Matthew 14:33). Matthew, therefore, invites preachers to use this story as a parable through which to view faith. In other words, Matthew transforms a christological story into one focused on discipleship.

The structure of the story is straightforward. The opening verses transition from the previous story and provide the setting for this scene (vv. 22-23). Sending the disciples across the sea and following by foot parallels the opening of the previous scene in which Jesus and the disciples cross the sea by boat and the crowd follows along the shore and passes them (14:13). The reader would begin reading this section, assuming it reverses what occurred earlier. But instead of doing as the crowd did, Jesus takes a short cut and walks across the sea.

In the next movement Jesus walks on water (vv. 25-27). In the ancient world, water represented mystery, danger and chaos—especially in the dark of night (v. 25). Seas were uncontrollable—they could be sailed across but never mastered. The Hebrew Bible speaks of the God who brought creation out of the void of water and made a path for the Israelites through the Red Sea alone as able to conquer the sea. Similarly in Greek literature, stories of walking on water was common. But in these stories only those with divine abilities—gods and heroes (sons of gods)—were able to do it. With these backdrops in place, the original readers of Matthew would recognize the claim being made about Jesus with his first step out on the water—he is of God. This becomes even more explicit when Jesus comforts the disciples saying, "Take heart, it is I; do not be afraid" (v. 27). The Greek for "It is I," is *ego eimi*, and is more literally translated, "I am." This expression recalls the language with which God of the Hebrew Bible identifies God's self (for example, Ex 3:14; Is 41:4; 43:10; 47:8, 10).

Not only can Jesus walk on water, however. He can empower others to do so as well. In the third and central section of the scene, Peter joins Jesus in walking on water (vv. 28-31). This is the first scene in Matthew in which Peter begins to gain a special voice and thus take on a representative role for all disciples (see also 15:15; 16:16; 17:4; 18:21; 19:27; 26:33, 35). Peter's address to Jesus, ("If it is you," v. 28) parallels the expression, "I am." Thus it is not meant to signal that Peter is unsure whether it is really Jesus (especially since Peter calls Jesus "Lord"), but to serve as the condition for the request: If/since you are able to walk on water, then command me to come to you one the water as well. Jesus' response is simply, "Come" (v. 29). He says nothing about Peter walking on water but only commands that Peter come to him.

Peter does so. This is the only miraculous act the reader sees a disciple perform in the entire gospel narrative. But then, upon reaching Jesus and attending to the wind, Peter begins to sink (v. 30). Rocks (16:18) do sink, after all. The Greek word translated here as "began to sink" (*katapontizō*) implies drowning, so preachers should not underplay the danger Peter is in now that he is away from the boat in the windstorm. Those in the boat cannot save him. Peter is truly at risk at this point. The language describing Peter's situation in the water and his fear resembles Ps 69:2-3. There the psalmist, with water up around his neck, cries out, "Save me, O God." Here, even in his fear, the apostle turns to Jesus as in his first request and calls him Lord once again: "Lord, save me." And indeed, the one who is able to walk on water and invite others to do so is also able to save. As he stretched out his hand toward the disciples when he named them as his true family (12:49; cf. 26:51) and as God is presented in the Psalms as stretching out a hand to rescue those in dangerous waters waters (Ps 18:15-16; 144:5-8), Jesus reaches out and saves Peter.

Finally, vv. 32-33 conclude the story, confirming both Jesus' divine ability (through the calming of the winds) and the disciples growing faith (in their worship of Jesus). Matthew has already identified Jesus as the Son of God for the reader in the birth story (1:20, 23; 2:15); has had the heavenly voice do so at his baptism (3:17); has presented the devil and demons as recognize him as such (4:3, 6; 8:29); and even had Jesus himself claim this identity (11:27). But this is the first time we see the disciples confess Jesus to be God's Son and foreshadows Peter's confession later in this narrative section in 16:16 (cf. 17:5; 27:54).

Whether they assume a literal nature miracle stands behind this story or not, most preachers have treated this story as a lesson about faith. Peter is presented as a figure similar to "doubting Thomas" in the Fourth Gospel (John 20:24-29). There is certainly exegetical justification for this. Jesus himself asks Peter rhetorically, "You of little faith, why did you doubt?" (14:31).

This, however, is not the only time Jesus calls the disciples ones of little faith (*oligopistoi*, cf. 6:30; 8:26, 16:8). One can read this term as accusatory (which is certainly is) or emphasize the way in which it calls the disciples to greater faith. Similarly, the word Jesus uses here for doubt (*distazō*) is used by the narrator in 28:17 to say that while some disciples worshiped Jesus on the Galilean mountain after the resurrection, others doubted. If doubt could be mustered in the presence of the resurrected Jesus, then it is certainly an understandable reaction when standing on wavy and windblown water.

Perhaps a better way to approach this text homiletically is to emphasize Peter's faith. In spite of the fear of initially thinking he sees a ghost, in spite of the rough seas, and in spite of the law of physics that says humans do not float, Peter calls Jesus "Lord" and steps out of the boat. None of the other disciples do this. And even when Peter falters, doubts and begins drowning, he calls Jesus "Lord" once again and trusts that only he can save him. All of this leads finally not only to Peter but to the whole group of disciples professing Jesus as God's Son. As finite beings, humans will always have finite faith. Doubt is an essential part of the experience of faith, and preachers can use this text to help congregations quit feeling guilty about their doubts and instead see that their faith, when placed as trust in Jesus as the Son of God, is greater than any doubt or danger they can ever face. Tell people they should have more faith, and they will feel guilty that they do not have enough. Simply show them that their faith is stronger than their doubts (as the text shows about Peter), and the faith of the congregation will grow.

Lection: Healing the Canaanite Woman's Daughter
15:(10-20), 21-28; Proper 15

Although the RCL offers vv. 10-20 as an optional part of this lection, it is best to focus only on vv. 21-28 because the earlier verses are from an earlier and different (albeit related) pericope. 15:21-28 is a difficult passage for preachers to help a congregation face honestly in the pulpit. There is no way around it: Jesus comes off looking pretty bad here. When a woman calls out to him in anguish over her daughter being demonized, he ignores and says nothing (v. 23). Were that this was as bad as it gets! When he does finally talk to her, her compares her to a dog (v. 26). Preachers will have everyone in the pews engaged if they name this portrayal of Jesus forcefully, with all its offensive character, as the "hook" of the sermon introduction. A good editor, after all, would have told Matthew this story should be omitted—it deconstructs the image of Jesus he has worked so hard to construct. Preachers who take such an approach to opening their sermons, however, must then offer an interpretation of the pericope that 1) makes sense of the offense and 2) has significance for today's people of faith. To be successful in these goals, preachers must have a sound understanding of the literary background of Matthew's story and the theological relation of it to his wider purposes as well as drawing on modern literary sensitivities to interpret the role of the characters in the story.

Concerning background, there is perhaps a literary relationship between this story and the scene in 1 Kings 17:8-24. There Elijah heals the child of a gentile woman in Sidon in a scene where bread is also referenced. This connection works christologically: Jesus is a prophet of Israel whose salvific power reaches beyond the Jews. But, of course, there is much more to this scene.

The most obvious background is Mark 7:24-30. While this Markan passage is Matthew's source for 15:21-28, Matthew edits the scene significantly, so that emphases are different than in Mark's version. Noting the most important differences in detail helps us get a handle on what Matthew is doing with the problematic story:

Mark 7:24-30	Matthew 15:21-28
V. 24a: Jesus arose and went away.	V. 21a: Jesus went away and withdrew (Matthew adds *anachoreō* as a signal that Jesus withdraws to avoid danger implied in the controversy with the religious authorities concerning what defiles in 15:1-20; cf. 2:12, 13, 14, 22; 4:12; 12:15; 14:13). This makes the connection of this scene with the previous controversy a little stronger than in Mark—with the issue of what makes one unclean in the reader's head, the narrator moves to a person who would have been considered unclean.
V. 24b: He entered a house and did not want anyone to know he was there.	Matthew omits this notice altogether, giving the sense that the scene takes place in public.
V. 25: Mark initially identifies the new character simple as "a woman," and then later describes her as "a gentile, of	V. 22: Matthew identifies the new character as "a Canaanite woman;" since there were no Canaanites in Jesus' day, the use of this anachronistic term signals a stronger sense of offense than simply "gentile"—the Canaanites were Israel's enemy.

Syropheonician origin" (v. 26).	
V. 25: Mark describes the woman's approach without attributing direct speech to her.	V. 22: Matthew gives the woman voice and allows her to name her concern (again in v. 25 over against Mark 7:26). Moreover, she addresses Jesus as "Lord, son of David" (she also uses *kyrios* in v. 25 and twice in v. 27). The fact that one described as a Canaanite uses such devotional, messianic labels for Jesus would have been striking to the original audience.
	Vv. 23-24: Matthew inserts into Mark's narrative an exchange between the disciples and Jesus. They request that Jesus dismiss her. Often read as annoyance, this request can be interpreted as signaling the disciples desire that that Jesus send her away with a blessing/healing (recall that Matthew presents the disciples as requesting that Jesus dismiss (*apoluō*) the crowd in 14:15 (cf. 14:22, 23) as an act of caring for them). This explains Jesus' negative response—he reminds them of what they should already know, that is, that he has been sent to the lost sheep of the house of Israel (cf. 10:6).
V. 27: Jesus says to the woman, "Let the children be fed first…"	V. 26: Matthew omits this opening clause of what Jesus says to the woman. This is a striking omission given that Matthew is concerned to explain salvation history in relation to two stages: the mission to the Jews/Israel during Jesus' ministry followed by the post-resurrection mission of the church that includes the nations.
V. 29: After the woman offers a retort to Jesus, he grants her request in recognition of what she has said.	V. 28a: Matthew intensifies Mark's version of Jesus' praise for the woman by having Jesus pronounce that her *faith* is great. This expression would seem to affirm both the wit and wisdom of her final pronouncement and the christological titles with which she addressed Jesus.
V. 30: The woman returns home and finds her daughter healed, implying a healing from a distance.	V. 28b: Matthew mentions simply that the woman's daughter is healed instantly. It is not clear whether the girl is present or not, but it is likely that if the readers were not familiar with Mark's versions, they would simply assume she was present as is the case in most healing miracles. Nevertheless, Matthew never presents Jesus as speaking to or touching the girl,

	indicating that the miracle is not the point of the story—it simply comfirms the point.

Noting that this story does not primarily focus on the healing raises the question of the story's central function. The focus is on the dialogue in the center of the story (vv. 23-27). In the Synoptic tradition, miracle stories are often transformed into pronouncement stories where the healing simply confirms what Jesus says (for example, 9:2-8). But that is not exactly what happens here. It is not Jesus' pronouncement that serves as the punch line for this story, but the woman's retort. Jesus' saying is the setup: "It is not fair to take the children's food and throw it to the dogs" (v. 26). The sting of Jesus metaphorically referring to this woman and her daughter (and all gentiles?) as dogs is troubling, and it is meant to be so. This sting gives the woman's saying all the more power: "Yes, Lord (*kyrios*), yet even the dogs eat the crumbs that fall from their masters' (*kyrios*) table" (v. 27). Jesus' declaration of the woman's faith and the healing that follows likewise point backward to this saying as the focal point of the entire story (v. 28).

There is another story in Matthew that parallels this structure. Interestingly, it is the other story in the Gospel in which Jesus heals a child of a gentile parent (8:5-13). A centurion approaches Jesus and asks him to heal his paralyzed child (most translations and commentaries interpret *pais* in vv. 6, 8 and 13 as servant, but compare 2:16; 12:18; 17:18; 21:15 where it is used for children). Jesus' response to the request is ambiguous. The NRSV translates Jesus as saying, "I will come and cure him" (v. 7). This presents Jesus as willing to enter a gentile home, which could have been seen as breaking the boundaries of purity codes (see Acts 10:28). But Jesus' line can also be translated as a question: "Shall I come and cure him?" This translation, on the other hand, could imply that Jesus is to be understood as questioning the appropriateness of his coming to heal a gentile, just as Jesus challenges the appropriateness of healing the Canaanite woman's daughter. Such a reading would better explain the centurion's speech about Jesus' authority and ability to heal from afar. It is the centurion's speech about authority (a christological claim about Jesus' authority) that is the punch line of the story. Jesus's declaration about the faith of the centurion ("Truly I tell you, in no one in Israel have I found such faith . . .") and the healing simply confirm the gentile's pronouncement.

The parallels between these two stories show that Matthew is concerned with presenting gentiles as possessing the ability to have and demonstrate faith in Jesus. It would seem, paradoxically then, that the very reason Matthew repeats the claim that Jesus' mission is directed only to the lost sheep of the house Israel within this story is so that the woman's response could be viewed in contrast, making this exorcism and the healing of the centurion's child exceptions to that rule. Therefore, the centurion and the Canaanite woman, in their own voices, justify the gentile mission which Jesus will later command the church to take up (28:19).

But preaching this pericope in today's world invites more than a discourse on Matthew's understanding of the inclusion of gentiles in the first century church. In a way contrary to what is found in almost every other pericope in the Gospels, Jesus is presented as the foil for someone else's character, actions and words to shine through. This is especially striking given that the character who shines here is someone whose outsider status in relation to Jesus and the disciples is doubled. She is an outsider by virtue of being a gentile, and not just any gentile but a Canaanite. And she is an outsider because she is a woman. In ancient Mediterranean society, patriarchy was such that not only were women not only not equal to men, they were not to approach men in public. At times in Matthew we see Jesus cross over cultural and purity boundaries to offer healing (for example 8:3), but here we see one crossing over those boundaries to get to Jesus and to get from him what she needs for another.

Note how far she goes to achieve this. When Jesus refers to her and her daughter (and all gentiles?) as nothing more than dogs, the woman does not name offense at what Jesus has said. She neither leaves in a huff nor argues with him about the nature of gentiles as children of God. We must be careful not to read the sting we readers feel into Matthew's characterization of the woman, but neither should we take her response as a sign of agreement with Jesus' characterization. She simply takes Jesus' metaphor to the next stage to get what she needs for her daughter. Call us dogs if you must, but at least offer my daughter a crumb of the healing you give to your children!

In preaching this text, pastors have the rare opportunity to offer their congregation a biblical role model of one who stands up to God/Christ, doing whatever it takes to get the salvation needed. She is one of the roundest, strongest characters in the Gospels besides Jesus and Peter—an amazing fact given the patriarchy of the day. Many of those sitting in the pew who feel sick, guilty, lonely, hated need such a role model. Her mixture of humbly approaching and recognizing Jesus' authority but yet refusing to be ignored can be empowering to those who need to know that a proper expression of faith, indeed an example of great faith, is to cry out and demand that God recognize our needs and the needs of others.

Lection: Peter's Confession
16:13-20; Proper 16

The importance of 16:13-28 for the theology and plot development of the First Gospel can hardly be overstated. Matthew edits and expands Mark 8:27-30 so that an incredible intersection of elements of Matthew's theology and storyline occurs here—christology, eschatology, hermeneutics, ecclesiology, persecution, passion, and resurrection. It is impossible for a preacher to do justice to all of them, even with the RCL (appropriately) splitting the dialogue into two lections. With each lection, preachers will need to have a sense of the whole complicated matter to determine what is most important for Matthew in order to determine the best way to focus the attention of their congregation.

Matthew 16:13-20 opens with Jesus and the disciples entering Caesarea Philippi. This setting is not inconsequential. The city is named, after all, for the emperor. And while reigning, a Caesar would be called the son of god. Thus professing Jesus to be the messiah, the Son of the living God and announcing that Peter has been given the keys to the reign of heaven (over against the reign of Caesar) is subversive language. The scene, then, like much of Matthew, is theo-political in nature.

Once the setting is established, Jesus asks the disciples who the people claim the son of the human is (v. 13). The populace's views show a high appreciation of Jesus. They think he is a resurrected prophet (v. 14). Recall that Herod the tetrarch had thought much the same (14:2), so even though the responses here are more varied (not only John the Baptist, but Elijah, Jeremiah, or one of the prophets), there is really nothing new here. The people have a high evaluation of Jesus, but ultimately misunderstand him.

Jesus then turns the question on the disciples, and Peter (vv. 15-16) answers as a representative for the group (and for the readers). Mark has Peter answer the question, saying, "You are the Messiah" (8:29). Matthew expands this to, "You are the Messiah, the Son of the living God." The reader, of course, already knows Jesus' messianic identity as the Son of God because it was firmly established in the opening chapters of the narrative (chapters 1–4). But not only is the content of the confession not new to the readers, the recognition of Jesus' true identity is not new for the disciples. After Jesus walks on water and calms the wind, the disciples in the boat worship Jesus and announce, "Truly you are the Son of God" (14:33). This is radically different from Mark's use of this title, where no human clearly recognizes Jesus as God's Son until the centurion watches him die on the cross (Mark 15:39). Thus, Peter's confession of Jesus really offers nothing new here. While christology is key to understanding the import of this passage for Matthew, to focus on it in a sermon is to miss Matthew's primary emphasis.

Matthew places the primary emphasis on vv. 17-19. This can seen through several lenses. First, the dialogue in 16:13-19 is in the form of a pronouncement story. In pronouncement stories, there is some kind of setup (in the shape of something Jesus sees or hears) that leads to a pronouncement Jesus offers. In this pericope, then, vv. 13-16 are all part of the setup. The christological content in these verses shape how readers understand the pronouncement in vv. 17-19, but clearly the pronouncement is what Matthew is emphasizing.

Second, this emphasis is made all the more obvious by the observation that Matthew inserts all of this material into Mark's version of the story. Mark moves immediately from Peter's confession to Jesus rebuking him, ordering them to tell no one. The implication in Mark is that even if Peter has used a proper title (messiah), he does not fully understand who Jesus is (as the Son of God). In Matthew, Peter gives precisely the right answer and receives a blessing for it.

And, third, whereas the ways the masses describe Jesus and the disciples' profession of Jesus is not new for Matthew, what Jesus says in his blessing of Peter in vv. 17-19 is radically new. Here, for Matthew, Jesus founds the church. The word *ekklesia* is anachronistic here (the only other use of *ekklesia* in the Gospels is in Matthew 18:17). There is no church in Jesus' day. Matthew is making a theological and not a historical statement with this language. The set up makes clear that the church is founded on the identity of Jesus as the messiah, the Son of the living God who stands over against the oppressive, evil powers of the world. Before his death and resurrection, indeed before his first pronouncement of his death and resurrection (v. 21), Jesus founds the church that is to come (that is, the church in which Matthew's readers dwell).

Matthew presents Jesus as blessing Simon as the rock (*petra*) upon which the church will be built (v. 18). Note Matthew does not present Jesus as giving Simon the name Rock (*petros*), but as taking his nickname (see 4:18; 10:10 for Simon already being called Rock) and using it metaphorically in this ecclesiological context. Note, however, that while the focus seems to be on Peter, Jesus is really the primary actor in the sentence (in the same vein that Peter does not profess Jesus as the messiah out of human intellectual ability, but only because God has actively revealed who Jesus is to the disciples, v. 17). Peter is the stone foundation of the church, but Jesus does the building. And what Jesus builds, he calls "*my* church." As his church, based in his identity as the Son of the *living* God, it will be even more powerful than the gates of the realm of the dead. In other words, Matthew claims it will endure forever.

This pronouncement is a mixture of metaphors that would drive English professors mad. Peter is in one breath the stone upon which the church is being built and in the next Jesus gives him the keys to the reign of heaven (v. 19). This second metaphor, and the language that follows, unpacks the first one. In other words, all of this language describes Peter's authority in the church. Before we analyze the specific nature of the authority given here, we need to note the long ecclesial debate concerning who is given this authority. Is it given specially to Peter (as the chief apostle) or is it given to the church (interpreting Peter here in his representative role in the Gospel)? The best answer is likely a both/and approach to the issue instead of taking a strong either/or stance. The Gospels, Acts and even Paul clearly identify Peter as a key figure for the early church. This is why he serves as a literary representative of the other disciples and of the church in the Gospels. Matthew presents Jesus as giving Peter authority here that he then gives to the church as a whole in the Community Discourse (18:18). Matthew likes to intimate and theologically legitimate the progression that leads to the life and work of the church. We have noted this repeatedly in reference to the mission beginning with the lost sheep of the house of Israel only (10:5-6; 15:24) and being extend to "the nations" after the resurrection (28:19). Similarly here, Jesus possesses authority (7:29; 8:9; 9:6, 8), passes his authority on to the disciples (10:1) and especially to Peter (16:18-19) and then onto the church (18:18).

But what is the nature of the authority implied in the gift of the keys to the reign of heaven and binding and loosing (v. 19)? In the Mission Discourse, Jesus gives the apostles authority over demons and illnesses (10:1) as well as the authority to proclaim the advent of the reign of heaven (10:7). The authority given here supplements that already given, instead of repeating it. Jesus builds his church and gives Peter the keys to the reign of God. The connection of a building and keys pictures Jesus as the master and Peter as his manager of the house. This metaphor has funded the image of Peter standing at the pearly gate controlling who does and does not get in. Clearly, this passage is not about the church as the funnel for who gets into the afterlife. Instead the language here stands in contrast to 23:13, where Jesus condemns the scribes and Pharisees for locking people out of the reign of heaven. The nature of the authority given here, then, is in relation to the interpretation of the *torah*.

Scholars have debated what is meant by binding and loosing but most contemporary interpreters make much of the fact that these terms were used in reference to halakic decisions made by rabbis concerning what was forbidden and permitted. Thus Peter (and in 18:18, the church) is given the authority to interpret the commandments of God. Remember that the Ethical Discourse ends with Jesus' exhortation to follow his teaching, saying that the one who hears and follows Jesus' ethical teaching is like one who builds his house on rock (7:24-25). It is hard to miss the connection here with Simon Rock as the foundation of the church being given authority to interpret *torah* in light of the hermeneutic and case studies Jesus offered in the Sermon on the Mount in 5:17-48. Matthew here continues building his case that the church is a legitimate heir of Israel's faith and traditions in its interpretation of the law and prophets over against that of the synagogue. Jesus gave the example of how to interpret God's will and then passed on the authority to continue interpreting it in that manner—first to Peter and then to the church as a body.

Given the extension of this authority to the church in 18:18, preachers are not out of line in asking their congregation (as a community) to identify with Simon Rock in this lection. While he is unique here, Matthew also uses him as our representative. We the church are to know and confess Jesus over against the world's confusion about him. He is not just a prophet; he is the Christ, the Son of the living God. And on the basis of that christological knowledge, we are to be/become a certain kind of community, living out the ethical principles Jesus has given. In other words, we are to strive to align the character of our community with the character of Jesus Christ. We are, after all, Christ's church, not a community/building of our own making. At best we are managers who hold on to Christ's keys that we might open the doors of God's reign to all who desire something other than living under the reign of Caesar.

LECTION: THE FIRST PASSION PREDICTION
16:21-28; PROPER 17

Although appropriately designated as a separate lection, 16:21-28 is really part of a dialogue that begins in v. 13. Some scholars have seen a major break in Matthew's narrative structure occurring at v. 21 with the phrase "From that time on . . ." because it is also used at 4:17. (See the Introduction for a more in-depth discussion of Matthew's structure.) These arguments, however, are not convincing and ignore the obvious connection in which the phrase designates what immediately follows as the result of what has immediately preceded. So Jesus foretells his death and resurrection and describes the nature of discipleship related to this event specifically as a result of the dialogue in which Simon Rock confesses Jesus as the Christ, the Son of the living God and Jesus blesses Peter as part of his declaration founding the church. Preachers focusing on this text, therefore, should review the commentary above on 16:13-20.

Consider how the previous lection ended in v. 20—Jesus orders his disciples to tell no one that he was the Messiah. In Mark 8:30, this silencing is part of the literary device of the "messianic secret" in which the narrator portrays the disciples (and all other humans) as unable to fully understand Jesus' identity as the Son of God until the crucifixion (see 15:39). Here, however, Jesus' beatitude offered to Peter shows that Matthew wants the reader to know that Peter did understand. Instead of silencing them due to their misunderstanding, Matthew's Jesus orders the disciples to keep quiet in order to protect their insider knowledge of his true identity until after the resurrection and the Great Commission (see 17:9; 28:18-20). In vv. 21ff, then, Jesus continues the dialogue by offering them *further* insider instruction, now concerning his death and resurrection and how this shapes their role as disciples. Confirming this reading of the text as focused on insider-dialogue is the fact that Matthew omits the reference to the crowd as being present in Mark 8:34.

Matthew 16:13-28 as a whole, then, brings together christology, soteriology, ecclesiology, eschatology and discipleship in a way not found anywhere else in the Gospel. Preachers will need to remind their congregations of this lection's role in the broader passage in order to help them hear how this passion prediction functions as part of Matthew's story. In fact, if congregations identified with Peter in a sermon on 16:13-19, in which he received a blessing from Jesus, they will be primed to identify with him here where he is rebuked by Jesus even to the point of being called Satan.

It may also be helpful to remind congregations reading this passage in late August or early September of the fact of having read major portions of Matthew's passion and Easter narratives months ago during Holy Week. It is an odd situation to be reading a section that has as one of its main purposes preparing the readers for the narrative climax when that material has already been read as part of the liturgical climax of the church year. But in truth this scenario is not that different than the experience of the original readers/hearers of Matthew's Gospel. They already knew of Jesus' death and resurrection, so hearing this first passion prediction (v. 21) gave them no new data. What was new for them was how Matthew would tell that story, so hearing this passion prediction (and the others) set them up to hear Matthew's particular interpretation of Jesus' suffering, death and resurrection.

This is the first time in the narrative that Jesus mentions his death and resurrection explicitly, but he has referred to them before (12:40). Moreover, Matthew includes all three of Mark's predictions (Mk 8:31/Mt 16:21; Mk 9:30-32/Mt 17:22-23; Mk 10:32-34/Mt 20:17-19; see also Mk 9:12/Mt 17:11-12) and adds one other (26:1-2). A reader cannot miss where Jesus' story is ultimately headed. Moreover, a Greek reader would recognize a theological hint about the inevitability of that ending in the word *dei* (translated simply as "must" by the NRSV: "Jesus began to show that he *must* go to Jerusalem"). While *dei* can mean "must" or "should," it often carries the weight of "it is necessary." So the ending Jesus foretells here is the necessary ending to his life and ministry—one who proclaims the reign of God in word and deed will be opposed by authorities who profit from the status quo but will also be redeemed by God. Implied in this use of *dei* is that God is in control of what will happen. (It is paradoxical that the living God has a son who must *die*.) This fits with Matthew's theology but not to the point of removing human agency. Both the authorities and Jesus choose the paths they take. So in this short foretelling of what is to come, Matthew brings together divine providence and human culpability.

Even though the narrator and reader know the passion is necessary, Peter is presented as desiring that it were not so (v. 22). The one just affirmed as the Rock of the church is presented as crumbling (as earlier Rock was presented as sinking, 14:30). Some sympathy for Peter's reaction is called for. Jesus has just said the gates of the realm of death will not prevail against the church (v. 18), and then in the next breath says he is going to die. Peter's response can be seen, at least in part, as a confused, literalizing of Jesus' words about the impotence of death (which sets up the coming metaphorical/eschatological interpretation of life prevailing over death in vv. 24-28). Nevertheless, we must beware of assigning intent or emotions to Peter not made clear in the text. In Mark, Peter's rebuke of Jesus is presented as being due to his misunderstanding of who Jesus fully is (8:32). But since Matthew presents Peter as clearly understanding who Jesus is, his motivation is not as clear here. Conjecture in the pulpit about Peter speaking out of love, fear, disappointment, doubt or concern takes away from what Matthew does emphasize. Jesus tells us not Peter's motivation for speaking as he did, but the reason for it: Peter has his mind on human things instead of the things of God. This accusation is meant as a contrast to earlier where Jesus blessed Peter saying that flesh and blood (human things) did not reveal Jesus' identity to Peter but God did. Peter looks real here. As he is representative of the church in his confession, he is representative here when he missteps.

Peter's rebuke of Jesus serves as the set up for Jesus' pronouncement (vv. 23-28). The pronouncement begins by addressing Peter directly (v. 23) and then expands to address all of the disciples (vv. 24-28). In the address to Peter, Matthew gives us a stronger indication of how Jesus experiences Peter's language. By calling Peter Satan with the rebuke language, it sounds very similar to end of the temptation scene where Jesus sends Satan away, saying

"Away with you, Satan!" (4:10; not found in Mark). He further calls Peter a stumbling block (Greek, *skandalon*). Everywhere in Matthew this term is used, it refers to a cause for someone to sin (5:29,30; 11:6; 13:21, 41; 17:27; 18:6-9; 24:10; 26:31, 33). So Jesus experiences Peter's desire that he not suffer as a test or a temptation, and rejects it.

Moreover, Jesus then turns his necessary fate back on the disciples. Remember in the Mission Discourse, when speaking about coming persecution of those sent out, Jesus told the disciples not to expect better treatment than their teacher received. If he was accused of casting out by Beelzebul, so would they be (10:24-25). Here, then, in vv. 24-28, Jesus extends that logic: if the Christ, the Son of the living God is willing to die, so must the disciples be willing to lose their life. Self-denial and suffering are characteristic of discipleship defined by Christ. As in the previous lection where the character of the church is determined by the character of Jesus, here the fate of disciples is determined by the fate of Jesus (cf. 10:38-39).

It is paradoxical to claim that losing one's life is the way to gain life (vv. 25-26). A careful reading of this pronouncement makes clear that Matthew understands this claim metaphorically. In other words, Jesus is *not* talking about life after death, in some literal sense of getting into heaven. He is talking eschatologically, which we have argued is experiential talk for Matthew. Notice the claim Matthew presents Jesus as making in vv. 27-28. On first reading, the shift to talking about the *parousia*—the son of the human coming in glory—seems to come out of nowhere. Narratively speaking, however, it is the natural extension of the salvation-history plot laid out in 16:13-28: (1) Jesus is the Christ, the Son of the living God; (2) Jesus must suffer and die; (3) Jesus will be raised from the dead; and (4) the son of the human will return. More importantly, though, it explains what is meant by gaining one's life in the face of losing it, because in v. 28 Jesus says that some of the disciples standing there (at that moment in Jesus' presence) would not die before witnessing the *parousia*. Matthew, writing some fifty years after Jesus' crucifixion, knew this statement adapted from Mark 9:1 was not literally true but kept it in his Gospel anyway. Matthew must have assumed the saying was true in a different way or he would have omitted it. This is the already-not yet of Christian existence. To not live under the power of death but to live authentically and fully as a disciple of Christ even in the face of death is to know Christ in the full glory of the reign of heaven, even while Caesar is still on his throne in Rome and lesser religio-political power mongers thrive in the shadow of that throne.

But we do not live this way perfectly because we, like Peter, turn our minds toward human things too often. Peter himself embodies the already/not yet in first confessing Jesus to be the Son of God (already) and then resisting what that claim implies (not yet). In Peter and the disciples in this scene, Matthew offers preachers the opportunity to explore who we are (and can be) as faithful but faltering disciples shaped by the character of the fully faithful and unfaltering Jesus Christ. But preachers must avoid the trap of equating a metaphorical reading of the language of losing and gaining one's life with making the demands of discipleship easier. Matthew clearly assumes death (including death at the hands of persecutors) is literal for Christians. To be a Christian living toward the reign of heaven in and over against the reign of Caesar is both the reward and the challenge.

LECTION: THE TRANSFIGURATION OF JESUS
17:1–9; TRANSFIGURATION

The final lection drawn from 13:54—17:27 is the only one not part of the semi-continuous series of readings used in Propers 13–17 during Ordinary Time after Pentecost. Transfiguration Sunday in most Protestant traditions falls on the last Sunday after Epiphany. The heavenly voice that here at the end of this season proclaims Jesus as God's Son echoes back to the voice that was heard doing the same in 3:17 on Baptism of the Lord, the First Sunday after Epiphany. Even though the RCL follows the pattern of semi-continuous readings fit for Ordinary Time on the Sundays in-between these two occasions, the bookend readings from Matthew give the period a thematic focus on God's revelation in and of Christ.

Our familiarity with this story should not keep us from recognizing how odd it is among the Gospel traditions. The appearance of the two immensely important figures from the distant past of the Hebrew Bible take the reader into a whole different sort of genre and feel compared to anything else in Matthew, including the resurrection. The presence of Moses and Elijah, along with the cloudy mountaintop setting, the dialogue between Jesus and the disciples, and the heavenly voice all point to a very complex intertextual background to this story. There are numerous echoes with the Hebrew Bible woven together into this story:

- Mountains play a key symbolic role for designating places of divine revelation (Ps 74:2). The story of the exodus and wandering in the wilderness is especially full of mountain experiences. Both Moses (for example, Exod 3 & 24) and Elijah (1 Kings 19) have epiphanic

experiences on mountains. And one of Moses' experiences includes coming down with his face shining (Exodus 34).
- Moses and Elijah can be seen to represent the law and the prophets or both can be seen as prophets.
- Throughout Matthew Jesus is presented in the typology of Moses and John the Baptist is said to be Elijah. So Elijah is forerunner of the Messiah and Moses is the messianic prototype.
- Both Moses and Elijah were claimed not to have died. Elijah in 2 Kings 2:11 ascends in a whirlwind into the heavens. Moses' death on a mountaintop (Nebo) overlooking the promised land, on the other hand, is reported in Deut 34. But later midrashic tradition re-tells this story in terms, for instance, of a cloud surrounding Moses followed by his sudden disappearance.
- The heavenly voice (here and in 3:17) resembles God's decree in Ps 2:7 declaring the king/anointed one as God's son.
- Peter's suggestion about building three tents can be seen as echoing the Feast of Tabernacles which begins on the sixth day after the Day of Atonement (Lev 23:27, 34).

No single one of these references supplies the background for the story of the transfiguration. The matrix of echoes, instead, fills the story with mythological and theological weight signaling to the reader the importance of the scene. Indeed, Matthew gives us a clue that readers were to interpret this story on a different level than others. As Jesus leads the disciples down the mountain after the epiphany, he orders them to tell no one about "the vision" (Greek, *orama*; not found in Mark 9:9; Matthew's version of the story is a redaction of Mark 9:2-10). Thus the images weave together to create an apocalyptic vision that offers an impressive christological picture: Jesus is prophet and lawgiver, messiah and Son of God, who reveals God's glory and power and should be attended to closely.

This christological epiphany on the mount of transfiguration stands at the center of Matthew's narrative horizons. The revelation accords with the biblical past as seen in the list of intertextual echoes above. It leans forward toward the crucifixion and resurrection (as seen in the fact that this passage follows on the heels of Jesus' first passion prediction, 16:21ff). And it is a narrative exploration of Jesus' claim that ended the previous chapter in which he said some of the disciples standing with him would not taste death before seeing the son of the human coming in his reign (16:28). To preach this text, then, is to preach a grand christology.

The scene opens with Jesus leading the disciples up the mountain. Mountains play an important role in Matthew's narrative (4:8; 5:1; 8:1; 14:23;

15:29; 17:20; 18:12; 21:21; 24:16; 28:16). Perhaps the most relevant parallel (or better, contrast) for this ascent up the mountain is Jesus' experience on the mountain with Satan during the third and climactic temptation. If Jesus would only worship Satan, Satan would give him reign over all the world (4:8-11). Jesus rejected Satan and yet stands here on a different mountain with God claiming him as God's Son, using enthronement language from the Psalter.

Once on the mountain, Jesus' appearance becomes a dazzling white (similar to the description of the angel at the resurrection in 28:3; note the reference to the resurrection in 17:9). It is important to recognize what does and does not happen in v. 2 when Jesus' clothes and face are transfigured (Greek, *metamorphoō*). It is Jesus' appearance that is changed, not Jesus himself. In other words, for Matthew the changed appearance reveals who he really is, who he has been all along; it does not transform him into someone new. The voice does not claim Jesus as God's Son, it reveals (reminds) the disciples and the readers of the identity of which they should already be aware.

In v. 3, Moses and Elijah appear and converse with Jesus. Matthew does not tell us what they discuss, and conjecture about such matters leads the preacher away from Matthew's intended focus (contrast Luke 9:31). Their very presence, with all of the symbolic import the characters hold, points to the unimaginable importance of Jesus as the culmination of God's salvific, providential care for Israel. Elijah, as the forerunner of the Messiah, confirms that Jesus is the Christ. Moses, as the lawgiver, confirms Jesus' (and the church's) authority and hermeneutic for interpreting the *torah*. Moses and Elijah spoke with God on mountaintops, but God did not call them God's sons. The scene presents continuity with Israel's past while making clear that, nevertheless, something radically new is occurring in Jesus.

Peter responds to the vision by volunteering to build three tents for the three (this includes Jesus) heavenly beings (v. 4). Marks explains that Peter does not know what to say and speaks out of fear (Mark 9:9), but Matthew omits this explanation. Instead, by having Jesus call this event a "vision" (*orama*) after the fact, Matthew indicates that Peter did not understand the epiphany in categories of apocalyptic visions while he was experiencing it. The fact that Jesus does not respond to Peter and instead the voice overshadows what he has said, warns readers against literalizing the scene. It provides meaning the way visions do in scripture, not the way historical events do.

The disciples, upon hearing the voice, fall on their faces out of exceeding fear (v. 6-8). And with their faces buried the visual and auditory epiphany draws to a close without their knowing it. Jesus (returned to his normal visage) tells them, "Have no fear." This saying need not be read as rebuke that they should not have been afraid. Whereas in Mark, fear is presented as the opposite of faith, for Matthew this is a more appropriate response to the direct presence of God than was the suggestion to build dwellings for the heavenly beings. The fact that Matthew adds this closing moment to Mark's version so that Jesus touches the disciples and tells them to arise (much as he does in healing stories) indicates that he offers them comfort. "Have no fear," then, can be read as there is *no longer* reason to be afraid.

Preachers often ask congregations to identify with the disciples and particularly Peter when this story is brought into the pulpit. Their witness and response to the epiphany makes this a logical and appropriate location from which the congregation can listen to the story. But we must be careful not to focus on the disciples' experience as if that is the climax of the story. The story is not about them. Jesus is not transfigured for their benefit; he is simply transfigured. Moses and Elijah do not talk to the disciples but to Jesus. Even when the heavenly voice finally addresses the disciples, it speaks to them about Jesus, putting a bright, white exclamation point on Peter's confession of Jesus as the Christ, the Son of the living God (16:16). So while there are strong experiential and epistemological elements of this passage, the experience is one of the new revelation of Jesus as God's Son. In other words, the divine voice interprets their experience christologically, and this is what the preacher should do as well.

CAPERNAUM-BASED MINISTRY: COMMUNITY DISCOURSE (18:1-35)

INTRODUCTION

Following the longest narrative section in the Gospel (13:54—17:27), Matthew now slows down again and turns to the fourth and shortest of Jesus' discourses. The discourse flows directly out of the content of that narrative section. While Matthew primarily reinforced theological and plot developments started earlier in the story in that narrative section, one element was significantly new: in 16:18-19 Jesus explicitly founded the church. (Recall Jesus' anachronistic use of the term *ekklesia* there.) The Community Discourse (which uses the term *ekklesia* twice in v. 17) comes at this point in the narrative because with the church founded, Jesus is now in a place to explicitly talk about aspects of its behavior.

Moreover, the Community Discourse concludes the longer division of Matthew's narrative dealing with Jesus' Galilean ministry based in Capernaum (4:12—18:35). This portion of the story begins with Jesus' entry into ministry and call of the disciples following the arrest of John the Baptist. It includes four out of five of Jesus' discourses (the Ethical, Mission, Parables and Community Discourses). It presents Jesus healing the sick, exorcising demons, feeding the crowds, walking on water, and foretelling his passion and resurrection. In the last narrative scene of this section just before the Community Discourse—the very last time Jesus returns to Capernaum—Matthew introduces the Jerusalem temple into the narrative for the first time (17:24-27). Immediately after the discourse in 19:1, Jesus will leave Galilee and head to Judea.

Thus, although this is the shortest of the discourses, it represents Jesus' final word in Galilee (that is, until after the resurrection, see 28:16-20). In 16:18-19, Jesus builds his church on Simon Rock, and gives Peter authority to bind and loose. The Capernaum section now ends with instructions for the church, dispersing the authority to bind and loose in relation to reconciliation and expulsion to the community as a whole. This placement of the discourse indicates that the result of Jesus' ministry and conflict with religious authorities (who represent the synagogue in Matthew's day) is the church. In other words, theologically speaking, for Matthew, Jesus' ministry culminates in the life of the church. As the Mission Discourse in chapter 10 had implicitly dealt with the church in its relation to the world, here Matthew explicitly deals with the internal life of the church as a community, in which sin occurs and reconciliation is sought.

Matthew has composed this discourse using materials taken from several sources in a way that shows his skill as an author and theological thinker. The opening of the discourse (vv. 1-9) comes from Mark 9:33-50, which in Mark's storyline follows on the heels of the second passion prediction (Mark 9:31-32). There the disciples' argument is about who is the greatest—in other words, given that Jesus is going to die, they are debating who is next in line to be in charge. But Matthew has broken the question of greatest apart from that context, reframed it to be about greatness *in the reign of heaven*, and used it to serve as the set up for a discourse concerning the church and the way it should deal with sin. (Even though this beginning is not as formal as that found in the previous three discourses, the formulaic ending—"When Jesus finished saying these things," 19:1— makes it clear Matthew wants this material to be interpreted in the same vein as the other discourses, that is, as central and exemplary teachings of Jesus.)

In addition to changing the context in which the opening scene occurs, Matthew omits a scene from the middle of the Markan material:

	Mark	Matthew
Question about Greatness	9:33–37	18:1–5
Strange Exorcist	9:38–41	
Warnings against being Stumbling Blocks	9:42–50	18:6–9

The result of this omission is that Matthew forges together the revision of the scene in which Jesus uses a child as an example to address the disciples' concern about who is the greatest (8:1-5) and the logion warning against placing stumbling blocks (that is, tempting or causing someone to sin) before the "little ones" (9:6-9). In other words, the use of a child as an example gives way to the metaphorical use of "little ones" to describe members of the church—that they are members of the community is made clear by the qualifier, "little ones *who believe in me*, (v. 6.) Matthew then adds to this discussion the parable of the lost sheep (vv. 10-14) from "Q" (see the parallel in Luke 15:3-7) to show God's extravagant concern for the little ones.

Building on the issue of sin, Matthew then expands a saying from "Q" (see Luke 17:3-4) that deals with forgiveness by breaking the logion into the opening and closing of the paragraph and inserting material that specifically addresses how the Matthean church is to handle the situation when one member of the community sins against another member:

	Luke	Matthew
"If your brother sins against you…"	17:3	18:15
Steps for Reconciliation		18:16-20
Forgive seven/ seventy-seven times	17:4	18:21-22

To this material, then, Matthew adds a parable that is unique to the First Gospel (vv. 23-35) that highlights the extravagance of God's forgiveness and the forgiveness expected of those in the church.

The resulting structure of the Community Discourse, therefore, is a two-part discourse. Each of the two parts includes a question from disciples (vv. 1 and 21). Each is made up of three pieces (vv. 1-5, 6-9, 10-14 and vv. 15-20, 21-22, 23-35). And each ends and climaxes with a parable (vv. 12-14, 23-35).

As important as this structural outline is, so also is the glue holding the individual pieces of the discourse together. The overarching theme is clearly sin and reconciliation within the church. But within the various movements of the discourse, repetition of different keywords holds and connects the section together. *Paidion* ("child" or "children") is used 4 times in the opening paragraph (vv. 2, 3, 4, 5). Although preachers have long sentimentalized this reference to children as indicating a need for childlike faith or innocence, in the first century children were at the bottom of culture's ladder, with no legal rights or social status. Relinquishing status is what Jesus lifts up as exemplary for those wanting to be greatest in God's reign.

Paidion, then, is replaced with *mikros* ("little one," vv. 6, 10, 14). Matthew does not make clear to whom he is referring with this term, likely because its reference was clear to his original readers (cf. similar terms in 10:42 and 25:40, 45). What we can say with certainty is that he has in mind members of the church who are in some way vulnerable, especially vulnerable to being led astray into sin.

Thus another key word that begins being used at this point is *skandalon* (vv. 6, 7 [three times], 8, 9). *Skandalon* is literally a snare or something that makes one stumble. Matthew uses it primarily to indicate making one stumble into sin (cf. 5:29, 30; 13:21, 41 16:23; 17:27; 24:10; 26:31, 33 [twice]). In the parable of the lost sheep, the word equivalent to stumbling into sin is *planaō*, "wander astray" (vv. 12 [twice], 13; for the similar use of this term in the final discourse, see 24:4, 5, 11, 24).

In the second half of the discourse, the metaphorical term "little ones" gives way to the broader metaphor for community members: "brother" (vv. 15 [twice], 21, 35). [The NRSV poorly translates *adelphos* (which is literally "brother") in this context as "member of the church." The reason for this choice is because the New Testament writers clearly used the masculine term *adelphos* to refer to both male and female members of the Christian community. A better inclusive translation would be "brothers and sisters." (On the importance Matthew places on the use of familial language for the community of Jesus' disciples, see the comments on 12:46-50.] While Jesus starts using *adelphos* for individual members of the church, he is also presented as using *ekklesia* ("church") for the community as a whole (v. 17 [twice]).

As more technical language for the community and its members begins being used in the second half of the discourse, so also Matthew explicitly names "sin" here (*hamartanō*, vv. 15, 21) instead of "stumbling block" or "wandering." But the focus is less on the sin and more on dealing with the sin. Thus "forgive" (*aphiēmi*, vv. 21, 27, 32, 35) becomes the final key word gluing the discourse together.

What our analysis of structure and vocabulary shows, is that Matthew has constructed this discourse to present Jesus' last word in Galilee as being concerned with the (future) church being both an ethical community in which some should not cause others to sin (in the first half of the discourse) and a reconciling community in which one forgives another when sinned against (in the second half). The discourse is, therefore, thoroughly ecclesiological from beginning to end.

The lectionary only draws on the second half of the discourse. This is due to the RCL's harmonizing tendency to reduce overlapping readings from the Synoptics. Consider the following:

Matthew	Mark	Luke
18:1-5	9:33-37 (9:30-37 is read in Proper 20, Year B)	9:46-48
18:6-9	Mark 9:42-50 (9:38-50 is read in Proper 21, Year B)	17:1-2
18:10-14		15:3-7 (15:1-10 is read in Proper 19, Year C)
18:15-20 (Proper 18, Year A)		Luke 17:3-4
18:21-35 (Proper 19, Year A)		

The lectionary choices, therefore, do not do justice to the structural development of the Community Discourse, but they do focus our attention on the material that is unique to Matthew.

PASSAGES OMITTED FROM THE LECTIONARY

The RCL omits readings from the first half of the Community Discourse. The section opens (18:1-5) with a discussion of who is the greatest in the reign of heaven. Jesus uses a child as a model in this story, setting up a discussion avoiding placing stumbling blocks before "little ones" in the material that follows (vv. 6-14).

To Be Greatest Become Humble Like Children (18:1-5):
Omitted from Lectionary

The opening paragraph of the Community Discourse is a pronouncement story. The disciples ask Jesus a question (v. 1) and Jesus answers them (vv. 2-5). But this answer is not the end of Jesus' pronouncement. He simply keeps talking, taking his use of a child as an example to launch into a discourse about stumbling blocks placed before "little ones" (vv. 6ff). So while Matthew valued this passage enough to use it as the introduction to the Community Discourse, it is in some ways tangential to the development of the rest of the Discourse.

In Mark's version of this story (Mark 9:33-37), Jesus has just foretold his coming death for the second time (Mark 9:30-32). The disciples then begin arguing among themselves about who is the greatest (among the members of the group). The implication is that they are arguing about who is second-in-command, as it were, and thus about who will take control of the movement after Jesus is gone. Matthew, however, has omitted all of this negative tone from the story. He has separated it from the second passion prediction (17:22-23) and has presented the disciples as coming to Jesus with a question. They are not arguing about which one of them is the greatest disciple but are asking a theological question concerning how to become great in the reign of heaven (v. 1).

Jesus offers a child as the answer: whoever becomes humble like a child is greatest (v. 4). One way to preach this text is to offer a new hearing of its message over against the way it has traditionally been preached. The image of the humble child is often sentimentalized in art and pulpits. But the Greek word *tapeinoō*, which New Testament translators usually render as "humble," can mean "make low." In this sense, the term indicates a low stature instead of a posture of humility (compare 23:11-12). One who is low is insignificant, impotent, and poor. Jesus, then, is not talking about one's attitude but about one's place in the world. In the patriarchal society of the ancient Mediterranean world, children were at the bottom of the cultural ladder, with no legal rights, social stature or economic means. To become low voluntarily, then is the point of the pronouncement. Those who want to become great in the reign of heaven must eschew the standards of greatness lifted up in the reign of Caesar (compare 19:30; 20:16, 25-28). To preach the call to become low in this manner is radically different than the usual homiletical invitations to become childlike in our faith.

STUMBLING BLOCKS FOR THE LITTLE ONES (18:6-10):
OMITTED FROM LECTIONARY

The opening of this short passage (vv. 6-7) raises many questions for the modern preacher. Who are the "little ones": all of those in the church; a certain group within the church such as those new to or weak in faith; or those who have "become low" in the sense of the previous passage (v. 4)? Who are those who cause the little ones to stumble: a specific group such as false prophets or potentially anyone in the community? And what constitutes "stumbling" and "causing someone to stumble"?

But even with these ambiguities, the point of vv. 6-7 is clear enough. It is a warning for the church. Within the church, one person or group should never be the reason another person or group sins. To reflect on this in light of contemporary congregational dynamics involving conflict offers the preacher much soil to plow.

On first glance, vv. 8-9 seem to shift perspective from causing others to sin to dealing with causes of one's own sin. Matthew's readers will remember this saying from 5:29-30. In that earlier context, the saying was used as part of the antithesis dealing with adultery and lust (5:27-30). The very different context in the Community Discourse should lead us to understand the parallel saying as functioning differently here. Likely in relation to warning about stumbling blocks for the little ones, this saying is to be read as removing from the community those who become such stumbling blocks. While Matthew wants all invited into the reign of heaven (contrast 16:18-19 with 23:13), the church cannot do this with destructive forces in its midst. Matthew's expectations of the church as an ethical and holy community are higher than modern expectations for behavior in the church. To protect the community and its most vulnerable members, at times we must be willing to exclude from membership and participation those who use the church for their own unhealthy and sinful ends. This passage, then, sets up the discussion of disciplinary procedure in vv. 15-20.

Still it should be noted that this call to remove from the community causes of sin (meaning people who cause others to sin) is not the last word of the Community Discourse. The last word deals with God's extravagant forgiveness and our call to forgive in like manner (vv. 21-35). Held in tension in the discourse then is avoidance of including everyone regardless of consequences on the one hand and cheap grace on the other. Matthew calls the church to remove sin in order to avoid sin, but his highest values here are reconciliation and forgiveness.

Parable of the Lost Sheep (18:12-14): Omitted from Lectionary

Matthew ends each half of the Community Discourse with a parable that offers a theological rationale for the community ethic being proposed in the section preceding it (see vv. 23-35). In the material before this parable, Jesus has warned against placing "stumbling blocks" before "little ones" that cause them to sin and has said that such causes (that is, people who cause such things) need to be removed from the community of faith (vv. 6-9). The parable of the shepherd leaving the flock of ninety-nine to recover the single lost sheep, then, names God's concern for the vulnerable one as a model for the same concern that should be held by the church as a community (contrast this with Luke's use of the parable in the triad of parables about recovering the lost as a response to religious leaders who scorned his practice of associating with tax collectors and sinners, Luke 15).

A flock of sheep as a metaphor for the people of God would have been familiar to Matthew's original readers (for example, Ps 23:1; 100:3; Is 40:10; Jer 31:10; Ezek 34). But the situation in the parable goes against common sense. Shepherds were business people. They would not leave a large flock on a mountain unattended and at risk to go in search of one lost sheep. They might return with one and have lost the ninety-nine. But this odd detail (see the commentary on chapter 13 for such twists as common to parables) highlights the level of concern God has for the "little ones."

While the parable highlights the extravagance of divine care for the vulnerable, preachers need to remember that the context in which Matthew uses this parable is thoroughly ecclesiological. The closing verse (v. 14) clearly connects the parable back to the issue from the previous section (vv. 6-9), so the parable is not about individualistic salvation. Matthew wants to instill in his church the same kind of extravagant, risky care for the "little ones" God has. A contemporary preacher should use this text as an opportunity to instill the same concern in today's church.

Lections

The RCL chooses two lections from the Community Discourse that come from the second half of the sermon, with its emphasis on dealing with sin and reconciliation in the church. The two lections serve as tensive counterpoints if preached on two consecutive weeks. The first focuses on an approach for calling to accountability one who has sinned against another in the community of faith. The second, then, focuses on the call to forgive extravagantly within the community as God does. Preachers will do well to study these two lections in tandem and work on the sermons on them together.

LECTION: OVERCOMING SIN IN THE CHURCH
18:15-20; PROPER 18

This passage is at times compared to a church order or discipline, but the comparison is imprecise. Matthew presents Jesus as neither giving instructions for church hierarchy nor prescribing a system of church rule. Matthew uses this passage specifically to advance the discussion begun in the first half of the discourse concerning sin within the community of faith. In the first half of the discourse (vv. 1-14), the point of view relates to those who are tempted or caused to sin. Now in the second half, the point of view shifts to that of the ones within the community against whom a sin is committed. How are they to respond to the one who has sinned against them?

This passage answers the question in terms of a procedure laid out to try to bring about reconciliation between the sinner and the one who was wronged. The structure of the passage is such that the procedure is actually laid out in vv. 15-17 and the theological basis for the procedure is given in vv. 18-20. One of the problems for preachers is that vv. 18, 19, and 20 individually have been used as common proof texts for theological claims that have little to do with Matthew's use of them in this context. Congregations will be well served by sermons that offer a new hearing of these well-known lines.

The procedure offered in vv. 15-17 is unique to Matthew. Jesus' instructions for the disciples explain what is to be done in the church when one brother or sister in the community sins against another. The three steps Jesus describes are actually quite simple and straightforward. The person who has been offended first approaches the offender in private (v. 16). The stated intent is to "gain" your brother or sister. The implication of this language is that the offense has resulted in the loss of the person as a sibling in the faith, that is, the familial nature of the relationship of those in the church has been broken. Thus reconciliation and the repair of the community of faith is the desired outcome. It is only if the offender will not "listen," that is, repent and be reconciled, that one moves to the second stage.

The second stage (v. 17) simply involves bringing one or two others (that is, brothers or sisters) into the conversation to confront the offender and serve as witnesses. The goal of reconciliation is not restated in the description of this step, not because it is no longer the goal, but because the intent is assumed from the first step on. Instead, all that needs to be named is the possibility that the offender still not "listen" to the one offended and the witness(es).

If it does happen that the sinner will not listen, a third stage is implemented in which the situation is reported to the entire *ekklesia* (v. 18, clearly meaning the local community of faith, at this point; perhaps in contrast to the broader use of *ekklesia* in 16:18). Again, the implied purpose is to effect reconciliation for the two in conflict and to repair the damage done to the community. But if the offender will still not "listen" even when the community speaks as a whole, then expulsion from the community is the only option left. This is not meant as punishment so much at it is a recognition that the deeply desired reconciliation between the two persons involved cannot be reached, and the only way the community can be repaired as a family unit is to remove the offender (cf. vv. 6-7 earlier in the discourse).

Next comes in vv. 18-20 the theological basis for the authority of the church asserted in v. 17. The three lines that make up this second half of the lection are closely related in ways often ignored in the pulpit. The opening line (v. 18) echoes back to 16:18 where Jesus grants Peter the authority to bind and loose. Indeed, the entire rationale offered in vv. 18-20 is derivative of Jesus' blessing given to Peter. (See the commentary on 16:13-20 above.) There Jesus gives Peter the keys to the reign of heaven and the authority to bind and loose (which we argued refers to interpretation of *torah*—that is, determining what interpretations are binding for the church and what is not—in order to open the reign of God to all who would accept the invitation to enter). Here that authority is extended to the church as a whole and is applied specifically to the issue of setting the appropriate boundaries of the community in terms of inclusion and exclusion when it comes to issues of sin and reconciliation.

The second line (v. 19) simply repeats in a different way what was just said in v. 18. The signal that this line is a reassertion as opposed to stating something new can be seen in the parallel opening of the two lines. V. 18 opens with "Truly I tell you," and v. 19 opens with "*Again* [truly] I tell you." Moreover, the logic of both verses is dependent on the connection between what happens "on earth" and what God does "in heaven." Thus the reassertion in v. 19 is clarifying who the "you" is in v. 18 when Jesus says, "Whatever *you* bind on earth… whatever *you* loose in heaven…" Jesus is speaking in the second person plural and is referring to the church as mentioned in v. 17. But it is not simply the church; it is the church in agreement about dealing with a sinner who is offered the opportunity to repent in order to be reconciled to a brother or sister in the community.

In other words, v. 19 is not simply about prayer in general as people often misunderstand it to be. If context did not make this clear, experience would certainly raise questions about whether the statement could be true. How often do people (plural) pray to God in agreement and God does not answer the prayer as it has been asked! Moreover, theologically speaking, what kind of a God would we be picturing if this God can simply be persuaded by having more people join together in praying about something? To preach this verse as it is often heard by congregations is pastorally irresponsible. It sets up hearers either to have a skewed view of the all-loving, omnipotent, omniscient God; lose trust in God; or see themselves as unworthy since God did not answer their prayers. Whatever theology we hold, it is illegitimate to assume God's ways are based on our majority opinion. The verse, instead, is figurative language affirming that God honors the church's authority (indeed the church's vocation) to attend to the health and holiness of the community.

Verse 20, then, is not about Christ being present in small gatherings of the faithful in all circumstances (although this can theologically and pastorally be asserted responsibly apart from this text). It is specifically about Christ as present in (that is, as authorizing) the church in its reconciling and boundary-setting work. The reference to the "two or three" gathered (joined with references to "one or two" in v. 16 and "two of you" in v. 18) is figuratively asserting the requirement of consensus in making such important decisions. The small size of the numbers may indicate the role leaders must take in this work of the community.

To preach this lection, then, is to preach about the hope for the church to be a familial community in which all are invited into relationships of reconciliation, but in the full recognition of the reality of human sin. The church is more than a club, association or institution. Remember that when Jesus founds the church, he calls it "*my* church" (16:18). It is not *our* church. Like Peter we are to be only managers of the master's house. It is not our place to set the rules of inclusion. We are to run the affairs of the church as its builder and owner—the Christ, the Son of the living God—desires. And what is clear here is that Jesus desires reconciliation but will not accept a refusal of reconciliation. This tension between being a community of grace and a community of call should characterize the boundaries and standards of church membership and participation. Being church in this manner is easier said than done, but it cannot be done without being said. This is the challenge for the preacher.

LECTION: HOW MUCH FORGIVENESS IN THE CHURCH?
18:21-35; PROPER 19

This lection serves as a tensive counterpoint to the previous passage (vv. 15-20). This is different, however, than saying that this passage contradicts the previous one. The first passage focuses on an approach for calling to accountability and into reconciliation one who has sinned against another in the community of faith. The second, then, focuses on the call to forgive extravagantly within the community as God does assuming the procedure has been successful and the offender has "listened." Matthew's construction of this structure of tensive counterparts may echo Leviticus 19:17-18, where the command to reprove one's neighbor is followed by the command to love one's neighbor.

Peter's question (v. 21), then, is not asking about forgiveness in general. Given the process named in vv. 15-20 and assuming it is successful in effecting reconciliation with an offender, how many times should one forgive a brother or sister in the community of faith? Peter asks whether it should be seven times. This is meant to represent a significantly high number. In numerological traditions of the ancient world, seven was sometimes seen as the number of perfection.

But Jesus answers that in the church we must go beyond a significantly high number to an extraordinarily high one. There is a translation issue with Jesus' answer. The Greek number he offers can either mean seventy-seven or seventy times seven. The meaning is the same either way, however. In this context both are huge numbers. The figurative response implies there is to be no limit to the forgiveness offered within the community of faith, given that the offender "listens," that is, assumes accountability, repents, and seeks reconciliation. In other words, Jesus calls those in the church to offer to one another grace that is extraordinary and extravagant but not cheap.

This is further illustrated in the parable that follows (vv. 23-35). The parable offers the theological justification for v. 22. This is a parable of the reign of heaven connecting (but not equating) life in the church with life in God's eschatological reign.

The parable has three scenes. The first two are parallel in structure so that the hearers/readers cannot miss the differences and development in content. The structure is as follows:

	King & Slave #1	Slave # 1 & Slave #2
Debt owed and demanded	vv. 23-24: 10,000 talents	v. 28: 100 denarii

| Plea for leniency | v. 26: "Have patience with me, and I will pay you everything." | v. 29: "Have patience with me, and I will pay you." |
| Response | v. 27: debt forgiven | v. 30: thrown into prison |

The common structure highlights the two radical differences in the scenes. The first is the difference in the amount of debt owed. In the second scene, the slave owes his fellow slave one hundred denarii. A denarius was a common day's wage for a laborer (see 20:1-16, where the NRSV translates a denarius as "usual daily wage"). For the sake of analogy, the preacher can think of this as minimum wage for a day of work, and thus one hundred denarii would be analogous to three and a half month's worth of wages at minimum wage. This is an amount that a debtor could realistically be able to repay. A talent, on the other hand, was equivalent to around 6,000 denarii or 6,000 days of work. Ten thousand talents, then, would be worth 60,000,000 denarii. To pay this back on minimum wage, one would have to work for over 164,000 years without spending any of the wages or taking any weekends off. In other words, 10,000 talents is meant to be an unimaginably large sum that a king would loan to a slave only in the world of fairy tales and parables (where twists are to be expected—see the discussion of parables in the introduction to ch. 13).

The difference between the financial amounts sets up the second difference—that of the responses of the lenders. The king not only has patience with the slave's inability to pay back the loan at that moment, he forgives the debt altogether—unimaginable grace related to an unimaginable debt. But the slave then, in turn, has no patience toward his fellow slave, and has him thrown in debtors' prison immediately.

The reign of heaven, however, is not just highlighted in this different level of forgiveness but in what is illustrated in the third scene of the parable (vv. 31-35). It is in this scene that Jesus' answer to Peter in v. 22 is justified. Upon hearing of the slave's refusal to offer a small amount of grace after having received an extraordinary amount of grace, the king recalls the slave and revokes the forgiveness of his immense debt. He is not simply sent to debtors' prison but handed over to a torturer. This image is not offered as some literal reference to eschatological punishment. It is meant to show the level of God's offense at one not forgiving as he or she has been forgiven. The final verse of the Discourse takes this explicit: "So my heavenly Father will also do to every one of you, if you do not forgive your brother or sister from your heart" (v. 35). The theological justification for forgiving our brother or sister seventy-seven or seventy times seven times is that we are to forgive others as God forgives us—and God has forgiven us more than seventy time seven times. In other words, here the Community Discourse echoes back to the Ethical Discourse, where Jesus stated explicitly, "For if you forgive others their trespasses, your heavenly Father will also forgive you; but if you do not forgive others, neither will your Father forgive your trespasses" (6:14–15). A sermon on this text is really an exposition of what we pray every Sunday in worship, "Forgive us our debts, as we also have forgiven our debtors" (6:12).

3

Traveling to Jerusalem (19:1—20:34)

In the Introduction, we argued that, based on geography, Matthew can be seen as having five major narrative divisions:

1:1—4:11	Beginnings: From Bethlehem to Nazareth
4:12—18:35	Capernaum-Based Ministry
19:1—20:34	Traveling to Jerusalem
21:1—28:15	Passion, Death, and Resurrection in/around Jerusalem
28:16-20	Beginning Again in Galilee

Having just completed the longest division—Jesus' itinerant ministry in and around Capernaum in Galilee—we now turn our focus to the shortest division except for the tiny but substantial return to Galilee at the tail-end of the narrative.

Most of the material in this division comes straight from Mark 10:1-52 (similar to Luke 18:18-43; see the chart below). While Matthew editorially shapes the material somewhat and adds a couple of elements to Mark's work, the division does not have a particularly Matthean feel to it. There are neither discourses nor new literary or theological developments in this section. In terms of broad narrative purposes, the primary function of this section is simple and straightforward: Jesus and the disciples travel from Galilee to Jerusalem, where the climax of the story is to occur. In other words, this division primarily serves to transition from the last major division to the next major division.

That, of course, is not to say that in chapters 19–20 there is no material of theological, ethical or narrative significance or are no literary connections holding the material together. For instance, while this material does not break down into an obvious outline, the manner in which it flows is clear.

19:1-2 These verses serve as the formal conclusion to the Community Discourse and transition to the new section. Moreover, here the primary geographical purpose of the section is named: moving from Galilee to Jerusalem.

19:3-9 Pharisees test Jesus with a question concerning divorce. Religious leaders have not appeared in the narrative in conflict with Jesus since 16:1-12. Starting this new section with such conflict reminds readers why the narrative is headed toward Jerusalem.

19:10-12 After Jesus' conflict with the Pharisees concerning divorce, the disciples ask whether his response means it is better not to marry at all. Jesus answers that celibacy is not for all but names that some make themselves eunuchs for the reign of heaven.

19:13-15 Topics shift in this scene as little children are brought to Jesus so that he might lay hands on them and pray. The disciples rebuke them but Jesus invites them to draw close for a blessing. The connection with what has preceded, however, is the reference to the reign of heaven—as there are those who make themselves eunuchs for the reign of heaven, so does the reign of heaven belong to little children.

19:16-22 Another shift in topics occurs as a man comes to Jesus asking what he must do to gain eternal life. As with the discussion of divorce, this scene involves interpretation of the *torah*. Then, however, the discussion of commandments moves to a call for the young man to sell his possessions, give to the poor and follow Jesus.

19:23-26 Following the rich young man's rejection of Jesus' call, Jesus continues to deal with the topic of possessions by commenting on the difficulty the wealthy have entering the reign of heaven (thus connection the earlier use of language concerning the reign of heaven with the discussion of eternal life).

19:27-30 The discussion of possessions is further extended when Peter asks Jesus what his previous declarations mean for those who (unlike the young man) have left possessions behind and followed him. Jesus answers in eschatological terms by assuring the disciples that they will be rewarded when the Son of the human is seated on the throne of his glory and they are placed on twelve thrones judging the tribes of Israel. The language of eternal life is raised again in this context. The rationale he provides for this reward over against the reward of possessions is that many who are first will be last and the last will be first.

20:1-16 Continuing his response to the disciples, Jesus tells the parable of the vineyard owner, exploring the meaning of the rationale he provided. The parable involves work and pay (echoing the discussion of possessions) but is clearly about more than literal wages. It concludes with a reiteration of the rational concerning the last and the first.

20:17-19 Although the narrator indicates a change in setting, Jesus continues teaching his disciples, now repeating the instructions from prior to the Community Discourse about the fate that awaits him in Jerusalem, reminding the reader of the geographical purpose of the section as a whole. Pharisees are not mentioned here, but religious leaders are named as Jesus' opponents as are the gentiles in power.

20:20-23 The Mother of John and James come to Jesus asking that he place them on his right and left in his reign (recalling the earlier language of the reign of heaven as well as the eschatological language using the imagery of thrones). Jesus rejects the request but does name that the two disciples will drink the same cup he is to drink (that is, suffer death as described in the previous passage).

20:24-28 When the other ten apostles hear of what just transpired, they become angry at James and John. But Jesus uses this as a teaching moment that brings together many of the threads of the section. He critiques the gentiles who are in power and instructs the disciples to act differently (that is, when they sit on their thrones). He continues by saying that whoever wants to be first must become a servant, recalling the reversal language earlier concerning the first and the last. And, finally, he grounds this claim in his own example of giving his life as a ransom, recalling the passion prediction and reminding the reader once again where the narrative is headed.

20:29-34 The section concludes with a healing story in which two blind men call Jesus "Son of David." While this messianic title has not appeared in the section, it will appear in the scene of the triumphant entry into Jerusalem (2:9). As with the earlier scene involving the little children, the blind men are rebuked but Jesus calls them nevertheless. After being healed, they follow Jesus—something the rich young man was unable to do.

What this brief survey of the flow of the division shows is that while Matthew has not constructed it with a single narrative or theological goal in mind, the development and shared vocabulary across the pericopes reinforce several key concepts of the First Gospel: the events in Jerusalem as the climax of Matthew's narrative; the eschatological reign of heaven as connected with Jesus' death and resurrection; and the call to radical discipleship as related to the reign of heaven.

One can also make a case that a central theme of the section is the way status, and especially the reversal of status, is portrayed. At the center of this portrayal is the claim that the status of the last and first will be reversed (19:30; 20:16). These two verses form an *inclusio* around the parable of the vineyard owner (20:1-15) that explores this reversal as a divine act.

Healing of the blind men reverses the low status they would have held in ancient society (20:29-33), as does Jesus' acceptance of little children who hold not social or economic status (19:10-12). The same might be said (although it is not as explicitly represented in the text) of Jesus' protection of women who had few rights protecting them from divorce in ancient Judaism (19:1-9) and of eunuchs (castrated males being used as a metaphor for celibacy?) who would have been scorned in a day when male virility was highly valued in society (19:10-12).

On other hand, other passages deal with relinquishing of high status to become low. The rich man is called to give up wealth to gain eternal life and the rich have difficulty entering the reign of heaven (19:16-27). The disciples are rewarded with thrones for having left behind possessions (19:27-30) but also have to be reminded that they are to become slaves to be great (20:20-28).

PASSAGES OMITTED FROM THE LECTIONARY

Only one passage from this division (20:1-16) appears in the lectionary. As we have seen repeatedly in our analysis of such omissions, part of the reason is related to the economic, harmonizing tendencies of the RCL. Over the course of the three-year cycle, the RCL often avoids reading parallel passages from the different Synoptic Gospels in order to cover more material over all. Since Matthew borrows almost all of this material from Mark 10, and almost all of Mark 10 is used by the RCL in Year B, no material in Matthew 19–20 that is paralleled in Mark is used. Only the parable that is unique to Matthew is found in Year A. Consider the following:

Passage	Matthew	Mark	
Controversy about Divorce	19:1-9 (not in RCL)	10:1-12	(Proper 22B)

Teaching about Celibacy	19:10-12 (not in RCL)		
Jesus Blesses Children	19:13-15 (not in RCL)	**10:13-16**	
Rich Young Man Seeking Eternal Life	19:16-22 (not in RCL)	**10:17-22**	**(Proper 23B)**
Difficulty of Rich entering the Reign of Heaven	19:23-26 (not in RCL)	**10:23-27**	
Reward for Those Who Have Left Possessions to Follow Jesus	19:27-30 (not in RCL)	**10:28-31**	
Parable of the Vineyard Owner	**20:1-16 (Proper 20A)**		
Third Passion Prediction	20:17-19 (not in RCL)	10:32-34	
Request for James and John	20:20-28 (not in RCL)	**10:35-45 (Proper 24B)**	
Healing of Two Blind Men	20:29-34 (not in RCL)	**10:46-52 (Proper 25B)**	

CONFLICT OVER DIVORCE (19:1-9): OMITTED FROM LECTIONARY

The issue being discussed in this conflict story is divorce, but for Matthew more is at stake than the particular topic. This is a debate about the interpretation and application of *torah*. Different schools of thought in Jesus' day interpreted Deuteronomy 24:1ff differently. In other words, Matthew presents Jesus as a rabbi participating in Jewish halakhic discussions of the day. He weighs Genesis 1:27 and 2:24 over against Deuteronomy 24. This portrayal legitimizes the church in Matthew's day as an heir and interpreter of Israel's history, traditions and practices. Jesus is presented as arguing consistently in terms of his hermeneutic of fulfillment presented in the Ethical Discourse in 5:17-20 when he bases his interpretation on the intent behind the certificate of divorce described in *torah*—Moses gave it because of men's hardness of heart not because divorce is the way God intended creation to be.

Even though the passage fits into the struggle between the church and synagogue (represented by the Pharisees) in Matthew's day, the fact that the Gospel returns to the topic of divorce after already using it as a case study for that hermeneutic in the series of antitheses in the Ethical Discourse (see 5:31-32) shows it is an important issue for his community. In 12:46-50 Jesus is presented as redefining familial ties in relation being his disciple (see also, 10:21, 34-38; as well as the use of *adelphos* "brothers and sisters" for members of the community, 5:22-24, 47; 7:3-5; 18:15, 21, 35). In today's world, where divorce has become commonplace, preachers may wish to explore Jesus' words on divorce once again. But in the process it is extremely important to note that what Jesus rejects here is a *man* divorcing a *woman*. Although in Roman law, women had some rights concerning divorce, in Jewish law only the husband could divorce the wife. Jesus here protects the one of lower status in the relationship in a way that fits well with the concern that the last shall be first (19: 30; 20:16).

Celibacy and the Reign of Heaven (19:10-12): Omitted from Lectionary

This is one of only two passages that Matthew adds to Mark 10 to make up this division (chs. 19–20). The content here is as odd as it is unique, making it little wonder the RCL avoids the pericope. Matthew constructs a terrible segue between the debate concerning divorce with the Pharisees and this discussion with his disciples. Upon hearing Jesus condemn the patriarchal practice of divorce, the disciples ask whether, then, it is better not to marry at all. In other words, the question sounds like men asking why one should consider marriage if he does not have an easy escape hatch available.

Jesus' answer, however, does not deal with their concern about getting out of marriage but instead with the issue of celibacy in the church. In some ways, Jesus' response here deconstructs the picture of him as concerned with the status of women in the earlier scene because the metaphor he uses for celibacy—being a eunuch—is a term applicable only to men. That said, Matthew seems to affirm the value (for some) of remaining unmarried and celibate in the life of the church (cf. 1 Cor. 7:1-17) in line with his redefinition of familial commitments in terms of discipleship (12:46-50).

CHILDREN BROUGHT TO JESUS (19:13-15): OMITTED FROM LECTIONARY

Earlier Matthew presents Jesus as using children as an example of the low status which one should assume to become great in the reign of heaven (18:1-4) and thus as a representative of the "little ones" in the community of faith who are vulnerable to stumbling blocks (18:5-14). Here Matthew uses Mark 10:13-16 to express literal concern about the inclusion of children (who have no social or economic status in culture) in the life of the community of faith. This connection with the church in Matthew's day is especially signaled by a change Matthew makes to Mark's version of the story. In Mark 10:13, the little children are being brought to Jesus that he might "touch them." Matthew references a more concrete ritual act by saying that they were bringing the children to Jesus that he might "lay his hands on them and pray" (v. 13).

While this likely signals something of historic practice of the early church concerning children, the pericope again supports the wider theme of the way status is turned upside down in the reign of heaven (19: 30; 20:16), and shows something of how the church lives into that reign. Preachers should avoid sentimentalizing children in this passage or in a sermon calling hearers to become childlike in their faith. This is about status in society being reversed in the life of the church. Children can still remind us of the need for such reversal today.

YOUNG MAN SEEKING ETERNAL LIFE (19:16-22): OMITTED FROM LECTIONARY

This passage (taken from Mark 10:17-22) sends the division in a somewhat new thematic direction by focusing on the surface-level topic of wealth for the next few pericopes instead of familial relations. Indeed, 19:16—20:16 is a single, new scene. Nevertheless, the underlying issue in this scene still concerns the relation of status and inclusion in the reign of heaven and the church. Perhaps the reason Matthew describes the man as young (an attribution not found in Mark) is to lead the reader to connect this story with that of the little children that it follows. The contrast of status could not be more marked: little children with no status and a rich young man with great status.

Also, continuing on from the earlier debate with the Pharisees at the beginning of the division is the issue of appropriate interpretation and application of *torah*. The young man asks what good thing (Matthew changes Mark's use of good where the man refers to Jesus as good instead of the deed to be done) he must do to have eternal life. The discussion that ensues concerns the commandments. When the young man asks which commandments he must uphold, Jesus lists those from the second half of the Decalogue (see Exod 20:13-16 and Deut 5:17-20). Matthew clearly presents Jesus as a law-keeping Jew as part of his argument for the legitimacy of the church as heir to Israel. This list should be interpreted as representative instead of exhaustive. But what is especially important about the list is that Matthew (over against Mark) has Jesus add the command to love one's neighbor from Leviticus 19:18 to the commandments from the Decalogue (cf. 22:34-40). Again we see Jesus "fulfilling" the *torah* in the sense of intensifying it (see the earlier commentary on 5:17-48).

This intensification goes a step further, however, due to the man's question concerning what else he is lacking (v. 20). The fact that he is following the commandments Jesus lists and yet still needs to ask this question, shows he experiences his life as indeed lacking something. Jesus now answers not only in terms of possessing eternal life but in terms of being "perfect" (Greek, *teleios*; cf. the command to be perfect as God is perfect in 5:48). Preachers should note the order of Jesus' advice. First, the man should sell his possessions and give the proceeds to poor and the result will be treasure in heaven. *Then*, the man should follow Jesus. In other words, following Jesus is not the road to having treasure in heaven but having treasure in heaven leads one to follow Jesus. The issue is not about how to get into the afterlife but an invitation into the quality of life in God's grace and service. Following Jesus is reward, not test.

Difficulty of Rich entering the Reign of Heaven (19:23-26): Omitted from Lectionary

In the previous passage, Jesus tells the wealthy young man to sell his possessions, give the proceeds to the poor, and follow him. The man leaves in grief because he has many possessions (19:22). This departure leads Jesus to comment more generally to his disciples about the difficulty the wealthy have entering the reign of heaven. This passage, combined with the previous one (and the next one), offers preachers the opportunity to speak honestly about the struggles to lead the Christian life facing their congregations in our age of materialism and commercialism.

The reason the wealthy have an impossible time (never can a camel pass through the eye of a needle) entering the reign of heaven is because their social standing and self-identity utterly rely on the status quo of the reign of Caesar. To give these up is not simply to see themselves differently but to become someone different.

The logion using the metaphor of the camel unable to pass through the eye of the needle is vivid and has intrigued interpreters throughout the history of the church. Some scribes have tried to water down the saying by changing camel (Greek *kamēlon*) to rope (Greek *kamilon*). Some commentators have tried to make the saying easier to swallow by claiming "needle" refers to a small gate in the Jerusalem wall through which a camel could barely fit. But the disciples' question, "Then who can be saved?" shows they understand fully the meaning of the saying.

This question sets up the real punch line of the passage. While the image of the camel is provocative, the failure of the rich is not the last word. Even though it may be impossible for the rich to enter the reign of heaven through their own efforts (remember the young wealthy man walks away grieving; 19:22), "for God all things are possible" (v. 26). Sermons on this text need to move from naming the bad news of the wealthy's inability to save themselves to celebrating the good news of God's ability to save and transform the rich (after all, earlier Matthew the tax collector does follow Jesus; 9:9).

THOSE WHO HAVE LEFT POSSESSIONS TO FOLLOW JESUS (19:27-30): OMITTED FROM LECTIONARY

Peter's question about the fate of those who have left all to follow Jesus (v. 27) is a response to Jesus' commentary on the plight of the rich in the previous passage—their being possessed by their possessions. In other words, it should not be read as the disciples simply following Jesus (and leaving possessions behind) in order to get a reward. The question sets up a contrast Matthew wants to make between those who are not able to accept Jesus' invitation (as seen in the departure of the rich young man, 19:22) and those disciples (that is, those in the church) who have accepted that invitation.

Jesus' answer is eschatological, but preachers should beware of interpreting this tone in terms of afterlife. Matthew changes Mark's version of this pericope (Mark 10:28-31) in several ways. One is to omit the explicit contrast Mark has Jesus make between the reward the disciples receive "now in this age" and the eternal life they will receive "in the age to come" (Mark 10:30), because of the way Matthew compresses the present and future in his understanding of eschatological experience of the already/not yet. Another is to add language concerning the twelve disciples sitting on twelve thrones judging Israel. Vv. 28-29 make clear that those who have left much behind for Jesus' sake will gain much more. This "much more" is not some kind of materialistic reward (in the sense of pearly gates, streets of gold, and mansions in the sky) but new, added responsibility for those to whom they have been sent (that is, the lost sheep of the house of Israel, see 10:6). On this sense of those eschatologically saved gaining added responsibility, see the Introduction and the commentary on the Eschatological Discourse (chs. 24–25).

The pericope transitions to the Parable of the Vineyard Owner (20:16) with the closing statement that "Many who are first will be last, and the last will be first" (v. 30). With the repetition of this language in 20:16 an inclusio is formed around that parable, so that the parable draws this section (19:16—20:16) of the division to a close, making clear that it is all about God's salvific reversal of status and thus of the status quo.

Third Passion Prediction (20:17-19): Omitted from Lectionary

Matthew includes all three of Mark's passion predictions (Mk 8:31/Mt 16:21; Mk 9:30-32/Mt 17:22-23; Mk 10:32-34/Mt 20:17-19; see also Mk 9:12/Mt 17:11-12) and adds one other time Jesus reminds the disciples of his coming crucifixion (26:1-2). In Mark, the three Passion predictions structure and focus chapters 8–10. Matthew, in contrast, uses his four to indicate how each phase of Jesus' ministry leads to his crucifixion and resurrection: the first two predictions appear near the end of his ministry in Galilee, this one during his journey from Galilee to Judea, and the last one just after the Eschatological Discourse while Jesus is on the Mount of Olives outside of Jerusalem. While none of the times Jesus foretells suffering, death and resurrection are identical, it is less the individual elements of the predictions that are important and more their cumulative effect on the reader. Readers are not allowed to get lost in the details of Jesus' teaching and healings and forget that those details will eventually result in what it will take for Jesus to save his people (1:21).

A Request Is Made for James and John (20:20-28): Omitted from Lectionary

This scene is made up of two related parts—Jesus' dialogue with James, John and their mother (vv. 20-23) and his teaching of the other ten after they hear about this dialogue (vv. 24-28). The whole of the passage should be understood as a response to the third time Jesus foretells his passion and resurrection. Recall that Mark uses the pattern of each passion prediction being followed by the disciples inappropriately responding to show their misunderstanding of Jesus and his mission, which in turns gives Jesus the opportunity to offer teaching about the radical nature of discipleship (Mk 8:31-9:1; 9:30-37; 10:32-45). Matthew followed this pattern with the first passion prediction but toned down the negative impression of Peter's response (16:21-28). Matthew broke the pattern with the second passion prediction, using the discussion concerning who is the greatest in the reign of heaven instead to introduce the Community Discourse (17:22-23; 18:1-5). In this third passion prediction, Matthew returns to Mark's pattern but again tones down the negative impression of the disciples by having the mother of James and John make the request concerning the places of honor and power instead of the disciples themselves and by describing her as simply asking "something" from him (the Greek *aitousa ti ap autou* is poorly translated by the NRSV as "she asked a favor of him") as opposed to asking him to "do for us whatever we ask of you" (v. 20; cf. Mk 10:35).

The use of the pattern (passion prediction, inappropriate response, teaching about discipleship) shows the rhetorical weight of the passage falls on the last element—Jesus' teaching—even though preachers might be drawn to the opening scene because of its vividness as a story. In sermons on this text, then, the preacher can use the opening elements (vv. 20-24) to create pathos for the congregation in hearing Jesus' pronouncement in vv. 25-28.

That said, the teaching offered here is not radically new for Matthew, but instead reasserts what Jesus has already taught the Twelve concerning their mission and leadership. It reasserts that after Jesus the Messiah has departed, the twelve are to judge the twelve tribes of Israel (see 19:28; see Ps 122 for the combination of approaching Jerusalem and thrones of judgment). It reminds the reader that the role and authority of the apostles (and thus of the church) are in rooted in imitation of Jesus (see the commentary on the Mission Discourse). It contrasts their leadership with that of gentile authorities (building on Matthew's repeated contrast between the reign of heaven and the reign of Caesar). And it explicitly applies the themes of the reversal of status that is prevalent throughout chapters 19–20 to the disciples themselves.

HEALING TWO BLIND MEN (20:29-34): OMITTED FROM LECTIONARY

The journey to Jerusalem opened with an explicit geographical reference in 19:1: Jesus left Galilee and went to Judea. Not until the closing scene of the division does another geographical reference appear (v. 29). Jericho, about 18 miles northeast of Jerusalem, represents the final leg of Jesus and the disciples' journey. Similarly, the crowd following Jesus mentioned in 19:2 is reintroduced here (vv. 29, 31). These elements set up the next scene in which Jesus enters the city to the voices of the crowd declaring him to be the Son of David (21:1-11; cf. the blind men calling Jesus the Son of David in vv. 30-31).

Matthew's story of Jesus healing the two blind men is a revision of Mark 10:46-53, the healing of the blind beggar, Bartimaeus. For Mark the story functions as a key narrative moment illustrating Mark's theology of faith and radical discipleship. Matthew does not use the story in this way. His redactions, including substituting two blind men for the man named Bartimaeus (see Matthew's two blind men in 8:28, cf. Mk 5:2; and two demoniacs in 9:27), simply turn this into another example of Jesus' compassion (in v. 34 Matthew adds *splagchnizomai* to Mark's version, see 9:36; 14:14; 15:32; 18:27).

Preachers should not think, however that this means the story is unimportant for Matthew. Remember that when John had his disciples ask Jesus whether he was the "coming one," Jesus' proof that he was the one John expected included his acts of healing the blind (11:5). This evidence is rooted in the claims of Isaiah 29:18 and 35:5 that the blind receiving sight is a sign of the nearness of the day of the Lord. Thus, placing this healing story just as Jesus is about to enter Jerusalem serves as a reminder of the nearness of the eschatological reign of heaven.

LECTIONS

Only one passage (20:1-16) from this division of Matthew (chs. 19–20) is utilized in worship by the RCL. One lection taken from two chapters of material that is not as central to Matthew's narrative and theological message as other parts of the Gospel does not seem so bad. But when one thinks of chapters 19–20 as a major geographical division of the Gospel, the choice seems more problematic. Congregations reading through Matthew using the RCL can completely miss out on the fact that in this division, Jesus is heading toward his fate in Jerusalem. Preachers will do well to name Jesus' movement as part of contextualizing the parable of the vineyard owner.

LECTION: PARABLE OF THE VINEYARD OWNER
20:1-16; PROPER 20

To interpret this parable properly, it must be read in the context of 19:16—20:16. These verses make up a single scene in which the surface issue is wealth:

19:16-22: Rich Young Man Seeking Eternal Life

19:23-26: Difficulty of Rich Entering the Reign of Heaven
19:27-30: Reward for Those Who Have Left Possessions to
Follow Jesus
20:1-16: Parable of the Vineyard Owner

The *inclusio* surrounding the parable (in 19:30 and 20:16) concerning the last becoming first and vice versa indicates that the deeper purpose of the scene, however, is to indicate the way in which God overturns the status quo by lifting up those of low social and economic status and vice versa. Matthew, therefore, adds the parable comparing the reign of heaven to a vineyard owner to his revision of Mark 10:17-31 to draw to a close this complex socio-theological scene.

Another context must also be kept in mind to properly preach on this parable. In the Hebrew Bible, the vineyard is often used as a prophetic metaphor for Israel (for example, Is 5:1-7; 27:1-6; 32:10-15; 34:4; Jer 8:13; Ezek 15:1-7; 17:1-10; Joel 1:11-12). It is no surprise then that Jesus is represented as using the vineyard in his parables (in addition to this parable, see Matthew's use of the metaphor in the temple conflicts; 21:28-31, 33-44). Matthew's original readers, therefore, would have been primed to relate the vineyard to the reign of heaven.

The parable is divided into two main parts: hiring the workers (vv.1-7) and paying the workers (8-16). In the first part the vineyard owner goes to the marketplace where day laborers wait to be hired. He goes early (6:00 a.m.?), at the third hour (9:00 a.m.), sixth hour (noon), and ninth hour (3:00 p.m.). Finally he returns one last time at the eleventh hour (5:00 p.m.). Already, the reader knows we are dealing with unusual practices (see the introduction to the Parables Discourse, for discussion of twists and oddities in Jesus' parables). No farmer hires workers with only one hour left in the workday!

The formulaic repetition of the visits to the market place stands out in what changes with each hiring. In the early morning hiring session, the vineyard owner and workers agree on the wage of a denarius, the standard pay for a laborer's day (v.2). At 9:00 a.m., however, the vineyard own simply promises the "idle" men "whatever is just/right" (v. 4; *ho ē dikaion*). At noon and at 3:00 p.m., we are simply told the vineyard owner "did the same" (vv. 5-6). Without an explicit mention of wages, the reader assumes the same promise of "whatever is just/right" is offered. At 5:00 p.m., we hear the dialogue between vineyard owner and the men in the marketplace (v. 7). But there is no mention of pay whatsoever.

The second part of the parable explicitly reverses the order of engagement so that those hired last are paid first. When those who worked only an hour are paid a full denarius (v. 9) it sets up those who have worked all day (and the readers) to assume they will get more pay (v.10a). But they do not. When they complain, the vineyard owner offers a response that recalls the offer he made to those who began working later in the day. He says, "I am doing you no injustice/wrong" (v. 13; *ouk adikō se*).

The parable is a difficult passage to preach, because it does not look (according to our standards) as if God has been fair here. But the final twist in the parable is meant to invite the readers to question their conceptions of the justice/righteousness of God. We must remember the context in which Matthew uses this parable. The surface level topic has been wealth, but the underlying issue is about status in the reign of heaven. Similarly, the parable seems to be about wages, but something else must be at play.

Too often we think of the life of discipleship as a means to an end: living the Christian gets us a reward (blessing, prosperity, heaven, etc.). The parable, however, invites preachers to offer congregations a view of the Christian life itself as the reward. It is the end not the means. In other words, while everyone got paid the same at the end of the day, those hired earliest in the morning received an extra blessing in that they got to be productive and valuable for a longer period of time than the others. They entered and worked in the vineyard (that is, in the God's reign) longer than those who came in late. In Matthew's eschatology in which the saved are left behind with more responsibility while the damned are taken away to weeping and gnashing of teeth (for example, 24:37-41, 45-47; 25:14-30; see the discussion of eschatology in the Introduction), this reversal of the status quo is good news. Life in the already/not yet is less about what we get when "yet" arrives and more about the blessing of living toward the "yet" in the "already."

4

Passion, Death, and Resurrection in and around Jerusalem (21:1—28:15)

Readers working their way through the Gospel according to Matthew from the beginning will have seen Jesus' messianic identity established through christological titles, geographically symbolic movements, and fulfillment of scripture in the opening (1:1—4:11). They would have seen Jesus live out this identity as he called disciples and taught them in four discourses around Capernaum in Galilee; as he healed the sick and exorcized demons; as he took on religious authorities in ways that transparently represented and informed the struggle between Matthew's church and the synagogue in the late first century; and as he foretold his passion, death and resurrection in Jerusalem (4:12—18:35). They would have followed Jesus on his short journey from Galilee to Judea (19:1—20:34). And now they are ready for the climax of the story.

This division opens with Jesus coming into Jerusalem in a parade and heading immediately into the temple, where over the course of some time he teaches the crowds and engages religious leaders in conflict (21:1—23:39). Upon leaving the temple, Jesus predicts its destruction and delivers his fifth and final discourse in which the eschatological threads of the gospel are brought together in a summative fashion (24:1—25:46). Having said his last word, as it were, Jesus prepares for his fate with his disciples (26:1-46). And then it arrives: Jesus is arrested, tried, mocked, killed and buried (26:47—27:61). Of course, the last scene in Jerusalem is that of the empty tomb (27:62—28:15). God gets the last word in Jerusalem.

Congregations following the lectionary, however, may not feel the full force of this division as the climax of Matthew's work. The triumphant entry (21:1-11) and the extended story of Jesus' last days (26:14—27:66) are read all in one day near the height of the liturgical calendar in the spring (Palm/Passion Sunday). But then various passages from the temple conflicts and the Eschatological Discourse are read months later in the fall during Ordinary Time

(Propers 21-28). Preachers will have to make the connections between these two sections for those in the pews if they are to understand the full significance of the individual passages and get a sense of Matthew's broader theological and literary purposes.

PASSION, DEATH, AND RESURRECTION IN AND AROUND JERUSALEM: CROWDS AND CONFLICTS IN THE TEMPLE (21:1—23:39)

INTRODUCTION

Conflicts between John the Baptist, Jesus and his disciples on the one hand and the religious leaders on the other have peppered the narrative since John first attacked the Pharisees and Sadducees who came out to him for baptism by calling them a "brood of vipers" and accusing them of not producing "good fruit" (3:7-10). This peppering led to the Pharisees conspiring to destroy Jesus in 12:11. Now as Jesus enters Jerusalem and moving his headquarters from the house in Capernaum to the temple, the conflict hits the fan, if you will.

We have repeatedly noted that Matthew does not present Jesus as the passive victim in these conflicts but as much of an initiator of them as are his opponents. Thus we should not be surprised that he ratchets up the conflicts by bringing it into the temple. The Jerusalem temple was symbolically the house of God. In other words, it was the locus of God's providential presence with Israel. As such it was the center of religious activity and political power for Jews.

Therefore, Jesus' conflicts now expand beyond the Pharisees and scribes to involve others. First are the chief priests. Priests' function was to serve in the sacrificial cult of the temple. Chief priests were likely the aristocracy of the group—the priests with money and power who controlled the temple, from whose ranks the high priest was chosen, and who had influence in circles of Roman political power. Before now they only showed up as active characters in Matthew at the opening of the story when they and the scribes advise Herod in Jerusalem that the messiah was to be born in Bethlehem so that Herod could try to kill the child Jesus (2:4). When Jesus enters Jerusalem for the first time, they engage him immediately and become major players in bringing about Jesus' execution. This is no surprise to the reader since Jesus mentioned them in his passion predictions (16:21; 20:18).

Second are the elders of the people. What specific historical group Matthew has in mind here is not entirely clear. What is obvious, however, is that the group is important to Matthew. In Mark's version of the Jerusalem narrative, the elders appear four times (11:27; 14:43, 53; 15:1) while Matthew has them show up in his ten times (21:23; 26:3, 47, 57; 27:1, 3, 12, 20, 41;

28:12; see also 16:21). They are always paired with scribes and/or chief priests, however. They seem to represent a leadership role in the Jerusalem Jewish community, perhaps being those men on the Sanhedrin who were not of the priestly class. The particular type of leadership Matthew envisions as part of the combination of leaders may be more social than religious. All of this is speculative, but in the narrative they certainly represent those who profit from the political and economic privilege they experience as part of the status quo of the reign of Caesar.

Third, Matthew introduces Herodians into the mix of those conspiring against Jesus in 22:16. Again, who this group is in a Jerusalem ruled by Pilate is anything but clear. But the designation identifies them as a political power. So Matthew indicts the religious, social and political leadership of the Jews in this section, and not the Jewish people as a whole. This strategy is certainly part of Matthew's agenda of legitimizing the church as an heir and interpreter of Israel's faith, traditions and practices over against the synagogue of his day after the fall of the temple in 70 C.E.

It is interesting that following Mark, Matthew does not present the Pharisees as playing any actual role in Jesus' arrest, trial and crucifixion in the chapters following this section. He may have assumed their presence, but they are not explicitly named in 24–27, except when they come with the chief priests to Pilate after the crucifixion to ask that guards be placed at Jesus' tomb (27:62). Their absence during the passion narrative is striking given their role in conflict with and conspiring against Jesus throughout his ministry centered in Capernaum and in the temple controversies. But certainly the overall effect is clear enough—*all* of the Jewish leaders are against Jesus, and thus against the church.

A sketch of the structure of the section shows how this opposition to Jesus coalesces in the temple and how it is contrasted with Jesus' attraction to the Jewish people represented by the crowds. (This contrast is a reminder to preachers to counter the anti-Semitic manner in which these texts have often been interpreted.)

The section opens with Jesus' "triumphal entry" not just into the city but into the temple (21:1-16). Jesus enters as the messianic king in the line of David conquering the temple that it might become his new headquarters for the end of his ministry. His entrance is accompanied and acclaimed not just by the "crowds" (Greek, *ochloi*; used 32 times in Matthew) or even the "large crowds" (Greek, *ochloi polloi*, used sixteen times in Matthew) that have flocked around him in Galilee, but by the "largest crowd" (Greek, *pleistos ochlos*, used only in 21:8). The blind and lame come to him in the temple now as they did to his house in Galilee (v. 14). And all of this leads the chief priests and scribes (who thought they were in control of the temple) to become angry at Jesus (vv. 15-16).

Next, Jesus who has slept outside the city, returns to teach in the temple and comes into immediate conflict with the chief priests and elders of the people (21:23); the chief priests and Pharisees (21:45-46); the Pharisees, their disciples and the Herodians (22:15-16); the Sadducees (22:23); one of the Pharisees (22:34-35); and the Pharisees (22:41). Jesus passed each test that was posed to catch him and turn the crowds against him, and the conflict ends with the notice that no one dared to ask Jesus anymore questions (22:46).

Jesus' time in the temple closes not in further conflict with the religious leaders—that is left to be reintroduced with Jesus' arrest in the next section. Instead, the temple scene concludes with a lengthy final condemnation (seven woes!) of the leaders as hypocrites (specifically of the "scribes and Pharisees," ch. 23) offered to the crowds and his disciples (23:1). Even though Jesus has bested the religious leaders to the point that they no longer speak with him, he continues to talk about them (recalling the warnings in 15:10-20; 16:5-12).

This structure focused on conflict serves not only Matthew's need to advance the plot toward Jesus' arrest, trial and execution but also the evangelist's theological purposes. There are three overarching aspects of Matthew's theology that are brought together in this section.

The first is christology. Although Matthew, following Mark, portrays Jesus as making only one journey to Jerusalem, it is important to remember that for the First Gospel this is a return to the region (Judea) in which Jesus was born and declared the messianic king (2:1-12). Born in the city of David, the son of David (20:30-31; 21:9, 15) and yet one who is more than the son of David (22:41-46) enters the city and the temple as the (symbolic) conquering hero. As with the introduction of Jesus in the birth narrative, Jesus' introduction to Jerusalem here is confirmed by a prophecy fulfillment citation (21:4-5). The royal motif cannot be missed, but neither is it the whole of Matthew's christological offering in this section. Indeed, several scriptural passages are echoed or cited in significant ways to underline Jesus' identity and purpose here in ways reminiscent of the density of scripture used in the opening chapters of the Gospel (for example), in chapter 21: v. 9 from Ps 118; v. 13 from Is 56:7, Jer 7:11; v. 16 from Ps 8:2; vv. 33ff based on Is 5:1-7; v. 42 again from Ps 118; v. 44 as an allusion to Isa 8:4).

The extensive use of scripture points to another theological Matthean emphasis that is reasserted in this section: Jesus is the legitimate interpreter of scripture. In the Ethical Discourse, Jesus presented his hermeneutic of fulfillment (intensification based on the intent of the scripture) of the *torah* followed by antitheses that served as case studies for the hermeneutic (5:17-48). Because this portrayal of Jesus serves to legitimize the way Matthew's church interprets scripture as an heir of Israel's history and traditions, this theme shows up repeatedly throughout the Capernaum division of the narrative. It is compressed in this section, however, in a way not seen by the reader since the Sermon on the Mount. Consider the conflicts in light of relation to scripture:

Jesus reclaims the purpose of the temple in relation to Isaiah 56:7 and Jeremiah 7:11 over against the chief priests and scribes.

Jesus uses Isaiah 5:1-7 to shape the parable of vineyard owner and tenant farmers in the dispute with the chief priests and elders concerning his authority.

The disciples of the Pharisees and the Herodians try unsuccessfully to trap Jesus by asking whether it is lawful (*exesti*)—that is, fitting according to the *torah*—to pay taxes to the empire.

The Sadducees try to trap Jesus with a question meant to show the absurdity of belief in resurrection by referring to a commandment concerning levirate marriage (Deut 25:5-6), but Jesus argues for resurrection in light of a new interpretation of Exodus 3:6.

One of the Pharisees tests Jesus by asking which is the great commandment, but Jesus answers with what most Jews of the time would have expected: Deuteronomy 6:5. He then adds to it, however, Leviticus 19:18.

Finally, Jesus turns the tables and asks the Pharisees a question about the identity of the messiah as the son of David only to show their answer as incorrect by quoting Psalm 110:1.

Having presented Jesus to be the better interpreter of *torah*, Matthew has Jesus indict the Pharisees and scribes specifically on these terms in the final chapter 23, pressing the issue even harder. Jesus describes them as ones who "sat on Moses' seat" (23:2)—in other words, they served (past tense) as authoritative interpreters of the Mosaic law. He then, however, criticizes them for the manner in which they interpret the law and especially the way they apply their interpretation to others' lives but fail to follow that application themselves. Jesus' tone here is uncomfortable for modern ears. Preachers must remember (and remind their congregations) that Jesus is not attacking the Jewish people here but those who hold social, political and religious power over them. And they must remember that Jesus' attacks on the Jewish authorities in the narrative are transparently intended to legitimate Matthew's church in its struggle with the synagogue in the period following the destruction of the temple, so his presentation of them often does not accord with what we know to be historically true. One of the reasons Matthew places Jesus' strongest condemnation against the scribes and Pharisees in the temple is because both the synagogue and the church are trying to present themselves as the proper heir to the temple's role of representing God's presence with Israel once the temple ceases to function. Perhaps the line that best focuses Matthew's argument is found in 23:13, where the Pharisees and scribes are accused of offering interpretations of scripture that lock people out of the reign of heaven whereas the interpretations proffered by Jesus and the church give people access to the eschatological experience of God's reign (see the earlier comments on 16:19 and 18:18).

Lectionary preachers can fairly easily present these theological emphases to a congregation because the material in the temple section of Matthew's narrative is covered well by the RCL. Most of Matthew's material here is drawn from Mark, but in its economic, harmonizing approach to the Synoptics, the RCL gives preference to Matthew's version of the materials:

Matthew, Year A	Mark, Year B	Luke, Year C
21:1–11: Triumphal Entry; Liturgy of the Palms	11:1–11: Triumphal Entry; Liturgy of the Palms	19:28–40: Triumphal Entry; Liturgy of the Palms
21:12–22: Cleansing the Temple 21:23–32: Conflict concerning Authority; Proper 21A 21:33–46: Parable of Vineyard Owner and Tenants; Proper 22A 22:1–14: Parable of the Wedding Banquet; Proper 23A 22:15–22: Conflict concerning Taxes; Proper 24A		
22:23–33: Conflict concerning Resurrection		20:27–38: Conflict concerning Resurrection; Proper 27
22:34–46: Conflict concerning Great	12:28–34: Conflict concerning Greatest	

Commandment; Proper 25A	Commandment; Proper 26B	
23:1-12: Warning about Scribes and Pharisees; Proper 26A	12:38-44: Warning about Scribes and the Widow's Offering; Proper 27B	
23:13-39: Woes to Scribes and Pharisees		

This strong use of Matthew allows preachers to offer a fairly solid cumulative view of the temple conflicts to a congregation near the end of the liturgical year.

What makes preaching cumulatively through the section as a whole difficult is the way the section is broken apart in relation to the structure of the liturgical year. The scene of the triumphal entry (with the cleansing of the temple unfortunately omitted) is read on Palm/Passion Sunday. A congregation must then wait over a quarter of a year to return to the temple conflict stories. Since the tone of the conflicts is set with Jesus' entry into the city and temple, preachers will need to remind them of both the triumphal entry and the cleansing of the temple when the readings in Ordinary Time appear. [It is a grave oversight that the RCL does not include any of the synoptic versions of the "cleansing" of the temple. John's version (2:13-22) is assigned for the Third Sunday in Lent in Year B, but the story functions quite differently in John (placed at the beginning of Jesus' ministry instead of at the end) than in the Synoptics.]

Passages Omitted from the Lectionary

Overall, the RCL does a good job covering Matthew's temple section (chs. 21–23). Only three passages are not included, although the third is quite lengthy. The first passage omitted is the most significant, especially given the fact that no synoptic version of the cleansing of the temple is used in the three year lectionary cycle.

Cleansing the Temple (21:12-17): Omitted from Lectionary

For Matthew, this passage is really the second half of the scene that begins in 21:1. It is understandable, but regrettable, that the two halves are separated due to liturgical tradition related to Palm Sunday. In Mark 11:1-11, Jesus enters the city, peeks in on the temple and leaves. The "cleansing" does not happen until the next day when Jesus returns to the temple. But in Matthew, Jesus does not only enter the city triumphantly, he enters the temple as the messianic conqueror, evidenced by children continuing to shout hosannas of praise inside the temple.

More than "cleansing" the temple (the traditional label given to this scene), Jesus claims it as his Jerusalem headquarters, similar to the way his home in Capernaum functioned. Matthew follows Mark's description (11:15-18) of Jesus turning over tables and running out those buying, selling and changing money—all tasks important to the sacrificial purpose of the temple and not symbols of corruption, as often misinterpreted. For Matthew, these actions and Jesus' words about the temple as a house of prayer are less about cleansing the temple than prophetically condemning the religious leadership Jesus has been fighting all along now in the locus of religious, social and political power. Indeed, he comes in and out of the temple, he heals there, teaches there, and engages in conflict with the religious authorities there. He has claimed the temple as the arena of his public ministry in Judea.

Cursing the Fig Tree (21:18-22): Omitted from Lectionary

One effect of Matthew connecting the Triumphal Entry into Jerusalem and the entry into and "cleansing" of the temple (contrasted with Mark 11:1-11, which keeps them separate; see the discussion of the previous passage) is that the story of the Cursing of the Fig Tree is disconnected from Jesus' actions in the temple. Sandwiching one story inside the other, Mark presents Jesus as heading into the city on the day after the triumphal entry, cursing the fig tree along the way. Then Jesus "cleanses" the temple (or better causes it to stop functioning), reclaiming it as a house of prayer for all nations. The next morning the disciples notice the fig tree has withered, and Jesus comments on prayer (Mark 11:12-26). The Markan intercalation encourages readers to see in the cursing of the fig tree a prophetic symbolic act related to the destruction of the temple. Matthew, instead, uses the fig tree scene as the opening to the temple disputes, so that any symbolic importance of the tree withering is directed not toward the temple (as an institution) but to the religious leadership (including those having authority over the temple).

There are other changes Matthew makes to Mark's version of the story that are important to notice. First, in Mark the fig tree has no figs because it is not the season for figs (Mark 11:13). Matthew omits this element, likely because it makes Jesus look irrational. Second, in Mark the fig tree is withered the next day (Mark 11:20), which fits with the narrative need of surrounding the temple story with two parts of the fig tree story but which also symbolically indicates a temporal distance between Jesus' curse of the temple and its withering in the year 70. Matthew, on the other hand has the tree wither immediately (v. 19), perhaps indicating that the authority of the religious leaders is taken away immediately when Jesus confronts them in the temple.

Preachers will likely (and appropriately) be drawn to focus on the conclusion of the story if it is to be addressed homiletically. Here the withered fig tree is turned into a lesson about the power of faith and prayer. The lesson here duplicates 17:20, but it also connects with the conflicts that follow. Faith to move a mountain is a demonstration of authority (the topic of the next passage, (vv. 23-27). The authority Jesus exhibits in dealing with both the fig tree and the religious leaders is offered here to his disciples.

SADDUCEES' CONFLICT CONCERNING RESURRECTION (22:23-33): OMITTED FROM LECTIONARY

Mark's version of this story (12:18-27) is the only time the Sadducees are mentioned in the Second Gospel. They appear only because of the topic of resurrection. They were known to be opposed to the doctrine of resurrection that appeared in later Judaism but was not found in the Pentateuch, the only part of the Hebrew scriptures they considered as canon. In Matthew, however, the Sadducees have appeared before (3:7; 16:1, 6, 11, 12). They appear as part of the complex of Jewish political, religious leaders with whom Jesus is in conflict. Thus the specific topic of resurrection is not the most important reason Matthew includes this scene in the context of the temple conflicts (although Jesus' stance clearly fits with what Matthew holds concerning resurrection in general and Jesus' resurrection specifically).

The more important purpose for Matthew is (once again) to present Jesus as a legitimate interpreter of scripture and thus to legitimize the church as an heir of Israel's history and traditions. Two things are especially striking about Jesus' biblical interpretation in this scene. First, even though the earliest mention of the idea of resurrection in Jewish scriptures is in the apocalyptic writing of Daniel (12:12), Jesus answers the Sadducees challenge (based on Deut 25:5-6) by applying Exodus 3:6 to the issue. The hermeneutical approach may seem questionable by modern exegetical standards, but Jesus represents a standard first century rabbinical interpretive approach well. The second striking element of Jesus' assertion is that he represents a view with which the Pharisees would be in complete agreement. Nevertheless, they continue to conspire against him in the very next scene (22:34). Matthew wants to show that their conflict with Jesus is based less on a theological difference and more on a desire to hold on to social, political and economic power rooted in the status quo, to which Jesus and his message of the reign of heaven is a challenge.

Preachers will be tempted to focus on resurrection and try to interpret this passage either as a defense of Jesus' resurrection or of contemporary understandings of life after death. To stay closer to Matthew's purposes and relate the passage to the wider narrative, though, preachers should help the congregation make sense of the hermeneutical arguments at play in the conflict.

WARNING ABOUT SCRIBES AND PHARISEES (23:13-39):
OMITTED FROM LECTIONARY

Chapter 23 is a lengthy address warning the crowds and disciples about the hypocrisy of the scribes and Pharisees as interpreters of Israel's faith and practices. This warning is not new (see, for instance, 15:10-20; 16:5-12). Instead, this address is the culmination of the conflicts between Jesus and the religious leaders (especially the conflicts in the temple in the previous two chapters) used to legitimize the existence and ways of Matthew's church over against the synagogue.

The RCL includes only the first eleven verses of the address (see commentary below). This opening of the discourse is an expansion of (Mark 12:38-40) omitting the critique of the temple found in the story of the widow's offering, (Mk 12:41-44). From there Matthew adds seven woes against the religious leaders unique to the First Gospel that intensify the attack considerably. To the modern ear this material can sound vitriolic, and it is no wonder the lectionary avoided it.

Preachers who work through the Matthean lections in Year A will have had many chances to address the theme of Jesus in conflict with the religious leaders and do not lose much by ignoring these verses in the preaching cycle. Still, the strong tone here will serve as a reminder to preachers and congregations alike how much was at stake in the sibling rivalry between the church and the synagogue in the early post-temple era. Moreover, the anti-

Semitic ways in which this chapter has been used throughout the history of the church serve as an invitation to preachers to re-contextualize the material as part of the church's attempt to improve its relationship with contemporary Judaism.

LECTIONS

The readings drawn from this section of Matthew's narrative are extensive. Preachers have the opportunity during Ordinary Time to offer their congregations a cumulative view of the temple controversies and overturn the view that the gospel presents a contrast between Jesus and the Jews. Over and over again, preachers working through this material will have to name the way Matthew presents the religious leaders negatively in order to legitimate the church in the late first century (as opposed to representing their stances and behavior in a journalistic fashion).

LECTION: TRIUMPHAL ENTRY
21:1-11; LITURGY OF THE PALMS

During the Sundays after Epiphany, congregations following the RCL made their way through semi-continuous readings drawn from the Ethical Discourse. On the First Sunday in Lent, the temptation story (4:1-11) was read, following longstanding liturgical tradition. Throughout the rest of Lent, Matthew was abandoned to make room for readings from John—the Fourth Gospel does not have a year dedicated to it as do the Synoptics. Thus, with Palm/Passion Sunday, congregations return to Matthew for the first time since the story of Jesus' temptation was read (4:1-11). Moreover, in Year A, they will not have yet heard a single story of Jesus performing a miracle or being in conflict with the religious authorities. What this means for a cumulative homiletical approach to Matthew is that, without significant work on the part of the preacher, a congregation will hear this passage only in its (significant) liturgical context instead of its narrative context. Preachers focusing on this passage will need to fill in some gaps so congregations can make sense of the full importance of this passage and the liturgical occasion related to it.

However, as Protestant congregations have shifted from celebrating this day simply as Palm Sunday to Palm/Passion Sunday, that is, as moving from the triumphal entry to the cross, this story takes on the role of prelude during the gathering portion of the ordo more than focal point during the proclamation portion of the service. Palm/Passion Sunday has become a day more for reading through extended texts in the Jerusalem narratives than preaching on a short portion of it (see comments on 26:14—27:66 below). Yet even if the service does not include a full-blown sermon, preachers will need to be aware of exegetical issues related to 21:1-11 and the passion narrative in designing the service and perhaps in providing some commentary for the congregation.

Having just been called "the Son of David" twice by the blind men in Jericho (20:29-34), Jesus is acclaimed as such by the crowds as he enters the city. The use of this messianic title, combined with the prophetic fulfillment citation taken from Zechariah 9:9 and Isaiah 63:11, makes it clear that this passage is a christological scene with political implications. Jesus is (symbolically) returning to Judea (where he was born, 2:1ff) to claim the throne of his forefather David. Thus he parades into Jerusalem and goes straight to the temple (the locus of religious and political power for first-century Jews).

Although Mark has Jesus enter the city one day and then overturn tables in the temple on the next (11:1-25), Matthew has the two not only occur on the same day but combines them so they are part of the same event (21:1-17). Because this text is used (as it should be) for the Liturgy of the Palms at the beginning of Palm/Passion Sunday, however, the story of Jesus entering the temple is omitted from the lection. Even though we will focus only on the entry into the city, it is helpful to see how Matthew's version of the material is structured to lead into the temple scene:

> Setting (1a)
> Making Arrangements for Entry (vv. 1b-6)
>> Instructions to Disciples (vv. 1b-3)
>> Prophecy Fulfillment Citation (vv. 4-5)
>> Disciples Do as Instructed (v. 6)
> Entering the City (vv. 7-11)
>> Mounting the donkey and colt (v. 7)
>> The Crowd's Acclamation (vv. 8-9)
>> The City's Question (vv. 10-11)
> Entering the Temple (vv. 12-17)
>> Claiming the Temple as House of Prayer (vv. 12-13)
>> Healings in the Temple (v. 14)
>> Religious Leaders' Challenge Due to Continued Acclamation (vv. 15-16)

Matthew makes other changes to Mark's entry story in addition to the structural one. Noting these help preachers identify Matthew's particular purposes. Three are significant changes. First, Mark's scene is a midrash of sorts based on Zechariah 9:9, but Matthew makes the intertextual relationship explicit by adding in a prophecy fulfillment citation (vv. 4-5) composed of language from Zechariah 9:9 and Isaiah 62:11. This is the first such formula since 13:35, highlighting the significance of this scene for Matthew's christology. Indeed, so important is the fulfillment motif to Matthew in this scene that he alters Mark's details so that the story corresponds more exactly to the elements of the quotation. The prophetic text uses poetic parallelism in which the animal is mentioned twice, using different language. Matthew want to present Jesus as fulfilling the letter of the prophecy, if you will, and thus has Jesus riding two animals—a full-grown donkey and its colt—at the same time!

The second significant change Matthew makes to Mark is the language the crowd uses in its acclamation. In Mark, the crowd celebrates the "coming reign of our father David" (11:10). Matthew changes the wording so that the celebration is specifically about Jesus: "Hosanna to the Son of David!" (21:9). This change, coupled with the previous one, points preachers toward a christological focus when preaching on this scene. Jesus fulfills scripture and comes to Jerusalem to save his people and as a sign of God's presence with them (cf. 1:21-23). Thus, the passion and resurrection of Jesus are to be interpreted in social, political and theological terms. Individualistic interpretations of what follows do an injustice to Matthew's intent.

A third change Matthew makes to Mark's version of the triumphal entry confirms the assertion that what follows in the stories of Jesus' crucifixion and resurrection should be understood at least in part through the lens of this politico-christological scene. Matthew adds to the end of the parade into the city, a dialogue between the crowds of pilgrims and the "whole city" (vv. 10-11; cf. the lament over Jerusalem in 23:37-39). Another element that is easily missed in the NRSV, however, is that the whole city "shook" (Greek, seiō; cf. the NRSV, "the whole city was in turmoil"). The reason this notice of shaking is important is that the language echoes the earthquakes and shaking that appear later in the story (24:7; 27:51, 54; 28:2, 4; cf. 8:24). The only use of such language in Mark is found in the Eschatological Discourse in 13:8, paralleled by Matthew 24:7. Thus all of this other references to quaking are unique to Matthew, tying the entry into Jerusalem and the temple to earthquakes at Jesus' death when the temple curtain rips in two and at the resurrection. Preachers can highlight these connections to help a congregation on Palm/Passion Sunday (and on Easter Sunday) see the unity of all that happens in Matthew's story.

Lection: Conflict concerning Authority
and the Parable of Two Sons
21:23-32; Proper 21

The last gospel lection in the semi-continuous readings in Ordinary Time was the Parable of the Vineyard Owner (20:1-16) and was the only reading drawn from the larger division involving Jesus' journey to Jerusalem (chs. 19–20). The two lections before that were taken from the Community Discourse in chapter 18 (vv. 15-20 and 21-35). All of these, in different ways, can be seen as dealing with the theology and life of discipleship.

A major shift, therefore, occurs with this passage. The RCL moves into the temple conflicts and keeps the church there for six weeks. The shift is somewhat of a jolt for those concerned with preaching Matthew in a cumulative fashion since the story of the entry into Jerusalem (21:1-11) was read months ago on Palm/Passion Sunday and the stories of the "cleansing" of the temple (21:12-17) and the cursing of the fig tree (21:18-22) were not read at all. These three passages together set the tone for all that follows in Matthew's Jerusalem narrative, especially the conflicts with the religious leaders in chapters 21–22. Thus preachers will need to use some time in especially the first sermon on a lection from this temple section reminding the congregation of this broader narrative context if they are to understand why Matthew piles these conflicts on top of each other and why the RCL spends so much time focusing on them.

Moreover, this lection in which Jesus is challenged by the chief priests and elders of the people is intimately related to the next two. 21:23—22:15 comprises a single dialogue. Once Jesus bests those challenging his authority (21:23-27), he continues addressing them in three parables (21:28-32, 33-46; 22:1-14), with the last one perhaps expanding the audience. The flow of the material is as follows:

> The chief priests and elders attempt to trap Jesus with a question about his authority (21:23).
>> Jesus offers a counter-question (which is a similar trap): if they will answer a question about the authority of John the Baptist, he will answer them (vv. 24-25a).
>>> The leaders refuse to answer because they recognize the question is the same sort of logical trap they laid for Jesus (vv. 25b-27a).
>> Jesus refuses to answer but tells a parable (the Parable of the Two Sons—in which the son who speaks disobediently but in the end acts obediently is lifted up over the son who says speaks obediently but acts disobediently) through which the

leaders expose their hypocrisy after initially trying to conceal it (vv. 27b-32).

Having indicted the leaders, Jesus uses the Parable (allegory) of the Vineyard Owner and Tenants, in which original tenants who act disobediently are replaced by new tenants, to intensify the indictment and pronounce judgment on the leaders (vv. 33-44).

The chief priests and Pharisees conspire to arrest Jesus but must wait due to fear of the crowd (vv. 45-46; cf. v. 26).

Jesus offers "them" (the chief priests and elder, the chief priests and Pharisees, or the religious leaders and the crowds?) another parable (the Parable of the Wedding Banquet) in which those who reject the king's invitation are replaced (similar to the first two parables). However, the parable continues as a warning to the replacements not to take their new position for granted (22:1-14).

This material is unified in that the narrator never tells the reader that Jesus is addressing anyone different than the chief priests and elders introduced in 21:23—although the Pharisees surprisingly appear in 21:45 and are likely included in the reference to "them" in 22:1. In 22:15-16, nevertheless, an explicit change is noted in that Jesus is engaged by the disciples of the Pharisees and the Herodians. Moreover, while the conflicts that continue throughout the rest of chapter 22 are closely related in approach to the material in 21:23—22:14, the focus here is especially on the idea of the torch of leadership being passed from the Jewish authorities to the post-resurrection church. Thus, this opening lection is quite important for preachers contextualizing the readings to follow, even if it offers little that is new theology or information on its own.

The scene opens after Jesus has returned from his evening in the suburbs of Jerusalem and begins teaching in the temple. The fact that he is teaching the crowds in the temple and that the religious authorities stand over against them afraid of their opinion (see v. 26) serves as a reminder to contemporary readers that Matthew does not present Jesus as being in conflict with the Jews but with the religious leaders as part of his narrative goal of legitimizing the existence, theology and practices of his church over against the synagogue in a post-temple era. Those who have power in the temple, therefore, are presented as being threatened by Jesus' return to the temple following his actions of the previous day. So they challenge him, asking by what and by whose authority he is doing "these things" (v. 23). The reference to "these things" is ambiguous, but in the narrative context the leaders are likely referring to the triumphal entry into the city and temple at which Jesus is praised as the Son of David coming in the name of the Lord, the "cleansing" of and healing in the temple, and now the teaching in the temple. The readers, of course, have known since the birth narrative—in which Jesus was declared the Messiah, Emmanuel who was conceived by the Holy Spirit (1:16, 18, 23)—by what and whose authority Jesus does *all* things. Moreover, they have heard Jesus' authority explicitly lifted up during his ministry in and around Capernaum (7:29; 8:5-13; 9:1-8; 10:1). It is not important, for the reader, that Jesus answer the question.

What Matthew intends to portray, instead, is the religious leaders struggling to hold on to the authority they have claimed for themselves, that is, in Matthew's eyes authority that comes only from humans. Their question is meant to trap Jesus. If he says his authority is from God, they can accuse him of blasphemy. If he says it is from humans, they can dismiss him. But Jesus refuses to play their game unless they will abide by the same rules, so he asks them by what and whose authority did John baptize (vv. 24-25). They are trapped as they hoped to trap Jesus, and they, too, refuse to give any answers.

But Jesus will not let things end here. As we have seen repeatedly in Matthew, Jesus is willing to spar aggressively with the religious leaders. He tells a parable in which a vineyard owner—recalling the vineyard owner of the previous lection (20:1-16) and foreshadowing the one of the next lection (21:33-46)—instructs his sons to go work in the vineyard (21:28-30). The first son refuses but ends up behaving obediently. The second son answers affirmatively, even to the point of calling his father *kyrios* (the NRSV translates this as "sir" instead of "lord," which disguises the connection of this parable with 7:21, "Not everyone who says to me, 'Lord, Lord,' will enter the kingdom of heaven, but only the one who does the will of my Father in heaven"). But then he does not go work in the vineyard.

Jesus then asks the chief priests and elders which of the sons did the will of the father. Now they answer Jesus, and they answer correctly, naming what is obvious in the story. But in doing so they step into the trap they tried to avoid with the previous question and condemn themselves (cf. their similar willingness to answer the question at the close of the next parable, 21:41). And then Jesus makes clear that tax collectors and sinners will enter the reign of heaven before the religious authorities will (vv. 31-32; cf. 9:10-13).

In the course of this dialogue, two things about Jesus' authority are re-affirmed: First is what we have already mentioned, but is worth naming differently at the end of the reading. By seeing through the trap being set and turning it back on the religious leaders, Jesus is portrayed as having authority they do not. This, in turn, lifts up the authority of Matthew's church over against the post-temple synagogue, since Jesus has passed his authority on to the disciples as representative of the church (see ch. 10; 16:17-19; 18:18-20). And, second, Jesus' authority is linked closely to the authority John possessed, reminding readers of the similarity of their proclamation shown earlier in the narrative (compare the summary of John's message in 3:2 with that of Jesus's preaching in 4:17; see also 11:1-15; 17:13).

Preachers will do well to attend in their sermon to Jesus' refusal to answer the question placed before him, because a similar approach arises in other conflicts with religious leaders. In truth, for Matthew this scene is less about the christological issue of Jesus' authority (although it is about that) and more about the ancient rhetorical sparring that is taking place in laying bare the impotence of the religious leaders. Matthew continues to legitimize his church through the lens of such conflicts Jesus wins, but he also sets the path to the cross in place. Because they cannot overcome Jesus's teaching (concerning the reign of heaven), they will be forced to turn to the power of Caesar to attempt to silence him by death (which of course fails as well).

Moreover, the religious leaders did not seek an honest answer to their question, so they did not deserve one. Jesus has over and over again offered his message to those with ears willing to hear. Being willing to hear involves risk—risk of having one's world-view radically altered and life utterly redirected. Otherwise, Jesus' teaching (especially in the form of parables seen in ch. 13 and immediately following this passage) is unbearable for those who listen but do not understand, who look but do not perceive because their hearts have grown dull. Even though Matthew moves in a different direction for his original readers, preachers may wish to ask contemporary hearers to identify with the religious authorities in the passage and ask whether we do not also try to box Jesus in so that we need not risk what true discipleship will mean for our lives.

LECTION: PARABLE OF THE VINEYARD OWNER
AND THE TENANTS
21:33-46; PROPER 22

This parable is fraught with problems for the preacher. Some of the troubles are found in the text—for example, what is one to make of the enigmatic saying in v. 44? But the primary hurdle the preacher must help the congregation jump over is the supersessionist fashion in which this parable has been interpreted throughout the history of the church. In other words, the parable has been understood to be an allegory in which the tenants represent the Jews who reject and kill the prophets (slaves) and Jesus (the son), so that God (the landowner) condemns and destroys the Jews, handing over the reign of God (the vineyard) to the gentiles (the new tenants). An effective way to preach this parable would be to name this interpretation, reject it, and then offer a new one.

Matthew does indeed present the parable as thoroughly allegorical. But we must remember that Jesus is in conflictual debate here with the religious leaders *of* the Jews, not with the Jewish people as a whole—remember Matthew presents Jesus as a faithful Jew. The allegory unfolds, then, in the following manner:

The image of the *vineyard* represents Israel. In the past, interpreters have sought a symbolic significance for every element of the description of the vineyard—the fence symbolizes the law; the tower, the temple; etc. But this is allegorical overkill. The vineyard was a common symbol for Israel in the ancient world, and the particulars of the description of the vineyard in this parable derive from Isaiah 5:1-7 (see especially vv. 2, 7).

The *absentee landowner* represents the transcendent God. God "builds" Israel. God's transcendence does not mean, however, that God is not concerned for Israel.

The *tenants* to whom the landowner leases the vineyard represent the religious leaders in whose care God has placed Israel. They are to nurture the people and return its "fruits" to God.

The *slaves* sent at harvest time represent the prophets of the past whom God sent to the people but who were rejected by the leaders (as illustrated in their rejection of John the Baptist in the previous passage, 21:23-32; see also 23:37). As with the description of the vineyard, we should resist looking for particular symbolic correlations for the two waves of prophets and the different references to their being beaten, killed, and stoned. Remember that many parables have strange elements or twists in them that raise questions for the hearer (see the introduction to the Parables Discourse in ch. 13). No real landowner would keep sending his slaves (that is, his property) much less a son into harm's way, when he has the power to destroy the tenants as signaled later in the story. The two waves, then (along with the sending of the son) show God's patience with and desire for the repentance of the religious authorities.

Finally, the landowner sends his *son* to collect the portion of the harvest due him. The son obviously represents Jesus. That he is treated in the same fashion as the prophets is fulfilled not only in the passion narrative but in the narrator's conclusion to the scene (v. 46). The rejection of the son, whom the landowner assumed would receive the respect of the tenants, results in the judgment of tenants. It is important in countering an anti-Semitic reading of this passage to point out that it is the tenants and not the vineyard who are condemned. The vineyard (Israel) is appropriately producing fruits. The tenants (religious leaders) are not appropriately offering those fruits to God. In other words, Matthew presents Jesus as condemning the religious leaders here out of concern for Israel, not as a rejection of the Jews. Thus the care of the vineyard is given over to other tenants, who represent the church. [Many still argue that the new tenants represent gentiles because in v. 43 Jesus speaks of the reign of God being given to a "nation" (Greek, *ethnos*). While the plural, nations (*ethnoi*) is used for gentiles, the singular here indicates something else is meant. Given that Jesus enters Jerusalem and the temple in the manner of a royal conqueror, his "nation" is the church.]

The power of this allegory as Matthew uses it hinges on a change he makes to the version he found in his primary source (Mk 12:1-12). In Mark, Jesus tells the parable and then draws the conclusion from it (Mk 12:9). Matthew, however, presents Jesus as telling the parable and asking a question (21:40). The religious leaders answer the question (v. 41). To understand the significance of this shift, it is helpful to think of the scene as a trial scene. Jesus parabolically presents the evidence against the "tenants" (vv. 33-40). The religious leaders serve as the jury and pronounce the tenants as guilty (40). They use stern language in doing so because as the religious, political, and economic elite, they identify with the landowner in the story. Jesus then hands down the sentence but in doing so turns the tables on the jury (21:42-44). He identifies them with the tenants instead of the landowner, and thus places the religious leaders in the position of having convicted themselves.

This allegorical reading of the parable fits with Matthew's narrative flow as the plot draws closer to the point at which the religious leaders will choreograph Jesus' arrest and crucifixion and fits with his theological goal of legitimizing the church over against the synagogue as an heir to and interpreter of Israel's practices, traditions, and faith. But overturning the supersessionist misreading of the passage should only be part of a sermon on this lection. One appropriate way to help today's congregations experience the parable is to model the sermon on Jesus' technique of turning the table on the hearers. As Jesus takes the religious leaders' scorn of the tenants and turns it back on them, so preachers might begin by having the congregation take a critical stance over against the religious elite and then shift to identifying with them. By recognizing ways the church today has assumed the role of the religious powers-that-be, the parable can serve as a call to a new stance for caring for God's vineyard (understood more broadly than Israel in our context to include all of God's children).

LECTION: PARABLE OF THE WEDDING BANQUET
22:1-14; PROPER 23

The Parable of the Wedding Banquet is troubling, to say the least. Most of us prefer Luke's more domesticated version of the parable (Luke 14:16-24). In that version a man (not a king) throws a dinner (not a wedding feast for his son) and sends a slave (only once) to tell those he invited to come. They all offer excuses (without harming the slave), and so in anger the man sends the slave out to bring in the dispossessed (without first killing those who rejected the invitation). Luke's version ends there (whereas Matthew continues on with the king throwing out into apocalyptic punishment one of the second-round invitees for failing to wear a wedding robe).

In the wider context of the discussion about greatness and position around the table (Luke 14:1-24), Luke's version is a parabolic expression of the gospel's soteriological concern for the poor, sick and oppressed. On the other hand, in the wider context of the temple disputes with the Jewish religious authorities (especially 21:23—22:14), Matthew's version is (or at least starts out as) an allegory condemning the religious leaders (as have the previous two parables). Assuming that the king in the allegory represents God, we are given an image of God as acting in violent (throughout the parable) and precarious (in the last scene) ways. The king's punishment of the wedding guest who was brought in off the street for not wearing a wedding robe he could not have been expected to be wearing in the first place is not an appealing lens through which to view God.

But preachers must remember that parables, by their very definition, contain strange elements and unexpected twists that are meant to provoke questions in the hearer/reader through which new insights about God and God's reign can be gained. Thus, even though this parable functions as an allegory, interpreters should not get caught up in the characterization of the king as indicating in any straightforward fashion the character of God. The fact that the narrative world of the parable (a human kingdom) is broken apart in the final scene with the apocalyptic, other-worldly reference (outer darkness) signals that the story is intentionally twisting reality for literary effect. Preachers will need to find a middle path to help their congregations experience the shocking character of the parable without getting so stuck on the details that they miss the big picture.

While we have asserted that this parable flows out of the Parables of the Two Sons (21:28-31) and of the Vineyard Owner and the Tenants (21:33-44) addressed to the chief priests and elders of the people (21:23), we should also recognize that the Matthew marks this parable off from them. The narrator breaks into Jesus' speech with commentary on the response of the religious leaders to the first two parables (21:45-46) and an introduction to this third one (22:1). In this introduction, we are told that "Once more Jesus spoke to *them* in parables" (italics added). The antecedent to the pronoun seems to be the religious leaders with whom Jesus is in conflict. After all, consider how closely this parable parallels the structure of the Parable of the Vineyard Owner and Tenants:

Vineyard Owner	Wedding Feast
Landowner prepares a vineyard	King prepares a wedding feast
Slaves are sent twice to collect the due portion of the harvest	Slaves are sent twice to invite guests
The landowner's son is sent to collect the harvest.	(The feast is for the son of the king.)
The tenants reject and kill the slaves.	The tenants reject and kill the slaves.
The landowner destroys the tenants.	The king destroys the invitees.
The land is given to new tenants.	New invitees are brought into the feast.

But Matthew's parable then continues on with that strange interaction of the king and the inappropriately garbed guest in the wedding hall (vv. 11-13) and a conclusion (v. 14). Given the parallel structures between the two parables, the first round of invitees clearly represents the Jewish authorities but the second round represents the church. Thus the man in the wedding hall is a member of the church. Instead of simply representing the church in this parable as in the first two, Matthew seems to present Jesus as *addressing* the church as part of "them." By way of analogy, we may recall the way the Ethical Discourse was introduced as being addressed to the disciples (5:1-2) but closed with a response by the crowds (7:28-29). Add to this the fact that of the three only this parable is explicitly compared to the reign of heaven (v. 2). Clearly, Matthew intends this parable to speak directly to his readers in a way the first two do not.

Thus for the preacher, the weight of the sermon should focus on the final scene of the parable, especially if the congregation has examined the previous two lections over the course of the previous two Sundays. You see, in comments on the last two lections, it has been suggested that one homiletical approach to dealing with the tradition of anti-Semitic, supersession misuse of Matthew's presentation of Jesus in conflict with the religious leaders in the temple is to ask the congregation to identify with those very religious leaders

Jesus criticizes. This makes sense given that, unlike Matthew's church, which was marginalized and persecuted by those very religious leaders who profited by the status quo of Caesar's reign, the North American church (especially individual Christians, congregations, and denominations of European descent) has a privileged position in society.

But this homiletical move is also exegetically suggested by the Parable of the Wedding Feast. In the preceding lections, the self-serving motives of the religious leaders are unmasked and critiqued through a parabolic reversal—the son who speaks obediently but acts disobediently is replaced by the one who speaks disobediently but acts obediently (21:38-41) and the tenants who reject and kill the slaves and son of the landowner are replaced by new tenants. For Matthew, the church replaces the religious leaders. This parable begins with a similar type of narrative strategy and thus seems to serve the same apologetic purpose, but then a whole new scene (a whole new twist) is introduced into the parable—inside the feast a guest unexpectedly brought in from the streets is kicked out because he is not wearing a wedding robe. (Compare this literary method of adding a new element to otherwise parallel parables to the parables of the lost sheep, lost coin and lost son in Luke 15.)

The key to interpreting the significance of this added element is the note that the second round of invitees includes both the good and the bad (v. 10). Inviting the bad into the reign of heaven fits with what the reader has seen of Jesus' Capernaum-based ministry (summed up for example in 9:9-13) and what has just been punctuated in the temple discourse in 21:32). The invitation is presented as completely undeserved. But as any reader of the earlier discourses (especially the Ethical Discourse) knows, Matthew's grace is not cheap grace. God requires much of those entering the reign of heaven and participating in the life of the church (for example, 7:21-27). Perhaps, the closing scene of this parable makes that point in the shocking manner that it does to temper any self-righteousness they may feel in Matthew's presentation of Jesus besting the representatives of their contemporaneous opponents. Not a bad message for congregations today.

LECTION: CONFLICT CONCERNING TAXES
22:15-22; PROPER 24

Preachers who have led their congregation through Matthew in Year A by this point well know that Jesus' ministry is characterized as proclaiming the reign of heaven from beginning to end (see 4:17). The reign of heaven is a threat to the reign of Caesar and those who profit by it. So the trap laid here by the Pharisees' disciples and the Herodians is a serious one. Paying taxes is a hermeneutical issue (signaled by the language, "Is it lawful?") and a political one and has the potential to strike at the heart of Jesus' ministry.

The scene begins (22:15-16a) with a notice transitioning from Jesus' opening temple conflict with the chief priests and elders (21:15—22:14) to his confrontation with the next group. The Pharisees conspire against him again (cf. 21:45) but instead of confronting him themselves, they send their disciples and Herodians to do the job (perhaps because Jesus supposedly did not already know them as he did the Pharisees themselves and thus might not suspect a trap). Who Matthew envisions historically with these two groups is uncertain, but their symbolic significance is clear enough—together they represent a partnership of the religious and political opposition to Jesus.

The new opponents begin by offering Jesus praise (v. 16b). The praise functions ironically. Characterized as trying to entrap Jesus, the Pharisees' disciples and Herodians speak insincerely; but the readers know what they do not—that their words about Jesus are actually accurate. Thus whatever answer he gives will be truth without regard for those who ask.

Thinking the ground has been prepared with flattery, the trappers set down the snare: Is it lawful to pay the poll tax to the emperor (v. 17)? If Jesus answers negatively, he risks prosecution by the ruling powers. If he answers yes, he betrays his message and risks rejection by the crowds.

The type of logic at work in the trap is similar to that found in the opening temple conflict where the religious leaders ask Jesus by what authority he is acting—any answer gets Jesus in trouble (21:23-27). Since in that setting Jesus refuses to answer if those challenging him refuse to risk anything themselves, we should expect that same sort of response here. Many interpreters of the past, however, have not recognized this. They have sought in Jesus' response an ethic for relating the church and the state (similar to Romans 13:1-17). Indeed, the text has appeared in many a sermon in recent years justifying the payment of taxes to the government.

Jesus, however, is not responding to questioners truly concerned about the matter of how an oppressed people should respond to the taxes imposed on them by their imperial conquerors (much less about the civic responsibilities in a democratic society). They want to trap Jesus, and Matthew wants to show how Jesus escapes the trap and bests his opponents. Thus, as the narrative moves toward Jesus' arrest, the reader is clear that the religious leaders had no justification for their actions. Jesus' response, therefore, is a non-answer of sorts.

He asks for a coin that would be used to pay the tax, and the opponents produce one (v. 19). He asks whose image is on the coin, and they answer that it is Caesar's (vv. 20-21a). These actions have already thrown some of the weight of the issue back on them—they are carrying around (as would have all people in the Roman Empire) the coin carrying the emperor's image that is used to pay the poll tax.

But as in all pronouncement stories. Jesus gets the last word: "Give therefore to the emperor the things that are the emperor's, and to God the things that are God's" (22:21). The last word has two parts. He seems to answer the question with the first clause, asserting that the law does permit the paying of the Roman taxes. But then Jesus offers another line—the last word of the last word. With this second clause, Jesus reorients the entire discussion theologically and escapes the trap. While it may be permitted to give (back) the coin to the emperor because it is already his (at times interpreters have made much of the fact that the Greek verb *apodidōmi* can mean "return" or "pay back," but its more common definition is simply "to give"), we are also to give to God that which is God's. Here, of course, is the point and the puzzle: what is there that is not God's? Caesar's image may be on the coin, but God's imprint is on all of God's creation. The second clause trumps the first—our highest priority is to give all to God. But does this affirm or discount the first clause? Is paying the tax part of giving to God what is God's or is it taking from God what is God's? That question is intentionally left unanswered because the initial question of the opponents was not a sincere one.

Given that this scene is in many ways a game of wits with rhetorical rules that do not translate well into our modern idiom, what are preachers to do with this text? Those concerned with the cumulative picture Matthew offers readers should find a way to walk the congregation through the logic of Jesus' non-answer as part of the ongoing struggles with the religious authorities. But this narration can be used to raise the question, "So what?" The answer to that (sincere) question lies in the final clause of the passage. Instead of inviting a sermon on church-state issues, this lection invites a stewardship sermon. It gives a preacher and congregation the chance to explore the implications of what it means to give to God that which already belongs to God when everything belongs to God. Even in a passage focused on the trickery of the powers-that-be, Matthew turns the table on the readers reminding us of Jesus' continuous call to radical discipleship.

LECTION: THE GREAT COMMANDMENT AND DAVID'S SON
22:34-46; PROPER 25

When first glancing at this lection as a possible text on which to preach, preachers will generally focus on the first section (the discussion of the great commandment) and ignore the second (the question concerning the Messiah as David's son). We might even think this is one of those places where the RCL has done a poor job of combining two unrelated pericopes simply to get more of the Gospel narrative read in a year's time. After all, the second dialogue pales in comparison to the first when it comes to the importance for the modern Christian life.

This focus on the first pericope is a justified move, but before preachers zoom in on the commandments to love God and neighbor, we should at least recognize that Matthew does connect the two conversations in a significant way to draw a close to the temple controversies. For a final time, a representative of the religious powers-that-be test Jesus with a hermeneutical question. This time, however, the test does not concern *a* commandment or a piece of the law. The Pharisee who tests Jesus a final time asks him to evaluate the whole of the law and name the great [not greatest] commandment. Jesus answers as would have any pious Jew of his time who quoted the Shema (Deut 6:4-9) twice a day: love God wholly. But then Jesus adds to this the command to love one's neighbor from Lev 19:18 (cf. 5:43; 19:19). Such an addition would not have been offensive, or perhaps even surprising, to Jews of the day. But Matthew's presentation of *how* Jesus combines the two is important. Changing Mark 12:31, which refers to the command to love one's neighbor as the "second" command with the commandment to love God the "first" (see Mark 12:28-29), Matthew has Jesus call the commandment to love God "the great and first commandment" (v. 38) and then say that Lev 19:18 is "like" it (v. 39). In other words, Matthew goes further than Mark is willing to in portraying Jesus as equating the two commandments in the fashion exemplified in the foundational hermeneutical proposal in the Ethical Discourse (5:17-48). The commandment from Leviticus 19:18 *fulfills* the commandment from Deuteronomy 6:5 (that is, intensifies it in relation to its intent). It is a striking thing indeed for Jesus to be standing in the very center of Israel's devotional and ritual life and claim that loving God is fulfilled by loving one's neighbor.

It is after this dialogue that Mark 12:34 says that no one dared to question Jesus any longer before he presents Jesus as raising the question concerning whether the messiah is David's son (Mark 12:35-37). Matthew, however, moves that notice so that it follows the christological conversation (22:46). Matthew thus connects the two dialogues. In the first, the representative of the Pharisees tests Jesus with a hermeneutical question that gets to the heart of the law. In the second, Jesus asks the Pharisees who were gathered (vv. 34, 41) a hermeneutical question (interpreting Ps. 110:1) that gets to the heart of the identity of Jesus. So in Matthew's configuration of these two scenes, the second dialogue represents Jesus turning the table set by the religious authorities in the first back on them.

This logic of the second dialogue (vv. 41-45) may seem odd to modern readers. It is helpful to recognize that in some ways, Jesus is playing a rhetorical/ exegetical game in order to best the religious authorities. Clearly, with the entry into Jerusalem and the temple, Matthew has affirmed the idea that Jesus is David's heir (see the above discussions of 21:1-17; cf. also 1:1, 6, 17, 20; 9:27; 12:23; 15:22; 20:30, 31). The point here is not to counter that christological affirmation for the reader but to expose the religious authorities' misunderstanding of the idea of the messiah as David's son as leading to their failure to recognize the one in their presence as the messiah (after all, Matthew has even portrayed blind men and a Canaanite woman as recognizing Jesus as the Son of David; 9:27; 15:22; 20:30, 31).

All of this is not to say that preachers should not focus on vv. 34-40 in their sermon but instead to suggest that as part of that focus, preachers concerned with offering a cumulative view of Matthew's plot need to name for the congregation that these two controversies together represent the closing conversation with the religious authorities. In the next chapter, Jesus turns to the crowds and his disciples and indicts the Pharisees and scribes as hypocrites with the strongest language found in the narrative. All of the various ways Matthew has presented the church as a legitimate heir of Israel's faith, tradition and practices are punctuated here with a final and irrevocable narrative break between Jesus and the religious leaders who, in Matthew's view, have failed as shepherds of God's people (recall 9:36). This is a key moment in Matthew's long narrative approach to this issue and should not be passed over lightly.

However, this in and of itself is not enough for a sermon. Focusing on the commandment to love God wholly as fulfilled by the command to love our neighbors as we love ourselves will more than fill the sermon. The preacher will have to deal with two interpretive issues much discussed in the history of interpreting 22:34-40. The first we have already named—the relation of the call to love God with one's whole emotion, life (a better translation of *psyche* than "soul"), and intellect and the call to love our neighbor as ourselves. This has been an interpretive issue because the three Synoptics do not all use the same language to name this relationship (cf. 22:38-29 to Mk 12:31 and Lk 10:27).

The second issue is what is meant by "love." This is in some ways less an exegetical problem and more one of how the word "love" is used in contemporary society. In a culture inundated with romantic notions of love, we tend to think of love as a feeling or attitude toward another (that is, do we "like" the other person?). In the ancient world (both in the Hebrew Bible and New Testament manifestations of these commandments), however, these commandments are concerned with behavior. Love is not about how we feel but about how we act toward God and neighbor. As in so many places in the Bible, and in Matthew specifically, the line between religious devotion and ethics is erased.

Lection: Warning about Scribes and Pharisees
23:1-12; Proper 26

Preachers, tread carefully when approaching this lection in the pulpit! Repeatedly throughout this commentary, flares have been shot in the air to warn against ways that Matthean passages involving conflict with religious leaders have been interpreted in the history of the church to support (conscious or unconscious) anti-Semitic and supersessionist claims (especially in the temple controversies just prior to this speech in 21:23—22:45; but for explicit warnings against religious leaders similar to this speech, see 15:10-20; 16:5-12). We have noted that Matthew's concern is with the religious leaders, not with the Jewish people, and that this concern is rooted in the sibling rivalry between the church and the synagogue in the decades following the fall of the temple and leads Matthew to contort the image of the religious leaders in a negative fashion. In other words, Matthew has presented Jesus as taking on the religious leaders to legitimate the church as heir to and interpreter of Israel's faith, traditions and practices. But chapter 23 ratchets up the rhetoric significantly. Not only is the picture of the Pharisees and scribes skewed for Matthew's purposes, their character is skewered.

First, then, preachers need to explicitly name that Matthew unfairly misrepresents and stereotypes the religious leaders of the first century as part of his family battle with the synagogue. This will help the congregation see the difference between historical description and the Gospel's advocacy for the early church.

Second, then, preachers can make it clear that the hyperbolic nature of indicting the leaders for everything from hubris to murder was typical rhetoric used in religious and philosophical polemic in the ancient Mediterranean world. Indeed, one can create a catalogue of all the charges Jesus is presented as making against the scribes and Pharisees in chapter 13 and find parallels spread through literature in which one Jewish group indicts another group within Judaism using the same accusations. Thus, what we find here is really an inter-Jewish conflict: Jesus (a Jew) and the church (heir of Israel and including Jewish Christians) over against the beginnings of Pharisaic Judaism. A helpful analogy might be the way hyperbolic polemics are used during political elections in today's world. Standard types of accusations and attacks are made in the most strident of terms. The audience knows this is what is happening and likely dismisses much of the content expressed in the advertisements on an intellectual level. Nevertheless, the rhetorical effect is still real and influences the way people vote.

Framing the tone of the speech in such a fashion will allow the preacher to lead the congregation past some of the specific accusations in the indictment of the religious leaders and perhaps hear a word addressed to them. After all, while Jesus is presented as addressing the scribes and Pharisees directly starting in v. 13, this is really an apostrophe—a rhetorical/literary technique in which an absent person or inanimate object is addressed for the benefit of the reader/hearer (for example, "Jerusalem, Jerusalem," in 23:37). Jesus' polemic is presented as being aimed at the Jewish religious leaders, but Matthew writes this speech for the church.

This is especially clear in the opening section of the speech, vv. 1-12. Following the narrative introduction (v. 1), the passage addresses two topics. The first is the hypocrisy of the scribes and Pharisees (vv. 2-4). Notice in the midst of the indictment, Matthew has Jesus instruct the crowd to follow their teaching (v. 3). Remember, Jesus has made it clear that he has not come to abolish the law and prophets but to fulfill them (5:17-19). Even though Matthew presents Jesus' (and the church's) interpretation of the law as being at odds with that of the synagogue, we should not be surprised that the Gospel presents Jesus as having some appreciation of their teaching. After all, when Jesus declared his commitment to fulfilling the law he added the warning, "Unless your righteousness exceeds that of the scribes and Pharisees you will never enter the reign of heaven" (5:20). The scribes and Pharisees are not condemned as unrighteous, but simply as not righteous enough. At least part of Matthew's concern here, then, is to promote the righteousness of his readers by encouraging them to do as the leaders of the synagogue have taught. (The use of the past tense here is intentional. Note that v. 2 literally reads, "The scribes and the Pharisees *sat* on Moses' seat," even though most English translations render it using the present tense, "sit." From Matthew's perspective, the Pharisees and scribes' authority to interpret the law is in the past.)

An even more explicit turn from description of the faults of the religious leaders to prescription for Jesus' disciples and Matthew's readers is found in the relation to the second topic, the desire for prominence (vv. 5-12). Jesus begins (vv. 5-7) by describing the actions of the scribes and Pharisees as being done to be seen by others and gain recognition (recall 6:1-18). But then with an emphatic linguistic signal at the beginning of v. 8, Jesus shifts from third person description to second person exhortation: "But you" (the Greek is just as emphatic in starting the sentence with *Humeis de*). Then, in material about twice as long as the indictment (vv. 8-12), Jesus warns his followers against such actions, especially as seen in being called rabbi, father, or leader, when such honor should be reserved for Christ and God. The general call to humility and service that concludes the section is familiar to the reader (5:5; 18:1-4; 20:25-28). So what we find here projected onto the scribes and Pharisees is a concern Matthew obviously has with leadership in the church that is taking on trappings of hierarchical rank which he finds problematic.

This is the best point of contact for preaching this text in today's church. In what ways do we still need to hear the call to humility and service within the community of faith? The text invites both a communal (ecclesiological) and individual reflection on this question.

Passion, Death, and Resurrection in and around Jerusalem: Eschatological Discourse (24:1—25:46)

Introduction

Matthew 21–23 has focused on Jesus getting into the temple and besting the religious authorities in conflicts dealing with interpretations of the *torah*. In 22:46, the narrator told us that the religious leaders finally give up on their strategy of trapping Jesus in hermeneutical battles of wit, which led Jesus to turn to the crowds and disciples (who presumably have been listening in on the controversies) and condemn the scribes and Pharisees (as representatives of the religious leaders as a whole) in scathing terms (23:1-36) that transparently reveals Matthew's approach to the conflict between his church and the synagogue in the post-temple era of the later first century. Jesus' condemnation ended with a lament over Jerusalem, the city that kills prophets and those sent to it (23:37-39). The way the temple conflicts end set the stage for Jesus to leave the temple never to return (24:1) and to look forward . . . all the way forward to the *eschaton*.

The Eschatological Discourse is Matthew's fifth and final collection of Jesus' core teachings. As we have noted before, Matthew's use of discourses is likely suggested by Mark's shorter parables and eschatological discourses (Mark 4:1-34; 13:1-37). Thus the placement of this discourse in Matthew follows Mark's placement. Still, preachers should not miss the way Matthew uses, edits and expands Mark's discourse to give it a climactic role in Jesus' teaching in the First Gospel. Following the Ethical (chs. 5–7), Mission (10), Parables (13) and Community (18) Discourses, this teaching on the "end" is the end of Jesus' teaching (signaled by the expansion of the formulaic conclusion to the discourses with the words, "When Jesus had finished saying *all* these things," 26:1; cf. 7:28; 11:1; 13:53; 19:1). Moreover, while the other four discourses are all presented as occurring in Galilee, Jesus delivers this one in Jerusalem: Jesus' sermon on the "end" comes at the end of his life and at the end of Matthew's story.

Of course, this is not the first appearance of Matthew's eschatological outlook. We have noted throughout the commentary how thoroughly eschatological the gospel is, and especially how often eschatological themes have played significant roles in the other discourses. In this final discourse, however, the eschatological voice that has all along been singing the descant takes over the melody line.

A specific illustration of this dynamic is helpful. Throughout the Capernaum-based ministry, Jesus here and there refers to himself using the christological title, "Son of the human." In addition to some nonspecific uses of the title (8:20; 11:19; 12:8; 13:37), Matthew presents Jesus as using the term in two primary ways. First, he uses it in an apocalyptic context (related to inheriting the title from Daniel as described in the Introduction) to speak of the *parousia* (10:23; 16:27-28). Second, Jesus speaks of the Son of the human primarily in the context of foretelling his impending death and resurrection (12:40; 13:41; 16:13 connected with v. 21; 17:9; 17:12, 22; 19:28; 20:18, 28). Nowhere during the temple scenes does Jesus use this language. Instead, the dominant christological title at play once Jesus begins approaching the temple is the "Son of David" (20:30, 31; 21:9, 15; 22:41-45). Connected with this emphasis are allegorical references to Jesus as God's Son (21:27-39; 22:2). Jesus then, speaking to his disciples alone, returns to the title "Son of the human" dramatically (24:27, 30, 37, 39, 44; 25:31; Son of David is not present at all and Son of God is implied only in 24:36). Matthew's use of this title here as Jesus leaves the temple and heads toward the cross brings together the two dominant uses of the title we noted above. Placed in Jerusalem, then, the discourse makes clear that the death and resurrection are eschatological events.

Given this complex dynamic, it is important before looking at specific passages in the Eschatological Discourse to recall our description of Matthew's use of eschatology. Matthew's eschatology is best understood in the context of the gospel's broad picture of salvation history. Although Matthew's plot extends from the conception to the resurrection of Jesus, his story world extends from Abraham (1:1) to the end of time (28:20). Put differently, at all times in his narrative, Matthew has in view both Israel's past and the church's future, and the story of Jesus serves as the hinge between the two. Jesus leans toward the future of the church (and indeed of the cosmos) in that even the eschatologically charged death and resurrection narrated within the storyline is not the end of his work—the *parousia* is.

All of the uses of "then" in chapter 24 (Greek, *tote*: vv. 9, 10, 14, 16, 21, 23, 39, 40) and especially the use of "immediately" in v. 29 might lead a reader to assume that Matthew is laying out an orderly chronology of end-time events building up to the *parousia,* but this is not the case. After all, Matthew makes a point not to overstate his knowledge of the end (24:36). Moreover, consider the structure of the first half of the Eschatological Discourse. The disciples ask, "What will be the sign of your *parousia* and the consummation of the age?" (v.3) and Jesus begins with a lengthy descript of hardships to be expected—political violence, natural disasters, persecution of the church, and the destruction of Jerusalem and its temple (vv. 4-26). But the very purpose of these descriptions is to show that they are *not* signs of the end, of the *parousia*, as signaled by the opening warning that the disciples not be led astray (v. 4).

The section concludes instead with a description of the *parousia* as a cosmic event (vv. 27-31). It will be accompanied by cosmic signs described in scripture—that is, the destruction of the lights in the sky (24:29). If there is any question whether the Son of the human has come, then he has not yet come. When he does come, it will be unmistakable and undeniable. So events that have parallels in history (and which can be listed in a chronological order) should not be confused with the *parousia*.

This does not mean such events have no eschatological import, however. Matthew's wants them to be understood eschatologically even if they are not literal signs of a literal end of time. Indeed, the evangelist takes very seriously the level of suffering that can be found in such times (see vv. 19-21). These types of events only make sense in light of the "already/not yet" of eschatological Christian existence. God's salvation and judgment have already arrived in Christ (as seen in the existence of the church), but they are not fully consummated (as seen in the continuing reign of evil in the world). For Matthew, it is incorrect to view the first coming of Jesus as historical and the second as eschatological. To speak the name Jesus is, in Matthew's view, to make an eschatological statement.

Thus while Matthew surely held to a literal understanding of the parousia as a literal event that would bring an end to the world (in the sense that it would transform history by ending the reign of Caesar/Satan and consummating God's reign), he is most concerned with an eschatological worldview that calls his readers to live eschatologically in the present (whenever that present is). The First Gospel presents Jesus as repeatedly predicting that the *parousia* would occur during the lifetime of some of those in the story (that is, in his generation—see 10:23; 16:28; 24:34). Matthew and Matthew's church, of course, know this did not occur or they would not be around to write and read this Gospel. The presence of the motif, then, points to a metaphorical interpretation of his eschatological themes alongside any literal interpretation one might propose. After all, one does not edit Mark's Gospel to include teaching to give a foundation for the hermeneutics and practices of the church for the long run with the expectation that the Son of the human is literally surfing in on the clouds any minute.

In other words, Matthew wants to offer his readers a view of living in the "already/not yet" of following Jesus Christ. Already: the birth, teachings, healings/exorcisms, death and resurrection of Jesus as a whole mark the incursion of the end of the ages, in which we currently live and which we wait to see fulfilled. Not yet: we also currently live in a day when Caesar (as a symbolic representation of human power enforced on others) and his demonic allies rule with intimidation, oppression, violence and death and long faithfully for the consummation of God's reign. As long as we can say Christ has come, we live as a saved people. As long as the sun is up in the sky in the same way it was yesterday, we need to keep living toward God's future in which the Son of the human will bring salvation to entire cosmos. Thus the Eschatological Discourse is in many ways another ethical discourse. In it Jesus provides instructions on living out this in-betweenness that is characteristic of Christian experience.

In today's theological climate, and given the passing of two thousand years without the *parousia*, preachers will do best to interpret Matthew's eschatological themes in experiential terms instead of chronological ones. Eschatological existence can be compared to driving a car on a lonely country road (with no street lamps) at night. With no oncoming traffic, you put your high beam lights on and ease toward the center of the road a little. But then as you begin to rise up a slope, you see headlight beams coming from the other side of the hill. You move back to the right some and turn off the high beams.

This is a simplified metaphor for the experience already/not-yet. You have not yet met the vehicle coming your way, but you have already adjusted your driving in relation to its approach. To be a Christian shaped by the Christ event but living in a world shaped also by evil forces is to live every day in relation to having already experienced and responded to the oncoming headlights but having not yet experienced but preparing for meeting the full reality of the vehicle.

The second half of the Eschatological Discourse is a series of parables that unpack this eschatological experience and the responsibility that comes with it in a variety of ways. As we recall from the discussion of the Parables Discourse in chapter 13, parables are "narrative metaphors, drawn from nature or common life, which arrest the hearer by their vividness or strangeness and leave the mind in sufficient doubt about their precise interpretation or application to tease it into active thought even to the point of altering one's worldview."

This definition is especially important to keep in mind when dealing with parables that offer eschatological ethics. For example, one element of Matthew's eschatology found in the parables will force a serious reader today to reconsider what we have assumed to be the standard New Testament apocalyptic view. This view can be illustrated with 1 Thessalonians 4 in which Paul answers the concern of the young church in Thessalonica about what happens to the faithful who have died when the *parousia* occurs. Paul assures the church that the dead in Christ will rise first. But he goes on to say in v. 17, "Then we who are alive, who are left, will be caught up in the clouds together with them to meet the Lord in the air; and so we will be with the Lord forever." This language has been interpreted (through connections with imagery in Revelation) to mean that the faithful will be taken away and the unfaithful will be left behind. This view of being left behind as being damned has won the day in contemporary popular theology.

Matthew has been read in these terms, but incorrectly so. The parables in Matthew's final discourse are about eschatological responsibility (in the present). This can be seen in the fact that the ones "left behind" in the parables are those who are saved, and an element of being saved is being given more responsibility. In the parable of the flood (24:37-42), Noah is left behind while the others are swept away. In the parable of the faithful or unfaithful servant (24:45-51), the master rewards the faithful one with added responsibility and cuts the unfaithful one in pieces, putting him "with the hypocrites, where there will be weeping and gnashing of teeth." In the parable of the talents (25:14-30), the slaves who received five and two talents from the master before he went and doubled the amount by his return are "put in charge of many things," but the master throws the slave who received one talent and did nothing but bury it "into the outer darkness, where there will be weeping and gnashing of teeth." And in the parable of the judgment of the gentiles, the Son of the human (the king) gives the reign of heaven to those who have cared for the king by caring for those in the church who are hungry, thirsty, a stranger, naked, sick and imprisoned, and sends those who did nothing "away (*aperchomai*) into eternal punishment" (cf. the same dynamic of the saved being left behind and the condemned being taken/cast away in 7:21-23; 13:24-30, 36-43, 47-50; 22:1-14.)

The idea of eschatological responsibility for those "left behind" is summed up near the end of the parable of the talents: "For to all those who have [faithfulness in responsibility], more [responsibility] will be given, and they will have an abundance; but from those who have nothing, even what they have will be taken away" (25:29). The image, then, of eschatological experience offered by Matthew is one of patient, faithful service in the already/not yet of the Christian life. The sun is still shining so the consummation of the age has not occurred. God/Christ is present with us (1:23; 28:20) but not as fully present as we long for in the face of pain, violence, poverty and oppression. What then are we to do? We live daily working toward "the end" over whose arrival we have no control. We struggle with mercy against injustice and suffering not because we can bring it to an end by our own doing, but simply because that is who (that is, signifies "whose") we are. We are a people who in Christ have had a foretaste of God's future reign, and thus can never again live comfortable with the state of the present. The eschatological reward we *have been* given is the work to be done *until*.

In truth it is a much more difficult responsibility to preach good news that involves this tensive understanding of eschatological experience than either the literalist (mis)interpretation of eschatological language of the New Testament or the mainline de-eschatologizing of the New Testament altogether. But, then again, to those who have, more responsibility will be given, and they will have an abundance.

The homiletical difficulties related to the Eschatological Discourse only begin there for the lectionary preacher. The RCL ignores the tight logical structure of the discourse—introduction/question (24:1-3); events that are not signs of the *parousia* (24:4-26); the *parousia* as an undeniable cosmic event (24:27-31); parables concerning eschatological ethics (24:32—25:46)—and instead draws its four lections from the discourse only from the final parabolic section. As we have noted repeatedly, this selection is related to the RCL's economic, harmonizing strategy of using as much of the synoptic material as possible with as little duplication of parallel passages from the three Gospels over the three years of the lectionary cycle as possible. Consider the material from the synoptic eschatological discourses used across the three-year cycle:

	MATTHEW, YEAR A	MARK, YEAR B	LUKE, YEAR C
Prediction of the Destruction of the Temple and Beginning of the Birth Pangs	24:1–8	13:1–8, Proper 28	21:5–11, Proper 28
Coming Persecutions	(10:17–22), 24:9–14	13:9–12, 13:13	21:12–16, 21:17–19, Proper 28
The Desolating Sacrilege	24:15–22	13:14–20	21:20–24
Beware False Messiahs	24:23–24, 24:25–28	13:21–23	(17:23), (17:24, 37)
The *Parousia*	24:29–31	13:24–27, Advent 1 (vv. 24–37)	21:25–28, Advent 1 (vv. 25–36)
Parable of the Fig Tree	24:32–36	13:28–32, Advent 1 (vv. 24–37)	21:29–33, Advent 1 (vv. 25–36)
Parable of the Returning Master		13:33–37, Advent 1 (vv. 24–37)	
Parable of the Flood	24:37–44, Advent 1 (vv. 36–44)		(17:26–36)
Parable of the Faithful or Unfaithful Servant	24:45–51		(12:41–46), Proper 14 (vv. 32–48)
Parable of the Ten Bridesmaids	25:1–13, Proper 27		
Parable of the Slaves Given Talents	25:14–30, Proper 28		(19:11–27)
Parable of the Judgment of the Gentiles	25:31–46, Reign of Christ; New Year ABC		

While there is merit in this liturgical approach, it makes it harder for congregations to get a cumulative exegetical picture of Matthew's theological and plot development. Preachers will need to name something of the argument and structure of 24:1-31 to help the congregation fully appreciate what is being asserted in the parables selected as lections.

Yet another hurdle for cumulative preaching of these lections is that the first reading from the Eschatological Discourse is the very first gospel lection of Year A and the last three lections from it are the last three gospel lessons for the year. The First Sunday in Advent is and has traditionally been associated with eschatology. The hope and expectation for the coming of Christ does not begin with the birth story. The liturgical year begins at the End. Only in Year A is this beginning not specifically Jesus' announcement of the *parousia* in the eschatological discourse (Year B: Mk 13:24-37; Year C: LK 21:25-36). Instead Year A starts with the parable of the flood (24:36-44).

Regardless, the church must wait eleven months before returning to the discourse. The liturgical year traditionally ends on an eschatological note as it heads toward the final Sunday, the Reign of Christ, and returns to Advent. Thus interestingly, the final three gospel lections of Matthew in Year A that are drawn from the concluding verses of the Eschatological Discourse lead into Mark's proclamation of the *parousia* as the opening for Year B. This dynamic invites a thematic approach to preaching cumulatively in connecting the end and beginning of the calendar, even it if causes problems for hearing Matthew's unique eschatological orientation cumulatively.

Passages Omitted from the Lectionary

The RCL omits the first half of the Eschatological Discourse in which Jesus answers the disciples' question: "What will be the sign of your coming and of the consummation of the age?" (24:3). The answer is first offered in the negative (describing what are not signs), and is followed by the positive (what are signs). The RCL's choice to focus on the parables at the end of the discourse (with only 24:45-51 omitted) is essentially a good one. It focuses on Matthew's eschatological ethics instead of the material that might be considered more speculative. On the other hand, proper understanding of the parables is dependent on the argument found in the opening section.

Hardships That Are Not Signs of the End (24:1-26): Omitted from Lectionary

This section is actually several passages but they are worth considering together because they comprise the first part of Matthew's argument. The section begins with Jesus and the disciples departing from the temple, and Jesus predicting its destruction (vv. 1-2). The disciples question Jesus about this, but ask more than just that: "Tell us, when will this [the destruction of the temple] be, *and* what will be the sign of your *parousia* and of the consummation of the age?" (v. 3) The first part of Jesus' response (vv. 4-26) subordinates the issue of the temple to the other two questions.

But what is really at stake for Matthew in this section is explaining what are *not* to be considered as signs of the end or the *parousia* (which are really synonymous for the First Gospel). Jesus offers three categories that some confuse with signs of the *telos* (vv. 3, 6, 13, 14): political violence and natural disasters (vv. 4-8), persecution of the church (vv. 9-14), and the destruction of the temple (vv. 15-26; drawing heavily on Daniel, see 9:27; 11:31; 12:11).

Focusing on this section in a sermon will allow preachers to critique the popular voices in the media that scour the news and identify this event and that disaster as signs of God's judgment and the end coming in twenty-four days and at 3:17 AM. In contrast, then, preachers can offer their congregations an outlook that names eschatology as an understanding of Christian experience that fits with the fact that after two thousand years the world is still here that builds on Jesus' *via negativa* argument. An important element of doing this is to help the congregation see how seriously Matthew takes evil and suffering in the world. There is here no pie-in-the-sky denial of the hardships of Christian existence (or of human existence, for that matter). Indeed, holding on to the type of eschatological behavior that Matthew promotes (in the "already") only makes sense when we look at the frailty and faults of the world honestly (the "not yet").

The *Parousia* as an Unmistakable Cosmic Event (24:27-35): Omitted from Lectionary

This short passage is really the crux of the Eschatological Discourse. It answers the question posed in v. 3 directly and positively (following vv. 4-26, in which Jesus describes what should not be considered signs of the *parousia* and consummation of the age). And it sets up the series of parables that provoke reflections on what it means for Christians to live eschatologically in the present age. The importance of the text's description of the *parousia* of the Son of the human is especially seen in the fact that when Jesus is on trial before the Sanhedrin and is asked directly if he is the Messiah, the only answer he gives echoes the language used here: "From now on you will see the Son of the human seated at the right hand of Power and coming on the clouds of heaven" (26:63-64).

Moreover, nearly every word and image in the passage echoes the Hebrew scriptures—for example, Isaiah 11:12; 13:10, 13; 27:12-13; 34:4; 49:22; Ezekiel 32:7-8; 37:9; Daniel 7:13; Joel 2:10; Amos 8:9; Zechariah 2:6; 12:10—adding to the weight readers should give to this moment in the discourse. The use of this biblical language, filled with its cosmic imagery, makes clear that any prophetic claims that the Messiah has already returned (24:4-5, 23-26) or will return in relation to human or natural events are false. There will be no guessing when the *parousia* occurs. There will be no denying its occurrence. It will be as obvious as a fig tree in season (v. 32). The cosmos will be transformed, and angels will gather the elect. If the sun is still shining and no one from the church has been gathered in, we must continue waiting.

To keep the reader from becoming misguided in focusing on the expectation of the *parousia* in too literal of a fashion, Matthew tempers the apocalyptic biblical imagery with Jesus' claim that, "this generation will not pass away until all these things have taken place" (v. 34). The problem with this claim, of course, is that by Matthew's day (around 80 C.E.), it was already clear that this line (taken from Mark 13:30) could not be considered literally true. Jesus' generation had already passed away, but Matthew chose to keep the comment intact nonetheless. The line is true, but it so in metaphorical, experiential (as opposed to chronological, temporal) terms. Preachers focusing on this text can use its apocalyptic language as a lens through which the congregation can see the radical existence offered to those who live in the already/not yet of salvation brought into the reign of Caesar through Jesus Christ.

Parable of the Faithful or Unfaithful Slave (24:45-51): Omitted from Lectionary

The parables in the eschatological discourse are of the "two ways" sort (cf. Josh 24:15). They lay out two options for responses to the calling to live in light of the eschatological reality initiated by Christ: to fall asleep and be ethically irresponsible or to keep awake and act ethically in a way that exhibits our readiness for Christ to come. This parable is an especially clear example in that vein, with the faithful and unfaithful slaves exemplifying the two ways. This parable flows out of and expands upon the parable of the flood (24:36-44).

Clearly, Matthew is concerned that his readers have become lax in their ethical lives in some way because they have a literalized understanding of the *parousia* and view it as delayed so that there is no urgency to be obedient. Matthew, thus, presents Jesus as raising the eschatological stakes even while offering a metaphorical interpretation of eschatology. Key for preaching this parable is recognizing that responsibility is the reward for being responsible. The unfaithful slave is dismissed in quite the mythic fashion, but the faithful slave is rewarded with more responsibility. Too often we see the Christian life as the test for which rest is the eternal reward. In this parable (and the others in this grouping), the Christian life, the ethical life, *is* the gift of grace.

LECTIONS

Although the first half of the Eschatological Discourse (which lays the foundation for the second half) is missing from the RCL, the parables that are chosen have merit. The two parables that are read on the First Sunday of Advent open the year with an appropriate eschatological tone (foreshadowed by eschatological readings from Luke at the end of Year C). And the three parables assigned to the Sundays at the end of the Year A overlap and reinforce each other's perspective on eschatological responsibility well.

LECTION: THE PARABLES OF THE FLOOD
AND OF THE THIEF IN THE NIGHT
24:36-44; ADVENT 1

Verse 36 is best understood as the conclusion to vv. 32-36 rather than the beginning of the piece of argumentation under consideration in this lection. Consider how the reference to the coming of the Son of the human is used similarly in vv. 39b, 42 and 44 to conclude and punctuate each section of the passage. Nevertheless, because of this repetition, v. 36 works well as the introduction to the passage as a reading in worship. No one knows the time, so quit listening to those who prophesy about when the *parousia* will take place and instead simply be ready . . . any time . . . all the time.

Thus this passage functions as exhortation to be ready (vv. 42, 44); but it also lays out Matthew's (metaphorical) understanding of what happens to those who are ready and those who are not. This is the element of the argument often misinterpreted in popular apocalyptic preaching in today's world. Matthew's theology is assumed to line up with views of the rapture in Revelation or 1 Thessalonians. But preachers need to allow Matthew's voice to speak on its own terms. Matthew reverses the language of who is saved and who is not. In rapture imagery, the saved are taken away and the damned are "left behind." This is not so in Matthew. Moreover, it is important to remember that Jesus is addressing his disciples and thus Matthew is addressing his church. The two groups contrasted in the parable, therefore, are both within the church—not the saved who are inside the church and those not saved who are outside the church.

The structure of the passage is clearly demarcated by references to the coming of the Son of the human as noted above. It is a fine homiletical structure: biblical text, application, exhortation. Following the transitional statement in v. 36, then, Jesus references the story of Noah as an example of people not knowing when something (the flood) was going to occur and thus not being ready (vv.37-39a). V. 39b applies the example as precedent to the *parousia*, so we should expect to find the saved being left behind.

And indeed this is what is found in the next movement of the argument (40-42). Jesus applies the logic of his scriptural example to the experience of those ready and those not ready in his own day. Notice that these are presented as being in work settings. Preachers have usually assumed those taken (*paralambanō*) from the field and the grinding mill are saved and the ones left behind (*aphiēmi*) are forsaken. But this reading ignores the analogy Jesus is presented as offering in the story of Noah. When Noah enters the ark, those who were not ready are "swept away" (*airō* = taken) by the flood. Noah is the one left behind, the one who is saved. So, too, here the one saved are left behind to continue the work in the field and the mill, only now they do it without those taken away. (This element of being left behind with added responsibility is a motif that gets more explicit imaging the Parable of the Faithful or Unfaithful Slave (24:45-51) and in the Parable of the Talents (25:14-30). The movement ends then with another exhortation to keep watch for no one knows when the *parousia* will occur.

Finally then, Jesus concludes this pericope with a metaphorical exhortation (vv. 43-44). The image of the householder keeping watch lest a thief comes serves as a good reminder to preachers that we should be careful about interpreting Matthew's parables in an allegorical fashion without warrant. Jesus is not symbolically representing the Son of the human as a thief in any way meant to comment on the nature of the Son of the human (see the violent king as a symbol for God in the parable of the wedding feast, 22:1-14; or the unjust master as a symbol for the Son of the human in the parable of the talents, 25:14-30). Instead, the image is meant to highlight the dynamic—the experience—of being ready for the unknown, as is made explicit in the final word of the movement (v. 44).

Pastors choosing to preach on this passage on the First Sunday in Advent will do well to establish Matthew's eschatology as primarily experiential instead of literally chronological right at the beginning of the lectionary year focusing on Matthew. They will have opportunity over and over again to repeat this assertion and to unpack its significance for the contemporary Christian life. Moreover, this emphasis is a good start to Advent, the season in which we wait and hope for the coming of Christ. On the first Sunday, we focus on the eschatological expectation of the coming of the Son of the human. On the second and third Sundays in Advent we attend to the expectation of Jesus' ministry as symbolized in John the Baptist. And only on the fourth Sunday does the church turn its attention to the expectation of the birth of the Christ child, as the Son of God. In terms of temporal sensitivities, the season works backward from the future to the past. Theologically and existentially, this is where the church is: between the not yet and the already.

LECTION: PARABLE OF THE TEN WEDDING ATTENDANTS
25:1-13; PROPER 27

When the church turns to this passage in worship as the Season after Pentecost begins to wane, there has been a jump from 23:1-12, the warning about scribes and Pharisees, over the first half of the Eschatological Discourse in chapter 24, to this parable. Moreover, if All Saints was celebrated on the first Sunday of November, the last text from the temple controversies was read two weeks ago (22:34-46) with the Beatitudes read on the week in-between (5:1-12). [Another possibility is that the All Saints Sunday takes the place of this lection.] Preachers will need to offer context to introduce the congregation to the Eschatological Discourse and the significance of this parable in it. Coming at the end of the year, they should have heard much of Matthew's eschatological worldview interpreted by now, but the RCL punctuates the end of the liturgical year with an exclamation point in the form of three eschatological parables.

This first parable in the series comes with some interpretive problems that cannot be overcome. Remember that parables have twists or strange elements that are meant to provoke the hearer/reader into questioning the meaning of both the parable and that to which it is compared (usually the reign of heaven). The problem with this parable is that we do not know enough about first century Jewish wedding customs to recognize which elements of the story reflect real practices and which are twists. Did wedding attendants wait at the groom's house as described instead of being part of the wedding procession? What kind of lamps would have been used instead of torches? Would a groom come late at night? These kinds of questions mean we miss some of the impact the parable likely had for the gospel's original readers. Nevertheless, the parable's meaning is clear enough, due in part to the way Jesus gives clues all along the way as to exactly how the parable is going to end.

The parable functions as an allegory. The bridegroom is the Son of the human, and the bridegroom's delay represents the delay of the *parousia*. Awaiting the groom is a group of ten female wedding attendants (while *parthenos* is best translated as "virgin" it is unclear whether the term is used literally of virgins or figuratively of a role similar to "bridesmaids," but since they are waiting on the groom and not the bride, the more generic view of the women as wedding attendants is best). While ten is a number of symbolic importance in the Hebrew Bible, what is more important here is that the group is divided into two: the wise and the foolish. In past supersessionist interpretations of this parable the foolish attendants have been assumed to be Jews and the wise ones, Gentiles. But the ten as a whole await the bridegroom, thus signifying that they all represent followers of Jesus Christ, that is, the church. Both the wise and the foolosih ones, therefore, are to be found in the church, and represent "two ways" of approaching eschatological existence.

This means that the parable is not an allegory about those inside the church (who enter the wedding hall) in contrast to those outside the church (who are left outside the wedding hall), but an allegory exhorting those inside the church. As with the other wedding parable that appeared in the lectionary about a month ago, just being invited does not mean one gets to stay (22:1-14). Those not properly robed (22:11-14) or not having enough oil for the long wait (25:3, 10-12) will not enter the reign of heaven. Those not living the ethical life taught by Jesus are not experiencing God's reign (see 7:13-27).

On the surface level, then, the parable exhorts the church (as Jesus does repeatedly in the Eschatological Discourse) to vigilantly do good works in preparation for the impending (albeit delayed) *parousia* (v. 13) given that the Son of the human can arrive at any unexpected moment (v. 6).

Parables, however, are never only to be understood at the surface level. Preachers need to help their congregations see that Matthew is not arguing against Paul for justification by works in the sense that good works are the test we must pass to enter into God's grace. Instead, the good works, the ethical life, is the gift of God's reign. It is the way we experience the already of the reign of heaven in the face of the not yet represented by the reign of Caesar. The life of discipleship, for Matthew, is not a test leading to salvation. It *is* the gift of salvation.

Preachers might be tempted to shape a sermon in a way that invites members of the congregation to choose whether to identify with the wise or the foolish attendants. But the parable is told in a way that the hearers/readers are specifically led to identify with the foolish attendants—notice how much focus is on them as compared to the wise ones. In truth, all need to be "wiser" in the sense of the parable, so following the parable's lead in this identification is a sound homiletical approach. Preaching this text invites the congregation to ask not, "Are we ready?" so much as "*In what ways* are we not prepared to meet Christ ever anew?"

Lection: Parable of the Slaves Given Talents
25:14-30; Proper 28

There are three problems with preaching this parable. First, too often this parable has been misused by preachers to talk about financial stewardship in general (since in the ancient world a "talent" was a large amount of money) or stewardship of our talents (that is, since in the modern world a "talent" is an innate gift or ability). Matthew uses the parable quite differently, but congregations likely are so familiar with these interpretations that they assume they already know what the text means.

Second, the parable of the talents has a parallel in Luke's Parable of the Pounds/*Minas* (Lk 19:11-27). But the parallel version is quite different, and preachers must not get lost in scholarship trying to construct an original form of the parable and miss Matthew's particular slant on it and what that message offers a congregation.

Third, the style of the parable is boring. One can get lost, nearly fall asleep, in the parallel structures and repetition of descriptions of the master handing down the money to the slaves and their giving account of what they earned while he was gone (the parallelism and repetition is even more monotonous in the Greek than in English). But this boring element has its function. It focuses the hearers'/readers' attention on the elements that are different, specifically on the exchange between the slave given one talent and the master (vv. 24-30).

As with the previous parable, this one divides the church into two groups. Since Jesus is instructing his disciples there is no reason to assume the different slaves represent those inside and outside the church or gentiles and Jews. Matthew is concerned with inspiring eschatological responsibility within the church in light of the delay of the *parousia*, imaged in the parable by the note that the master did not return from his journey until after a long time (vv. 14, 19). While the master, therefore, represents Jesus and the slaves represent groups within the church, we should be careful about going too far down the allegorical slide. In v. 24, the final slave says that the master is a hard man who reaps where he has not sown. In other words, the master is accused of acting unjustly. The surprise is that the master does not deny the accusation (v. 26). Thus the master's going away, coming back after a delay, and holding his slaves accountable at that point symbolize the dynamic of eschatological experience Matthew wants his readers to understand in the metaphorical promise of the *parousia*. The master's character does not, however, serve as a lens into Jesus' character (see the king in the parable of the wedding feast as a symbol for God, 22:2-14; or the thief in the night, 24:43).

As with the Parable of the Wedding Attendants, this parable divides the slaves who represent the church into two groups—those who are good and faithful (vv. 21, 23) and those who are lazy and wicked (v. 26). What is different about the division here, however, is that it is not even. Five prepared wedding attendants and five unprepared ones now gives way to two faithful slaves and one unfaithful slave. This is significant homiletically because the master has chosen the amount of talents to give each slave on the basis of the slave's ability (v. 15). Two ideas can be drawn from this nuance that may help preachers think about how to invite their congregation into the parable. First, the parable presents a majority of the church as faithful and ready. This means that even though we should follow the parable in asking the whole of the congregation to focus on the final slave (see the homiletical strategy suggested for the Parable of the Wedding Attendants) and ask whether they are like him, we should be careful not to characterize the church as a whole as "worthless" (v. 30).

Second, we have seen that for Matthew the parables in the Eschatological Discourse are about responsibility in the already/not yet that characterizes Christian existence. The note that the master gave different slaves different amounts of talents should remind us not to assume all members of the church must carry equal loads of responsibility to be considered faithful. The slave who doubles two talents is considered just as good and faithful as the one who doubles five (note the parallel wording in vv. 21, 23). Indeed, the slave who was given only one talent could also have been faithful if he had at least earned a little interest on that for which he was responsible (v. 27). The question to ask those sitting in the pew then is not, "Have you carried as much of the load as the person sitting next to you?" but "Have you carried the load appropriate to your abilities?"

Again, we should note that as with other aspects of Matthew's eschatological outlook, the one who is condemned in the story is not left behind while the other are taken away. The one condemned is cast into outer darkness where there is only weeping and gnashing of teeth (cf. 8:12; 13:42, 50; 22:13; 24:51). The ones who are "left behind" are the responsible ones. Indeed, they are given more responsibility for their faithfulness (vv. 21b; 23b; 28). V. 29 sums this up, but the sentence is often misunderstood in light of a prosperity gospel of sorts. It should be understood as referring to responsibility, not to gifts. After all, the text does not speak of the master *giving* (as a present or reward) talents to the slaves but of placing responsibility for his talents in their hands. The line is best read as "For to all those who have [responsibility; that is, acted responsibly], more [responsibility] will be given, and they will have an abundance [of responsibility]; but from those who have nothing [that is, have not acted responsibly], even what [little responsibility] they have will be taken away." This reasserts what we have already heard from Matthew: the ethical Christian life is not a test for which we are rewarded, the ethical Christian life *is* the reward. The more we live it, the more of it we get.

Lection: Parable of the Judgment of the Gentiles 25:31–46; Reign of Christ A/New Year's Day ABC

This final parable of the Eschatological Discourse is assigned to New Year's Day because it invites the question, "Have I been a sheep or a goat, and how do I plan to live my life in the coming year?" It is assigned to the Reign of Christ because the Son of the human is pictured as sitting on the throne of glory (v. 31) and is called king (vv. 34, 40). It also fits for the final gospel reading of the year because it flows out of the two eschatological parables assigned to the previous two weeks.

Like those parables, this one offers a view of "two ways" (dividing the righteous sheep on the right and the unrighteous goats on the left) with one way leading into God's reign (v. 34, 46) and the other to eternal punishment (vv. 41, 46). Like those parables, this scene is filled with parallelism and repetition (cf. vv. 34-40 with 41-45). Like those parables where the wedding attendants were judged on the basis of whether they were prepared for the bridegroom and where the slaves were judged on the basis of whether they brought their master profit, the basis of judgment here is how well the two groups have served the king. The twist, however, is that unlike the earlier parables, the way the two groups serve or fail to serve the king is through acts of mercy performed on behalf of others. This difference signals that there may be others to which we should attend.

Indeed, to understand this parable properly, preachers must recognize the way this parable changes the context from those two parables. First, we have an explicit reference to the Son of the human as a character in the parable instead of simply in the application/interpretation of it. Second, we have shifted from imagery rooted in normal existence (for example, weddings and master-slave relations) to an apocalyptic setting. These two differences already hint that Matthew is doing something different with this parable than the previous two.

A third shift, the most important one and the one that has most been missed by preachers, is that this parable, unlike the previous two, does not divide the church into two groups. Instead, it focuses on the two ways available to the gentiles (that is, those outside the church). Traditionally, when we have preached this parable, we have asked out congregation: are you a sheep or a goat? This interpretation follows the pattern of the previous parables offering two ways to live in the already/not yet of Christian, eschatological existence, and is certainly not a bad message to offer a congregation. But it does not fit with the way Matthew uses this parable.

This shift should not surprise us. Remember, Matthew often presents Jesus as ending a series of similar items with a shift in perspective. In the Mission Discourse, after all the warnings about hardships the church will endure, Jesus reminds the disciples that the mission will be a success and some will welcome them (10:40-42). After two parables indicting the religious leaders in the temple conflicts (21:28-31; 21:33-41), Jesus tells the parable of the wedding banquet and shifts attention to those in church needing to be responsible with the image of the man not wearing a wedding robe (22:2-14). Here, Jesus shifts from parables exhorting the church on how to act ethically and responsibly in the already/not yet of Christian existence to a concluding parable about those outside the church.

This shift is signaled first in the Greek word *ethnoi* used for those who are gathered to be judged (v. 2). There is a translation problem here. The word can mean either "gentiles" (as opposed to Jews and sometimes to the church) or more neutrally "nations" (in other words all nations, including Israel). Although there are a couple of incidents where there is some ambiguity, a case can be made that every time Matthew uses the plural form of the word, he is referring to gentiles (4:15; 6:32; 10:5, 18; 12:18, 21; 20:19, 25; 24:9, 14; 28:19; contrast the use of the singular *ethnos* in 21:43; 24:7). Two of these incidents of the use of the plural form are especially instructive. In 10:5 the disciples are specifically instructed to go only to Israel and not to the *ethnoi,* and then in 28:19 the post-resurrection mission is extended to the *ethnoi.* The most natural reading of those judged in this parable, then, is gentiles.

This is supported, secondly, by the use of the phrase, "the least of these who are my brothers and sisters" (Greek, *toutōn tōn adelphōn mou elachistōn*) in v. 40 and its shortened version, "the least of these" (*toutōn tōn elachistōn*) in v. 45. These labels for those whom the *enthnoi* have or have not treated with acts of mercy echoes earlier terms in Matthew used for members of the church community (cf. "brothers and sisters" (*adelphoi*) in 5:22-24, 47; 7:3-5; 12:46-50; 18:15, 21, 35; 23:8; 28:10; and "little ones" (*mikroi*) in 10:42-44; 18:6 [explicitly names members of the community with the phrase, "little ones who believe in me"], 10, 14). That the Son of the human identifies with them as his brothers (v. 40) echoes specifically 12:50 and 28:10.

If this reading is correct, then what Matthew presents Jesus as doing in this parable is shifting focus from calling those in the church to judge which group (the fruitful or unfruitful) they are in and instead showing them that those outside the church will be divided in a similar fashion. Specifically, they will be judged on the basis of their treatment of those in the church who are in need. If the outsiders have treated those in the church with compassion—feeding, welcoming, clothing and visiting them—then they are accounted as righteous. If they have not done such, they are not righteous. (Remember that Matthew is willing to present Jesus as recognizing the righteousness of those outside the church; 5:20). Seeing those judged as people other than us (that is, the audience of the parable) is a radically different orientation to this text than the way it is usually preached.

In comments on earlier passages in which Jesus indicts the religious leaders, I have suggested that it is appropriate to ask the congregation to identify with them in ways Matthew's original readers would not have. This is due to the fact that the church in North American today (to a certain degree) is in a position of power, privilege and protection that was not true of the early church. In other words, our situation and attitudes may be closer to the characterization of the religious leaders in Matthew than we may want to admit. Given this fact, it is certainly appropriate to ask the congregation to identify with the gentiles in this parable, and preach the same sort of sermon one might on the two preceding parables. The question would be: "Are you standing with the sheep or the goats?" And the sermon would lead the congregation to recognize ways they have failed to serve those who are hungry, strangers to us, naked, sick and in prison. This homiletical approach certainly fits with Matthew's overall eschatological concern that the world is not as it should be and the church should work on behalf of the poor and oppressed.

But the parable also invites a sermon in our pluralistic, globalistic society that might challenge the way the church at times views outsiders. Matthew is very clear here that those outside the church who perform acts of mercy are invited into God's reign (v. 34). The gospel is not here entering an imagined argument between Paul and James over justification by faith versus justification by works. Given his view of the ethical life as the gift of salvation instead of a test for who gets saved, Matthew here recognizes those outsiders who perform the very acts of mercy to which Jesus calls his disciples as living the eschatologically ethical life he offers to his disciples. What would happen if today's church applied the same standard used by the Son of the human to people who hold ideologies and beliefs that are contrary to ours, but who perform acts of compassion we hold as essential to the Christian life?

Passion, Death, and Resurrection in and around Jerusalem: The Passion (26:1—27:61; [26:14—27:66; Liturgy of the Passion])

Introduction

Dating back at least to the fourth century, there is a long history of reading the entire story of Jesus' passion in worship during Holy Week. By at least the eighth century, the passion narratives began to be chanted during Holy Week, evolving over the centuries into the various forms of sung Passions in worship and concerts. Moreover, by the thirteenth century, both liturgical and popular passion plays had begun to develop, which were performed during Holy Week. This historical backdrop helps contextualize the RCL's use of the passion narrative in the liturgical calendar. Instead of reading individual passages from the passion narrative over the course of a number of Sundays (that is, the pattern we see with every other part of the gospel narrative), the lectionary assigns a synoptic version of the passion narrative in its near entirety to the Liturgy of the Passion for Palm/Passion Sunday (with readings from John assigned for the weekdays of Holy Week).

This practice is not only historically established, but accords with the type of literature found in the passion narrative as compared to that in other parts of the Synoptic Gospels. The bulk of the gospel material is composed of short stories and sayings that circulated independently in oral and written form in the early church. The synoptic authors (with Matthew and Luke following the example of Mark) have artistically woven these together into narratives of Jesus' ministry. The passion narrative, on the other hand, has a very different feel to it. While there are distinct scenes in the passion narrative, as a whole it flows more like a unified narrative. Most scholars argue that the passion narrative was a full-blown story that Mark inherited and edited—even with different details and theological interpretations of the passion, John 18–19 matches Mark's passion narrative in terms of broad structure and flow of events narrated. Matthew then follows Mark 14–15 very closely (contrast Luke 22–23, with its many changes to Mark 14–15). Thus, while the cut and paste feel of most of the synoptic material invites reading pericope after pericope, Sunday after Sunday, the unified nature of the passion narrative invites reading it as a whole.

In Year A, then, the gospel lection for the Liturgy of the Passion is Matthew 26:14—27:66—omitting only the introductory summary of the religious leaders conspiring against Jesus (26:1-5) and Jesus' anointing by the woman in the house of Simon the leper (26:6-13). In all the other sections of this commentary, we begin with an overview of the section, glance at the pericopes omitted from the lectionary and then examine more closely those passages selected as gospel readings by the RCL. But such an approach is superfluous for the passion material given that the whole is used as a single lection. Therefore we will collapse the kinds of commentary separated into overview and examination into a single presentation. [While the RCL understandably includes the story of placing guards at Jesus' tomb in 27:62-66 as part of the reading for this liturgical occasion, it is best understood exegetically in association with the story of Jesus' resurrection and the empty tomb. For comments on this scene, see the next section.]

Before we turn to our commentary, however, it is important to note that the length of the reading creates a homiletical challenge: how is such an extensive lesson to be preached? One answer to this question is that we should not try to preach it. Following the liturgical history named above, we can let the reading stand on its own on Palm/Passion Sunday. Read effectively both the flow and pathos of the story of Christ's passion can be conveyed without homiletical exposition. There are two ways this can be done. First, the lection can be read dramatically using several voices—one person reads the lines of the narrator, another the opponents of Jesus, another the disciples, and so on. This need not grow into a full passion play (and should not), but simply reading Matthew's text as a script to help worshipers stay attentive through the longer sweep of reading (especially in an era when we no longer gather in the parlor as families to read aloud together). Second (and not exclusive of the first option), if the liturgical tradition of the congregation is flexible enough to allow, the lection can be broken into scenes and read throughout the service so that different scenes are related to different liturgical acts. The very restructuring of this Sunday's worship into a liturgy of the Palms and a liturgy of the Passion suggests this. As the triumphal entry is read in association with the gathering and praise at the opening of worship, the story of the last supper can be read in relation to the Eucharist, and the scene in Gethsemane read in connection with the prayers of the people. To allow the liturgy to follow the flow of the narrative, however, will likely require some creative rearranging of the usual order of worship for the Sunday. In some sense, the resulting service may seem like a Lenten hybrid of Lessons and Carols and Tennebrae.

To allow the reading of the passion narrative to stand on its own, however, is not without problems. If a congregation is lectionary-based in its worship, Palm/Passion Sunday is the only opportunity to hear a synoptic version of the passion interpreted homiletically. With Holy Week texts otherwise drawn from John and the passion narrative of the Synoptic Gospels not offered up again in Ordinary Time, there is no other opportunity to preach on this story than on Palm/Passion. Therefore, we need to name some homiletical strategies for ways one might preach in light of the length of this reading. First, one might follow the suggestion above of breaking the passion narrative into shorter scenes and instead of preaching a full sermon, the preacher might offer a short exegetical or homiletical comment before or after each reading. Second, a preacher might follow the long reading by focusing the congregation's attention in on a key passage. The choice of what counts as "key" would involve exegetical observations about Matthew as well what is being ignored and emphasized in other Holy Week services. Of course, one way to choose a key passage, is to read only the RCL's shorter alternative of 27:11-54 n the service. Yet this option is still a fairly long reading and will require some decision about where to attend homiletically. Finally, the length of the lection invites preachers to look for overarching themes or plot threads to use as a homiletical focus. For example, one could attend to the characterization of the disciples, the way Jesus acts in light of his impending death, or the way the story constructs for readers some element of the meaning of Jesus' suffering and death.

Given that pastors may choose either to use the passion narrative liturgically as an extended dramatic reading that stands on its own or as the basis of a sermon dealing with some element of Jesus' passion, what follows are some topics that will help them get a handle on key elements of Matthew 26–27.

PLOT STRUCTURE

Since nearly the whole of these two chapters serves as a single lection, we will not examine the material in the passion narrative scene by scene. Nevertheless, getting a sense of the structure and movement of this section of the Jerusalem narrative is essential to its appropriate liturgical and homiletical use.

One might be tempted to outline the material chronologically so that readings during the Liturgy of the Passion unfold in a way that foreshadows the unfolding of Holy Week. It is surprising to note that while the order of events in Matthew's version of the passion (following Mark 14–15) is clear, which event occurred on which day is not. The only two events we can be certain about in terms of determining Matthew's stance is that the crucifixion occurred on the day before the Sabbath (which correlates with our Friday) and the resurrection occurred on the day after (our Sunday). Backing all the way up to the beginning of chapter 26, much less to the triumphal entry into Jerusalem in 21:1-11, is impossible to do with certainty. There are several reasons for this (almost all of which are inherited from Mark).

The first is the ambiguity found in 26:2. Following the conclusion of the Eschatological Discourse (that is, supposedly on the same day of the temple controversies and Eschatological Discourse), Jesus says to the disciples, "You know that *after two days* (Greek: *meta duo hēmeras*) the Passover is coming, and the Son of the human will be handed over to be crucified." It is unclear how "after two days" is to be counted. Are there two days in-between the moment when Jesus speaks and Passover, with Passover occurring on the third day; or is the Passover to be understood as occurring on the second day? The reference to the Son of the human as being handed over for crucifixion does not clear up the ambiguity because while the Greek word *paradidōmi* is primarily used of Judas betraying Jesus in Gethsemane on the evening following the last supper (26:15, 16, 21, 23, 24, 25, 45, 46, 48; 27:3, 4, it also appears in reference to both the religious leaders handing Jesus over to Pilate (27:2, 18) and Pilate handing Jesus over to the soldiers to be crucified (27:26) on the next day. The ambiguity in 26:2 causes problems for identifying what happens on what day in-between the pronouncement and Jesus' death.

The second issue complicates the first one further. The transitions from one day to the next in the passion narrative are not always clearly demarcated. For instance, following the pronouncement in 26:2, the next clear temporal designation is 26:17 which sets the scene on "the first day of Unleavened Bread." It is simply not obvious to the reader on which days the chief priests and elders conspire against Jesus (26:3-5), Jesus is anointed (26:6-13), or Judas conspired to betray Jesus (26:14-16). How much time has passed?

A third issue is that the specific reference to "the first day of Unleavened Bread" in 26:17 is technically incorrect or Matthew (again following Mark 14:12) uses the language in a popular sense. Technically Passover occurs on the Hebrew date of Nisan 14 and is followed by the seven day Feast of Unleavened Bread. Matthew's use conflates Passover and the first day of the feast (that is, probably turning the Feast of the Unleavened Bread into an eight day celebration with Passover as the first day). There is some evidence that this designation was used in common parlance about the holy days, but it is difficult to tell precisely what Matthew has in mind.

The final issue is that it is unclear when a day begins for Matthew. In the Jewish calendar a day began at sundown, while the Roman reckoning of time marked the day as beginning at sunrise. During the crucifixion, for instance, Matthew 27:45-46 marks time in relation to sunrise—noon is referred to as the sixth hour (*hektēs hōras*) and 3:00 p.m. as the ninth hour (*enatēn hōras*). While this might seem that Matthew favors the gentile approach to time, it would have been common for Jews to divide the work day with such language. Therefore, this is inconclusive.

The reason this issue is important is that Matthew refers to events happening in the evening and it is unclear whether he is speaking of the beginning of a new day or the end of the previous day. For example, in 26:6-7, Jesus is described as reclining at the table in Simon the leper's house just before he is anointed. This is clearly a reference to the evening meal. But given Jesus' announcement that "after two days the Passover is coming) in 26:2, are we to assume this anointing occurs on the same day that Jesus made the announcement or the following day. Perhaps the distinction does not seem to be too significant, but when we come to the last supper this issue is more striking. Did Jesus institute the Lord's Supper on the same day he was crucified (assuming day started in the evening) or the day before he was crucified (assuming day started in the morning)? Given that the meal is presented as a Passover meal, it would appear to be the former, but Matthew's use of the word "evening" is imprecise (8:16; 14:15, 23; 16:2; 20:8; 26:20; 27:57). The two possible ways of counting the days in Matthew's passion narrative can be seen in the table:

ROMAN		JEWISH
Tuesday?	Triumphal Entry into Jerusalem and into the Temple (21:1-17)	Monday?
	Temple Controversies (21:18-23:39)	
	Eschatological Discourse (24:1-25:46)	
	Jesus' Prediction of His Death (26:1-2)	
"Two days before Passover" = Wednesday?	Religious Leaders Conspire against Jesus (26:3-5)	"Two days before Passover" = Tuesday? Wednesday?
	Anointing at Bethany (26:6-13)	
	Judas Conspires to betray Jesus (26:14-16)	
	Preparation for the Passover (26:17-19)	Thursday
	Passover Meal/Last Supper (26:20-29)	
Thursday	Prediction of Denial, Prayer ,and Arrest on Mount of Olives (26:30-56)	Friday = Passover (=Day of Preparation for Sabbath, see 27:62)
	Trial before Sanhedrin and Peter's Denial (26:57-75)	
Friday	Trial before Pilate (27:1-31)	
	Crucifixion and Death (27:32-56)	
	Burial (27:57-61)	
Saturday	Placing Guards at the Tomb (27:62-66)	Saturday = Sabbath
Sunday	Resurrection (28:1-15)	Sunday

This has been a lot of detail offered to basically argue that we cannot use the ambiguous chronology to outline the passion narrative in a definitive way. It is worth the time, however, because even though we cannot discern a clear chronology, sketching the material in this way does show how much Matthew slows down the narrative movement once he brings the story to Jerusalem. This is liturgically and homiletically significant for interpreting whatever texts are used on Palm/Passion Sunday. It is unclear how much time is supposed to have passed in chapters 3–20, but the pace of the narrative gives the reader the sense of at least numerous months whipping by. Then the brakes hit and Matthew spends the final bulk of eight chapters on no more than a week. This pace highlights how theologically important this week is and in what sense all the other material of the narrative is a prelude to what is found here.

If this is the nature of the movement and pace of the passion narrative, what is the best way to understand its structure? Because of the ambiguity in the chronology and because the passion narrative has more of the feel of a unified narrative than earlier material in the gospel, we should resist the temptation to draw rigid divisions in the material. Nevertheless, an argument can be made that chapters 26-27 fall into three somewhat thematically focused segments.

The first is 26:1-46 in which Jesus prepares his disciples and himself for his impending death. Certainly other things occur during this segment, such as the religious leaders conspiring against Jesus (26:3-5) and Judas making arrangements to betray Jesus (26:14-16), but these passages have the feel of asides or insertions that are necessary to move the plot toward the next segment more than contributing to the impression offered by the immediately surrounding material. Consider ways Jesus prepares for the crucifixion:

> In 26:2, Jesus reminds the disciples that the Passover and the crucifixion of the Son of the human are at hand.
>
> In 26:6-13, Jesus interprets for the disciples the woman's act of anointing as preparing his body for burial.
>
> At the Passover meal, Jesus obscurely announces Judas' betrayal and institutes the meal of bread and wine as one through which the church will remember his death (26:20-30).
>
> At the Mount of Olives, Jesus warns the disciples that they will desert him (including Peter's denial) but promises that after the resurrection, he will go before them to Galilee (26:31-35).
>
> In 26:36-46, Jesus goes to Gethsemane on the Mount of Olives to pray in preparation for the trial about to come. The angst Jesus expresses is immense but the submission to (and trust in) God's will overcomes it.

In the next segment, 26:47—27:26, Matthew tells of Jesus' arrest and trials. The progression of the story across the segment is straightforward: Jesus is arrested, tried before the Jewish religious authorities, tried before the Roman political authority, and condemned to death. Since the reader knows that Jesus is going to die, part of what drives the plot along at this point are hurdles in each part of the progression that seem to have potential for preventing the execution. As he is being arrested, someone with Jesus draws a sword to defend him and cuts off the ear of the high priest's slave (26:51). Jesus is the one who stops the resistance and interprets what is to happen to him in terms of the fulfillment of scripture (vv. 52-54). When Jesus is being tried before the Sanhedrin, the religious powers-that-be have trouble finding even false testimony that will justify having Jesus put to death (26:59-62). But when Jesus is asked directly if he is the Messiah, the Son of God (recalling Peter's confession in 16:16), Jesus answers with language about the *parousia* of the Son of the human (recalling imagery from the Eschatological Discourse in 24:30). This allows the council to accuse Jesus of blasphemy and hand him over to Pilate.

And, finally, when Jesus does appear before the Roman governor, the hurdles appear *en masse*. First, Pilate questions Jesus, but he gives no clear response that sounds like blasphemy or a threat to Rome (27:11-14). Second, Pilate attempts to release Jesus by giving the crowd a choice between Barabbas and him (27:15-17). And, third, Pilate's wife has a dream about Jesus and warns her husband to have nothing to do with "that innocent/righteous man" (*tō dikaiō ekeinō*, 27:19). But even though Pilate found no guilt in Jesus, he gave into the crowds (who had been urged on by the religious leaders, 27:20) and condemned Jesus to death (27:24-26).

The third and final segment of the passion narrative is 27:27-61, the narration of Jesus' crucifixion, death, and burial. Matthew's narrative has been leading to this moment since Jesus made the first passion prediction in 16:21. The significance of the event is especially seen in the way it confirms the eschatological identity of Jesus as the Son of God, Son of the human. This confirmation begins with mocking from opponents in which they speak insults that the reader knows to be ironically true:

> When the soldiers take possession of Jesus they mock him by dressing and addressing him as king of the Jews (27:27-31). The language recalls the royal imagery in the triumphal entry (21:1-11).
>
> Similarly, when Jesus is crucified, over his head is placed a sign mocking him as king of the Jews (27:37).
>
> This derision continues in words from passersby and religious leaders mocking him as the king of Israel and the Son of God (27:39-44).

Following the ironic confirmation of Jesus' messianic identity, Matthew offers several positive and dramatic confirmations. First, as Jesus begins to die, darkness covers the earth (27:45), recalling the image of the sun becoming dark at the *parousia* of the Son of the human (24:29). Second, when Jesus cries out "Eli, Eli" (an Aramaic transliteration of Ps 22:1), the crowd misunderstands it as a call for Elijah and waits to see if Elijah will come (27:46-49). Of course, Elijah as the forerunner of the Messiah does not come, because he already done so in John the Baptist as the forerunner of Jesus (3:3-4; 11:14; 17:3, 4, 10-13).

Third, at the moment Jesus dies, the curtain of the sanctuary in the temple is ripped from top to bottom (27:51a). This occurrence recalls Jesus' prediction of the destruction of the temple at the opening of the Eschatological Discourse (24:2, 15; see also 26:61). Fourth, an earthquake occurs as Jesus dies (27:51b). The image recalls the shaking of the powers of heaven that accompany the coming of the Son of the human in 24:29. More than that, the fact that it results in breaking open tombs from which many "saints" are raised (27:52-53) makes clear that Jesus' death is an eschatological event and foreshadows the earthquake at Jesus' resurrection in 28:2. And, finally, upon seeing Jesus' death and the accompanying events, the centurion and those with him recognize that, "Truly this man was God's son" (27:53-54). The fact that the very ones who mocked and crucified Jesus (27:27-31), those who most symbolize the oppressive power of Caesar's reign to cause suffering and death, declare Jesus to be the Son of God is extraordinary and should not be missed by preachers due to our familiarity with the story.

If there were any moment in the gospel that makes clear that Jesus Christ offers Christians the salvific experience of the "already" in the midst of the "not yet," it is the passion story. The death scene blurs the lines between God's future and the present even more than they have been blurred in earlier points of the narrative. The movement from preparation for dying, through the arrest and trials, to the crucifixion and death is the christological and eschatological crux of the gospel's proclamation.

CHARACTERIZATION

Throughout this commentary we have pointed to characters in scenes with whom the preacher might identify the congregation in order to gain a sharp point of view from which they can experience the story. Along with recognizing the way the structure and movement of the passion narrative functions theologically, it is homiletically helpful to note the way Matthew characterizes the main players at this climactic point of the story to fund such identification.

Jesus. We have noted above the way the scene of Jesus' crucifixion and death serves as a lightning rod to confirm the eschatological christology that Matthew has developed across the gospel narrative. It is also instructive to note the way Matthew presents Jesus as approaching his death. We must always be careful not impose emotions, attitudes or intentions on biblical characters when the narrator tells us nothing about them. But in the passion narrative, a cumulative picture of Jesus' responses to the progression of events leads us down that path in a way it has not earlier in the Gospel. Jesus keeps mentioning and interpreting his impending death in ways that make it difficult not to hear pathos in his voice.

Chapter 26 opens with Jesus reminding the disciples that the Passover is coming after two days "and the Son of the human will be handed over to be crucified" (v. 2). The two items are named almost as if they are both regular calendar items—no emotions noted.

When the woman anoints Jesus in Bethany, we are told what emotion the disciples experienced—they were angry/indignant (*aganakteō*) (26:8). The narrator does not tell us what Jesus is feeling, but it is clear what is on his mind. He interprets the anointing as preparation for his death (v. 12).

Similarly during the Passover meal we are told about the emotional state of the disciples—they are greatly saddened (*lupeō*) when Jesus announces that one of them will betray him (26:22). Matthew tells us nothing explicit about Jesus' emotional state, but the fact that he curses his betrayer (v. 24) even though his role is necessary for Jesus to fulfill scripture (that is, by dying) shows that Jesus is distressed about his situation.

Still at the table, Jesus again mentions his impending death in relation to the institution of the Lord's Supper (26:26-30). In language resembling an ancient last will and testament of sorts, Jesus asks his followers to remember him through the liturgical practice of sharing bread and wine after he has died, and offers the quite graphic terms of body and blood in making the request.

Even while being portrayed as understandably preoccupied with his coming death, Jesus is also presented as concerned for the fate of his disciples. He tells them that they will desert him, but before they can try to refute him, he promises that after the resurrection he will meet them in Galilee (26:31-32).

Finally, the narrator explicitly names Jesus' emotions in the scene in Gethsemane. Jesus withdraws with his inner circle of disciples (26:36-46). At the transfiguration (17:1-8), they saw his true glory. Now they see his deepest angst. Matthew describes Jesus as starting to become distressed (*lupeisthai*) and troubled or agitated (*adēmonein*) in 26:37. Jesus names himself similarly in the next verse when he tells the inner group of disciples how he is feeling. Translated woodenly, he says, "My life is grieved to death" (*perlupos estin hē psyche mou heōs thanatou*) and then throws himself on the ground in isolation (vv. 38-39). In today's idiom, Jesus is saying, "I feel like I am going to die," not in a flippant fashion but as one who has reached a state of depression where life feels like death. Jesus experiences knowing he is going to die as if death has already arrived. It is difficult to exaggerate the level of agony named here because nowhere else in the Gospel, before or after this scene, are Jesus' emotions highlighted in any comparable manner.

Yet, Jesus' emotions are not the last word on his character. His utter desire that God take away "this cup" of death is subordinated to his obedience to God's will (26:39, 42). His distress is real, but it does not win. Thus when the time for his betrayal arrives, Jesus is not hiding. In fact, he rouses the sleeping disciples so they are all ready for Judas and the religious authorities to come (vv. 45-46).

Then, in the arrest scene, Matthew adds the second largest insertion into Mark's passion narrative (the first largest is the description of Judas' death in 27:3-10) to show that Jesus could have stopped the arrest and crucifixion if he really wished to. When one of his followers cuts off the ear of the high priest's slave, Jesus explains that he has the authority to ask God to send legions of angels to defend him, but to do so would mean ignoring the scriptures that must be fulfilled with his death (26:52-54). In 5:17-18, Jesus claims that he has come not to abolish the law and the prophets, but to fulfill them. Here at the most difficult of his life, when he could choose another route, he holds true to that understanding of his purpose.

Disciples. Repeatedly throughout the commentary, we have noted places where Matthew redeems Mark's portrayal of the disciples. Mark presents them as consistently misunderstanding Jesus' message of the reign of God and who Jesus is. Matthew does allow the disciples to respond to Jesus inappropriately at times but overall makes them appear more insightful and faithful than in Mark. That is, until the passion narrative.

Here, their worst side comes out. When the woman anoints Jesus in preparation for his burial, they become angry (26:8). Judas betrays Jesus of his own initiative (26:14-17, 21-25, 46-49; 27:3-10). When Jesus tells the disciples that they will desert and deny him, they all promise they will not, even if it means their own death (26:31-35). But then in the very next scene in Gethsemane, they cannot even stay awake while Jesus prays in anguish (vv. 36-46). Immediately after that, when Jesus is arrested, they do all desert him (v. 56). Peter follows at a distance as Jesus is taken to the house of the high priest (v. 58), but hides his identity and denies even knowing who Jesus is (vv. 69-75). In contrast to Jesus overcoming his emotional distress, this scene ends with Peter weeping bitterly (v. 75). None of the disciples reappear in the passion narrative after this.

But unlike Mark they do reappear later in the Gospel, when the risen Jesus meets them in Galilee. Jesus promises that this will happen in 26:32. It is not their fear or distress that have the last word about their character; it is Jesus. Even with their failure at this point in the narrative, Jesus foreshadows that he will recommission them after the resurrection (28:16-20) to an even broader mission than they have been called thus far (10:1-42). While their behavior raises the level of pathos of the passion narrative in its isolation of Jesus in his time of suffering and death, they are not ultimately condemned for being human.

Religious Leaders. Throughout Matthew, the religious authorities have been contrasted with Jesus, especially in terms of their approach to interpreting and applying *torah*. They have been characterized as experiencing privilege resulting from the status quo of the reign of evil/Caesar that Jesus counters with the proclamation of the reign of heaven. In the division dealing with Jesus' Capernaum-based ministry, the Pharisees and scribes are presented as Jesus' primary opponents, but following the temple controversies, they disappear until after Jesus' death (27:62). Instead the chief priests and elders of the people (whoever this group is) take center stage. With the Herodians and Sadducees appearing in the temple controversies (22:16, 23), Matthew seems to be conflating the different parties. Following the Eschatological Discourse, the chief priests and elders conspire to arrest Jesus in secret and kill him (26:2-3), just as the Pharisees have been doing since 12:14.

We have repeatedly argued that the religious authorities in the narrative (especially the Pharisees and scribes) are transparent representatives for the synagogue leadership in Matthew's day. The conflicts between Jesus and these leaders is meant to inform how Matthew's church understands and deals with their sibling rivalry with the post-temple synagogue as both assert their legitimacy as an heir and interpreter of Israel's faith, tradition and practices over against the other. On this basis, we have made clear that Matthew is not anti-Jewish or supersessionist in the way the First Gospel is often interpreted. Matthew presents Jesus as a Jew who is not struggling against the Jews but against Jewish leadership.

This situation is complicated, however, in the passion narrative. When Jesus enters Jerusalem and the temple, there is still a clear distinction between religious leaders' negative response to him and the crowd's positive response (21:1-16). In the temple controversies, Jesus is in conflict with the variety of religious and political leaders, not with the crowds (21:23-46). Presumably the crowds overhear the controversies but still find Jesus appealing in that they remain around to hear Jesus condemn the Pharisees and scribes as hypocrites once the conflicts have ended (23:1).

This division between the leaders and the crowd seems to be in place as the chief priests and elders conspire against Jesus in 26:3-5. Otherwise, they would not be concerned about the people rioting during the feast if Jesus were arrested. The division seems to be maintained as Judas negotiates with the chief priests, and not with the people as a whole, in 26:14. But then when Judas comes to Gethsemane to betray Jesus, not only do the chief priests and elders come with him but also a "great crowd" with swords and clubs (26:47, 55). It is difficult to know who is assumed to be in this crowd, so this notice does not smear the line between the religious authorities and the crowds so much as it leads the reader to raise an eyebrow. But then the crowd reappears in the scene when Pilate fails in his appeal to the people hoping to release Jesus and execute Barabbas (27:15-25). They appear to be against Jesus in as strong of terms as have been seen in the Gospel. After the crowd has called for the release of Barabbas, Pilate asks what should be done with Jesus, and they respond, "Let him be crucified!" (v. 22). When Pilate follows up with the question, "Why, what evil has he done?" they do not answer but just shout stronger, "Let him be crucified!" (v. 23). If this were not bad enough, when Pilate washes his hands to declare his own innocence in dealing with Jesus "the people as a whole" (Greek, *pas ho laos*) respond, "His blood be on us and on our children!"

This response has been referenced throughout history to justify the church's persecution of the Jews. Would that Matthew had not added it to Mark's version of the story! But he did. Nevertheless, it should be interpreted in light of the narrative's presentation of the religious leaders as a whole and thus especially in light of the notice in v. 20: "Now the chief priests and the elders persuaded the crowds to ask for Barabbas and to have Jesus killed." Throughout the Gospel Matthew has portrayed the religious authorities as leading the people in directions that are self-serving, and this story is the most extreme example of that. Even though the history of interpretation has focused on the behavior of the crowds as a whole, Matthew really uses the story to show the level of the leaders' hypocritical abuse of power in their desire to maintain their status quo (see v. 18, where even Pilate recognizes the religious leaders are acting out of jealousy!).

In comments on various pericopes throughout Matthew involving religious leaders as opponents of Jesus, it has been suggested that a homiletical strategy appropriate for the church's current situation of privilege in society is to construct a sermon in which the congregation is led to identify with those religious leaders. Congregations, however, are unlikely to be able to make such an existential identification with them in the passion narrative. To see themselves as represented by those who conspired throughout the narrative to "destroy" Jesus is a place the imagination of the faithful may not be able to go. On the other hand, they may well be able to identify with the crowd, as those drawn to Jesus' person and ministry but who are too easily led astray, even to the point of turning on Jesus. If we are honest, we can see in ourselves both the crowd shouting hosannas during the triumphal entry and the one shouting, "Crucify him!" during the trial.

Roman authorities. In the previous discussion of the religious leaders, we described their conspiring role in bringing about Jesus' death (26:3-4). Even though they feared the crowd might riot if they were to arrest Jesus during the festival (26:5), they jump at the opportunity that arises when one of Jesus' own followers approach them (26:14-16). They fabricate evidence against Jesus (26:59-67). And both avoiding a riot against them and manipulating the Roman authorities, they persuade the crowd to become their voice so that Pilate ends up fearing the crowd in the way the religious leaders had originally (27:24).

In contrast, Pilate (along with his wife) recognizes Jesus' innocence (27:14, 18, 19, 24). He even looks for a way around executing Jesus by focusing the crowd's attention on Barabbas (27:15-21). This does not make him the saint in the story, however. Representing the power of Caesar's reign, the Roman governor is still the one who sentences Jesus to death. Washing his hands (27:24) did not, in Matthew's portrayal, cleanse him of any guilt. Instead, it showed he did not care about the issue of justice enough to resist the crowd's desire that Jesus be killed. Moreover, Pilate goes beyond just giving in to the crowd's demands: before he hands Jesus over to be crucified, he flogs him (27:26). Pilate is portrayed as a weak ruler; but a weak representative of the empire still holds the power of death (that is, as long as Jesus allows him to hold it; 26:52-54).

This display of power is manifested and intensified in Pilate's underlings as the story moves from trial to mocking and death. Whether he was innocent or not, the soldiers have no qualms about being brutal in their treatment of Jesus. Their behavior shows that crucifixion was not simply used to kill someone but to shame them publicly as a show of Rome's militaristic power. They mock him as king of the Jews before the entire cohort of the governor's forces (27:27-31). Then when they crucify him, they mock him again with a sign sarcastically declaring his royal identity (v. 37). Passersby, religious leaders and even the two thieves crucified with Jesus bow to the Roman power by joining in with their shaming of Jesus (vv. 39-44).

But then something extraordinary happens. Following the three hours of darkness, when Jesus dies and the temple curtain is torn from top to bottom and the earthquake occurs, the Roman soldiers (that is, the very centurion and those with him who crucified Jesus; cf. Mk 15:39 where it is only the centurion) declare Jesus to be God's Son (27:51-54). Note we are not told that they repented of their actions nor are the readers given any sign that they became converts to Christianity. Instead, we have here a moment—a single, brief moment—when the reign of evil is taken aback by a vision of the reign of heaven. For Matthew, when that happens, there can be no refuting that the cross is truly a revelatory occasion for any who will look at it. Even those who resist the good, know a good thing when they see it.

THEOLOGICAL SIGNIFICANCE

Having a handle on the literary characteristics of plot structure and characterization in Matthew's passion narrative invites theological reflection on Jesus' suffering and death that informs liturgical and homiletical use of the text on Palm/Passion Sunday. In such a process, we must be careful not to impose Paul's understanding of the cross onto Matthew or more broadly to try to make Matthew's presentation of the passion cohere with later theories of atonement proffered in church tradition. As a preacher who strives to offer a congregation a coherent theological worldview, Matthew should certainly be brought into to conversation with these soteriological expressions; but Matthew must be allowed to enter the conversation on his own terms.

We have already named a number of theological themes present in Matthew's version of the passion: the passion narrative reveals Jesus' full identity as Son of God and Son of the human (christology); the passion is presented as a necessary part of salvation history as seen in both the fact that the narrative has led to this moment all along and in Jesus' death as a fulfillment of scripture (providence); and the lines between the death of Jesus and the *parousia* of the Son of the human are blurred to indicate that the cross marks a turning of the ages so that we live in the already/not yet of Christian existence (eschatology). In what follows we reflect on three other theological elements of Matthew's passion narrative: 1) the relation of Jesus' suffering and his death; 2) the exemplary nature of Jesus in the passion; and 3) the redemptive nature of the cross.

Jesus' suffering. In the earlier discussion of Matthew's characterization of Jesus in the passion narrative, we examined the portrayal of Jesus' emotions. Clearly Jesus is presented as being in psychological anguish as he heads toward the cross. Even though this motif diminishes in the trial scenes, it can be seen as reaching its peak in 27:46 when Jesus cries out asking why God has forsaken him—in place of Mark's use of *boaō*, meaning "cry out" (Mk 15:34), Matthew substitutes the synonym *anaboaō* which intensifies the meaning somewhat to imply crying out in grief or lament.

But what does Matthew have to say about Jesus' physical pain during the trials and crucifixion? In a nutshell, the answer is nothing. Clearly there was pain. In his passion predictions Jesus not only named that the Son of the human would die, but also that he would suffer (16:21; 20:19). And, indeed, Jesus is hit, slapped and spat upon by the Sanhedrin (26:67-68). He is flogged by Pilate (27:26). He has a thorn of crowns forced on his head, is spat upon, and is hit on the head with a reed by the cohort of soldiers (27:29, 30). And he is, of course, crucified (27:35). But the narrator in no way elaborates on the pain Jesus experiences in these events. Indeed, it is instructive to note the way Matthew narrates Jesus' crucifixion. It is mentioned in a subordinate position as part of a sentence focused on the soldiers dividing up his clothes (in Greek, the participle *staurōsantes* provides the setting for the sentence instead of its focus).

Since the first crucifix was hung in a sanctuary, preachers have loved to dwell homiletically on the details of Jesus' crucifixion: the nails piercing his skin, the echo of the hammer, the blood dripping down his arms, the pressure on his lungs and heart, and on and on. Describing the gruesome elements of Jesus' suffering in as much detail as possible has been used by preachers to show the level of Christ's sacrifice and thus to evoke a deeper emotional response on the part of the hearers. Pathos gives way to emotionalism. But Matthew's presentation of the cross in no ways justifies such homiletical behavior. It is the *fact* of Jesus' crucifixion and death that is theologically important for Matthew, not its gory details. Noting this for a congregation offers them room to explore the significance of the cross for contemporary theology in new ways, moving beyond expressions of individualized, substitutionary atonement that feed on ramping up the amount and character of Jesus' pain.

Jesus' death as exemplary. The first time Jesus predicted his passion (16:21-23) he proceeded to exhort his disciples that to be his followers they would have to "deny themselves and take up their cross" (vv. 24-26). Even before this in the Mission Discourse, Jesus warned that the disciples/church will face persecution in the same forms he has (10:16-25). If those in Matthew's church will suffer as Jesus did, then the evangelist clearly intends in the passion narrative to offer his readers an example of how Christians should face suffering. As with Jesus they can expect to experience anguish, but like him they should also stand strong in God's will (26:36-46).

Theologically, and pastorally, there is a problem with the call to be willing to suffer as Christ has suffered. It has been too often been used to coerce people into accepting oppressive circumstances. Slaves have been told to suffer as Christ did in serving their masters. Women have been told to suffer as Christ did in serving their men. The list of such illegitimate and oppressive uses of Jesus' death as an example for those faithfully trying to walk in his footsteps is extensive, and they are not all in the past. There is good reason, then, to allow this theme of Matthew's portrayal of Jesus' death to lie fallow.

On the other hand, preachers can lift up Jesus' lament in the midst of his suffering (15:34-36) as a healthy model for those who suffer today. Jesus' utterance comes from Psalm 22:1—"My God, my God, why have you forsaken me?" At first glance, it looks like Matthew presents Jesus as ending his life in doubt. This has been a difficult biblical pill to swallow for many who believe that doubt is the opposite of faith. How could Jesus, the Son of God who knew in advance he was going to die, experience such anguish?

But what Jesus' lament does for the contemporary church is legitimate lament as an important element of the Christian faith. In his last moment, Jesus does not deny God. Indeed, his words acknowledge the silence of God at his moment of death *as* God. It is an incredible act of faith to trust God enough to question God concerning why we are suffering or why (more broadly) evil is at work in the world. Preachers who lift up Jesus' cry as a positive model for being faithful and connect his lament with the much-attested tradition in the Hebrew Bible of naming our pain to God and asking, "How long?" offer permission and absolution to those in the pews who feel this sort of angst and anguish at times but think they must repress it.

The cross as redemptive. As an eschatological event, Jesus' death is more than simply the end of his life, even more than the end of his life that is overcome on the third day with God raising him out of the tomb. The cross, for Matthew, is the occasion of God's redemption. This is named in three ways.

First, at the very beginning of the division, Jesus himself associates his crucifixion with Passover (26:2; see also vv. 17-30). Passover reminded Jews of the paradigmatic expression of God's salvation in liberating the Israelites from bondage in Egypt. To connect the cross with Passover is to claim that it is a similar paradigmatic moment of God's salvific care.

Second, in the scene of Jesus' death (27:50-54), as we have noted, the centurion and those with him recognize Jesus as God's Son when they see his death accompanied by darkness, the temple curtain being ripped, and an earthquake. While we are told nothing of how this affects the Roman soldiers, a soteriological statement is nevertheless clearly made: the cross is revelatory. To know the dying Jesus as the Son of God is to recognize that his very purpose as God's Son was/is to "save his people from their sins" (1:21).

This insight leads us to a third way Matthew names the redemptive aspect of the cross. Just after Jesus has made his last passion prediction and just before he enters Jerusalem, he instructs the disciples to serve with humility and says, "the Son of the human came not to be served but to serve, and to give his life as a ransom (Greek, *lutron*, that is, the price paid for the manumission of slaves) for many" (20:28). Similarly, at the last supper when he names what the cup is to signify, he says, "this is my blood of the covenant, which is poured out for many for the forgiveness of sins" (26:28; language echoing Is 53:12).

Clearly, Matthew interprets the cross as the means through which God offers forgiveness. What is not clear is how Matthew understands this to occur. Nowhere does Matthew engage in speculative theology concerning the way in which God's grace operates through the cross. Nevertheless, one thing is absolutely clear for Matthew that goes against the way the cross is often proclaimed as the moment of salvation: God did not need the cross to be able to forgive humanity of its sinfulness. Already, the birth, teachings, and healings of Jesus have been presented as expressions of God's forgiveness. Nowhere is this more explicit than in the scene where Jesus claims that the Son of the human has authority to forgive sins and heals the paralytic as proof (9:2-8). For Matthew, the cross is paradigmatic of God's forgiveness, but it represents neither the beginning nor the end of God's grace. Following Matthew, then, preachers will do well to name the cross as the central expression of divine forgiveness for the church but one which flows out of God's works as described in the Hebrew Bible and in the life and ministry of Jesus and which flows into to the work of the church as commissioned in 28:18-20.

Passion, Death, and Resurrection in and around Jerusalem: The Empty Tomb (27:62—28:15)

INTRODUCTION

In the Introduction to this commentary we were reminded that Matthew's appreciation for the Gospel according to Mark is seen in the fact that he used Mark as his primary source for constructing his own story of the Christ event. The very fact that Matthew wrote a gospel narrative while Mark was available to his community, on the other hand, shows that he thought Mark to be an inadequate Gospel for his community's needs. As opposed to the Gospel of Matthew being a natural evolution from Mark, we should see in Matthew's editorial changes a critique of Mark. Nowhere is this more obvious than in the ending to the Gospel.

Mark's Gospel is, in its entirety, a parable of sorts that intends to move the original readers to recognize that their triumphalist conclusion is misguided and offer a conclusion rooted in the cross for the post-temple church. Therefore, he concludes with an open ending, what many call a failed ending (Mk 16:1-8).

The women head to the tomb to anoint Jesus' body. They are concerned about who will move the stone for them, but when they arrive they find the stone already moved. There is a young man dressed in a white robe (reminiscent of the young man in 14:51-52) who tells them that Jesus has been raised and instructs them to tell the disciples and Peter (who is probably singled out because of his denial; 14:66-72) that Jesus will meet them in Galilee. All seems well with this story, but then Mark concludes: "So they [the women] went out and fled from the tomb, for terror and amazement had seized them; and they said nothing to anyone, for they were afraid." There is no appearance of the risen Christ, the women run away in fear (which throughout Mark is contrasted with faith), no one else hears that Christ has been raised, and the disciples do not meet Christ back in Galilee.

It is likely that Mark ends this way to invite his readers (1) to return to the Galilee narrative and reconsider the stories there in light of the cross and (2) to share the message that the women failed to pass on. After all, Mark affirms that the resurrection occurred (in addition to the empty tomb, see Mk 8:31; 9:9, 31; 10:32) and foreshadows Jesus' meeting with the disciples in Galilee (14:28). He takes a story his readers already know and twists the ending (in the vein that parables have twists) so that they ask (and answer) how their perception of the Christ event is misguided.

But this will not do for Matthew. He thoroughly edits Mark's scene at the empty tomb so that there is a clear and definite affirmation of the resurrection (27:62—28:15). He changes the young man to an angel and throws in an earthquake, so that it is clear we are in the realm of God's supernatural power. The women overcome their fear and respond faithfully to the instructions they are given. Jesus appears to them and they worship him. And Matthew even places guards at the tomb to confirm the resurrection by the opponents' very denial of it. And, as we shall see in the final division (28:16-20), the Gospel concludes with a scene in Galilee in which the risen Christ appears to and recommissions the disciples.

While Matthew edits Mark throughout the story, the two largest narrative additions to Mark's story (as opposed to sayings material) are the birth narrative and the story of the empty tomb. It is interesting to note ways Matthew relates these two sections through parallels:

In the birth narrative, the story of Herod's resistance to Jesus in Jerusalem results in Jesus eventually being displaced to Galilee (2:1-23). The passion narrative and the scene of the empty tomb take place in

Jerusalem (21:1-28:15) but the conclusion is that Jesus meets his disciples in Galilee (28:16-20).

In both the birth story and the story of the empty tomb (as well as the passion narrative) the political and religious authorities are partnered against Jesus (2:4; 27:62-66).

There is a strong apologetic motif in both sections to counter scandals concerning accusations made against Jesus. In the birth narrative, the scandal involves the tradition of Jesus' birth to a virgin. Matthew answers the accusation that Jesus was not born of a virgin through the genealogy that involves four scandalous biblical heroines and the story of Joseph deciding not to divorce Mary (1:1-25). In the story of the empty tomb, the accusation is that the disciples stole Jesus' body. Matthew answers the accusation with the story of the guards at the tomb (27:62-66; 28:11-15).

Although angels are mentioned by Jesus here and there throughout the Gospel (13:39, 41, 49; 16:27; 18:10; 22:30; 24:31, 36; 25:31, 41; 26:53), it is only in the birth and resurrection stories that angels appear as active characters who speak (1:20, 24; 2:13, 19; 28:2-5).

As the magi open the Gospel by paying homage to Jesus (2:2, 11), the women and disciples close the Gospel by worshiping him (28:9, 17).

Both sections emphasize the inclusion of the gentiles in Matthew's understanding of Christianity. In the birth narrative, the gentile magi come from the East (2:1-12). In the Great Commission the disciples are sent out to make disciples of all gentiles (28:19).

The most striking and explicit parallel is the reference to Jesus as Emmanuel, "God with us," in the birth narrative (1:23) as paralleled by Jesus promising to always be with the disciples to the consummation of the age (28:20).

The parallels (and the many others we could name if we compared the whole of the Beginnings division in 1:1-4:11 to the whole of the Jerusalem division in 21:1-28:15) show that Matthew has not simply added details to Mark's version of the empty tomb in some willy nilly fashion. He shapes the story of Jesus' resurrection to form an "*inclusio*" with the opening of the Gospel. *Inclusios* serve to enclose material in-between into some unified whole. The parallels remind preachers that Matthew assumes every piece of the narrative is most fully understood only in light of the whole.

The resurrection for Matthew then does not add something new to the identity or mission of Jesus as Son of God and Son of the human. Jesus has been "God with us" since his birth as opposed to becoming that now. The story of the resurrection confirms the presentation of the person and work of Jesus Christ throughout the preceding narrative *and* extends the experience of Christ into the life and times of Matthew's readers. In other words, the resurrection makes clear that the story of the Christ event is not an historical account for Matthew—it is the proclamation of the good news of the reign of heaven for Matthew's community, for us here and now, for all until the consummation of the age (28:20). The resurrection is eschatological but not in the sense of a break with the story of the past included in the rest of the narrative. Jesus' birth, life, ministry, teaching, and passion were (are) all eschatological. The resurrection is in continuity with the establishing of the "already" for the church as it struggles forever with the "not yet" of evil and pain in the world.

It is not surprising, then, that this section flows seamlessly out of the passion narrative. In the good news of the Christian faith, death leads to resurrection, signaled in Matthew by the earthquake occurring at both moments (27:51; 28:2). There are other ways Matthew connects the passion story and the Easter story. For example, while the disciples all desert Jesus (and remain absent from Jerusalem for the rest of the narrative), "many women" who had followed Jesus from Galilee were there watching from a distance when Jesus died (27:55-56). Moreover, two of them (the two Mary's) were watching from a distance (the text reads, "sitting opposite the tomb") when Jesus is buried (v. 61). This recurrence of the women and the distance they were forced to maintain during the passion foreshadows for the readers the desire of the two Mary's to go nearer to "see the tomb" on the day after the Sabbath (28:1)

Similarly, the chief priests and the Pharisees requesting that Pilate place a guard at the tomb (27:62-66) flows out of their manipulation of Pilate in killing Jesus in the first place. Pilate's characterization is consistent as well. He ordered Jesus' execution due to fear the crowd in Jerusalem might riot (27:24-26). There is no crowd present when the religious leaders make this request, so he gives them nothing more than his permission to place their own guards at the tomb.

The first action of the guards and the religious leaders at the tomb also recalls what has just occurred. When Joseph buries Jesus in his own (newly hewn) tomb, he rolls the "great stone" in front of the opening (27:60). In an act of overkill, the religious leaders and guards go a step further and seal the tomb, presumably with something like wax or ropes (v. 66).

Given that the story of the resurrection flows directly from the passion narrative, the division between the sections is debatable. Some would argue that 27:62-66 is best understood as the final scene of the passion narrative (as evidenced by its inclusion in the extensive reading on Palm/Passion Sunday; 26:14—27:66). But the fact that Matthew explicitly names that the story is set on a new day (after being ambiguous about some chronological elements earlier in the passion narrative) and concludes the story of the guards at the tomb in 28:11-15 suggests that 27:62-66 is better understood as part of the story of the empty tomb.

The structure of the section dealing with the empty tomb then is an "*inclusio,*" a sandwich structure, if you will. The story of the guards at the tomb serve as the bread of the sandwich and the story of the women's experiences of the angel and of Jesus (28:1-10) serve as the filling. The outside pieces frame and focus the readers' attention on the central matter. Moreover, the structure parallels the content: the inside material deals with the church's inner story in its focus on the women who have followed Jesus and the message to be given to the male disciples while the outside materials deals with external accusations about the church's message of resurrection.

The lectionary only includes one distinct reading from this section: 28:1-10 for either the Easter Vigil or Easter Sunday. However, 27:62-66 is the concluding scene of the extensive reading for the Liturgy of the Passion assigned to the preceding Sunday. Given the use of the placement of the guards on Palm/Passion Sunday, it would have made sense to include 28:11-15 as part of the lection for Easter. But if the previous story (27:62-66) is not read, 28:11-15 makes no sense.

Passages Omitted from the Lectionary

The only passage in the section dealing with the empty tomb that is excluded from the lectionary is the story of the bribing of the guards at the tomb (28:11-15) after the women have left to tell the disciples what they have seen and heard. The RCL likely omitted it because it only makes sense as the conclusion to the first half of the story presented at 27:62-66). Nevertheless, given that it is unique to Matthew, it is a shame that it is ignored.

Bribing the Guards at the Tomb (28:11-15):
Omitted from Lectionary

Since this scene is the conclusion to the plot that began in 27:62-66, preachers interested in focusing on this passage should consult the notes below on that text. Also important to attend to, however, is the notice in 28:4. The earthquake accompanying the angelophany continues with aftershocks in the guards (Greek, *apo de tou phobou autou eseisthēsan*); and ironically at the very moment that the fact that Jesus is alive is revealed, the guards become like dead men (*egenēthēsan hōs nekroi*).

Verse 11 states that the guards told "everything that had happened" (Greek, *apanta to genomena*) to the chief priests. It is unclear exactly to what "everything" refers. Does it mean the whole of 28:1-10? Or because they became like dead mean, could they only give witness to the earthquake and sight of the angel as narrated in vv. 2-3? It matters little, because even the earthquake and the angel without the conversation that followed was enough to confirm that whatever occurred was an act of God and not simply deceptions wrought by Jesus' disciples.

Thus the deception perpetrated by the religious leaders and their guards raises the stakes for the entire scope of conflicts throughout the gospel narrative. Throughout Jesus' Galilean ministry, his teaching in the temple, and even his trials, the religious leaders could have perhaps really believed him to be an imposter. No such consideration is possible any longer. By bribing the guards to lie and passing on the lie even into Matthew's day, the religious leaders are portrayed as being in direct and intentional conflict with God. This scene, then, is the final and strongest challenge Matthew makes toward the synagogue in his attempts to legitimate the church as heir and interpreter of Israel's faith, practice and traditions in light of the Christ event.

LECTIONS

This section of Matthew (27:62—28:15) is shorter than most in the Gospel and certainly shorter than the 136 verses of the passion narrative just preceding it. Yet it is exegetically essential to Matthew and existentially essential for the life and faith of the church. The lectionary's primary focus in the section is naturally on 28:1-10.

LECTION: PLACING GUARDS AT THE TOMB
27:62-66; LITURGY OF THE PASSION

This passage is actually the final scene included in the extensive reading for Palm/Passion Sunday (26:14—27:66) and does not stand alone as a lection offered by the RCL. Therefore, we will not comment on the passage extensively, but it is important to note how the passage functions (along with 28:11-15) to support Matthew's apologetic approach to the synagogue of his day as well as how it influences the way we read 28:1-10.

To get a handle on both of these, one must attend closely to the accusation made by religious leaders to Pilate in v. 63: "Sir, we remember what that imposter said while he was still alive, 'After three days I will rise again." First, note that they call Pilate *kyrios*. While this term was used as a common title of respect (as seen in being translated as "sir"), it is a clear indication here that they fail to recognize Jesus as "Lord." Second, their label for Jesus as imposter is meant to be heard as ironic, given that we have seen these religious leaders fostering false testimony against Jesus (26:59-61; contrast 22:16). And, third, their claim to remember Jesus' speaking of his resurrection seems odd given that all of Jesus' direct speech about his resurrection was offered in private to his disciples (16:21; 17:9, 23; 20:19; 26:32). In the trial before the Sanhedrin, however, part of the false testimony foreshadows the resurrection: "The fellow said, 'I am able to destroy the temple of God and to build it in three days'" (26:61). But more to the point when the scribes and Pharisees asked Jesus for a sign, he told them they would only be given the sign of Jonah who was in the belly of the sea monster three days and nights just as the Son of the human would be in the heart of the earth three days and nights (12:38-42; see also 16:4).

The religious leaders sought a sign earlier in the narrative, and here they are presented as attempting to stop the very sign promised them from occurring. Even when the sign does occur, they deny it for themselves and lie about it publicly.

LECTION: THE EMPTY TOMB
28:1-10; EASTER VIGIL; EASTER SUNDAY

Preachers facing a congregation on Easter Sunday morning often make two mistakes. First, they try to persuade their congregations that the resurrection should be important to them. This homiletical approach is ill-conceived because everyone sitting in the pews already knows the claim to be true. That is why they are present on this day even if they do not show up the rest of the 51 Sundays of the year. Second, they try to interpret that importance in terms of the historicity of the resurrection. Without denying the importance of the scientific and historical debates concerning this theological and hermeneutical issue, it should be said explicitly that people come to worship on Easter wanting and needing to experience the good news of the risen Christ in their lives and world in the twenty-first century instead of a history lesson. After all, in the liturgy of Easter we do not proclaim, "Christ was risen;" we proclaim, "Christ *is* risen."

Homiletically, then, preachers should construct a sermon in which the congregation is invited to identify with the women at the tomb, to experience resurrection as they do in the story. This does not mean, however, trying to place congregations back in an ancient cemetery and surprise them with the discovery of the ancient tomb. Everyone gathered for the Easter vigil or for Easter Sunday knows the tomb is empty. What many do not know (especially at an experiential level, thanks to so many sermons focused otherwise), is in what way the claim that Christ is risen can actually inform their existence and worldview. How does God bring life into the midst of death? How does God transform grief into joy? If preachers surprise their congregations with a meaningful vision of reality today seen through the lens of the resurrection of Jesus Christ, sanctuaries might be as full on the Second Sunday of Easter (Low Sunday) as they are on the first.

Matthew's story invites such an experience because it is presented as a vision in line with the visions/dreams in birth narrative (1:20; 2:12, 13, 19, 22). The women come to "see" the tomb (v. 1) and the angel descends with his "appearance" (Greek, *eidea*) described in detail (v. 3). The angel invites them to look into the tomb to "see" the [now empty] place where he had been laid (v. 6).

They are able to look into the tomb because when the angel descends with an earthquake (like the earthquake that accompanied the resurrection of "many saints" at the moment of Jesus' death; 27:51-53), he rolls the stone away from the tomb (v. 2) The guards' act of sealing the stone (27:66) had no power whatsoever to withstand God's will. But what is important to note at this point is why the stone is moved at all. In Mark, the stone was moved before the women arrived, apparently to let Jesus out (Mk 16:4). But in Matthew, the stone is not moved that Jesus might get out of the tomb; he is already gone. It is moved so that the women (and we as readers) might get in.

Matthew gives no insight at all into how God raised Jesus or how Jesus escaped from the tomb. Indeed, we do not even really know when the resurrection occurred; we only know when God chose to make it known. This shows that, theologically speaking, for Matthew the [historical, scientific] details of Jesus' resurrection are unimportant; instead what is emphasized is the proclamation and experience of Christ as the risen one.

The angel proclaims the gospel to the women in its purest and simplest form: Jesus was crucified; now he has been raised (vv. 5-6). But hardly a second ticks off the clock before proclamation turns to exhortation, and the angel instructs the women to go tell the disciples about the resurrection and that Jesus will meet them in Galilee.

The women in Mark's version of the story experience the news of Jesus' resurrection and with overwhelming fear (Mk 16:8). In Matthew's version that level of fear is transferred to the guards. The women, on the other hand, experience the good news and the commission to tell the disciples with fear and joy (Greek, *chara*) at the same time (28:8). Never was there a better expression of an appropriate emotional response to the presence of God. As they leave the tomb (v. 9) they meet Jesus who greets them (the word translated by the NRSV as "greetings" can also mean "rejoice;" Greek *chairete*). The women respond by falling to Jesus' feet and worshiping (Greek, *proskuneō*) him (as do the male disciples in 28:17). By his presence, Jesus confirms the angel's announcement that Jesus is risen. He then speaks to confirm the instructions the angel gave the women (v.10).

The women are the first to experience the resurrection, the first to be commissioned to proclaim the Easter message—Matthew does not tell the story of the women doing this but by including the story of Jesus meeting the disciples in Galilee in vv. 16-20 implies that they faithfully fulfilled their calling—and the first to worship the risen Christ. By asking congregations to identify with these women who pioneered the Easter faith, preachers are given the chance to make yet another chink in the armor of patriarchy in the church. However, the homiletical focus cannot be on the women themselves on Easter Sunday. The focus is on the risen Christ; and through an identification with the women, we are invited into the fear and joy of experiencing the resurrection, of being called to share the message of that resurrection, and to be inspired to worship the risen one.

5

Beginning Again in Galilee (28:16–20)

It may seem odd to consider five verses to be a major division of Matthew in the same way that sixteen chapters is—the Capernaum-based ministry is the longest division of the gospel narrative; chapters 4–19. Indeed, most commentators view the scene of the risen Jesus meeting his disciples as part and parcel of the Jerusalem narrative (beginning in chapter 21) or at least the empty tomb scene (28:1ff).

A clear geographical break occurs in 28:16, however. The setting shifts from Jerusalem to Galilee. This return to Galilee (Jesus' Capernaum-based ministry extended from 4:12—18:35 until Jesus departed for Jerusalem in 19:1) is no way incidental. Matthew has been foreshadowing this return with similar emphasis to the way he foreshadowed Jesus' passion and resurrection. Jesus promised to meet the disciples in Galilee after he is raised from the dead even as he tells them they are going to desert him (26:32; Matthew takes this from Mark 14:28, but in Mark the return to Galilee is never narrated). Then no less than three times is Galilee mentioned in the empty tomb scene as the place where the risen Jesus will meet the disciples (28:7, 10, 16).

Indeed, a whole new phase in Jesus' mission is marked by the return to Galilee. When Matthew first presented Jesus as beginning his ministry in Galilee, he justified the location with a prophecy fulfillment citation from Isaiah 9:1-2 which refers to the region as "Galilee of the gentiles" (4:12-16). This seemed an odd reference at the time, especially given that during his ministry in this locale, Jesus instructed his apostles not to minister to the gentiles but only to the lost sheep of the house of Israel (10:5-6). But now Jesus returns to Galilee to expand that commission to include making disciples of all the gentiles (28:19).

Beginning Again in Galilee:
The Great Commission (28:16-20; Trinity Sunday)

Because of its brevity, the entire closing division of Matthew serves as a single lection. This passage is used as the gospel reading for Trinity Sunday, the first Sunday after Pentecost. The reason for the assignment is clear: in this passage Matthew uses the only explicit formula reference to the Father, Son, and Holy Spirit (v. 19) in the Gospels (cf. 2 Cor 13:13). Even though the doctrine of the Trinity is a post-New Testament development in the church's faith, it is language such as this that, at least partly, funded that development. Moreover, the Trinitarian baptismal formula is considered standard, indeed required, liturgical practice for most denominations today, over against baptizing in the name of Jesus alone (as some argue is justified by the likes of Acts 2:38; 8:16; 10:48; 19:1-7).

Nevertheless, it is a terrible injustice to Matthew's Gospel to use this passage for the purpose of celebrating and exploring the doctrine of the Trinity alone in Year A. Even though the shift in setting exegetically justifies interpreting this scene as distinct from the empty tomb story, it belongs in the season of Easter. It is a story of the resurrection. The story of the empty tomb can be seen as the exclamation point punctuating the end of the Jerusalem division. But this text is the semicolon punctuating the end of the Gospel as a whole: it draws together and concludes much of what Matthew has offered the reader throughout the narrative while explicitly pointing forward to the unfinished story of the future of the church. The importance of the passage for the Matthew is difficult to exaggerate, and this importance is difficult for preachers to name appropriately on Trinity Sunday if they intend to attend to the emphasis of the liturgical occasion. Difficult, but not impossible. We will examine the passage in detail and suggest a homiletical approach for Trinity Sunday that honors the liturgical occasion while moving to the bigger picture of Matthew's narrative purposes.

The structure of scene is relative simple. It is similar to the twofold movement of pronouncement stories: set up and pronouncement. The set up involves the eleven disciples (that is, the twelve apostles minus Judas; 27:3-10) meeting the risen Jesus and worshiping him (vv. 16-17). The pronouncement is commonly known as the Great Commission and is Jesus' last word to the disciples (vv. 18-20). But even the last word has a last word, if you will. The pronouncement is composed of instructions (vv. 18-19) and promise (v. 20).

Even though the structure is simple, the passage is extremely dense. Nearly every phrase echoes earlier material in the Gospel and is filled with theological weight.

Let's begin with the set up. The disciples find Jesus on "the mountain" in Galilee to which they had been directed (v. 16; see 26:32). While Galilee is specific and real, the mountain is mythical. It recalls all the mountains of revelation in the Hebrew Bible and all the references to mountains earlier in Matthew. For example, in the temptation story, the devil takes Jesus to a mountain and promises him all the dominions of the world if Jesus will only worship him (4:8-9). Now Jesus stands on a mountain claiming all authority (28:18) and being worshiped by his followers (v. 17). Matthew first taught his disciples on a mountain (5:1), and now he offers his last teaching on a mountain. The inner circle of disciples first saw Jesus' true glory on the mountain of transfiguration (17:1-8), and now all the disciples see Jesus in his risen glory on a mountaintop.

This meeting in this setting leads the disciples to worship Jesus (v. 17). During Jesus' ministry the disciples are never presented as worshiping Jesus. This act is reserved for the risen Christ (as we saw the women do in 28:9). But Matthew does not exaggerate the disciples' devotion. He admits that some doubted (*distazō*). This dynamic of worship and doubt is paralleled in 14:25-31 by Peter's act of faith in stepping out on the water when Jesus calls him but sinking when he begins to doubt (these are the only two places the Greek word *distazō* appear in the New Testament). Moreover, this dynamic sets up Jesus' pronouncement of instruction and promise.

The disciples are not allowed to stay on this mountain any more than Peter, James and John were allowed to build tents and stay on the mountain of transfiguration. Jesus sends them down with his pronouncement, implying worship gives way to service. In his sending them out he claims authority (v. 18) but we should be careful not to assume this is new authority. Recall how many times Jesus' authority was asserted in the First Gospel (7:29; 8:9; 9:6, 8; 21:23ff). Indeed, Jesus has passed authority on to the disciples before in the Mission Discourse (10:1-8a). So the resurrection did not confer upon Jesus new authority, it confirmed authority he already had been given. But Jesus passes on authority to the disciples to act in ways now that he did not authorize them to act originally. Originally they were authorized to cast out unclean spirits, heal the sick, proclaim the reign of heaven, and even raise the dead—but all among the lost sheep of the house of Israel. What Jesus instructs here does not counter those previous instructions but adds to them.

There are three new, related tasks (vv. 19-20). First, the disciples (*mathētai*) are make disciples (*mathēteusate*). This is language of invitation. Recall the scribes and Pharisees were condemned for "locking" people out of the reign of heaven (23:13) whereas Peter had been given the "keys" to that reign in order to loose and bind, that is, to interpret the *torah* in ways that people know what is binding and in what ways they are binding (16:19; see also 18:18). The apostles are to invite people into God's reign. Given the references just cited, this instruction would not seem to be new. What makes it new is who is to be invited. The Jewish disciples are to make disciples of *ethnoi*. Even though *ethnoi* is usually translated "nations" here (as if it means the whole world), it is best to understand the word to refer specifically to "gentiles" as an extension of the mission to the lost sheep of the house Israel (See the discussion of the Greek word *ethnoi* in the comments on 25:31–46 above). This mission to the gentiles is not a replacement of the mission to the lost sheep of the house of Israel—Matthew never indicates that mission as being concluded. The reign of heaven is open to Jews and gentiles alike.

The second new task assigned to the disciples after the resurrection is to baptize these new disciples in the name of the Father, Son, and Holy Spirit. Whereas the first invitation they are to offer the gentiles is to enter the reign of heaven, baptism implies initiating them into the church.

The church, then, is the locale for the third new task—teaching those newly invited into God's reign and newly initiated into the church what Christ has taught. Remember, a major change Matthew made to Mark was to include much more of Jesus' teaching material in the story than Mark had. Matthew collects the bulk of these teachings into the five discourses (chs. 5–7, 10, 13, 18, 24–25). The disciples here are ordered to teach the *ethnoi* "all that I have commanded you," wording that echoes the conclusion to the final discourse, "When Jesus had finished saying all these things . . ." (26:1). The church is now to teach what Jesus taught—his hermeneutic, his parables, his mission, his way of being church, and his eschatological ethic.

Finally, following the instructions, Jesus concludes the pronouncement with a promise to the disciples/the church that, in the face of their doubt, he will be with them until the consummation of the age (Greek, *tēs sunteleis tou aiōnos*). Jesus' last word is an eschatological promise that echoes back to the announcement that the messiah to be born would be Emmanuel, God with us (1:23). With one simple promise, Matthew creates a long-arching *inclusio* drawing the narrative to a close and opening the church to a new beginning based on the whole of that narrative. The closing scene of the Gospel of Matthew, then, offers an ecclesiology rooted in the eschatological event of the resurrection of Jesus Christ. With disciples as the church's representatives in the narrative, Jesus' closing words are instructions and promise to the church in all times.

While Matthew offers this ecclesiological vision as the last word of his Gospel, it is not inappropriate that it be used liturgically as the first word of Ordinary Time, the season of the church, as it were. To preach Matthew's vision of the church on Trinity Sunday is to name the mission of the community of those baptized in the name of the Creator, Redeemer and Sustainer in light of the resurrection. This approach can start with some direct words about why Matthew's pericope is used on Trinity Sunday, and then move to a homiletical and exegetical approach that uses the text describe the church's devotion to the triune God exhibited in the new mission.

Appendix: Suggestions for Further Reading

As noted in the preface, this homiletical, lectionary-oriented commentary on Matthew is meant to help preachers as they begin to turn from detailed, critical commentaries toward the pulpit. Given that assumption, it seems prudent to recommend some recent, critical commentaries that preachers may find helpful in doing significant exegesis in the earliest stages of sermon preparation.

Boring, M. Eugene. "Matthew" in *The New Interpreter's Bible: Matthew-Mark*, vol. 8. Nashville: Abingdon, 1995.

As part of the popular *New Interpreter's Bible*, Boring's commentary is shorter than some in this list. Nevertheless, his exegetical and theological insight into the text is helpful for preachers. This should not be the only commentary a preacher consults, but it is worth having on one's desk.

Davies, W. D. and Dale C. Allison Jr. *Matthew*. 3 vols. International Critical Commentary. Edinburgh: T. & T. Clark, 1988.

This extensive three-volume commentary is one of the best exegetical works on Matthew. Although not engaging the most recent of critical hermeneutics, the authors closely examine the Greek text, exploring various levels of textual, source, historical, and literary issues.

France, Richard Thomas. *The Gospel of Matthew*. Grand Rapids: Eerdmans, 2007.

France takes a literary approach to his exegesis of Matthew, reading the Gospel as a unified narrative without being concerned about source and redaction issues that attract the attention of most synoptic scholars. This allows him to interpret Matthew's story as unique proclamation within and for the particular sociohistorical context in which it was composed.

Harrington, Daniel J. *The Gospel of Matthew*. Sacra Pagina. Collegeville: Liturgical, 2007.

Harrington's beginning point is similar to that in this commentary—that is, that Matthew writes from the perspective of a Jewish Christian who is concerned about the church's sibling rivalry with the synagogue. He offers a nuanced theological approach to the text, avoiding anti-Semitism and providing a good foundation for thinking about preaching on Matthean pericopes.

Hauerwas, Stanley. *Matthew*. Brazos Theological Commentary on the Bible. Grand Rapids: Brazos, 2006.

Hauerwas reads Matthew not as a biblical scholar but as a theologian. This means that many sociohistorical and literary elements of the text are ignored. Nevertheless, Hauerwas's reading usually stands in line with the broad history of scholarship on Matthew and is always theologically provocative.

Levine, Amy-Jill. "Gospel of Matthew." In *The Women's Bible Commentary*, 3rd ed. Louisville: Westminster John Knox, 2012.

As an entry in a one-volume commentary, Levine's essay on Matthew is hardly a detailed commentary. However, she raises feminist issues and a focus on women in the narrative in her reading that are often missed by the male scholars in this list of recommended commentaries.

Luz, Ulrich. *Matthew*. 3 vols. Translated by Wilhelm C. Linss and James E. Crouch. Hermeneia: A Critical and Historical Commentary on the Bible. Minneapolis: Fortress, 2001–2007.

Originally a German work, this three-volume commentary is one of the best contemporary works on the Gospel of Matthew. Not only does Luz provide historical and theological analysis of the Greek text, he also reviews the history of interpretation and the church's use of influential Matthean passages throughout the work.

Talbert, Charles H. *Matthew*. Paideia Commentaries on the New Testament.

Instead of dealing with the text verse-by-verse, Talbert focuses on the sense units of Matthew, offering a literary reading of the final form of the text instead of its historical development. Although offering a narrative reading, Talbert draws significantly on Jewish and especially Greco-Roman resources in ways helpful to the modern reader.